Illustrations
UNLIMITED

Illustrations Unlimited

JAMES S. HEWETT
EDITOR

Tyndale House Publishers, Inc.
Wheaton, Illinois

The editor gratefully acknowledges the assistance of his late wife, Avis, and his daughters, Marie and Janeen, in producing *Parables, Etc.* and *The Pastor's Story File.*

Acknowledgment is given to Guideposts Associates for material from "I'm Still Learning to Forgive," *Guideposts,* November 1972.

Acknowledgment is given to Linda Andersen for "Love Adds the Chocolate" (page 192), taken from her book *Love Adds the Chocolate* (Baker Book House, 1983).

"A Brother Like That" on page 235 is taken from *Iron Shoes* by C. Roy Angell. © Copyright 1953. Renewal 1981 Broadman Press. All rights reserved. Used by permission.

Contents

Introduction

EVERY writer, pastor, teacher, or speaker needs help in preparing material. Even the wisest person knows that his sermon or speech can use support in the form of quotations, historical anecdotes, personal testimonies, and even popular films and songs. None of us has unlimited experience, so our audiences deserve our taking the time to illustrate our written and spoken presentations with stories and quotations that draw from the vast treasury of human experience in general, Christian experience in particular.

James S. Hewett, himself a pastor for many years, launched *Parables, Etc.* in 1981 as a monthly newsletter to provide topical illustrations for pastors and others. In 1984 he launched *The Pastor's Story File,* another monthly newsletter. Both publications have been rich sources of ideas and insights for their readers.

Here in one volume are hundreds of stories, quotations, and anecdotes drawn from the many issues of *Parables* and *The Pastor's Story File.* In selecting materials for this volume, we have tried to present a broad selection of topics, most of which are especially pertinent for the Christian writer or speaker. Some topics are seasonal—Christmas and Easter, for example, and also Patriotism (illustrations appropriate for Independence Day), Fathers (for Father's Day), and Mothers (for Mother's Day). Some are theological— Atonement, The Bible, God's Love, Resurrection, and many others. Some, while not theological, relate to the life of the church—Ministry, Stewardship, Church Life, and others. Some relate to interpersonal issues—Family, Leadership, Youth, Optimism, Persuasion, Role Models, for example. In all there are 142 topical sections, arranged alphabetically, with each illustration numbered under each topical heading.

We have tried to arrange the material for the greatest ease of use. Recognizing that different readers will use different words to refer to a topic, we have carefully cross-referenced the book. A reader looking for illustrations on *kindness,* for example, can turn to the table of contents and see that the heading *Kindness* refers him to the section on *Compassion.* A reader looking for material on *wealth* will find in the table of contents that he should turn to the sections *Materialism* and *Money*. The table of contents also refers the reader to related sections—if he looks up the heading *Optimism*, he will see that heading also refers him to the section *Hope*. These cross-references appear not only in the table of contents, but also under the topical sections.

We hope that this system will prove helpful to the pastor, writer, speaker, or teacher who is searching quickly for just the right illustration. We also hope that any reader will find this book eminently "browsable." There is much material here, and much wisdom and humor also. There are quotations from Martin Luther, John Calvin, C. S. Lewis, and Peter Marshall. There are also quotations from Henny Youngman and Woody Allen. There are inspiring stories of dedicated missionaries, and there are knee-slapping accounts of the quirkiness of pastors and laypeople. And there is much, much more. Take time to browse through the table of contents and familiarize yourself with the wide variety of topics. Then spend some time thumbing through the sections. Above all, *use* the materials here. Sprinkle them like salt on your sermon, speech, or article. Be grateful that the word *experience* includes not only the events in your own life, but the events and insights in the life of the whole human race.

ONE

Accidents

1. KITCHEN DISASTERS
The worst thing about accidents in the kitchen is you usually have to eat them.

2. DESIGNED FOR DISASTER
A shin is a device invented for finding furniture in the dark.

TWO

Actions

1. NAUTICAL ACTION
The person who rows the boat usually doesn't have time to rock it.

2. ON THE NEED FOR ACTION
Gardens are not made by singing "Oh, how beautiful," and sitting in the shade. RUDYARD KIPLING

3. A STRATEGY FOR LIFE
You don't learn to hold your own in the world by standing on guard but by attacking and getting well-hammered yourself. GEORGE BERNARD SHAW

THREE
Adversity
(See also Failure, Handicaps)

1. THE GIVING OF BURDENS
God gives burdens, also shoulders. *Yiddish proverb*

2. BROKENNESS
A rabbi was asked a question by a pupil, referring to Deuteronomy 6:6—
"And these words, which I command thee this day, shall be upon thy heart."
"Why is it said this way?" the pupil asked. "Why are we not told to place
them *in* our heart?" The rabbi answered that it is not within man's power to
place the divine teachings directly in his heart. "All that we can do is place
them on the surface of the heart so that when the heart breaks they will drop
in."

3. LESSON FROM GOLF BALLS
When they first manufactured golf balls, they made the covers smooth. Then
it was discovered that after a ball had been roughed up one could get more
distance out of it. So they started manufacturing them with dimpled covers.
So it is with life; it takes some rough spots in your life to make you go your
farthest.

4. DANDELIONS
A gardener took great pride in caring for his lawn. But one year it grew full
of dandelions. He tried every method and product to get rid of them, but
nothing worked. Exasperated, he wrote the Department of Agriculture
explaining all he had done. "What shall I try next?" he wrote. "Try getting
used to them," came the reply.

5. SILLS ON SUFFERING
Beverly Sills, operatic great, tells of her two severely handicapped children in
her pictorial autobiography, *Bubbles*. Her own natural daughter is deaf and
her stepdaughter is also severely handicapped. She writes:
   "I was now only thirty-four, but a very mature thirty-four. In a strange
way my children had brought me an inner peace. The first question I had
when I learned of their tragedies was a self-pitying 'Why me?' Then
gradually it changed to a much more important 'Why them?' Despite their
handicaps they were showing enormous strength in continuing to live as

normal and constructive lives as possible. How could Peter and I show any less strength? After all that had happened, I felt we could survive anything."

6. OVERCOMING

Although the world is full of suffering, it is also full of the overcoming of it.
HELEN KELLER

7. THE PRIVILEGE OF SUFFERING

Joni Eareckson's story is now well known to us both through her books and the movie about her paralysis as a teenager and her amazing fight back to a useful and productive life of ministry through her art. From the preface of *Joni:*

"Isolated, by itself, what is a minute? Merely a measurement of time. There are sixty in an hour, 1,440 in a day. At seventeen, I had already ticked off more than 9 million of them in my life. Yet, in some cosmic plan, this single minute was isolated. Into these particular sixty seconds was compressed more significance than all the millions of minutes marking my life prior to this instant.

"So many actions, sensations, thoughts, and feelings were crowded into that fragment of time. How can I describe them? How can I begin to catalog them?

"I recall so clearly the details of those few dozen seconds—seconds destined to change my life forever. And there was no warning or premonition.

"What happened on July 30, 1967, was the beginning of an incredible adventure which I feel compelled to share because of what I have learned.

"Oscar Wilde wrote: 'In this world there are only two tragedies. One is not getting what one wants, and the other is getting it.' To rephrase his thought, I suggest there are likewise only two joys. One is having God answer all your prayers; the other is not receiving the answer to all your prayers. I believe this because I have found that God knows my needs infinitely better than I know them. And He is utterly dependable, no matter which direction our circumstances take us."

"In the Psalms we're told that God does not deal with us according to our sins and iniquities. My accident was not a punishment for my wrongdoing—whether or not I deserved it. Only God knows why I was paralyzed. Maybe He knew I'd be ultimately happier serving Him. If I were still on my feet, it's hard to say how things might have gone. I probably would have drifted through life—marriage, maybe even divorce—dissatisfied and disillusioned. When I was in high school, I reacted to life selfishly and never built on any longlasting values. I lived simply for each day and the pleasure I wanted—and almost always at the expense of others."

8. THE POTENTIAL OF TRIAL
When you are face to face with a difficulty, you are up against a discovery. LORD KELVIN

9. BUILDING CHARACTER
In the northeastern United States codfish are a big commercial business. Note the following facts: There is a market for eastern cod all over, especially in sections farthest removed from the northeast coastline. But the public demand posed a problem to the shippers. At first they froze the cod, then shipped them elsewhere, but the freeze took away much of the flavor. So they experimented with shipping them alive, in tanks of seawater, but that proved even worse. Not only was it more expensive, the cod still lost its flavor and, in addition, became soft and mushy. The texture was seriously affected.

Finally, some creative person solved the problem in a most innovative manner. The codfish were placed in the tank of water along with their natural enemy—the catfish. From the time the cod left the East Coast until it arrived at its westernmost destination, those ornery catfish chased the cod all over the tank. And, you guessed it, when the cod arrived at the market, they were as fresh as when they were first caught. There was no loss of flavor nor was the texture affected. If anything, it was better than before.

Each one of us is in a tank of particular and inescapable circumstances. It is painful enough to stay in the tank. But in addition to our situation, there are God-appointed "catfish" to bring sufficient tension that keeps us alive, alert, fresh and growing. It's all part of God's project to shape our character so we will be more like his Son. Understand why the catfish are in your tank. Understand they are part of God's method of producing character in your life and mine. CHARLES SWINDOLL

10. A SHIP'S CHALLENGE
A ship, like a human being, moves best when it is slightly athwart the wind, when it has to keep its sails tight and attend to its course. Ships, like men, do poorly when the wind is directly behind, pushing them sloppily on their way so that no care is required in steering or in the management of sails; the wind seems favorable, for it blows in the direction one is heading, but actually it is destructive, because it induces a relaxation in tension and skill. What is needed is a wind slightly opposed to the ship, for then tension can be maintained, and juices can flow and ideas can germinate; for ships, like men, respond to challenge. JAMES MICHENER, *Chesapeake*

11. THE USE OF BROKEN THINGS

God uses broken things. It takes broken soil to produce a crop, broken clouds to give rain, broken grain to give bread, broken bread to give strength. It is the broken alabaster box that gives forth perfume . . . it is Peter, weeping bitterly, who returns to greater power than ever. VANCE HAVNER

12. THE SKILLED BLOWS OF GOD

Many years ago, there was found in an African mine the most magnificent diamond in the world's history. It was presented to the king of England to blaze in his crown or state. The king sent it to Amsterdam to be cut. It was put into the hands of an expert lapidary. And what do you suppose he did with it? He took the gem of priceless value, and cut a notch in it. Then he struck a hard blow with his instrument and—lo!—the superb jewel lay in his hand cleft in two. Did he do this out of recklessness, wastefulness, and criminal carelessness? Indeed not! For days and weeks that blow had been studied and planned. Drawings and models had been made of the gem. Its quality, its defects, its lines of cleavage had all been studied with minutest care. The man to whom it was committed was one of the most skillful lapidaries in the world.

Was that blow a mistake? No! It was the climax of the lapidary's skill. When he struck that blow, he did the one thing which would bring that gem to its most perfect shapeliness, radiance, and jeweled splendor. That blow which seemed to ruin the superb precious stone was, in fact, its perfect redemption. From those two halves were wrought two magnificent gems which the skilled eye of the lapidary saw hidden in the rough, uncut stone as it came from the mine.

Sometimes, God lets a stinging blow fall upon your life. The blood spurts; the nerves wince. The soul cries out in agony. The blow seems to you an appalling mistake. But it is not, for you are the most priceless jewel in the world to God. And He is the most skilled lapidary in the universe.

Let us beware of questioning the methods and approaches of almighty God. We lie in His hands, and He knows just how to deal with us.

13. A BAD DAY WHEN . . .

You know it's going to be a bad day when you wake up in a hospital all trussed up and your insurance agent tells you that your accident policy covers falling off the roof, but not hitting the ground.

14. TESTING THE STABILITY

In order to realize the worth of the anchor, we need to feel the stress of the storm.

15. SURROGATE FEELING
Neurosis is always a substitute for legitimate suffering. M. SCOTT PECK, *The Road Less Traveled*

16. OVERCOMING THE IRRITATION
It is the wounded oyster that mends its shell with pearl.
RALPH WALDO EMERSON

17. ESCAPE
One day Linus and Charlie Brown are walking along and chatting with one another. Linus says, "I don't like to face problems head on. I think the best way to solve problems is to avoid them. In fact, this is a distinct philosophy of mine. No problem is so big or so complicated that it can't be run away from!"

18. PROSPECTS FOR THE FUTURE
A fortune-teller studied the hand of a young man and said, "You will be poor and very unhappy until you are thirty-seven years old."

The young man responded, "Well, after that, what will happen? Will I be rich and happy?"

The fortune-teller said, "No, you'll still be poor, but you'll be used to it after that."

19. THE BLINDED BOXER
An athlete was blinded in a freak boxing accident. The doctors told him, "You'll never see again." The social workers said, "Learn braille, stay home, accept the fact that you will be dependent on others for the rest of your life." But Morris Frank fought to regain his independence. The result was the development of "The Seeing Eye," the organization that trains seeing-eye dogs for the blind.

20. THE BITTER VIEW
The cynic says: "Don't bother telling people your troubles. Half of them don't care, and the other half figure you probably had it coming."

21. RECYCLING TRAGEDY
An artist went to visit a dear friend. When he arrived, she was weeping. He asked why. She showed him a handkerchief of exquisite beauty that had great sentimental value, which had been ruined by a drop of indelible ink.

The artist asked her to let him have the handkerchief, which he returned to her by mail several days later. When she opened the package she could hardly believe her eyes. The artist, using the inkblot as a base, had drawn on the handkerchief a design of great beauty with India ink. Now it was more beautiful and more valuable than ever.

Sometimes the tragedies that break our hearts can become the basis for a more beautiful design in our lives. Be patient with the hurts over which you have no control. They may become a source of healing, help, and beauty.
THOMAS LANE BUTTS

22. DIDN'T YOU KNOW I WOULD COME
Rufus Jones lost a son of eleven years who was all the world to him. He wrote many years later about the experience, concluding with this luminous parable of how his own heart was opened to God's love:

"When my sorrow was at its most acute I was walking along a great city highway, when suddenly I saw a little child come out of a great gate, which swung to and fastened behind her. She wanted to go to her home behind the gate, but it would not open. She pounded in vain with her little fist. She rattled the gate. The she wailed as though her heart would break. The cry brought the mother. She caught the child in her arms and kissed away the tears. 'Didn't you know I would come? It's all right now.' All of a sudden I saw with my spirit that there was love behind my shut gate."

If you suffer with God you will find love behind your shut gate, a love that can lead you through the gate to be at home with all the children of God.

23. PRAISE AND SUFFERING
Five or six years ago I visited a church in Connecticut. In the middle of the eucharistic liturgy, when the whole congregation was kneeling and singing the "Alleluia," I saw a woman near me with her hands lifted in praise. The thing was, those hands were terribly twisted and gnarled, and she had a pair of crutches near her. *Dear Christ,* I thought, *what makes Christians sing "Alleluia"?* Clearly there was something besides self-interest welling up from that woman in the act of praise.

24. THE GIFT OF TROUBLE
The ability to get into trouble and the ability to get out of trouble are seldom present in the same person.

25. FAILURE AND PERSEVERANCE
When he was seven years old, his family was forced out of their home on a legal technicality, and he had to work to help support them. At age nine, his mother died. At twenty-two, he lost his job as a store clerk. He wanted to go to law school, but his education wasn't good enough. At twenty-three, he went into debt to become a partner in a small store. At twenty-six, his

business partner died, leaving him a huge debt that took years to repay. At twenty-eight, after courting a girl for four years, he asked her to marry him. She said no. At thirty-seven, on his third try, he was elected to Congress, but two years later, he failed to be reelected. At forty-one, his four-year-old son died. At forty-five, he ran for the Senate and lost. At forty-seven, he failed as the vice-presidential candidate. At forty-nine, he ran for the Senate again and lost. At fifty-one, he was elected president of the United States. His name was Abraham Lincoln, a man many consider the greatest leader the country ever had. Some people get all the breaks.

26. THE HIGHEST OF JOYS
The highest joy to the Christian almost always comes through suffering. No flower can bloom in paradise which is not transplanted from Gethsemane. IAN MACLAREN

27. HOW YOU CAN TELL IT'S GOING TO BE A ROTTEN DAY
You see a "60 Minutes" news team in your office. You call Suicide Prevention and they put you on hold. You turn on the news and they're showing emergency routes out of the city. Your twin sister forgot your birthday. Your car horn goes off accidentally and remains stuck as you follow a group of Hell's Angels on the freeway. Your boss tells you not to bother to take off your coat. Your income tax check bounces. You put both contact lenses in the same eye.

28. CHANGE OF HABIT
With me, a change of trouble is as good as a vacation. DAVID LLOYD GEORGE

29. AGAINST THE WIND
Remember, if everything is coming your way, you're in the wrong lane. . . . When everything seems to be going against you, remember that the airplane takes off against the wind, not with it.

30. NO INFERIORITY
No one can make you feel inferior without your consent. ELEANOR ROOSEVELT

31. POLISHING TRIALS
The gem cannot be polished without friction, nor man perfected without trials. *Chinese proverb*

32. TESTING
The tree that never had to fight
For sun and sky and air and light,
Never became a forest king,

But lived and died a common thing.
The man who never had to toil,
Who never had to win his share
Of sun and sky and light and air,
Never became a manly man,
But lived and died as he began.
Good timber does not grow on ease.
The stronger wind, the tougher trees,
The farther sky, the greater length,
By sun and cold, by rain and snow,
In tree, or man, good timber grows. DOUGLAS MALLOCK

33. THE OYSTER

There once was an oyster whose story I tell,
Who found that sand had got under his shell;
Just one little grain, but it gave him much pain,
For oysters have feelings although they're so plain.
Now, did he berate the working of Fate,
Which had led him to such a deplorable state?
Did he curse out the government, call for an election?
No; as he lay on the shelf, he said to himself:
"If I cannot remove it, I'll try to improve it."
So the years rolled by as the years always do,
And he came to his ultimate destiny—stew.
And this small grain of sand which had bothered him so,
Was a beautiful pearl, all richly aglow.
Now this tale has a moral—for isn't it grand
What an oyster can do with a morsel of sand;
What couldn't we do if we'd only begin
With all of the things that get under our skin.

34. OVERCOMING AND ACHIEVING

Some of the world's greatest men and women have been saddled with
disabilities and adversities but have managed to overcome them. Cripple him,
and you have a Sir Walter Scott. Lock him in a prison cell, and you have a
John Bunyan. Bury him in the snows of Valley Forge, and you have a George
Washington. Raise him in abject poverty, and you have an Abraham Lincoln.
Subject him to bitter religious prejudice, and you have a Benjamin Disraeli.
Strike him down with infantile paralysis, and he becomes a Franklin D.
Roosevelt. Burn him so severely in a schoolhouse fire that the doctors say he

will never walk again, and you have a Glenn Cunningham, who set a world's record in 1934 for running a mile in 4 minutes, 6.7 seconds. Deafen a genius composer, and you have a Ludwig van Beethoven. Have him or her born black in a society filled with racial discrimination, and you have a Booker T. Washington, a Harriet Tubman, a Marian Anderson, or a George Washington Carver. Make him the first child to survive in a poor Italian family of eighteen children, and you have an Enrico Caruso. Have him born of parents who survived a Nazi concentration camp, paralyze him from the waist down when he is four, and you have an incomparable concert violinist, Itzhak Perlman. Call him a slow learner, "retarded," and write him off as ineducable, and you have an Albert Einstein.

35. THE POSITIVE FRUIT OF TENSION
Theodore E. Steinway, president of Steinway and Sons, once noted, "In one of our concert grand pianos, 243 taut strings exert a pull of 40,000 pounds on an iron frame. It is proof that out of great tension may come great harmony."

36. FINAL INSPECTION
God will look you over, not for medals or degrees, but for scars.
EDWARD SHELDON

37. STRUGGLE
A man confined to bed because of a lingering illness had on his sunlit windowsill a cocoon of a beautiful species of butterfly. As nature took its course, the butterfly began its struggle to emerge from the cocoon. But it was a long, hard battle. As the hours went by, the struggling insect seemed to make almost no progress. Finally, the human observer, thinking that "the powers that be" had erred, took a pair of scissors and snipped the opening larger. The butterfly crawled out, but that's all it ever did—crawl. The pressure of the struggle was intended to push colorful, life-giving juices back into the wings, but the man in his supposed mercy prevented this. The insect never was anything but a stunted abortion, and instead of flying on rainbow wings above the beautiful gardens, it was condemned to spend its brief life crawling in the dust. That gives me the idea that God knows what He is doing. It's a fact that you can depend on Him—even when it seems the struggle is hard and meaningless.

38. GOOD FRIDAY'S SUFFERING
Christ did not come to do away with suffering; He did not come to explain it; He came to fill it with His presence. PAUL CLAUDEL

39. MOTIVATION TO PUSH US
The Lord gives us friends to push us to our potential—and enemies to push us beyond it. JIM VORSAS

40. LIGHT AND SHADOW
Never fear shadows. That just means a light's shining somewhere nearby.

41. HOW BAD WAS IT?
A woman described a nerve-wracking ordeal: "It was like being trapped for four hours in a stuck elevator with a team of Jehovah's Witnesses."

FOUR
Advice

1. GOOD ADVICE FOR ANYONE
While she was enjoying a transatlantic ocean trip, Billie Burke, the famous actress, noticed that a gentleman at the next table was suffering from a bad cold.

She asked him sympathetically, "Are you uncomfortable?" The man nodded.

She said, "I'll tell you just what to do for it. Go back to your stateroom and drink lots of orange juice. Take two aspirins. Cover yourself with all the blankets you can find. Sweat the cold out. I know just what I'm talking about. I'm Billie Burke from Hollywood."

The man smiled warmly and introduced himself in return. He said, "Thanks. I'm Dr. Mayo of the Mayo Clinic."

2. NO HARM, NO BENEFIT
Free advice is like being kissed on the forehead. It doesn't hurt, but it doesn't do too much for you either.

3. BAD BUILDING
He who builds according to every man's advice will have a crooked house. *Danish proverb*

AFFLICTION *(See Adversity)*

FIVE

Aging
(See also Middle Age)

1. OUTLIVING ZEAL
None are so old as those who have outlived enthusiasm.

2. ASPECTS OF AGING
One of the most disturbing aspects of aging is the growing inability to recall vitally important information—such as the gross national product of Liberia, the Greek alphabet, and where you put your slippers. This affliction becomes particularly pronounced when you go upstairs to get something. Halfway up, you realize that you have no inkling of what you were going upstairs to fetch. Then—you have to decide whether to go back downstairs and try to remember what you needed, or continue on up and look for something that needs bringing down. Unable to decide, you resort to sitting on the landing and sulking, only to discover that you have completely forgotten whether you were originally upstairs going down or downstairs going up!

3. NO CONCERT
Maturity is when you're willing to stand in line to get out of going to a rock concert.

4. NEVER AGAIN
I was fired because of my age. I'll never make the mistake of being seventy again. CASEY STENGEL

5. PERSPECTIVE ON GROWING OLDER
Being as I'm now in my middle fifties, I occasionally give some thought to those years, down the road a ways, when I might want to retire. My financial advisor tells me I should give thought to making provision for those years if I want to stay out of the county poor farm. And whenever I have to attend to those sort of plans I sometimes get to thinking back over my career. I remember in particular 1956, more than thirty years back. I was a middler at Fuller Seminary, married and with three little kids. That was the year I had my first surgery, the year I was beginning to think about my future pastoral career. Since then I have served some five churches, and I review with nostalgia and warmth those years of service since then. And I think about my gray hair. And I start to remember how I'm growing older. And then I

remember that year in seminary and it dawns on me that in 1956 George Burns was already entering his sixties—and I don't feel so old after all!
JAMES S. HEWETT

6. GROWING OLDER
As people grow older they tend to become more quiet. They have more to keep quiet about.

7. AGED BUT HEALTHY
The denunciation of the young is a necessary part of the hygiene of older people and greatly assists in the circulation of the blood.
LOGAN PEARSALL SMITH

8. LESS THAN EXPECTED
Children are a comfort to you in your old age—but like your IRA, it's nowhere as much as you expected.

9. WELL PRESERVED
In a conversation with Woody Allen, Groucho Marx said he was often asked what he'd like people to be saying about him in a hundred years. "I know what I'd like them to say about me," responded Woody. "I'd like them to say, 'He looks good for his age.'"

10. OPEN AND READY TO LEARN
The Roman scholar Cato started to study Greek when he was over eighty. Someone asked why he tackled such a difficult task at his age. Cato said, "It's the earliest age I have left."

11. MORE FORMS
An elderly woman was filling out an application for residency in a retirement village. She was a bit nervous answering all the questions about her health, fearing she might be refused admission. But, she finally finished the form and then signed her name and filled in the place where it asked for her current address. After "Zip" she printed firmly: "Normal for my age."

12. SHARP AND OPEN FOR THE FUTURE
A woman in a convalescent home was given a party to celebrate her one hundredth birthday. Her pastor came to offer his congratulations. Later the pastor said, "Her mind was keen and alert. When I arrived, she was completely caught up in the excitement of the birthday party. A reporter had come to interview her. And when he asked that high-spirited, one-hundred-year-old woman, 'Do you have any children?' she replied without hesitation, 'Not yet!'"

13. AGES OF MAN
The seven decades of man: Spills, Drills, Thrills, Bills, Ills, Pills, and Wills.

14. CARE FOR ONE'S ASSETS
If I had known I was going to live this long, I would have taken better care of myself.

15. OLDNESS AND CONFORMITY
One good thing about becoming ninety years old is that you're not subject to much peer pressure.

16. ROSSINI IN RETROSPECT
You know you're a part of the older generation if you can't hear the "William Tell Overture" without thinking of the Lone Ranger.

17. HOW ARE YOU?
A common greeting of these days is, "How are you?" The stereotype reply is, "Fine, and how are you?" I frequently give this reply to my friends who would be dismayed and bored if I tried to tell them the truth, for the edition of this jalopy which I call my body is getting worse and worse, and my friends recognize it and make mental note, "He is slipping fast." No one comments on the obvious and colossal lie that it is.

This jalopy is getting into bad condition. The steering gear is so worn and wobbly that I have to use a cane to keep it from running off the road. The headlights are so dim that they show up only about a half or a third as much as they used to. The horn is a mere squawk. I only get about a tenth of the speed out of it that it gave a few years ago. And as for climbing hills, or even gentler slopes, the less said the better. It is clear that it is going to have to be junked one of these days. But the real person who lives inside this jalopy is a different story. God is much more real and his truth shines more brightly. The companionship of Christ is more constant through His Holy Spirit, and He holds out a hope for a new model, after this jalopy is junked.

This, I think, is what Paul had in mind when he spoke of the reward that God, the righteous Judge, would give him on that day. I think it is also what he was writing to the Philippians about his own body which was in a hazardous state: "I rejoice and I intend to rejoice. I hope all of you will rejoice with me." Paul labeled his new model spiritual and eternal, as compared with our present model, physical and decaying. This then is the lively hope that I can have. I know I do not deserve a new model, and if God, the righteous Judge, determines that I should not have it, that is all right, too. In any case, Righteous Judge is His middle name, sandwiched between His first and last

names, both of which are LOVE. So, I am fine, thank you. How are you?
DR. JOSEPH LEROY DODDS TO HIS GRANDDAUGHTER, MARGO

18. YOUNG IN THE MIND
People grow old only by deserting their ideals. Years may wrinkle the skin, but to give up interest wrinkles the soul.

You are as young as your faith, as old as your doubt; as young as your self-confidence, as old as your fear; as young as your hope, as old as your despair.

In the central place of every heart there is a recording chamber. So long as it receives messages of beauty, hope, cheer, and courage—so long are you young.

When your heart is covered with the snows of pessimism and the ice of cynicism, then, and only then are you grown old—and then, indeed, as the ballad says, you just fade away.

19. THE HARD TRUTH
We don't become more moral as we grow older, we just choose our sins more carefully.

20. YOU KNOW YOU'RE GETTING OLDER WHEN . . .
Almost everything hurts. What doesn't hurt doesn't work anymore. It feels like the morning after the night before, and you haven't been anywhere. All the names in your little black book end in M.D. You get winded playing chess. You look forward to a dull evening. You still chase women but have forgotten why. You turn out the lights for economic, not romantic reasons. Your knees buckle and your belt won't. You are 17 around the neck, 42 around the waist, and 126 around the golf course. You sink your teeth into a steak and they stay there. You try to straighten the wrinkles in your socks and you find you aren't wearing any. A little old gray-haired lady tries to help you across the street. She's your wife.

21. IF I HAD MY LIFE TO LIVE OVER
I'd dare to make more mistakes next time; I'd relax; I would limber up; I would be sillier than I have been this trip; I would take fewer things seriously; I would take more chances; I would climb more mountains and swim more rivers; I would eat more ice cream and less beans; I would perhaps have more actual troubles, but I'd have fewer imaginary ones.

You see, I'm one of those people who lives sensibly and sanely hour after hour, day after day. Oh, I've had my moments, and if I had it to do over again, I'd have more of them. In fact, I'd try to do nothing else, just moments, one after the other instead of living so many years ahead of time.

I've been one of those persons who never goes anywhere without a thermometer, hot water bottle, raincoat, and parachute. If I had to do it again, I would travel lighter than I have. If I had my life to live over, I would start barefoot earlier in the spring and stay that way later in the fall. I would go to more dinners; I would ride more merry-go-rounds; I would pick more daisies. *An elderly woman*

22. RETIREMENT PLANS
A newly hired consultant breezed into the personnel manager's office and interrupted his conversation with another employee to ask how many of the company's employees were approaching retirement age. The personnel manager said, "All of them. Not one of them is going the other way."

23. COUPLES APART
That time of life when a man will let his wife go anywhere as long as she doesn't insist on his coming along.

SIX
Ambition
(See also Determination)

1. TOO MANY BEETLES
Too busy? Distracted? When we attempt to do too many things at once we often get rattled and accomplish even less. The story is told of young Charles Darwin that one day he was eagerly holding one rare beetle in his right fist, another in his left and then suddenly he caught sight of a third beetle that he simply knew he must have for his collection. What to do? In a flash he put one of the beetles in his mouth for safekeeping and reached for the third beetle with his now free hand. But the mouth-imprisoned beetle squirted acid down Darwin's throat—so that in a fit of coughing he lost all three beetles.

2. FOUR STEPS TO YOUR DREAM
Years ago a young black child was growing up in Cleveland, in a home which he later described as "materially poor but spiritually rich."

One day a famous athlete, Charlie Paddock, came to his school to speak to the students. At the time Paddock was considered "the fastest human being alive." He told the children, "Listen! What do you want to be? You name it and then believe that God will help you be it." That little boy decided that he too wanted to be the fastest human being on earth.

The boy went to his track coach and told him of his new dream. His coach told him, "It's great to have a dream, but to attain your dream you must build a ladder to it. Here is the ladder to your dreams. The first rung is determination! And the second rung is dedication! The third rung is discipline! And the fourth rung is attitude!"

The result of all that motivation is that he went on to win four gold medals in the 1936 Berlin Olympics. He won the 100 meter dash and broke the Olympic and world records for the 200 meter. His broad jump record lasted for twenty-four years. His name? Jesse Owens.

3. THINKING BIG

It's tremendous to be learning that no matter how big you see things or how simple you keep them you'll never reach the ultimate. No man has ever seen things as big as they could have been or kept them as simple as they might be. Sometimes we do well in one area at the expense of the other—like the little boy on the corner with his flop-eared pup.

A salesman passed the corner each day, and after a week he began to pity the boy who was striving to sell his puppy. The salesman knew the boy didn't See It Big. He stopped and said, "Son, do you really want to sell this dog?"

The boy replied, "I certainly do."

"Well you're never going to sell him until you learn to See It Big. What I mean is, take this dog home, clean him up, doll him up, raise your price, make people think they're getting something big, and you'll sell him."

That noon the salesman came by and there was the boy with a puppy that was groomed, perfumed, and beribboned alongside a big sign: TREEMENNDOUS Puppy For Sale—$5,000.

The salesman gulped and realized he had forgotten to tell the boy about Keeping It Simple. That evening he stopped by to tell the boy the other half of the formula, only to discover that the boy was gone, the puppy was gone and the sign lay there with "SOLD" written across it in big letters.

The salesman couldn't believe it. This kid couldn't have sold the dog for $5,000. His curiosity got the best of him and he rang the boy's doorbell. The boy came to the door and the salesman blurted, "Son you didn't really sell that dog for $5,000 now, did you?"

The boy replied, "Yes, sir, I did and I want to thank you for all your help."

The salesman said, "How in the world did you do it?"

The boy replied, "Oh, it was easy. I just took two $2,500 cats in exchange!" CHARLES E. "TREMENDOUS" JONES, *Life Is Tremendous*

SEVEN

Angels

1. IF YOU WANT TO SEE THE ANGELS

Have you ever seen an angel? Dr. S. W. Mitchell thought he had. Dr. Mitchell was a well-known neurologist in Philadelphia. After one very tiring day he retired early, but he was awakened by a persistent knocking at the door. It was a little girl, poorly dressed and deeply upset. She told him that her mother was very sick and needed his help. Even though it was a bitterly cold, snowy night and he was bone tired, Mitchell dressed and followed the girl. He found the mother desperately ill with pneumonia. After treating her, Dr. Mitchell complimented the sick woman on her daughter's persistence and courage. The woman gave him a strange look and said, "My daughter died a month ago. Her shoes and coat are in the closet there." Dr. Mitchell went to the closet and opened the door. There hung the very coat worn by the little girl who had been at his front door. The coat was warm and dry and could not possibly have been out in the snowy night.

Have you ever seen an angel? John G. Paton believes he has. While he was a missionary in the New Hebrides Islands, hostile natives surrounded his mission headquarters one night, intent on burning the Patons out and killing them. Paton and his wife prayed all that night. At dawn they were amazed to see the attackers just turn and leave.

A year later the chief of that very tribe was converted to Christianity. Paton then asked him what had kept him and his men from burning down the house and killing them that night. The chief asked Paton a return question: "Who were all those men you had with you there?" Paton told him there had been no one except his wife and himself, but the chief insisted they had seen hundreds of men standing guard—big men in shining garments with drawn swords.

2. ANGELS ON ASSIGNMENT

This happened in 1956 during the Mau Mau uprisings in East Africa. The story is told by veteran missionary Morris Plotts.

A band of roving Mau Maus came to the village of Lauri, surrounded it, and killed every inhabitant, including women and children—three hundred people in all. Not more than three miles away was the Rift Valley Academy, a private boarding school where children were being educated while their missionary parents worked elsewhere. Immediately upon leaving the carnage at Lauri the Mau Maus came with spears, clubs, torches, and bows and arrows to the school, bent on destruction.

You can imagine the fear of those children at the school. Word had already reached them about the destruction of Lauri. There was no place to flee. The only resource was prayer.

Out in the night, lighted torches were seen coming toward the school. Soon there was a complete ring of these terrorists about the school, cutting off all avenues of escape. Shouting and curses could be heard coming from the Mau Maus. Then they began to advance on the school, tightening the circle, shouting louder, coming closer. Suddenly, when they were close enough to throw a spear, they stopped. They began to retreat, and soon they were running into the jungle. A call had gone out to the authorities, and an army had been sent in the direction of the school to rescue the inhabitants. But by the time the army arrived, the would-be assassins had dispersed. The army spread out in search of them and captured the entire band of raiding Mau Maus.

Later, before the judge at their trial, the Mau Mau leader was called to the witness stand. The judge asked him, "On this night did you kill the inhabitants of Lauri?"

The leader replied, "Yes."

"Was it your intent to do the same at the Rift Valley Academy?"

"Yes."

"Well then," asked the judge, "why did you not complete the mission? Why didn't you attack the school?"

The leader, who had never read the Bible and never heard the gospel, replied, "We were on our way to attack and destroy all the people at the school. But as we came closer, all of a sudden between us and the school there were many huge men, dressed in white with flaming swords. We became afraid and we ran to hide!"

3. GOD'S SPECIAL MESSENGER

In the spring of 1982 I was the speaker at a morning prayer group which meets in a town near Springfield, Illinois. Before I spoke, a neighboring pastor shared about his recent trip to Mexico. He, along with several others, had gone there on a preaching mission. While they were returning, their van developed mechanical problems. After jacking up the van, the pastor crawled underneath to check out the problem. The jack collapsed, and he suddenly felt the crushing weight of the van on his chest. His companions quickly grabbed the bumper to lift the van. They weren't able to budge it. He cried out, "Jesus! Jesus!" Within a few seconds a youthful-looking Mexican came running toward them. He was thin and small in stature. He was smiling. As he reached the van, he grabbed the van and lifted it. The others joined in, and the van lifted like a feather.

As he was freed, the pastor felt his chest expand and the broken bones mend. The visitor then lowered the van, waved to them, and ran in the direction from which he had come, until he disappeared on the horizon. No one knew who the mysterious visitor was or where he had come from.

"The Lord encamps around those who fear him and rescues them" (Psalm 34:7). KENNETH NORDVALL

4. THE TRAIN STOPS JUST IN TIME

The British express train raced through the night, its powerful headlamp spearing the black darkness ahead. The train was carrying Queen Victoria.

Suddenly the engineer saw a startling sight. Revealed in the beam of the engine's headlights was a weird figure in a black cloak, standing in the middle of the tracks and waving its arms. The engineer grabbed for the brakes and brought the train to a grinding halt.

He and his fellow trainsmen climbed out to see what had stopped them. They could find no trace of the strange figure. On a hunch, the engineer walked a few yards farther up the tracks. Suddenly he stopped and stared into the fog in horror. A bridge had been washed out and had fallen into a swollen stream. If he had not heeded the ghostly figure, the train would have plunged into the stream.

While the bridge and tracks were being repaired, the crew made a more intensive search for the strange flagman. But not until they got to London did they solve the mystery.

At the base of the engine's headlamp was a huge moth. The engineer looked at it for a moment, then on impulse wet its wings and pasted it to the glass of the lamp. Climbing back into his cab, he switched on the lamp and saw the "phantom flagman" in the beam. He knew what had happened: the moth had flown into the beam, seconds before the train reached the washed-out bridge. In the fog, it appeared to be a phantom figure waving its arms.

When Queen Victoria was told of the strange happening she said, "I'm sure it was no accident. It was God's way of protecting us."

5. BACK TO LIFE

A seventy-year-old woman in China was the only one who had knowledge of most of the daily operations of her family as well as the operations of a house church. She alone knew where the Bibles were, who the messengers were, who could or could not be trusted. Suddenly she died of a heart attack.

Her family felt lost. She had not been able to pass on the information that was so vital to all. They began to pray, "Lord, restore our mother back to life." After being dead for two days, she came back to life. She scolded her family for calling her back. They reasoned with her. They said they would pray that in two days she could return to the Lord. It would, they said, take that much time to set the matters straight.

After two days, the family and friends began to sing hymns and pray that the Lord would take her back. The mother's final words were, "They're coming. Two angels are coming." The incident caused the entire village to repent. CARL LAWRENCE, *The Church in China*

6. WITNESS TO ANGELS

Six Soviet cosmonauts said they witnessed the most awe-inspiring spectacle ever encountered in space—a band of glowing angels with wings as big as jumbo jets. Cosmonauts Vladimir Solovev, Oleg Atkov, and Leonid Kizim said they first saw the celestial beings during their 155th day aboard the orbiting *Salyat 7* space station. "What we saw, " they said, "were seven giant figures in the shape of humans, but with wings and mistlike halos, as in the classic depiction of angels. Their faces were round with cherubic smiles." Twelve days later the figures returned and were seen by three other Soviet scientists, including woman cosmonaut Svetlana Savitskaya. "They were smiling," she said, "as though they shared a glorious secret."

7. THE SOUND OF ANGELS

We so often hear the expression "the voice of an angel" that I got to wondering what an angel would sound like. So I did some research and discovered that an angel's voice sounds remarkably like a person saying, "Hurry up!"

Prior to my research, I thought that the voice of an angel would be beautiful. But the words "Get up and hurry!" are rarely beautiful, especially at seven in the morning. Yet the Bible records many instances of angels saying these words. An angel comes to Peter in jail and says, "Rise quickly." An angel says to Gideon, "Arise and go in this thy might." An angel says to

Elijah, "Arise and eat." An angel appears to Joseph in a dream, when Herod is slaughtering the infants, and says, "Go quickly." An angel appears to Philip and says, "Arise and go."

Really, the angels are monotonous talkers! They always say the same thing—"Arise, hurry!" But so is a fire bell monotonous. If we are to be saved, it will be by monotony, the reiterated command, "Get up and get going!" Listen carefully and you can hear the voice of angels above the contemporary din of the world, a voice that ought to get us out of lounge chairs and comfortable beds. "Arise, go quickly!"

8. THE INHABITANTS OF HEAVEN

Of all the supernatural beings mentioned in the Scriptures, it is the angels who are constantly depicted as being identified with heaven. When the angel of God called to Hagar in the wilderness, we read that this call was heard "out of heaven" (Gen. 21:17). When the angel appeared at the time of the vision which Jacob heard at Bethel, he saw a ladder reaching to heaven on which the angels of God were ascending and descending. Often the angels are called the "heavenly ones" (Ps. 29:1) or the "heavenly host" (Luke 2:13). When the angelic host had finished their song to the shepherds, we read that "the angels went away with them into heaven" (Luke 2:15). It was an angel "from heaven" that rolled away the stone at the tomb where our Lord was buried (Matt. 28:2). Our Lord Himself often spoke of "the angels in heaven" (Mark 12:25; 13:32; Matt. 22:30). Then we have such a phrase as "the angels of heaven" (Matt. 24:36), and in a most interesting passage our Lord said, "Angels do always behold the face of my Father which is in heaven" (Matt. 18:10). Wilbur M. Smith, *The Biblical Doctrine of Heaven*

EIGHT

Anger

1. TIME TO THINK

When you're angry always count to ten before you say anything. It'll give you more time to come up with the right insult.

2. HOLD ON TIGHT

Your temper is one of your most valuable possessions. Don't lose it.

3. A MEAN DRUNK

It seems this man had been drinking for awhile in one of those bars on the top floor of a skyscraper and he had become mean and surly. Another patron decided to cheer him up. He told him that life was really great and he wasn't going to leave until he started to smile. This obviously bugged the surly patron, but they did get into a conversation. Finally the drinker pointed out at the skyline and asked the unappointed cheerleader if he knew what happened to the winds when they swept through the big city's skyscrapers. He allowed as he didn't know. So he told him, "When the wind sweeps through the buildings of a big city it creates powerful updrafts. Sometimes, like today, they are so strong that you can hardly throw anything off the building without it being blown right back up to the top."

He walked out onto the penthouse, climbed up onto the wall, and said, "Look, I'll show you. I'll jump off, and the wind will bring me right back up." Before the man could stop him, the drinker had jumped off the building. The cheerful drinker looked over the edge as the man fell past the 80th floor, 70th floor, 60th floor, 50th floor and sure enough, down about the 40th floor the man's fall slowed and gradually he began to come back up to the top of the building and climbed back over the ledge safe and sound. He said, "See—isn't that amazing?"

Well, of course, the man was stunned. He said, "That is the most incredible thing I have ever seen. That must really be exciting. Do you think I could do it too?"

The surly patron said, "Of course you could."

So, the man climbed up on the ledge and jumped. And he fell like a rock, splat, all the way to the pavement below never pausing for even a moment during his drop. Meanwhile, the surly man went back to the bar and ordered another drink. As he sat down the bartender turned to another patron, pointed to the surly drinker and said, "That Clark Kent really gets mean when he drinks."

ANXIETY *(See Worry)*

NINE
Appearances
(See also Pretense and Hypocrisy)

1. BIG ISN'T EVERYTHING
It doesn't depend on size, or a cow would catch a rabbit. *Pennsylvania German proverb*

2. BEAUTY AND BRUTALITY
The beauty of the tiger's skin does not lessen the sharpness of his teeth. PAUL ELDRIDGE

3. THE BEAUTIFUL AND THE PRACTICAL
Remember that the most beautiful things in the world are the most useless; peacocks and lilies for instance. JOHN RUSKIN

TEN
Atonement
(See also Christ)

1. A PICTURE OF ATONEMENT
It was a mountain one-room school house where severe discipline was used to keep the rowdyism of uninterested pupils in check. The noon recess was ended and the teacher was interrogating the class with regard to the disappearance of Sally Jane's lunch. After a few minutes of verbal threats and demands, a sob was heard. It was little Billy—a thin, undernourished child. His family was the poorest of the poor.

"Did you take Sally Jane's lunch?" demanded the teacher.

"Yes, sir," mumbled Billy through his tears. "I was hungry."

"Nevertheless, you did wrong to steal and you must be punished," declared the teacher.

As the teacher removed the leather strap from its place on the wall, Billy was ordered to the front of the room and told to remove his shirt. The arm of the teacher was raised over the bent and trembling form of little Billy.

"HOLD IT, TEACHER!" shouted a husky voice from the rear of the room. It was Big Jim striding down the aisle removing his shirt as he came. "Let me take his whipp'n," he begged.

The teacher was aghast, but knowing that justice must be demonstrated, he consented and laid the belt to the back of Big Jim with such force that even the stronger boy winced and his eyes watered. But Billy never forgot the day that Big Jim took his place.

2. I HAVE THE PEACE
A friend visited an elderly woman badly crippled by arthritis. When asked, "Do you suffer much?" she responded, "Yes, but there is no nail here," and she pointed to her hand. "He had the nails, I have the peace." She pointed to her head. "There are no thorns here. He had the thorns, I have the peace." She touched her side. "There is no spear here. He had the spear, I have the peace." That is what the atonement of Jesus Christ means for us—He gave of himself so that we might have the peace. RALPH TURNBULL, *If I Only Had One Sermon to Preach*

3. A CURIOUS FEELING ABOUT THE CROSS
We crucified him on a stick, but we have always had a curious feeling that He somehow managed to get hold of the right end of it.
GEORGE BERNARD SHAW

4. THE HEART OF THE FAITH
Nikolai Berdyaev, who abandoned Marx for Christianity, insists that neither history nor theology nor the church brought him to the Christian faith, but a simple woman called only Mother Maria. He was present at a concentration camp when the Nazis were murdering Jews in gas chambers. One distraught mother refused to part with her baby. When Maria saw that the officer was only interested in numbers, without a word she pushed the mother aside and quickly took her place. This action revealed to Berdyaev the heart of Christianity—and what atonement means.

5. COVERING SINS
The story of Christ's coverage for sins has been told so often to some of us that the message just doesn't seem to get through. We are jaded. Somehow we need to find ways to get the message through in vital and fresh and arresting ways.

There is a wonderful story about a young family moving into a new house. The move had been scheduled weeks in advance, but when the day approached the husband announced that an important meeting had been called at the office, and he would be unable to help. Consequently, the wife had to handle the move by herself. After the moving van had pulled away, the wife found herself standing in the living room of the new house surrounded by boxes to be unpacked, appliances to be hooked up, a screaming baby, and a five-year-old who decided to throw one of his metal toys through the picture window. Fortunately, the child wasn't hurt, but the jagged glass was scattered everywhere and a brisk wind was blowing through the opening. The wife was now so upset that she simply had to tell her husband what was happening. When she called him on the telephone, a secretary informed her that he was tied up in the meeting and could not be disturbed. The secretary asked, "Would you like to leave a message?" This didn't help her at all because from past experience the wife knew that he could be extremely lax about returning telephone calls home. So she figured out a way to get to him. She replied, "Just tell him the insurance will cover it. Call home for details."

The moment he got the message, he called home.

Maybe we need to learn from this some ways to arrest people with the message of God's coverage for sin. Maybe we need to rephrase the headlines of our faith for each generation in ways that will seize their minds and demand their attention!

6. THE SUBSTITUTE

There was a law in Tokyo about 1900 that no foreigner could take up residence there unless he had a "substitute." There were natives who hired themselves out for this purpose. If the foreigner broke any law, the substitute suffered the penalty for it, even if the penalty were death. In a similar way, our standing before God and his law is only obtainable through the substitutionary work of His Son. And this substitutionary work is obtained without any fee—only faith in Him. JAMES M. GRAY

7. APPROPRIATING THE SOLUTION

A Japanese soldier by the name of Shoichi Yokoi lived in a cave on the island of Guam to which he fled in 1944 when the tides of war began to change. Fearing for his life, he stayed hidden for twenty-eight years in the jungle cave, coming out only at night. During this self-imposed exile he lived on frogs, rats, snails, shrimp, nuts and mangoes. Even when he figured out the war was over he was afraid to come out for fear he would be executed. Two hunters found him one day and escorted him to freedom. He was living all this time under the indictment of sins that had all been dealt with—but he simply had not appropriated the atonement that was available.

8. PURSUED BY THE ATONING LOVE

One evening a woman was driving home when she noticed a huge truck behind her that was driving uncomfortably close. She stepped on the gas to gain some distance from the truck, but when she sped up the truck did too. The faster she drove, the faster drove the truck.

Now scared, she exited the freeway. But the truck stayed with her. The woman then turned up a main street, hoping to lose her pursuer in traffic. But the truck ran a red light and continued the chase.

Reaching the point of panic, the woman whipped her car into a service station and bolted out of her auto screaming for help. The truck driver sprang from his truck and ran toward her car. Yanking the back door open, the driver pulled out a man hidden in the backseat.

The woman was running from the wrong person. From his high vantage point, the truck driver had spotted a would-be rapist in the woman's car. The chase was not his effort to harm her but to save her even at the cost of his own safety.

Likewise, many people run from God's provision of atonement on the cross, fearing what He might do to them. But His plans are for good not evil—to rescue us from the hidden sins that endanger our lives.

9. BUYING BACK THE BOAT

One of the old favorites is the story of the father and son who worked for months to build a toy sailboat. Every night when he came home from work the man and his boy would disappear into the garage for hours. It was a labor of love—love for each other and for the thing they were creating. The wooden hull was painted bright red and it was trimmed with gleaming white sails. When it was finished, they traveled to a nearby lake for the boat's trial run. Before launching it the father tied a string to its stern to keep it from sailing too far. The boat performed beautifully, but before long a motorboat crossing the lake cut the string, and the sailboat drifted out of sight on the large lake. Attempts to find it were fruitless, and both father and son wept over its loss. A few weeks later as the boy was walking home from school he passed his favorite toy store and was amazed to see a toy sailboat in the window—his sailboat! He ran inside to claim the boat, telling the proprietor about his experience on the lake. The store owner explained that he had found the boat while on a fishing trip. "You may be its maker," he said, "but as a finder I am its legal owner. You may have it back—for fifty dollars." The boy was stunned at how much it would cost him to regain his boat, but since it was so precious to him he quickly set about earning the money to buy it back. Months later he joyfully walked into the toy store and handed the owner fifty dollars in exchange for his sailboat. It was the happiest day of his life. As he left the store he held the boat up to the sunlight. Its colors gleamed as though newly painted. "I made you, but I lost you," he said. "Now I've bought you back. That makes you twice mine, and twice mine is mine forever."

10. THE SON AND THE DRAWBRIDGE

A man had the duty to raise a drawbridge to allow the steamers to pass on the river below and to lower it again for trains to cross over on land. One day, this man's son visited him, desiring to watch his father at work. Quite curious, as most boys are, he peeked into a trapdoor that was always left open so his father could keep an eye on the great machinery that raised and lowered the bridge. Suddenly, the boy lost his footing and tumbled into the gears. As the father tried to reach down and pull him out, he heard the whistle of an approaching train. He knew the train would be full of people and that it would be impossible to stop the fast-moving locomotive, therefore, the bridge must be lowered! A terrible dilemma confronted him: if he saved the people, his son would be crushed in the cogs. Frantically, he tried to free the boy, but to no avail. Finally, the father put his hand to the lever that would start the machinery. He paused and then, with tears he pulled it. The giant gears began to work and the bridge clamped down just in time to save the train. The passengers, not knowing what the father had done, were laughing and making merry; yet the bridgekeeper had chosen to save their lives at the cost of his son's.

In all of this there is a parable: the heavenly Father, too, saw the blessed Savior being nailed to a cross while people laughed and mocked and spit upon Him and yet, "He spared not his own Son, but delivered him up for us all."

11. RECONCILIATION, HAND IN HAND

There was a little girl whose parents had had a miserable marriage and were divorced, having nothing in common save their affection for the child. One day as the girl was playing in the street she was knocked down by a bus and seriously injured. Taken to the hospital, she was examined by the doctors but was found to be beyond human aid. Hastily summoned to the hospital, her parents heard the sad news and stood silently, one on either side of the bed, looking down helplessly at the little girl. As they stood there, the child's eyes suddenly opened and seeing her parents she tried to smile. Then drawing one arm from under the sheet, she held it out in the direction of her father. "Daddy," she said, "give me your hand." Turning to her mother, she stretched out her other arm. "Mummy," she said, "give me your hand." Then with a final effort of her fast-ebbing strength she drew them close together. This is a picture of what Christ did on the cross. The Savior took the hand of sinful hateful humanity and placed it in the loving hand of God. Jesus reconciled us to God; He broke down the barrier; He restored the broken fellowship caused by sin or turning our backs on God. Just as in this little girl's dying to bring her parents together, Jesus was dying to bring God and us together, but we have to make the effort to keep the relationship going.

12. A KEEN JUSTICE
Zaleusus flourished about 500 B.C. His government over the Locrians was severe but just. In one of his decrees he forbade the use of wine unless it were prescribed as medicine; and in another he ordered that all adulterers should be punished with the loss of both their eyes. When his own son became subject to this penalty, the father, in order to maintain the authority of the laws, but to show parental leniency, shared the penalty with his son by ordering one of his own eyes to be thrust out along with one of his offending son. In this way, the majesty of his government was maintained, and his own character as a just and righteous sovereign was magnified in the eyes of his subjects.

ELEVEN
Attitude
(See also Point of View)

1. THE FAULT
One man gets nothing but discord out of a piano; another gets harmony. No one claims the piano is at fault. Life is about the same. The discord is there, but so is the harmony. Study to play it correctly, and it will give forth the beauty; play it falsely, and it will give forth the ugliness. Life is not at fault.

2. FEAR ENLARGES
Fear makes the wolf seem bigger than he is.

3. DONE WITH RELUCTANCE
There is nothing so easy but that it becomes difficult when you do it with reluctance.

4. THINK IMPOSSIBLE

Attempt something so impossible that, unless God is in it, it is doomed to failure. JOHN HAGGAI

5. AIMING HIGH

Who shoots at the midday sun, though he be sure he shall never hit the mark, yet as sure he is he shall shoot higher than he who aims at a bush. SIR PHILIP SIDNEY

6. THE IMPULSE

One can never consent to creep when one feels an impulse to soar. HELEN KELLER

7. EYES TO SEE

Gutzon Borglum, the sculptor, was once working on a head of Lincoln. A woman who was sweeping out his studio wondered what he was doing. One day she finally recognized the face of Abraham Lincoln emerging from the stone. Very much surprised, she turned to Borglum and asked, "How did you know that Mr. Lincoln was in that piece of stone?"

8. POSITIVE MENTAL ATTITUDE

A little boy was overheard talking to himself as he strutted through the backyard, baseball cap in place, toting ball and bat. He was heard to say, "I'm the greatest hitter in the world." Then he tossed the ball into the air, swung at it and missed. "Strike one!" Undaunted he picked up the ball, threw it into the air and said to himself—"I'm the greatest baseball hitter ever," and he swung at the ball again. And again he missed. "Strike two!" He paused a moment to examine his bat and ball carefully. Then a third time he threw the ball into the air. "I'm the greatest hitter who ever lived," he said. He swung the bat hard again, missed a third time. He cried out, "Wow! Strike three! What a pitcher! I'm the greatest pitcher in the world!"

9. LIFE'S DEEPER MEANING

Examining life for Deeper Meanings is a twentieth century preoccupation. We assume that things are not what they seem. Words disguise Hidden Feelings. Actions symbolize Something Else. We sometimes try too hard to discover the hidden meanings when there just might not be anymore to it than what is on the surface. Tom Mullen illustrates this at the very beginning of his book:

An engineer, a psychologist, and a theologian were hunting in the wilds of northern Canada. They came across an isolated cabin, far removed from any town. Because friendly hospitality is a virtue practiced by those who live in the wilderness, the hunters knocked on the door to ask permission to rest.

No one answered their knocks, but, discovering the cabin was unlocked, they entered. It was a simple place—two rooms with a minimum of furniture and household equipment. Nothing was surprising about the cabin except the stove. It was large, potbellied, and made of cast iron. What was unusual was its location: it was suspended in midair by wires attached to the ceiling beams. "Fascinating," said the psychologist. "It is obvious that this lonely trapper, isolated from humanity, has elevated his stove so he can curl up under it and vicariously experience a return to the womb." "Nonsense!" replied the engineer. "The man is practicing the laws of thermodynamics. By elevating his stove, he has discovered a way to distribute heat more evenly throughout the cabin." "With all due respect," interrupted the theologian, "I'm sure that hanging his stove from the ceiling has religious meaning. Fire 'lifted up' has been a religious symbol for centuries." The three debated the point for several minutes without resolving the issue. When the trapper finally returned, they immediately asked him why he had hung his heavy potbellied stove by wires from the ceiling. His answer was succinct: "Had plenty of wire, not much stove pipe!" Tom Mullen, *Laughing Out Loud and Other Religious Experiences*

10. WHAT ARE YOU LOOKING FOR?
If you only look for holes, you will think a screen is useless; yet it keeps the flies out.

11. CHOOSING ONE'S WAY
We who lived in concentration camps can remember the men who walked through the huts comforting others, giving away their last piece of bread. They may have been few in number, but they offer sufficient proof that everything can be taken from a man but one thing: the last of human freedoms—to choose one's attitude in any given set of circumstances, to choose one's own way. Viktor Frankl, *Man's Search for Meaning*

12. THE DIFFERENCE
There are two types of people in the world—those who come into a room and say, "Here I am!" and those who say, "Ah, there you are!"

13. NAPOLEON'S ADVERTISING
When Napoleon was an artillery officer at the siege of Toulon, he built a battery in such an exposed position that he was told he would never find men to man it. But Napoleon had a sure instinct for what was required. He put up a sign saying The Battery of Men without Fear, and the battery was always manned.

14. THE ATTITUDE OF YOUTH

Youth is not a time of life, it is a state of mind, a product of the imagination, a vigor of the emotions, a predominance of courage over timidity, an appetite for adventure.

Nobody grows old by living a number of years. People grow old when they desert their ideals. Years wrinkle the skin, but to give up enthusiasm wrinkles the soul.

Worry, self-doubt, fear, and anxiety—these are the culprits that bow the head and break the spirit.

Whether seventeen or seventy, there exists in the heart of every person who loves life the thrill of a new challenge, the insatiable appetite for what is coming next. You are as young as your faith and as old as your doubts.

So long as your heart receives from your head messages that reflect beauty, courage, joy, and excitement, you are young. When your thinking becomes clouded with pessimism and prevents you from taking risks, then you are old.

15. PLEASURE SEEKING

Thinking the world should entertain you leads to boredom and sloth. Thinking you should entertain the world leads to bright clothes, odd graffiti, and amazing grace in running for the bus. *The Next Whole Earth Catalog*

16. PERCENTAGE PRAYERS

Three Indians—a Navajo, a Hopi and an Apache—were speaking about how powerful their prayers were. The Navajo said, "You know, we Navajos pray for healing, and the patients get well about half the time." The Hopi said, "Well, we Hopis pray for rain, and it happens about 70 percent of the time." Finally, the Apache spoke up: "Yes, but we Apaches have the sunrise prayer dance, and it works every time."

TWELVE
Authority
(See also Leadership)

1. FORM AND SUBSTANCE

A young second lieutenant at Fort Bragg discovered that he had no change when he was about to buy a soft drink from a vending machine. He flagged down a passing private and asked him, "Do you have change for a dollar?" The private said cheerfully, "I think so, let me take a look." The lieutenant drew himself up stiffly and said, "Soldier, that's no way to address an officer. We'll start all over again. Do you have change for a dollar?" The private came to attention, saluted smartly, and said, "No, sir!"

2. POTENCY IN THE JUNGLE
The jackass brays mightily but the forest does not tremble. The tiger's paw barely presses the fallen leaf, and all rush for shelter. PAUL ELDRIDGE

THIRTEEN
The Bible

1. THE BONES OF BELIEF
A clergyman took a seat in a dining car on a train traveling along the Hudson River. Opposite him was an atheist who, seeing his clerical collar, started a discussion. "I see you are a clergyman." "Yes," came the reply. "I am a minister of the gospel." "I suppose you believe the Bible." The clergyman, orthodox in his views, responded, "I certainly do believe the Bible to be the Word of God." "But aren't there things in the Bible you can't explain?" With humility the minister answered, "Yes, there are places in the Bible too hard for me to understand." With an air of triumph as though he had cornered the preacher, the atheist asked, "Well, what do you do then?" Unruffled, the clergyman went on eating his dinner—which happened to be Hudson shad, a tasty fish but noted for its bony structure. Looking up, he said, "Sir, I do just the same as when eating this shad. When I come to the bones, I put them to the side of the plate and go on enjoying my lunch. I leave the bones for some fool to choke on."

2. THE DEEPER MEANING OF SCRIPTURE
Sign in the church nursery: We shall not all sleep, but we shall all be changed. (1 Corinthians 15:51)

3. SO MUCH TIME TO READ
How much time does it take to read from Genesis to Revelation? If you would read the Bible at standard pulpit speed (slow enough to be heard and

understood) the reading time would be seventy-one hours. If you would break that down into minutes and divide it into 365 days you could read the entire Bible, cover to cover, in only twelve minutes a day. Is this really too much time to spend reading about God?

4. THE BIBLE AND ITS CHRIST

We have an almost superstitious attitude to Bible reading as if it had some magical efficacy. But there is no magic in the Bible or in the mechanical reading of the Bible. No, the written Word points to the Living Word and says to us, "Go to Jesus." If we do not go to the Jesus to whom it points, we miss the whole purpose of Bible reading.

Evangelical Christians are not, or ought not to be, what we are sometimes accused of being, namely, "bibliolaters," worshipers of the Bible. We do not worship the Bible; we worship the Christ of the Bible. Here is a young man who is in love. He has a girlfriend who has captured his heart. As a result he carries a photograph of his beloved in his wallet because it reminds him of her when she is far away. Sometimes, when nobody is looking, he might even take the photograph out and give it a surreptitious kiss. But kissing the photograph is a poor substitute for the real thing. And so it is with the Bible. We love it only because we love him of whom it speaks. JOHN R. W. STOTT

5. RULE FOR PRUDENT RELIGION

On the whole subject of religion, one rule of modesty and soberness is to be observed, and it is this: In obscure matters not to speak or think, or even long to know, more than the Word of God has delivered. A second rule is that in reading the Scriptures we should constantly direct our inquiries and meditations to those things which tend to edification, not indulge in curiosity, or in studying things of no use. JOHN CALVIN

6. THE POTENT WORD OF GOD

The Epistle to the Hebrews is difficult to translate because so much of the content concerns the Jewish culture and religious rituals that are totally foreign to the Agta people who live in the northern Philippines. However, some parts of the epistle really make sense to them, like the verse in Hebrews 4:12, "The Word of God is living and potent."

Depending upon the context, the Agta word *madagat* can mean stinging, venomous, or potent. A poisonous snake is *madagat,* but so are some medicines that can heal. My translation assistant explained his understanding of how the Word of God is potent: "It depends upon how we approach it. If we disregard it, it's like the poisonous snake. But if we live by it, its potency is like medicine."

7. SIMPLE UNDERSTANDING

There was no gymnasium on our seminary campus, so we played basketball in a nearby public school. The janitor, an old black man with white hair, would wait patiently until the seminarians had finished playing. Invariably he sat there reading his Bible.

One day I went up to him and inquired, "What are you reading?"

The man did not simply reply, "The Bible." Instead he answered, "The Book of Revelation."

With a bit of surprise, I asked, "The Book of Revelation? Do you understand it?"

"Oh yes," the man assured me. "I understand it."

"You understand the Book of Revelation! What does it mean?"

Very quietly that old janitor answered, "It means that Jesus is gonna win."
BERNARD TRAVAIEILLE

8. THE AGE OF ELIZABETH I

No greater moral change ever passed over a nation than passed over England during the years which parted the middle of the reign of Elizabeth from the Long Parliament. England became a people of the book, and that book was the Bible. It was read at churches and read at home, and everywhere its words, as they fell on ears which custom had not deadened, kindled a startling enthusiasm. As a mere literary monument, the English verson of the Bible remains the noblest example of the English tongue. But far greater was the effect of the Bible on the character of the people. Elizabeth might silence or tune the pulpits, but it was impossible for her to silence or tune the great preachers of justice and mercy and truth who spoke from the Book. The whole temper of the nation felt the change. A new conception of life and of man superseded the old. A new moral and religious impulse spread through every class. JOHN RICHARD GREEN, *A Short History of the English People*

BRAVERY *(See Courage)*

FOURTEEN
Chance

1. LOOK AGAIN
If everything is coming your way, you must be in the wrong lane.

2. SERENDIPITY
Even a blind hog occasionally turns up an acorn.

3. YOU MUST DO YOUR OWN THING
Question: How many psychiatrists does it take to change a light bulb?
Answer: Only one, but the light bulb must really want to change.

4. SOMETIMES THERE IS JUSTICE
In Czechoslovakia, Vera Czermak of Prague discovered her husband was cheating on her. She contemplated both murder and suicide, and chose the latter, blindly leaping out of her third-story window. She incurred only minor injuries, however, because she landed on her husband in the street below, killing him.

FIFTEEN
Change and Conversion
(See also Repentance)

1. HOW GOD BRINGS CHANGE
Charles Colson told the following story in an address at Reformed Theological Seminary in Jackson, Mississippi:

I love the illustration about a man named Jack Eckerd. A few years ago I was on the Bill Buckley television program, talking about restitution (one of my favorite subjects) and criminal justice. Bill Buckley agreed with me. A few days later I got a call from Jack Eckerd, a businessman from Florida, the founder of the Eckerd Drug chain, the second largest drug chain in America. He saw me on television and asked me to come to Florida. He agreed Florida had a criminal justice crisis, would I come down and do something about it? And we did. We got the attorney general of the state, the president of the senate; we got on Jack Eckerd's Lear jet; we went around the State of Florida advocating criminal justice reforms, and everywhere we would go Jack Eckerd would introduce me to the crowds and say, "This is Chuck Colson, my friend; I met him on Bill Buckley's television program. He's born again, I'm not. I wish I were." And then he'd sit down. We'd get on the airplane and I'd tell him about Jesus. We'd get off at the next stop, he'd repeat it, we'd do the same thing again, and I'd talk to him about Jesus. When we left I gave him some of R. C. Sproul's books and I gave him C. S. Lewis's *Mere Christianity,* which had such an impact on me. I sent him my books. About a year went by and I kept pestering Jack Eckerd. And eventually one day he read some things including the story of Watergate and the Resurrection out of my book, *Loving God,* and decided that Jesus was, in fact, resurrected from the dead. He called me up to tell me he believed that, and I asked him some other things. When he got through telling me what he believed I said, "You're born again!" He said, "No, I'm not, I haven't felt anything." I said, "Yes, you are! Pray with me right now." After we prayed he said, "I am? Marvelous!" The first thing he did was to walk into one of his drugstores and walked down through the book shelves and he saw *Playboy* and *Penthouse.* And he'd seen it there many times before, but it never bothered him before. Now he saw them with new eyes. He'd become a Christian.

He went back to his office. He called in his president. He said, "Take *Playboy* and *Penthouse* out of my stores." The president said, "You can't mean that, Mr. Eckerd. We make three million dollars a year on those books." He said, "Take 'em out of my stores." And in 1,700 stores across America, by one man's decision, those magazines and smut were removed from the shelves because a man had given his life to Christ. I called Jack Eckerd up. I said, "I want to use that story. Did you do that because of your commitment to Christ?" He said, "Why else would I give away three million dollars? The Lord wouldn't let me off the hook."

Isn't that marvelous? *God wouldn't let me off the hook.* I don't know any theologian who's better defined the Lordship of Christ than that. And what happened after that is a wonderful sequel and a wonderful demonstration of what happens in our culture today.

We are caught up with this idea that we've got to have big political institutions and big structures and big movements and big organizations in order to change things in our society. And that's an illusion and a fraud. Jack Eckerd wrote a letter to all the other drugstore operators, all the other chains, and he said, "I've taken it out of my store. Why don't you take it out of yours?" Not a one answered him. Of course not—he'd put them under conviction. So he wrote them some more letters. But then Eckerd's drugs began to get floods of people coming in to buy things at Eckerd's because they'd taken *Playboy* and *Penthouse* out. And so People's removed the magazines from their shelves and then Dart Drug removed them from their shelves and then Revco removed them from their shelves. And over the period of twelve months while the pornography commission in Washington was debating over what to do about pornography, and while they're trying to come up with some recommendations for the president about what to do which will result in laws which if Congress ever passes them will be sued by the ACLU and will be tied up in the courts for 10 years—meanwhile, across America, one by one, stores are removing them. And the 7-11 chairman, who sits on Jack Eckerd's board, finally gave in two weeks ago and 5,000 7-11 stores removed it. And in a period of twelve months, 11,000 retail outlets in America removed *Playboy* and *Penthouse*, not because somebody passed a law, but because God wouldn't let one of his men off the hook. That's what brings change.

2. MOODY'S CONVERSION

In May 1855, an eighteen-year-old boy went to the deacons of a church in Boston. He had been raised in a Unitarian church, in almost total ignorance of the gospel, but when he had moved to Boston to make his fortune, he began to attend a Bible-preaching church. Then, in April of 1855, his Sunday school teacher had come into the store where he was working and simply and persuasively shared the gospel and urged the young man to trust in the Lord Jesus. He had, and now he was applying to join the church. One fact quickly became obvious. This young man was almost totally ignorant of biblical truth. One of the deacons asked him, "Son, what has Christ done for us all—for you—which entitles Him to our love?" His response was, "I don't know. I think Christ has done a great deal for us, but I don't think of anything in particular as I know of."

Hardly an impressive start. Years later his Sunday school teacher said of him: "I can truly say that I have seen few persons whose minds were spiritually darker than was his when he came into my Sunday school class. I think the committee of the church seldom met an applicant for membership who seemed more unlikely ever to become a Christian of clear and decided views of gospel truth, still less to fill any space of public or extended usefulness." Nothing happened very quickly to change their minds. The deacons decided to put him on a year-long instruction program to teach him basic Christian truths. Perhaps they wanted to work on some of his other rough spots as well. Not only was he ignorant of spiritual truths, he was only barely literate, and his spoken grammar was atrocious. The year-long probation did not help very much. At his second interview, there was only a minimal improvement in the quality of his answers, but since it was obvious that he was a sincere and committed (if ignorant) Christian, they accepted him as a church member.

Over the next years, I am sure that many people looked at that young man and, convinced that God would never use a person like that, they wrote off Dwight L. Moody. But God did not. By God's infinite grace and persevering love, D. L. Moody was transformed into one of the most effective servants of God in church history, a man whose impact is still with us. GARY INRIG, *Hearts of Iron, Feet of Clay*

3. PENNEY'S CONVERSION

J. C. Penney was a man of advanced years before he committed his life fully to Jesus Christ. He had been a good man, honest, but primarily interested in becoming a success and making money. "When I worked for six dollars a week at Joslin's Dry Goods Store back in Denver," he confessed as he looked back on his life, "it was my ambition, in the sense of wealth in money, to be worth one hundred thousand dollars. When I reached that goal I felt a certain temporary satisfaction, but it soon wore off and my sights were set on becoming worth a million dollars."

Mr. and Mrs. Penney worked hard to expand the business, but one day Mrs. Penney caught cold and pneumonia developed, which claimed her life. It was then that J. C. Penney realized having money was a poor substitute for the real purposes in living. "When she died," he said, "my world crashed about me. To build a business, to make a success in the eyes of men, to accumulate money—what was the purpose of life? What had money meant for my wife? I felt mocked by life, even by God Himself." After several more fiery trials, J. C. Penney was financially ruined and, naturally, in deep distress. That is when God could deal with his self-righteous nature and his love for money. After his spiritual conversion he could testify of God's working.

"I had to pass through fiery ordeals before reaching glimmerings of conviction that it is not enough for men to be upright and moral. When I was brought to humility and the knowledge of dependence on God, sincerely and earnestly seeking God's aid, it was forthcoming, and a light illumined my being. I cannot otherwise describe it than to say that it changed me as a man." *Submitted by* REV. JOHN FITTS, *Clearwater Community Church, Clearwater, Florida*

4. THE MIRACLE OF CHANGE

When we tell ourselves "I can never change," or "That will never happen," we presume too much and believe too little. In Jesus Christ God renders all of our final conclusions premature and all of our talk of determinism as simply bad faith. In Christ, God opens closed doors, brings resurrection, reveals possibilities, reclaims the lost, liberates the cursed and possessed, and changes the unchangeable. DON SHELBY

5. WESLEY AND THE ROBBER

As John Wesley rode across Hounslow Heath late one night, singing a favorite hymn, he was startled by a fierce voice shouting, "Halt," while a firm hand seized the horse's bridle. Then the man demanded, "Your money or your life."

Wesley obediently emptied his pockets of the few coins they contained and invited the robber to examine his saddlebags which were filled with books. Disappointed at the result, the robber was turning away when evangelist cried, "Stop! I have something more to give you."

The robber, wondering at this strange call, turned back. Then Wesley, bending down toward him, said in solemn tones, "My friend, you may live to regret this sort of a life in which you are engaged. If you ever do, I beseech you to remember this, 'The blood of Jesus Christ, God's Son, cleanseth us from all sin.'" The robber hurried silently away, and the man of God rode along, praying in his heart that the word spoken might be fixed in the robber's conscience.

Years later, at the close of a Sunday evening service with the people streaming from the large building, many lingered around the doors to see the aged preacher, John Wesley.

A stranger stepped forward and earnestly begged to speak with Mr. Wesley. What a surprise to find that this was the robber of Hounslow Heath, now a well-to-do tradesman in the city, but better still, a child of God! The words spoken that night long ago had been used of God in his conversion.

Raising the hand of John Wesley to his lips, he affectionately kissed it and said in tones of deep emotion, "To you, dear sir, I owe it all."

Wesley replied softly, "Nay, nay, my friend, not to me, but to the precious blood of Christ which cleanseth us from all sin."

6. CATERPILLAR TRANSFORMATION

Two caterpillars were crawling across the grass when a butterfly flew over them. They looked up, and one nudged the other and said, "You couldn't get me up in one of those things for a million dollars."

7. WHO WAS THAT?
At a college reunion, thirty years after graduation, one man said to another, "See that fellow over there? Well—he's gotten so bald and so fat he didn't even recognize me!"

8. TRUE CONVERSION
Paul's testimony is repeated over and over again as persons respond in faith to God's gift of Christ, as they are given His Spirit and become new creations. I heard of such a miracle recently. The American Red Cross was gathering supplies, medicine, clothing, food and the like for the suffering people of Biafra. Inside one of the boxes that showed up at the collecting depot one day was a letter. It said, "We have recently been converted and because of our conversion we want to try to help. We won't ever need these again. Can you use them for something?" Inside the box were several Ku Klux Klan sheets. The sheets were cut down to strips and eventually used to bandage the wounds of black persons in Africa.

It could hardly be more dramatic—from symbols of hatred to bandages of love because of the new creation. Nothing else matters, says Paul.
MAXIE DUNNAM, *Commentary on Galatians*

9. JUST THE SITE!
London businessman Lindsay Clegg told the story of a warehouse property he was selling. The building had been empty for months and needed repairs. Vandals had damaged the doors, smashed the windows, and strewn trash all over the place. As he showed a prospective buyer the property, he took pains to say that he would replace the broken windows, bring in a crew to correct any structural damage, and clean out the garbage. The buyer said, "Forget about the repairs. When I buy this place, I'm going to build something completely different. I don't want the building; I want the site."

That's God's message to us! Compared with the renovation God has in mind, our efforts to improve our own lives are as trivial as sweeping a warehouse slated for the wrecking ball. When we become God's the old life is over. He makes all things new. All He wants is the site and the permission to build. There are still some trying to "reform," but God offers "redemption." All we have to do is give Him the "property" and he will do the necessary "building."

10. SAD BUT TRUE
In a famous experiment with nursery school children, psychologist F. T. Merei organized relatively passive children into play groups and let them play for several days with the same toys and games. Each group developed its own

behavior patterns as well as its own traditions of who played with which toys. Once these patterns were set, Merei added an older child to each group, introducing the newcomer as the leader. For this role, he chose children who were eighteen months older than the others and who had shown signs of dominance in other situations at the nursery school. All of these new leaders tried to take charge, but most failed. Merei's explanation: "The group absorbed the leader, forcing its traditions on him." The one leader who succeeded did so only after several group members spent several days smoothing the way.

Corporations are not nursery schools, of course, and a chief executive's position carries considerably more weight than the nominal power Merei conferred simply by announcing to the group that the new member would be its leader. But the enormous pull exerted by a group makes it hard for new leaders to effect any change at all, much less act as quickly as corporate saviors are expected to.

11. BEHAVIOR CHANGE

A friend of mine tells the story of having counseled a man who was falling out of love with his wife. My friend advised the man to think of all the ways he could make life happier for his wife and then do them. A few days later my friend received a phone call in which the husband related the following:

"Every day I leave for work, put in a hard day, come home dirty and sweaty, stumble in the back door, go to the refrigerator, get something to drink, and then go into the rec room and watch television until supper time. After talking to you, I decided I would do better than that in the future. So yesterday, before I left work, I showered and shaved and put on a clean shirt. On the way home I stopped at the florist and bought a bouquet of roses. Instead of going in the back door as I usually do, I went to the front door and rang the doorbell. My wife opened the door, took one look at me, and started to cry. When I asked her what was wrong she said, 'It's been a horrible day. First Billy broke his leg and had to have it put in a cast. I no sooner returned home from the hospital when your mother called and told me that she is coming to stay for three weeks. I tried to do the wash and the washing machine broke and there is water all over the basement. And now you have to come home drunk!'" Tony Campolo

12. WHAT A DIFFERENCE A CHANGE MAKES

Once upon a time there was a prince who fell in love with a fair maiden. But his enemy captured the fair maiden and held her captive in a tower. Now the prince had a plan to rescue her, so he recruited the help of two small animals to send a message to the maiden. First there was Claude Caterpillar. Claude was a nice guy, and he didn't mind helping fair maidens in distress. But Claude was kind of a crusty old character. You might wonder, *Did he get up on the wrong side of the bed? Maybe he has a migraine headache or something.* Anyway, the prince gave him the message, and he started inching along toward the tower. Being a fat little caterpillar, he had to work hard to get there, even sweat a bit. He thought to himself, *Wouldn't you know it, the sun would have to be shining today!* Just then the weather began to change. Clouds moved in and little drops started coming down all around him. He grumbled, "Rain, of all things. And I just had this suit cleaned." But Claude wasn't a quitter. He made it to the tower and searched for a way up. A vine growing along one side was the obvious answer. Inch by inch up the vine Claude went, only to discover that it was a climbing rose bush. All the way up you could hear, "Ouch! Ouch! Ouch!" When he finally reached the window he heaved himself onto the ledge and said to the fair maiden, "Hey, lady! Come here! Are you the maiden in distress?" She nodded as she looked down at this sweaty, muddy little caterpillar. Claude gave her the once-over and said, "You're kidding. You mean I came all the way up here for the likes of you. I don't know what the prince sees in you. He sent me with a message, and you wouldn't believe how hard it was for me to get here. His message was: 'Get Ready.' He's coming to get you. Five o'clock sharp! Understand? All right! Good-bye!" And off went Claude.

Next the prince sent Barney Butterfly. Barney was not so sure of himself with the rain and wind, but he said he would try. His soft wings lifted him gracefully into the air. He struggled with all his might against the wind as it blew him back and forth. Just as he was about to reach the window, a bird swooped down and nearly ate him alive. After a frantic chase, Barney flew inside the window beyond the bird's snapping beak. He flew about the room until the maiden noticed him. She reached out her hand, and he landed softly on her finger. She brought him close as he relayed the Prince's message: "Lovely and favored maiden, the prince loves you dearly. At the sound of his voice, jump from the window and into his arms." The maiden replied, "Thank you, beautiful butterfly. You are very sweet. But tell me, why did the caterpillar bring the good news in such a nasty manner? He seemed so rude and rough."

The butterfly replied, "Oh, you mean Claude? Well, that's just Claude. I used to be that way, too, until I was transformed."

13. PURPOSE EMERGING
It is in changing that things find purpose. HERACLITUS

SIXTEEN
Character
*(See also Dignity, Integrity,
Nobility)*

1. RULE FOR LIFE
Always do right. This will gratify most people, and astonish the rest.
MARK TWAIN

2. DOING RIGHT ANYWAY
People are unreasonable, illogical and self-centered. Love them anyway.

If you do good, people will accuse you of selfish ulterior motives. Do good anyway.

If you are successful, you will win false friends and true enemies. Succeed anyway.

Honesty and frankness make you vulnerable. Be honest and frank anyway.

The good you do today will be forgotten tomorrow. Do good anyway.

The biggest people with the biggest ideas can be shot down by the smallest people with the smallest minds. Think big anyway.

People favor underdogs but follow only top dogs. Fight for some underdogs anyway.

What you spend years building may be destroyed overnight. Build anyway.

3. VARIETIES OF POVERTY
Rudyard Kipling once advised a group of students not to make money, power, or fame their goals. For one day they would meet a man who did not care for any of these things. "Then you will know how poor you are."

4. CLOSE SCRUTINY
A prosperous young Wall Street broker met and fell in love with a rising young actress of gentility and dignity. He frequently escorted her about town and wanted to marry her. But being a cautious man, he decided that before proposing marriage he should have a private investigating agency check her background and present activities. After all, he reminded himself, I have both a growing fortune and my reputation to protect against a marital misadventure.

The young man requested that the agency was not to reveal his identity to the investigator making the report on the actress. In due time the investigator's report came back. It said the actress had an unblemished past, a spotless reputation, and her friends and associates were of the best repute. The report concluded, "The only shadow is that she is often seen around town in the company of a young broker of dubious business practices and principles."

5. HUMILITY AND GENTLENESS
I have three precious things which I hold fast and prize. The first is gentleness; the second is frugality; the third is humility, which keeps me from putting myself before others. Be gentle and you can be bold; be frugal and you can be liberal; avoid putting yourself before others, and you can become a leader among men. LAO-TSE

6. THE RICH VARIETY OF PEOPLE
Some people are like wheels—they don't work unless they're pushed
Some people are like trailers—they have to be pulled!
Some people are like kites—always up in the air, and if you don't keep a string on them, they fly away!
Some people are like canoes—they have to be paddled.
Some people are like footballs—you never know which way they are going to bounce next!
Some people are like balloons—always puffed up, and you never know when they are going to blow up!
Some people are like flat tires—they have to be jacked up!
Some people are like good watches—pure gold, open faced, always on time, dependable, quietly busy and just full of good works!

7. THE DAILY PUSH
I long to accomplish a great and noble task, but it is my chief duty and joy to accomplish humble tasks as though they were great and noble.... For the world is moved along, not only by the mighty shoves of its heroes, but also by the aggregate of tiny pushes of each honest worker. HELEN KELLER

8. REVEALING CHARACTER
It is not true, as some writers assume in their treatises on rhetoric, that the personal goodness revealed by the speaker contributes nothing to his power of persuasion; on the contrary, his character may almost be called the most effective means of persuasion he possesses. ARISTOTLE

9. THE RIGHT MAN
They were burying a rather unsavory character who had never been near a place of worship in his life. The services were being conducted by a minister who had never heard of him. Carried away by the occasion, he poured on praise for the departed man. After ten minutes of describing the late

lamented as a father, husband, and boss, the widow, whose expression had grown more and more puzzled, nudged her son and whispered: "Go up there and make sure it's Papa."

10. JEFFERSON'S PLAN
Thomas Jefferson's ten rules for the good life:
1. Never put off till tomorrow what you can do today.
2. Never trouble another for what you can do yourself.
3. Never spend your money before you have it
4. Never buy what you do not want because it is cheap; it will be dear to you.
5. Pride costs us more than hunger, thirst, and cold.
6. Never repent of having eaten too little.
7. Nothing is troublesome that we do willingly.
8. Don't let the evils which have never happened cost you pain.
9. Always take things by their smooth handle.
10. When angry, count to ten before you speak; if very angry, count to one hundred.

11. SELF-MADE?
He who says, "I'm a self-made man," simply demonstrates the horror of unskilled labor.

12. THE BOTTOM LINE
I do the very best I know how—the very best I can; and I mean to keep doing so until the end. If the end brings me out all right, what is said against me won't amount to anything. If the end brings me out wrong, then angels swearing I was right would make no difference. ABRAHAM LINCOLN

13. ADDING VIRTUES
It is easier to enrich ourselves with a thousand virtues than to correct ourselves of a single fault. JEAN DE LA BRUYERE

14. THE ACID TEST
Live in such a way that you would not be ashamed to sell your parrot to the town gossip. WILL ROGERS

16. LOSS OF AN EMPIRE
Our whole Roman world had gone dead in its heart because it feared tragedy, took flight from suffering, and abhorred failure. In fear of tragedy we worshiped power. In fear of suffering, we worshiped security. During the rising splendor of our thousand years, we had grown cruel, practical, and

sterile. We did win the whole world, but in the process, we lost our souls.
St. Ambrose

17. TAKING STOCK

When I went to jail, nearly two years after the cover-up trial, I had a big self-esteem problem. I was a felon, shorn and scorned, clumping around in a ragged old army uniform, doing pick and shovel work out on the desert. I wondered if anyone thought I was worth anything. . . . For years I had been able to sweep most of my shortcomings and failures under the rug and not face them, but during the two long criminal trials, I spent my days listening to prosecutors tell juries what a bad fellow I was. Then at night I'd go back to a hotel room and sit alone thinking about what was happening to me. During that time I began to take stock. . . .

I stayed about two weeks. Every day I read the Bible, walked on the beach, and sat in front of my fireplace thinking and sketching, with no outline or agenda. I had no idea where all this was leading or what answers I'd find. Most of the time I didn't even know what the questions were. I just watched and listened. I was wiped out. I had nothing left that had been of value to me—honor, credibility, virtue, recognition, profession—nor did I have the allegiance of my family. I had managed to lose that too.

Since about 1975 I have begun to learn to see myself. I care what I perceive about my integrity, my capacity to love and be loved, and my essential worth. I don't miss Richard Nixon very much, and Richard Nixon probably doesn't miss me much either. I can understand that. I've made no effort to be in touch. We had a professional relationship that went as sour as a relationship can, and no one likes to be reminded of bad times. Those interludes, the Nixon episodes in my life, have ended. In a paradoxical way, I'm grateful for them. Somehow I had to see all of that and grow to understand it in order to arrive at the place where I find myself now.
John Ehrlichman

18. KEEPING A SECRET

The severest test of character is not so much the ability to keep a secret as it is, when the secret is finally out, to refrain from disclosing that you knew it all along. Sydney J. Harris

19. REVELATION OF CHARACTER

People seem not to realize that their opinion of the world is also a confession of character. Ralph Waldo Emerson

20. AN EMPEROR'S RULES OF LIFE

Marcus Aurelius, the Roman emperor and philosopher, identified the following traits of a successful person:

Consciousness of an honest purpose in life. A just estimate of himself and everyone else. Frequent self-examinations. Steady obedience to what he knows to be right. Indifference to what others may think or say.

21. BLEMISHES AND CHARACTER

Someone took the time to analyze the faces of 90 famous people who had been photographed by Yousoff Karsh and included in his book, *The Faces of Greatness*. According to the study, 70 of the men who posed for Karsh were physically unattractive—35 had moles, wens, and warts; 13 had noticeable freckles or liver spots; 20 had obvious traces of acne or other pimples; 2 had highly visible scars.

These blemishes did not deter them. Picasso, the renowned painter; Thornton Wilder, the great playwright; Richard Rogers, the composer of many popular and other musicals; Christian Dior, the honored designer—all had imperfections that were obvious to the world. What might have embarrassed lesser men just added character when they posed before the ever-truthful lens of the portraitist.

22. THE PLAGUE OF MEDIOCRITY

Miss Jones, an elderly spinster, lived in a small Midwestern community. She had the distinction of being the oldest resident of the town. One day she died, and the editor of the local newspaper wanted to print a little caption commemorating Miss Jones's death. However, the more he thought about it, the more he became aware that while Miss Jones had never done anything terribly wrong (she had never spent a night in jail or been drunk), yet she had never actually done anything noteworthy. While musing over this, the editor went down to have his morning coffee and met the owner of the tombstone establishment in the little community. The tombstone proprietor stated that he had been having the same problem. He wanted to put something on Miss Jones's tombstone besides just her birthday and death date, but he couldn't think of anything of significance that she had ever done.

The editor decided to go back to his office and assign to the first reporter he came across the task of writing up a small article suitable for both the paper and the tombstone. Upon returning to the office, the only fellow around was the sports editor, so he gave him the assignment.

They tell me if you pass through that little community you will find the following statement on her tombstone:

Here lies the bones of Nancy Jones,
For her life held no terrors.
She lived an old maid.
She died an old maid.
No hits, no runs, no errors.

23. THE NINE TESTS OF CONFUCIUS

"Man's mind," says Confucius, "is more treacherous than mounts and rivers, and more difficult to know than the sky. For with the sky you know what to expect in respect of the coming of spring, summer, autumn, and winter, and the alternation of day and night. But man hides his character behind an inscrutable appearance. There are those who appear tame and self-effacing, but conceal a terrible pride. There are those who have some special ability but appear to be stupid. There are those who are compliant and yielding but always get their objective. Some are hard outside but soft inside, and some are slow without but impatient within. Therefore those who rush forward to do the righteous thing as if they were craving for it, drop it like something hot.

"Therefore (in the judgment of men) a gentleman sends a man to a distant mission in order to test his loyalty. He employs him nearby in order to observe his manners. He gives him a lot to do in order to judge his ability. He suddenly puts a question to him in order to test his knowledge and makes a commitment with him under difficult circumstances to test his ability to live up to his word. He trusts him with money in order to test his heart, and announces to him the coming of a crisis to test his integrity. He makes him drunk in order to see the inside of his character, and puts him in female company to see his attitude toward women. Submitted to these nine tests, a fool will always reveal himself." *The Wisdom of Lao-tse*

24. DISPROVING THE RUMOR

When men speak ill of you, so live that nobody will believe them. PLATO

25. MAKING THE MOST OF LIFE

If I can throw a single ray of light across the darkened pathway of another; if I can aid some soul to clearer sight of life and duty, and thus bless my brother; if I can wipe from any human cheek a tear, I shall not have lived my life in vain while here.

If I can guide some erring one to truth, inspire within his heart a sense of duty; if I can plant within my soul of rosy youth a sense of right, a love of truth and beauty; if I can teach one man that God and heaven are near, I shall not then have lived in vain while here.

If from my mind I banish doubt and fear, and keep my life attuned to love and kindness; if I can scatter light and hope and cheer, and help remove the curse of mental blindness; if I can make more joy, more hope, less pain, I shall not have lived and loved in vain.

If by life's roadside I can plant a tree, beneath whose shade some wearied head my rest, though I may never share its beauty, I shall yet be truly blest— though no one knows my name, nor drops a flower upon my grave, I shall not have lived in vain while here. AUTHOR UNKNOWN

26. A REAL CHRISTIAN

A real Christian is an odd number, anyway. He feels supreme love for One whom he has never seen; talks familiarly every day to Someone he cannot see; expects to go to heaven on the virtue of Another; empties himself in order to be full; admits he is wrong so he can be declared right; goes down in order to get up; is strongest when he is weakest; richest when he is poorest and happiest when he feels the worst. He dies so he can live; forsakes in order to have; gives away so he can keep; sees the invisible, hears the inaudible, and knows that which passeth knowledge. A. W. TOZER

27. A REAL GRIND

Life is a grindstone. Whether it grinds you down or polishes you up depends upon what you are made of.

28. MENTAL HEALTH

Do you realize that one in every four Americans is unbalanced? Think of your three closest friends. If they seem OK, you're the one! ANN LANDERS

29. DIRECTION

It is more important to know where you are going than to see how fast you can get there. MARTIN VANBEE

30. YOUR LOT

Whatever your lot in life, build something on it.

31. DOING RIGHT ANYWAY

People are unreasonable, illogical and self-centered. Love them anyway.

If you do good, people will accuse you of selfish ulterior motives. Do good anyway.

If you are successful, you will win false friends and true enemies. Succeed anyway.

Honesty and frankness make you vulnerable. Be honest and frank anyway.

The good you do today will be forgotten tomorrow. Do good anyway.

The biggest people with the biggest ideas can be shot down by the smallest people with the smallest minds. Think big anyway.

People favor underdogs but follow only top dogs. Fight for some underdogs anyway.

What you spend years building may be destroyed overnight. Build anyway.

SEVENTEEN
Children
(See also Family, Youth)

1. CHILD REARING

In the biography *Blackberry Winter* by Margaret Mead, she tells of her grandma who was a wonderful storyteller and who had a "set of priceless, individually tailored anecdotes with which American grandparents of her day brought up children."

There was the story of little boys who had been taught absolute, quick obedience. One day when they were out on the prairie, their father shouted, "Fall down on your faces!" They did, and the terrible prairie fire swept over them and they weren't hurt. There was also the story of three boys at school, each of whom received a cake sent from home. One hoarded his, and the mice ate it; one ate all of his, and he got sick; and who do you think had the best time? Why, of course, the one who shared his cake with his friends. Then there was the little boy who ran away from home and stayed away all day. When he came home after supper, he found the family sitting around the fire and nobody said a word. Not a word. Finally, he couldn't stand it anymore and said, "Well, I see you have the same old cat!"

2. CRIME AND PUNISHMENT

A group of kindergarten children visited the local police station and viewed the pictures of the ten most-wanted men. One child pointed to a picture and asked if it really was the photograph of the wanted person. The policeman guide replied that it was.

The youngster inquired, "Well, why didn't you keep him when you took his picture?"

3. IT'S YOUR DAD

Two boys were walking home from church and sharing their reflections on the lesson. They had been studying the temptation of Christ in the wilderness. Little Peter said to his friend John, "Do you believe that stuff about the Devil? Do you think there really is a Devil?" John looked at him and said, "Naah, it's just like Santa Claus—it's your dad."

4. SONSHIP

A promising young executive quit his job and before leaving, stopped in to say good-bye to the boss. The boss lamented, "I'm sorry to see you go. Actually, you've been like a son to me—sassy, impatient, demanding, and loud."

5. PICTURE OF GOD

A little boy was working hard on a drawing and his daddy asked him what he was doing. The reply came back, "Drawing a picture of God." His daddy said, "You can't do that, honey. Nobody knows what God looks like." But the little boy was undeterred and continued to draw. He looked at his picture with satisfaction and said very matter-of-factly, "They will in a few minutes."

6. UNPREDICTABLE

You never know how far up the wall they're going to drive you.

7. SCHOOL PRAYER

Whether legal or not, kids have been praying in school for as long as anyone can remember.

We prayed that the school would burn down the night before the math exams. We prayed the teacher would break her leg on the way to our house to talk to Mom. We prayed that Dad would not notice the D on our report card. We prayed the music teacher would not ask us to sing the scale. We prayed the most popular classmate would ask us to the prom. We prayed the bus carrying the rival team would go into the ditch. We prayed for good marks so we could go to summer camp. We prayed for laryngitis so we would not have to dress like a tree and recite that silly Arbor Day poem. Oh, yes, we prayed in school.

8. NOT MOLDED

Children are not things to be molded but are people to be unfolded.

9. SPELLING INTEGRITY

At a national spelling contest in Washington an incident occurred that made me feel good—and made me wonder. In the fourth round of the contest, Rosalie Elliot, then an eleven-year-old from South Carolina, was asked to spell *avowal*. In her soft Southern accent she spelled it. But did the seventh grader use an *a* or an *e* as the next to last letter? The judges couldn't decide. For several minutes they listened to tape recording playbacks, but the critical letter was accent-blurred. Chief Judge John Lloyd finally put the question to the only person who knew the answer, "Was the letter an *a* or was it an *e?*" he asked Rosalie. Surrounded by whispering young spellers, she knew by now the correct spelling of the word. Without hesitating, she replied she had misspelled it. She walked from the stage.

The entire audience stood and applauded, including half a hundred newspaper reporters, one of whom was heard to remark that Judge Lloyd had put quite a burden on an eleven-year-old. Rosalie rated a hand and it must have been a heartwarming and proud moment for her parents. The thing that makes me wonder, however, was the apparent feeling on the part of so many that the issue might have been in doubt and that honesty might have bowed to temptation. Have we in this age stopped taking honesty for granted, even from our children?

10. A MODERN FATHER'S PERSPECTIVE
A cartoon in *Forbes* magazine shows a modern father talking with his young boy, giving him some fatherly perspective: "Remember, Son, these are your tax-free years. Make the most of them."

11. TEACHING OR VIOLENCE?
At the hockey game, I was rinkside when one of the players rammed into the boards. As he struggled to regain his balance, he gasped, "There must be an easier way to make a living." "I'll trade jobs," I retorted. "What do you do?" he queried. "I teach sixth grade." "Forget it," he said, and was gone.

12. FRESH AND SPOILED
If a growing object is both fresh and spoiled at the same time, the chances are it's a child.

13. ABSENT CREED
Each Sunday morning as they began class, the fifth graders would line up and recite their one section of the creed in the order that it was written. That teaching method worked well and went on about four months, until one Sunday. They began the class the same way. The first girl as usual recited her line flawlessly: "I believe in God the Father Almighty, maker of heaven and earth." The second, a boy, stood up and said his sentence: "I believe in Jesus Christ, His only Son, our Lord." But then silence descended over the class. Finally, one girl, who felt she had discovered the problem, stood up and loudly said, "I'm sorry, sir, but the boy who believes in the Holy Ghost is absent today!"

14. GET THE STORY STRAIGHT

A group of four-year-olds were gathered in a Sunday school class in Chattanooga. Their enthusiastic teacher looked at the class and asked this question: "Does anyone know what today is?" A little four-year-old girl held up her finger and said, "Yes, today is Palm Sunday." The teacher exclaimed, "That's fantastic! That's wonderful! Now does anyone know what next Sunday is?" The same little girl held up her finger and said, "Yes, next Sunday is Easter Sunday." Once again the teacher said, "That's fantastic! Now, does anyone know what makes next Sunday Easter?" The same little girl responded and said, "Yes, next Sunday is Easter because Jesus rose from the grave." But before the teacher could congratulate her, she continued, "But if he sees his shadow, he has to go back in for seven weeks."

15. BECOMING POSSIBLE

The teacher asked her class what each wanted to become when they grew up. "President." "A fireman." "A teacher." One by one they answered until it came Billy's turn. The teacher asked, "Billy, what do you want to be when you grow up?" "Possible," Billy responded. "Possible?" asked the teacher. "Yes," Billy said, "my mom is always telling me I'm impossible. When I grow up I want to become *possible*."

16. IT'S TOUGH TO BE A SAINT

Young Brian, age five, had been told the story of the "pillar-monk," Symeon the Stylite, in Sunday school. He was captivated by this godly man's approach to seeking God's approval. Early Monday morning he decided to imitate Symeon. He placed the kitchen stool on top of the table and climbed to his perilous perch and began his journey toward sainthood. Mother, entering the kitchen, interrupted his holy pilgrimage by explaining, "Brian, get down off that stool before you break your neck." Brian complied but went storming from the room announcing, "You can't even become a saint in your own home!"

17. TEN COMMANDMENTS FOR PARENTS

1. My hands are small; please don't expect perfection whenever I make a bed, draw a picture, or throw a ball. My legs are short; slow down so that I can keep up with you.
2. My eyes have not seen the world as yours have; let me explore it safely; don't restrict me unnecessarily.
3. Housework will always be there; I'm little only for a short time. Take time to explain things to me about this wonderful world, and do so willingly.

4. My feelings are tender; don't nag me all day long (you would not want to be nagged for your inquisitiveness). Treat me as you would like to be treated.

5. I am a special gift from God; treasure me as God intended you to do—holding me accountable for my actions, giving me guidelines to live by, and disciplining me in a loving manner.

6. I need your encouragement (but not your empty praise) to grow. Go easy on the criticism; remember, you can criticize the things I do without criticizing me.

7. Give me the freedom to make decisions concerning myself. Permit me to fail, so that I can learn from my mistakes. Then someday I'll be prepared to make the decisions life will require of me.

8. Don't do things over for me; that makes me feel that my efforts didn't measure up to your expectations. I know it's hard, but don't compare me with my brother or my sister.

9. Don't be afraid to leave for a weekend together. Kids need vacations from parents, and parents need vacations from kids. Besides, it's a great way to show us kids that your marriage is something special.

10. Take me to Sunday school and church regularly, setting a good example for me to follow. I enjoy learning more about God. KEVIN LEMAN

18. CHILDREN OR WEALTH?
A person with six children is better satisfied than a person with $6 million. Reason: The man with $6 million wants more.

19. MAKE UP YOUR MIND!
My eight-year-old son, Noah, was discussing parent problems with his little friend. Of course, they had a lot of complaints. Dustin was overheard grumbling, "First they teach you to talk, then they teach you to walk, and as soon as you do it, it's 'Sit down and shut up!'"

20. GENETIC FLAW
Insanity is hereditary. You can get it from your children. SAM LEVENSON

21. LOSS OF THE BELOVED CHILD
Excerpt from an interview with the late Joe Bayly of David C. Cook Publishing Company and his wife, Mary Lou. The Baylys lost three children.

Joe: We are stewards of the children God gives us, and at any time God can interrupt that stewardship.

Mary Lou: Although this isn't something you can say to somebody else who has just lost a child or is in the process of losing a child, it's still true that if Jesus Christ is the Creator and has planned in intricate detail each of

His creations—especially His own people—then if we love one of them how much more He must. How can we compare our love to His? Our assignment from God is to simply prepare our children as a skilled craftsman fashions an arrow. But you always have to remember that the arrows may not always be shot out into adulthood.

22. A CHILD IN HEAVEN
We have eight children. And they're all living: one's in heaven and seven are on earth. *Father of missionary* CHET BITTERMAN, *killed by terrorists in Colombia in March 1981*

23. CONSIDER THE CHILDREN
A distinguished elderly gentleman, walking through the toy department, stopped to admire a toy train. It whistled, belched smoke, deposited milk cans, in fact did virtually everything a real freight train does. After looking at it for some time he finally said, "I'll take it. Please have it wrapped." The clerk said, "Fine, I'm sure your grandson will love it." The elderly gentleman said thoughtfully, "That's right. Maybe you'd better give me two of them."

24. ONCE IN A LIFETIME
When I was around thirteen and my brother was ten, Father promised to take us to the circus. But at lunch there was a phone call. Some urgent business required his attention downtown. My brother and I braced ourselves for the disappointment. Then we heard him say, "No, I won't be down. It will have to wait." When he came back to the table, Mother smiled and said, "The circus keeps coming back, you know." "I know," said Father, "but childhood doesn't." ARTHUR GORDON

25. PRIMITIVE?
One of the first things one notices about any backward country is that the children obey their parents.

26. A TEACHER'S PRAYER
Lord, give me the wisdom to discover in each child his spark of divinity, the gift that You have given him, and through love and guidance nurture this spark into a glowing flame.

Let me not favor any one child at the expense of others. Let all be equally worthy of my devotion without regard to their intelligence, their religion, their race, or their wealth.

Let me teach a love of America by keeping ever alive her commitment to the greatest good for the greatest number in the belief that these children are Your greatest good and Your greatest number.

Lord, help! They're coming into the room right now, all thirty-two of them. Any small miracle will be greatly appreciated. Amen.

27. CHILDISH VIRTUE
One thing you can say for small children—they don't go around showing off pictures of their grandparents.

28. JUST LIKE FAMILY
The secretary was leaving to get married and the boss gave her a big hug and a kiss. "You've been like a daughter to me—insolent, surly, unappreciative."

29. TEST DRIVE
When my brother and his wife were considering adopting some children they first took two little boys into their home as foster children to see how they would all relate to each other before moving toward adoption. I was explaining this to my wife's twelve-year-old daughter, who responded spontaneously: "Gee, that's like test-driving a little kid."

EIGHTEEN
Christ
(See also Atonement,
Christmas, Incarnation)

1. A NAIL FOR REMEMBERING
One time at the City Temple in London, there was in the congregation a restaurateur named Emil Mettler, who was a close friend of Albert Schweitzer and a kind of agent for Schweitzer in Britain. Mettler would never allow a Christian worker to pay for a meal in his restaurant, but once he did happen to open his cash register in the presence of a secretary of the London Missionary Society. The secretary was astonished to see among the bills and coins a six-inch nail. What was it doing there? Mettler explained, "I keep this nail with my money to remind me of the price that Christ paid for my salvation and of what I owe Him in return."

2. THOUGHT FOR REFORMATION SUNDAY
Martin Luther had a dream in which he stood on the day of judgment before God Himself—and Satan was there to accuse him. When Satan opened his

books full of accusations, he pointed to transgression after transgression of which Luther was guilty. As the proceedings went on, Luther's heart sunk in despair. Then he remembered the cross of Christ—and turning upon Satan, he said, "There is one entry which you have not made, Satan."

The Devil retorted, "What is that?"

And Luther answered, "It is this—the blood of Jesus Christ, his Son, cleanseth us from all sins."

3. THE RELEASE I LONG FOR

In *God's Smuggler,* Brother Andrew tells in the first couple of chapters the story of his early life—one section of which dealt with his hell-for-leather days in the Dutch army in Indonesia. While serving in that area, fighting against Sukarno in the late 1940s he bought a young ape, a gibbon, who took to him, and Andy treated him as a pet in the barracks. He hadn't had the gibbon for many weeks before he noticed that when he touched it in some areas around the waist it seemed to hurt him. So he examined the gibbon more closely and found a raised welt that went around his waist. He carefully laid the animal down on his bed and pulled back the matted hair from this welt until he could see what was causing the problem. He discovered that evidently when the gibbon had been a baby someone had tied a piece of wire around his middle and had never taken it off. As the monkey grew larger the wire became embedded in his flesh. Obviously, it must have caused him a great deal of discomfort. So that evening Andrew began the operation, taking his razor and shaving off all the monkey's hair in a three-inch-wide swath around his middle. While the other boys in the barracks looked on, he cut ever so gently into the tender flesh until he exposed the wire. The gibbon lay there with the most amazing patience. Even when he obviously was hurting him the gibbon looked up with eyes that seemed to say, "I understand," until at long last he was able to get down to the wire, cut it, and pull it away. Instantly, as soon as the operation was over, the gibbon jumped up, did a cartwheel, danced around his shoulders, and pulled Andy's hair in joyful glee to the delight of all the boys in the barracks. "After that, my gibbon and I were inseparable. I think I identified with him as strongly as he with me. I think I saw in the wire that had bound him a kind of parallel to the chain of guilt still so tight around myself—and in his release, the thing I too longed for."

4. THE GOOD HUNTER

During hard times in the darkness of winter in an Alaskan Eskimo village a young man of unequaled courage might go out into the bitter cold in search of food for his people. Armed only with a pointed stick and his compassion for his starving village, he would wander, anticipating the attack of a polar bear. Having no natural fear of humans, a polar bear will stalk and eat a man. In the attack the Eskimo hunter would wave his hands and spear to anger the bear and make him rise up on his hind legs to over ten feet in height; and then, with the spear braced to his foot, the hunter would aim for the heart as the weight of the bear came down upon his spear. With heart pierced, the bear might live long enough to maim or kill this noble hunter. Loving family and friends would then follow his tracks out of the village and find food for their survival and evidence of profound courage.

Early missionaries proclaimed to attentive ears that Jesus Christ is the "Good Hunter" who lays down his life for the world.

5. THOUGH I DRIVE THROUGH THE VALLEY
It was 1972 and we had a Plymouth station wagon and a Chevrolet Malibu. Whenever I would ask my parents to help me drive, they each had a reply. Father would say, "Go ask your mother," and Mother would say, "Let's go." For months she would sit beside me as I practiced on the back roads of South Jersey. Sometimes she would drive and tell me what she was doing, and other times she would talk me through a particular operation of the car. I remember the first time I drove at night. We were returning from visiting my mom's brother and had to get on the Walt Whitman Bridge from an access ramp. It was nine o'clock at night, pitch dark, pouring rain. As I sat waiting to enter the six-lane highway, with all the headlights, taillights, rain, and noise, I was thoroughly confused. All my training, but mostly youthful pride, kept me from asking my mother to take the wheel.

I can remember pressing the accelerator, hearing the motor respond, hearing someone yell, "YEEEEHAHHHH," and suddenly finding ourselves following along in traffic with everyone else over the bridge.

Certain things remain a mystery, like how we got onto the lane as confused as I was, and which of us screamed, but certain things are not a mystery, like how reassuring it is to have your teacher go through things with you. Our temptation and our trials are not foreign to Jesus, nor are they ours alone to bear. The Teacher is with us. FRED GROSSE

6. CHRIST AND BUDDHA—THE GREAT DIFFERENCE
Frederick Buechner, in his book *Now and Then,* has a section on his comparison of the teachings of Buddha and of Jesus Christ, a topic he wrestled with when he was teaching at Phillips Exeter Academy:

"Finally, lest students of comparative religion be tempted to believe that to compare them is to discover that at their hearts all religions are finally one and that it thus makes little difference which one you choose, you have only to place side by side Buddha and Christ themselves.

"Buddha sits enthroned beneath the Bo tree in the lotus position. His lips are faintly parted in the smile of one who has passed beyond every power in earth or heaven to touch him. 'He who loves fifty has fifty woes, he who loves ten has ten woes, he who loves none has no woes,' he has said. His eyes are closed.

"Christ, on the other hand, stands in the garden of Gethsemane, angular, beleaguered. His face is lost in shadows so that you can't even see his lips, and before all the powers in earth or heaven he is powerless. 'This is my commandment, that you love one another as I have loved you,' he has said. His eyes are also closed.

"The difference seems to me this. The suffering that Buddha's eyes close out is the suffering of the world that Christ's eyes close in and hallow. It is an extraordinary difference, and even in a bare classroom in Exeter, New Hampshire, I think it was as apparent to everyone as it was to me that before you're done, you have to make a crucial and extraordinary choice."

7. HOW DO YOU RESPOND?

As you travel along I-10 in Louisiana there is a large billboard which catches your eye. It stands high above the city just as you start up the Mississippi River bridge. On it is a picture of Jesus Christ hanging on the cross of Calvary, head bowed. The caption underneath says in bold letters, "It's Your Move!"

What a powerful thought. God has already taken the initiative in salvation. Christ died for you. Now—it's your move!

8. PERFECTION OF HUMANITY

Christ's perfect life was the perfect manifestation of human life as God intended it.

9. ONLY ONE PLAN

There is a legend that recounts the return of Jesus to glory after His time on earth. Even in heaven He bore the marks of His earthly pilgrimage with its cruel cross and shameful death. The angel Gabriel approached Him and said, "Master, you must have suffered terribly for men down there." He replied that he did. Gabriel continued: "And do they know and appreciate how much you loved them and what you did for them?" Jesus replied, "Oh, no! Not yet. Right now only a handful of people in Palestine know." But Gabriel was perplexed. He asked, "Then what have you done to let everyone know about your love for them?" Jesus said, "I've asked Peter, James, John, and a few more friends to tell others about me. Those who are told will tell others, in turn, about me. And my story will be spread to the farthest reaches of the globe. Ultimately, all of mankind will have heard about my life and what I have done."

Gabriel frowned and looked rather skeptical. He well knew what poor stuff men were made of. He said, "Yes, but what if Peter and James and John grow weary? What if the people who come after them forget? What if way down in the twentieth-century people just don't tell others about you? Haven't you made any other plans?" And Jesus answered, "I haven't made any other plans. I'm counting on them." Twenty centuries later, He still has no other plan. He's counting on you and me. High on God's "To Do" list is the evangelization of the world. His early disciples adopted His priorities and devoted themselves to reaching the world. Christ counted on them, and they delivered. Have we done as well?

10. LET HIM PLAY

In a large stone cathedral in Europe there was a large, magnificent pipe organ. It was a Saturday afternoon, and the sexton was making one final check of the choir and organ loft high in the balcony at the back of the church. He was startled to hear footsteps echoing up the stone stairway, as he thought the doors were all locked and no one was around. He turned to see a man in slightly tattered traveling clothes coming toward him. "Excuse me, sir," the stranger said. "I have come from quite a distance to see the great organ in this cathedral. Would you mind opening the console so that I might get a closer look at it?" The custodian at first refused, but the stranger seemed so eager and insistent that he finally gave in. "May I sit on the bench?" That request of the stranger was met with absolute refusal by the cathedral custodian. "What if the organist came in and found you sitting there? I would probably lose my job!" But again the stranger was so persistent that the sexton gave in. "But only for a moment," he added.

The custodian noticed that the stranger seemed to be very much at home on the organ bench, so he was not completely surprised when he was asked by the stranger to be allowed to play the organ. "No! Definitely not!" said the custodian. "No one is allowed to play it except the cathedral organist." The man's face fell, and his deep disappointment was obvious. He reminded the custodian how far he had come and assured him that no damage would be done. Finally the sexton relented and told the stranger he could play the instrument, but only a few notes and then he would have to leave. Overjoyed, the stranger pulled out some stops and began to play. Suddenly the cathedral was filled with the most beautiful music the custodian had ever heard in all his years in that place. The music seemed to transport him heavenward.

In what seemed all too short a time, the dowdy stranger stopped playing and slid off the organ bench. And started down the stairway. "Wait!" cried the custodian. "That was the most beautiful music I have ever heard in the cathedral. Who are you?" The stranger turned for just a moment as he replied, "Mendelssohn." The man was none other than Felix Mendelssohn, one of the greatest organists and composers of the nineteenth century!

The cathedral sexton was alone now in that great stone edifice, the beautiful organ music still ringing in his ears. "Just think," he said softly, "I almost kept the master from playing his music in my cathedral!"

Each one of us has the opportunity to have a personal relationship with the Master of the universe, Jesus Christ. Let's not keep Him from "playing His music" and being Master of our lives!

11. THE ONE WHO INTERCEDES

There was a soldier in the Union army, a young man who had lost his older brother and his father in the war. He went to Washington, D.C., to see President Lincoln to ask for an exemption from military service so he could go back and help his sister and mother with the spring planting on the farm. When he arrived in Washington, after having received a furlough from the military to go and plead his case, he went to the White House, approached the doors, and asked to see the president. However, he was told, "You can't see the president! Don't you know there's a war on? The president's a very busy man. Now go away, son! Get back out there and fight the Rebs like you're supposed to." So he left, very disheartened, and was sitting on a little park bench not far from the White House when a little boy came up to him. The lad said, "Soldier, you look unhappy. What's wrong?" The soldier looked at this young boy and began to spill his heart out to this young lad about his situation, about his father and his brother having died in the war, and how he was the only male left in the family and was needed desperately back at the farm for the spring planting.

The little boy took the soldier by the hand and led him around to the back of the White House. They went through the back door, past the guards, past all the generals and the high ranking government officials until they got to the president's office itself. The little boy didn't even knock on the door but just opened it and walked in. There was President Lincoln with his secretary of state, looking over battle plans on the desk. President Lincoln looked up and said, "What can I do for you, Todd?"

And Todd said, "Daddy, this soldier needs to talk to you." And right then and there the soldier had a chance to plead his case to President Lincoln, and he was exempted from military service due to the hardship he was under.

Such is the case with our ascended Lord. We have access to the Father through the Son. It is the Son who brings us to the Father's throne and says, "Daddy, here is someone who wants to talk to You."

12. THE CHRIST OF BETHLEHEM

Some tell us that Jesus' earthly life was not very important. They say he wrote no books, composed no songs, drew no pictures, carved no statues, amassed no fortune, commanded no army, ruled no nation. And yet . . . He who never wrote a line has been made the hero of unnumbered volumes. He who never wrote a song has put music into the hearts of nameless multitudes. He who never established an institution is the foundation of the Church that bears his name. He who refused the kingdoms of this world has become the Lord of millions. Yes, He whose shameful death scarcely produced a ripple on the pool of history in his day has become a mighty current in the vast ocean of the centuries since He died. MACK STOKES

13. THE REAL CHRIST

The people who hanged Christ never accused Him of being a bore; on the contrary, they thought Him too dynamic to be safe. It has been left for later generations to muffle up that shattering personality and surround Him with the atmosphere of tedium. We have very efficiently pared the claws of the Lion of Judah, certified Him "meek and mild," and recommended Him as a fitting household pet for pale curates and pious old ladies. To those who knew Him, however, He in no way suggested a milk-and-water person; they objected to Him as a dangerous firebrand. True, He was tender to the unfortunate, patient with honest inquirers, and humble before heaven; but He insulted respectable clergymen by calling them hypocrites; He referred to King Herod as "that fox"; He went to parties in disreputable company and was looked upon as a "gluttonous man and a winebibber, a friend of publicans and sinners"; He insulted indignant tradesmen and threw them and their belongings out of the Temple, . . . He showed no proper deference for wealth or social position; when confronted with neat dialectical traps, He displayed a paradoxical humor that affronted serious-minded people, and He retorted by asking disagreeable questions that could not be answered by rule of thumb . . . But He had a "daily beauty in his life that made us ugly," and officialdom felt that the established order of things would be more secure without Him. So they did away with God in the name of peace and quietness. DOROTHY SAYERS

14. THE MARK OF FORGIVENESS

In my second year of seminary I worked as a dorm supervisor for the New Jersey School for the Deaf. On Sunday a worship service was held for the children remaining for the weekend. I remember the first time I saw the sign for "Jesus"— the right hand used the little finger to draw the letter *J*, then ending in the palm of the other hand to signify Jesus' nail imprint. The very name of Jesus tells us of Jesus' suffering and forgiveness of our sins!

15. A DUBIOUS BIRTHPLACE

Beneath the Church of the Nativity in Bethlehem, a silver star marks the alleged precise spot where Christ was born. A stone slab nearby is supposed to mark the exact site of the manger wherein he lay. The Holy Land is littered with such shrines, divided up like African territories in the old colonialist days, between the different sects and denominations—the Greeks, the Armenians, the Copts, the Latins, etc.—and often a cause of rancor among them. Most of the shrines are doubtless fraudulent, some in dubious taste, and none to my liking. Yet one may note, as the visitors come and go, ranging from the devout to the inanely curious, that almost every face somehow lights up a little. Christ's presence makes itself felt even in this dubious birthplace.
MALCOLM MUGGERIDGE, *Jesus Rediscovered*

16. GOD'S WAY

When God wants an important thing done in this world, or a wrong righted, He goes about it in a very singular way. He does not release His thunderbolts or stir up His earthquake. He simply has a tiny, helpless baby born, perhaps in an obscure home, perhaps of a very humble mother. Then He puts the idea or purpose into the mother's heart, she puts it into the baby's mind and then—God waits. EDWARD T. SULLIVAN

17. DEALING WITH THE DILEMMA

According to an old legend, a man became lost in his travels and wandered into a bed of quicksand. Confucius saw the man's predicament and said, "It is evident that men should stay out of places such as this." Next, Buddha observed the situation and said, "Let that man's plight be a lesson to the rest of the world." Then Muhammad came by and said to the sinking man, "Alas, it is the will of God." Finally, Jesus appeared. "Take my hand, brother," he said, "and I will save you."

18. TO SEE THE BEAUTY ABOVE

Norman A. McMurry tells about a palace in the city of Rome which has a great high dome. Inside that dome there is a painting known as *The Dawn* by Guido Reni. In order that visitors may see this masterpiece, a table has been placed directly beneath the dome, and on the table a mirror. When one looks into the mirror, he sees the majestic painting far above. Is that not what the Incarnation is all about? Jesus of Nazareth is the "mirror-image" of God.

19. A POINT OF CONTACT

Bob Weber, past president of Kiwanis International, told this story. He had spoken to a club in a small town and was spending the night with a farmer on the outskirts of the community. He had just relaxed on the front porch when a newsboy delivered the evening paper. The boy noted the sign Puppies for Sale. The boy got off his bike and said to the farmer, "How much do you want for the pups, mister?" "Twenty-five dollars, son." The boy's face dropped. "Well, sir, could I at least see them anyway?" The farmer whistled, and in a moment the mother dog came bounding around the corner of the house tagged by four of the cute puppies, wagging their tails and yipping happily. At last, another pup came straggling around the house, dragging one hind leg. "What's the matter with that puppy, mister?" the boy asked. "Well, Son, that puppy is crippled. We took her to the vet and the doctor took an X ray. The pup doesn't have a hip joint and that leg will never be right." To the amazement of both men, the boy dropped the bike, reached for his collection bag and took out a fifty-cent piece. "Please, mister," the boy pleaded, "I want to buy that pup. I'll pay you fifty cents every week until the twenty-five dollars is paid. Honest I will, mister." The farmer replied, "But, Son, you don't seem to understand. That pup will never, never be able to run or jump. That pup is going to be a cripple forever. Why in the world would you want such a useless pup as that?"

The boy paused for a moment, then reached down and pulled up his pant leg, exposing that all too familiar iron brace and leather knee-strap holding a poor twisted leg. The boy answered, "Mister, that pup is going to need someone who understands him to help him in life!"

Crippled and disfigured by sin, the risen, living Christ has given us hope. He understands us—our temptations, our discouragements, and even our thoughts concerning death. By His resurrection we have help in this life and hope for the life to come.

20. LIGHT REVEALING LIGHT

It would little avail to ask how we know. That would be like asking how we know that Beethoven's "Hymn to Joy" is joyous. If a man were to say, "It is not joyous to me," he would not condemn the music; he would tell only his morbidness. There is no logic to establish an axiom, for an axiom is the basis of all logic; and the soul of Jesus has axiomatic truth. Jesus is light, and there is no proof for light except light itself. GEORGE BUTTRICK

NINETEEN
Christmas
(See also Incarnation)

1. SIGN OF STRENGTH AND MAJESTY

The religious and political leaders who were in power at the time misread the events of Jesus' birth. When a woman is to have a baby, she goes to the best hospital she and her husband can afford. They find the best doctors and highly trained specialists. They get the best that money can buy. And they do this not because they feel strong, but because they feel weak.

When God's Son was born, He was born in a stable under very austere and unsanitary conditions. It happened this way not because God was poor, but because God was sure of himself.

The leaders misread the signs. The baby born in the stable is not a sign of a weak and ineffectual king. But it is a sign of a majesty who is secure and knows who He is. It's a sign of love. The leaders of that time didn't know anything about that. And so they missed it. EARL PALMER

2. THREE WAYS OF VIEWING CHRISTMAS

The basis for this tremendous annual burst of gift buying and parties and near hysteria is a quiet event that Christians believe actually happened a long time ago. You can say that in all societies there has always been a midwinter festival and that many of the trappings of our Christmas are almost violently pagan. But you come back to the central fact of the day and quietness of Christmas morning—the birth of God on earth.

It leaves you only three ways of accepting Christmas. One is cynically, as a time to make money or endorse the making of it. One is graciously, the appropriate attitude for non-Christians, who wish their fellow citizens all the joys to which their beliefs entitle them. And the third, of course, is reverently. If this is the anniversary of the appearance of the Lord of the universe in the form of a helpless babe, it is a very important day. It's a startling idea, of course. My guess is that the whole story that a virgin was selected by God to bear His Son as a way of showing His love and concern for man is not an idea that has been popular with theologians.

It's a somewhat illogical idea, and theologians like logic almost as much as they like God. It's so revolutionary a thought that it probably could only come from a God that is beyond logic, and beyond theology. It has a magnificent appeal. Almost nobody has seen God, and almost nobody has any real idea of what He is like. And the truth is that among men the idea of seeing God suddenly and standing in a very bright light is not necessarily a completely comforting and appealing idea. But everyone has seen babies, and most people like them. If God wanted to be loved as well as feared he moved correctly here. If He wanted to know His people as well as rule them, He moved correctly here, for a baby growing up learns all about people. If God wanted to be intimately a part of man, He moved correctly, for the experiences of birth and familyhood are our most intimate and precious experiences.

So it comes beyond logic. It is either all falsehood or it is the truest thing in the world. It's the story of the great innocence of God the baby—God in the form of man—and has such a dramatic shock toward the heart that if it is not true, for Christians, nothing is true.

So, if a Christian is touched only once a year, the touching is still worth it, and maybe on some given Christmas, some final quiet morning, the touch will take. *TV news commentator* HARRY REASONER

3. DICKENS ON CHRISTMAS
I have always thought of Christmas time, when it has come round . . . as a good time: a kind, forgiving, charitable, pleasant time: the only time I know of, in the long calendar of the year, when men and women seem by one consent to open their shut-up hearts freely, and to think of people below them as if they really were fellow passengers to the grave, and not another race of creatures bound on other journeys. And therefore . . . though it has never put a scrap of gold or silver in my pocket, I believe that it has done me good, and will do me good; and I say, God bless it! CHARLES DICKENS, *A Christmas Carol*

4. THE MIRACLE OF THE VIRGIN BIRTH
The grounds for belief and disbelief are the same today as they were two thousand or ten thousand years ago. If Joseph had lacked faith to trust God or humility to perceive the holiness of his spouse, he could have disbelieved in the miraculous origin of her Son as easily as any modern man; and any modern man who believes in God can accept the miracle as easily as Joseph did. C. S. LEWIS

5. SYMBOLS OF THE GREATER GIFT
At a Christmas celebration in a nursing home, I asked the folks to tell us about their favorite Christmas experience. The group seemed to light up. Spontaneously one by one they told their Christmas story. Each was different

except in one respect. Every experience was taken from their childhood. They did not remember Christmas as a parent, but as a child.

Then I turned the question on myself. I, too, returned to my childhood. The first, and perhaps most memorable, experience I recalled took place when I was seven years old. Early Christmas Eve, my mother took my brother and me out for a treat. It was her way to get us out of our fifth-floor apartment in the Bronx while my father prepared for the evening festivity.

As we climbed the stairs back to the apartment, the shrill sound of a whistle filled the hallway. What was that, and where did it come from? Our pace quickened and a second burst of the whistle could be heard. We dashed into the apartment. There was my father playing engineer with the biggest Lionel train ever made. It was so magnificent, so unexpected, so wonderful!

Some fifty years later, I still have the train set and cherish it as much as any material gift I ever received from my parents. The train is a warm reminder of the greater gift my parents gave me. This gift has nothing to do with any material advantages, or even with any piece of sage advice. Unconditional love was their gift. I never doubted their care for me, and from such grace sprang my own capacity to truth.

It was years later that I fully understood the gift my parents gave me had its source in God's gift of the Child to us all. The sound of the whistle and the song of the angels have become one and the same. They are both the signal of God's love. ANDREW WYERMANN

6. THE MARVELOUS PARADOX OF CHRISTMAS

The claim that Christianity makes for Christmas is that at a particular time and place God came to be with us Himself. When Quirinius was governor of Syria, in a town called Bethlehem, a child was born who, beyond the power of anyone to account for, was the high and lofty One made low and helpless. The One who inhabits eternity comes to dwell in time. The One whom none can look upon and live is delivered in a stable under the soft, indifferent gaze of cattle. The Father of all mercies puts Himself at our mercy.
FREDERICK BUECHNER

7. WHOSE BIRTHDAY?

There was once a family that celebrated Christmas every year with a birthday party for Jesus. An extra chair of honor at the table became the family's reminder of Jesus' presence. A cake with candles, along with the singing of "Happy Birthday" expressed the family's joy in Jesus presence.

One year a Christmas afternoon visitor asked five-year-old Ruth, "Did you get everything you wanted for Christmas?" After a moment's hesitation, she answered, "No, but then it's not my birthday!"

8. THE STORY OF THE CHRISTMAS CHILD

First heard above a lonely hill
By humble shepherd men—
Repeated down the centuries
Again—and yet again—
The story of the Christmas Child
Remains as near, as bright,
As filled with love and hope for all
As on that hallowed night. KATHERINE EDELMAN

9. NEW APPROACH TO GREETINGS

Couple to neighbors who have just opened their door for them: "To save postage, we're hand delivering our Christmas cards this year and dropping in for a bit of lunch and a cup of coffee."

10. CASTING THE PLAY

Announcement about a school play in Memphis: All of the cast will be played by members of the eighth grade, except the baby Jesus, who will be played by a concealed 40-watt light bulb.

11. THE PUSHY CHURCH

Just a few days before Christmas two ladies stood looking into a department store window at a large display of the manger scene with clay figures of the baby Jesus, Mary, Joseph, the shepherds, the wise men, and the animals. Disgustedly, one lady said, "Look at that, the church trying to horn in on Christmas!"

12. CHRISTMAS EVERYWHERE

Everywhere, everywhere, Christmas tonight!
Christmas in lands of the fir tree and pine,
Christmas in lands of the palm tree and vine,
Christmas where snow peaks stand solemn and white,
Christmas where cornfields stand sunny and bright.
Christmas where children are hopeful and gay,
Christmas where old men are patient and gray,
Christmas where peace, like a dove in his flight,
Broods o'er brave men in the thick of the fight;
Everywhere, everywhere, Christmas tonight!
For the Christ child who comes is the Master of all;
No palace too great, no cottage too small. PHILLIPS BROOKS

13. CHRISTMAS BELLS

There are sounds in the sky when the year grows old,
And the winds of the winter blow—
When night and the moon are clear and cold,
And the stars shine on the snow,
Or wild is the blast and the bitter sleet
That bleats on the window pane;
But blest on the frosty hills are the feet
Of the Christmas time again!
Chiming sweet when the night wind swells,
Blest is the sound of the Christmas bells!
Dear are the sounds of the Christmas chimes
In the land of the ivied towers,
And they welcome the dearest of festival times
In this Western world of ours!
Bright on the holly and mistletoe bough
The English firelight falls,
And bright are the wreathed evergreens now
That gladden our own home walls!
And hark! the first sweet note that tells,
The welcome of the Christmas bells! ANONYMOUS

14. THE MEANING OF CHRISTMAS

When the hustle and bustle is over
And the last of the gifts has been wrapped,
And the cookies and cakes are all ready
For the big Christmas plans you have mapped;
When the children are quiet and dreaming
Of the presents Saint Nick will bestow,
And the fire on the hearth burns less brightly,
And the clock has struck twelve long ago;
You relax by the embers and ponder
On this happiest evening of all . . .
On the meaning of Christmas to mankind
By Christ's birth in the low cattle stall.
In the giving of gifts upon Christmas,
People pattern the Father above
Who, in giving His Son, gave His best gift . . .
So the meaning of Christmas is love. DELPHIA CLINE FREEMAN

15. CHRISTMAS SPIRIT

I am the Christmas Spirit—

I enter the home of poverty, causing palefaced children to open their eyes wide, in pleased wonder.

I cause the miser's clutched hand to relax and thus paint a bright spot on his soul.

I cause the aged to renew their youth and to laugh in the old glad way.

I keep romance alive in the heart of childhood, and brighten sleep with dreams woven of magic.

I cause eager feet to climb dark stairways with filled baskets leaving behind hearts amazed at the goodness of the world.

I cause the prodigal to pause a moment on his wild, wasteful way and send to anxious love some little token that releases glad tears—tears which wash away the hard lines of sorrow.

I enter dark prison cells, reminding scarred manhood of what might have been and pointing forward to good days yet to be.

I come softly into the still white home of pain, and lips that are too weak to speak just tremble in silent, eloquent gratitude.

In a thousand ways, I cause the weary world to look up into the face of God, and for a little moment forget the things that are small and wretched.

I am the Christmas Spirit. E. C. BAIRD

16. THE INN THAT MISSED ITS CHANCE

The landlord speaks, A.D. 28
What could be done? The inn was full of folks:
His Honor, Marcus Lucius, and his scribes
Who made the census; honorable men
From farthest Galilee, come hitherward
To be enrolled; high ladies and their lords;
The rich, the rabbis, such a noble throng
As Bethlehem had never seen before
And may not see again. And there they were,
Close-herded with their servants, till the inn
Was like a hive at swarming time, and I
Was fairly crazed among them. Could I know
That they were so important? Just the two,
No servants, just a workman sort of man,
Leading a donkey, and his wife thereon,
Drooping and pale—I saw them not myself.
My servants must have driven them away.

But had I seen them, how was I to know?
Were inns to welcome stragglers, up and down
In all our towns from Beersheba to Dan,
Till He should come? And how were men to know?
There was a sign, they say, a heavenly light
Resplendent; but I had no time for stars.
And there were songs of angels in the air
Out on the hills; but how was I to hear
Amid the thousand clamors of an inn?
Of course, if I had known them, who they were,
And who was He that should be born that night,
For now I learn that they will make Him King.
A second David, who will ransom us
From these Philistine Romans—who but He
That feeds an army with a loaf of bread?
And if a soldier falls, He touches him
And up he leaps, uninjured. Had I known,
I would have turned the whole inn upside down,
His Honor, Marcus Lucius, and the rest,
And sent them all to stables.
So you have seen Him, stranger, and perhaps
Again may see Him? Prithee say for me
I did not know; and if He comes again,
As He surely will come, with retinue,
And banners, and an army—tell Him, my Lord,
That all my inn is His to make amends.
Alas, alas! to miss a chance like that!
This inn that might be chief among them all—
The birthplace of the MESSIAH—had I known! Amos R. Wells

17. SONG OF BETHLEHEM

I was a shepherd on that star-filled night
In Bethlehem. I thought of long ago ...
I thought of brave Naomi taking flight
From Moab's land, of Ruth who chose to know
A stranger's lot—a royal daughter, she.
"Entreat me not to leave thee," she had said,
"Thy people shall be mine—so let it be."
Humbly she gleaned the fields, and there she wed
Boaz, and there she bore him a son.

And from this line came David. In these hills
He roamed and played, and fought at last and won.
Ah, memories—my heart with rapture fills
For here of David's family Christ was born
And alleluias rang from night till morn!
Yes, I, a shepherd on that holy night
In Bethlehem, saw the bright, whirling star
Shatter the darkness like a shaft of light,
Shedding great gleams of glory from afar.
With fright, yet filled with dreams, I heard the song
"Come, find the Child." Joy overflowed the brim
Until I found I could not go along.
I sent instead a lamb to welcome Him.
Though mine shall be a humble walk for long,
I shall not sorrow, for I saw the Light,
And I shall hear the glory of the song—
My days shall always mark that one great height.
They told me that the blessed mother smiled,
And that she placed my lamb beside the Child.
Ah, Bethlehem, my home, my house of bread,
Here let my body and my soul be fed! MELVA ROREM

18. BAH HUMBUG DEPARTMENT

I am sorry to have to introduce the subject of Christmas in these articles. It is
an indecent subject; a cruel, gluttonous subject; a drunken, disorderly subject;
a wasteful, disastrous subject; a wicked, cadging, lying, filthy, blasphemous,
and demoralizing subject. Christmas is forced on a reluctant and disgusted
nation by the shopkeepers and the press; in its own merits it would wither
and shrivel in the fiery breath of universal hatred; and anyone who looked
back to it would be turned into a pillar of greasy sausages.
GEORGE BERNARD SHAW

19. THE MODERN UNDERSTANDING

Last November my choir director asked me if I would pick up the sheet
music for "How Great Thou Art." I happened to be in a shopping center the
next day, so I went in a record store and asked the clerk: "Do you carry any
religious sheet music?" The clerk (she looked like a high school student)
thought a moment and then said: "Some of the Christmas music might be
religious." LESTER WEEKS, *pastor, First Christian Church, Platte City, Missouri*

83

20. THE STAR

Back during World War II a little boy and his daddy were driving home on Christmas Eve. They drove past rows of houses with Christmas trees and decorations in the windows. In many of the windows the little boy noticed a star. He asked his father, "Daddy, why do some of the people have a star in the window?" His daddy said that the star meant that the family had a son in the war. As they passed the last house, suddenly the little boy caught sight of the evening star in the sky. "Look, Daddy, God must have a son in the war, too! He's got a star in his window." Indeed, God has a son who went to war, but Jesus came into our world to go to war with sin.

21. THE SPIRIT OF GIVING

A true story: Two weeks before Christmas a nine-year-old girl was walking with her friend down the street, sliding on the ice. The two of them were talking about what they hoped to get for Christmas. They stopped to talk to an old man named Harry, who was on his knees pulling weeds from around a large oak tree. He wore a frayed, woolen jacket and a pair of worn garden gloves. His fingers were sticking out the ends, blue from the cold.

As Harry responded to the girls, he told them he was getting the yard in shape as a Christmas present to his mother, who had passed away several years before. His eyes brimmed with tears as he patted the old oak. "My mother was all I had. She loved her yard and her trees, so I do this for her at Christmas." His words touched the girls and soon they were down on their hands and knees helping him to weed around the trees. It took the three of them the rest of the day to complete the task. when they finished, Harry pressed a quarter into each of their hands. "I wish I could pay you more, but it's all I've got right now," he said.

The girls had often passed that way before and as they walked on they remembered that the house was shabby, with no wreath, no Christmas tree or other decorations to add cheeriness. Just the lonely figure of Harry sitting by his curtainless window. The quarter seemed to burn a hole of guilt in the one little girl's mind as they returned to their homes. The next day she called her friend and they agreed to put their quarters in a jar marked "Harry's Christmas Present" and then they began to seek out small jobs to earn more. Every nickel, dime, and quarter they earned went into the jar.

Two days before Christmas, they had enough to buy new gloves and a Christmas card. Christmas Eve found them on Harry's doorstep singing carols. When he opened the door, they presented him with the gloves wrapped in pretty paper, the card and a pumpkin pie still warm from the oven. With trembling hands, he tore the paper from the gloves, and then to their astonishment, he held them to his face and wept.

22. THE CHRISTENING

The story is told of a christening that was to be held many years ago by a very wealthy European family. Many guests were invited to the home for the occasion and came in the very latest fashionable garb. Their wraps and coats were carried to a bedroom and laid upon the beds. After the usual lot of conversation and commotion, they were ready for the christening ceremony and someone asked, "Where is the baby?" The nurse was sent upstairs to look and returned in alarmed distress. The baby was nowhere to be found! After several minutes' search someone remembered that the child had last been seen lying on one of the beds, and after a frantic search the little child was found smothered under the wraps of the guests. The chief reason why they had come had been forgotten, neglected, and destroyed! This Christmas many will forget, neglect and even destroy the Christ child! He is smothered by the tinsel, wrapping paper, ribbon, and make-believe that surround the festive occasion reminding us of the words of Luke, "There was no room for them in the inn." Let's not crowd Christ out of Christmas. C. E. SMITH, *San Jose Mercury News*

23. ONE GOOD WORD FOR SANTA

Nicholas was born of wealthy parents in A.D. 280 in a small town called Patara in Asia Minor. He lost his parents early by an epidemic but not before they had instilled in him the gift of faith. Then little Nicholas went to Myra and lived there a life full of sacrifice and love and the spirit of Jesus. Nicholas became so Christlike that when the town needed a bishop he was elected. He was imprisoned for his faith by Emperor Diocletian and released later by Emperor Constantine. There have been many stories of his generosity and compassion: how he begged for food for the poor, and how he would give girls money so that they would have a dowry to get a husband. The story most often repeated was about how he would don a disguise and go out and give gifts to poor children. He gave away everything he had. And in the year 314, he died. His body was later moved to Italy where his remains are to this day.

But the story of Nicholas has spread around the world. There are more churches in the world named after St. Nicholas than any other person in all the history of the church. Oh, people have done strange things to him. The poet, Clement More, gave him a red nose and eight tiny reindeer. And Thomas Nast, the illustrator, made him big and fat and gave him a red suit trimmed by fur. And others have given him names—Belsnickle, Kris Kringle, Santa Claus. But what's important about him is that he had the mind of Christ. Because of his gentle selfless love, he touched the whole world. And this same mind of Christ is to be in us.

24. JESUS WITH A SWITCH

The kids were putting on the Christmas play. To show the radiance of the newborn Savior an electric light bulb was hidden in the manger. All the stage lights were to be turned off so that only the brightness of the manger could be seen, but the boy who controlled the light got confused—all the lights went out!

It was a tense moment, broken only when one of the shepherds said in a loud stage whisper, "Hey! You switched off Jesus!"

25. A DIFFERENT VIEW

It was just a few days before Christmas. Two men who were next-door neighbors decided to go sailing while their wives went Christmas shopping. While the men were out in their sailboat, a storm arose. The sea became very angry and the men had great difficulty keeping the boat under control. As they maneuvered their way toward land, they hit a sandbar and the boat grounded. Both men jumped overboard and began to push and shove with all their strength, trying to get the boat into deeper water. With his feet almost knee-deep in mud, and the waves bouncing him against the side of the boat, and his hair blowing wildly in the wind, one of the men said with a knowing grin, "It sure beats Christmas shopping, doesn't it?"

26. THE STUNNING IMPACT OF CHRISTMAS

An old pioneer traveled westward across the great plains until he came to an abrupt halt at the edge of the Grand Canyon. He gawked at the sight before him: a vast chasm one mile down, eighteen miles across, and more than a hundred miles long! He gasped, "Something musta happened here!" A visitor to our world at Christmas time, seeing the lights, the decorations, the trees, the parades, the festivities, and the religious services, would also probably say, "Something must have happened here!" Indeed, something did happen. God came to our world on the first Christmas.

TWENTY

Church Life
(See also Ministry)

1. THE CHURCH WITHOUT COMMITMENT

Emerson Colaw tells about doing some work with his church's nonresident membership list. He wrote a letter to one family that had been very active in his church. A letter came back saying, "Mr. Colaw, we now live near a university campus and we go every Sunday to the chapel service there. They have unusually fine music . . . they have nationally known preachers ever Sunday morning." And she added a note he didn't think necessary. "We had not heard such preaching as that before. The children are being taught in church school by seminary students." And then she ended, "But the best of all there is no membership, no pledging, and no women's society asking me to work. So if you don't mind, we'll just leave our membership at Hyde Park and continue to enjoy what we have here." No involvement, no bother. No crosses.

2. FAITHFUL ATTENDANCE

A pastor was once asked to define "Faithful Attendance at Worship," and this was his reply: All that I ask is that we apply the same standards of faithfulness to our church activities that we would in other areas of our life. That doesn't seem too much to ask. The church, after all, is concerned about faithfulness. Consider these examples:

If your car started one out of three times, would you consider it faithful? If the paperboy skipped Monday and Thursdays, would they be missed? If you didn't show up at work two or three times a month, would your boss call you faithful? If your refrigerator quit a day now and then, would you excuse it and say, "Oh, well, it works most of the time." If your water heater greets you with cold water one or two mornings a week while you were in the shower, would it be faithful? If you miss a couple of mortgage payments in a year's time, would your mortgage holder say, "Oh, well, ten out of twelve isn't bad"? If you miss worship and attend meetings only often enough to show you're interested but not often enough to get involved, are you faithful?

3. NO INVITATION NEEDED

A church member waiting to be asked to serve in his own church is just like the member of a family waiting to be invited to pull weeds in front of the house where he lives.

4. MEETING HIM IN CHURCH

I love to step inside a church,
To rest, and think, and pray;
The quiet, calm and holy place
Can drive all cares away.
I feel that from these simple walls
There breathes a moving sound
Of sacred music, murmured prayers,
Caught in the endless round.
Of all that makes our human life:
Birth, and the union blessed
Of couples at the altar wed,
And loved ones laid to rest.
Into my soul this harmony
Has poured and now is still,
The Lord's own benediction falls
Upon me as I kneel.
Once more, with lifted head, I go
Out in the jarring mart,
The spring of gladness in my step,
God's peace about my heart. DAVID W. FOLEY

5. LETTER ON ATTENDANCE, SENT TO A PASTOR

Dear Pastor,
You often stress attendance at worship as being very important for a
Christian, but I think a person has a right to miss now and then. I think
every person ought to be excused for the following reasons and the number
of times indicated:
Christmas (Sunday before or after) . . . 1
New Year's (Party lasted too long) . . . 1
Easter (Get away for the holidays) . . . 1
July 4 (National holiday) . . . 1
Labor Day (Need to get away) . . . 1
Memorial Day (Visit hometown) . . . 1
School closing (Kids need a break) . . . 1
School opens (One last fling) . . . 1
Family reunions (Mine and wife's) . . . 2
Sleep late (Saturday night activities) . . . 4
Deaths in family . . . 4

Anniversary (Second honeymoon) . . . 1
Sickness (One for each family member) . . . 5
Business trips (A must) . . . 3
Vacation (3 weeks) . . . 3
Bad weather (Ice, snow, rain, clouds) . . . 6
Ball games . . . 5
Unexpected company (Can't walk out) . . . 5
Time changes (Spring ahead; fall back) . . . 2
Special on TV (Super Bowl, etc.) . . . 3

Pastor, that leaves only two Sundays per year. So, you can count on us to be in church on the fourth Sunday in February and the third Sunday in August unless providentially hindered.

Sincerely,
Faithful Member

6. WHAT DOESN'T COUNT
Going to church don't make anybody a Christian, any more than taking a wheelbarrow into a garage makes it an automobile. BILLY SUNDAY

7. THE QUESTION ABOUT ATTENDANCE
If you don't go to God's house, why should He go to yours?

8. RARE APPEARANCES
Some people never come to church except for their baptism, their marriage, and their funeral, or when they're hatched, matched, and dispatched.

9. GETTING ATTENTION
Just before the beginning of the Sunday service at Saint Bartholomew's on Fifth Avenue, New York City, a man wearing a large hat was discovered sitting in the front row. An usher moved to his pew, leaned in, and discreetly asked him to remove his hat. The man replied that he would not. The head usher was then summoned, made the same request, and received the same answer. About that time the president of the women of the parish arrived and was asked to assist. She had the same dismal result. Finally, with only two minutes remaining before the opening hymn, the senior warden of the parish was summoned. He tiptoed up beside the man and tried to seize the hat, but the man nimbly dodged and there was not time for further attempts.

As the opening hymn began and the procession entered the church, the man stood, removed his hat and did not put it on again.

At the conclusion of the service, the four frustrated people waited for the man at the rear of the church. The senior warden approached him and said,

"Sir, about the hat: perhaps you don't understand, but in the Episcopal church men do not wear hats at worship." The man replied, "Oh, but I do understand. I've been an Episcopalian all my life. As a matter of fact, I've been coming to this church regularly for two years and I've never met a soul. But this morning I've met an usher, the head usher, the president of the church women, and the senior warden."

10. CHURCH FIGHTS
It often seems that the church is a place for contention, which seems to turn some people away. But some see fighting in the church as a healthy sign that people care enough to invest the energy in fighting. A few years ago two ministers got into a fight about what they considered to be an important doctrinal matter. They settled the fight when the first minister told the second: "Look, what are we fighting over? We're both striving to do the Lord's work. You do it your way and I'll do it His way!"

11. THE PERSONAL TOUCH
Some friends recently related an experience they had soon after they joined a new church. They had been assigned to a cell group in the congregation under the care of a church officer. They were excited about their new membership and really wanted to feel as though they were a part of the body.

The church, in an attempt to communicate their caring attitude toward new members, sent a letter that did everything but that. It began:

Dear _____,
We want you to know that we're concerned about you.

12. SEASON'S GREETINGS
The church choir director was being driven out of his mind at the rehearsals for the Christmas choral concert. It seemed that at least one or more members of the choir was absent at every rehearsal. Finally they reached the last rehearsal and he announced: "I want to personally thank the pianist for being the only person in this entire church choir to attend each and every rehearsal during the past two months." At this, the pianist rose, bowed, and said, "It was the least I could do, considering I won't be able to be at the concert tonight."

13. ACTIVE MEMBERS
The pastor of a small southern church was on his way home when he met an acquaintance from town who was not a member of his church. After chatting a while the man asked how many members he had. The pastor responded, "Fifty active members." The friend said, "My, that certainly speaks well for you." But the preacher responded, "Well, I wouldn't say that. All fifty are

active—but twenty-five are actively working for me and the other twenty-five are actively working against me!"

14. TOO MUCH CHRISTIAN VOCABULARY?

After hearing his dad preach on "justification," "sanctification," and all the other "-ations," a minister's son was ready when his Sunday school teacher asked if anybody knew what "procrastination" meant. The boy said, "I'm not sure what it means, but I know our church believes in it!"

15. MODERN HYBRID

Did you hear about the student, a follower of both theologian Paul Tillich and evangelist Billy Graham, who was asked to pronounce the benediction. He said: "And now may the Ground of All Being bless you real good!"
ANTHONY EVANS

16. A PASTOR'S EXCUSES

Twelve reasons why a local clergyman stopped attending athletic events:
Every time I went, they asked me for money.
The people with whom I had to sit didn't seem very friendly.
The seats were too hard and not comfortable.
The coach never came to call on me.
The referee made a decision with which I could not agree.
I was sitting with some hypocrites—they came only to see what others were wearing.
Some games went into overtime, and I was late getting home.
The band played some numbers that I had never heard before.
The games are scheduled when I want to do other things.
My parents took me to too many games when I was growing up.
Since I read a book on sports, I feel that I know more than the coaches anyhow.
I don't want to take my children because I want them to choose for themselves what sport they like best.

17. LET GEORGE DO IT

My eight-year-old son told me a joke one morning while I was frying eggs for the family's breakfast. "Dad, how can you eat an egg without cracking the shell?"

I thought about it for several moments before finally conceding that I did not know.

He replied, "Have someone else crack it for you."

Now this reminded me of some church people. They want the benefits the church has to offer without sharing the responsibilities. They want revival as long as someone else does the praying. They want good programs as long as someone else does the work.

If you want to eat eggs, you're going to have to break some shells.

18. WHAT IS THE CHURCH?
I think that I shall never see
A church that's all it ought to be;
A church whose members never stray
Beyond the straight and narrow way;
A church that has no empty pews,
Whose pastor never has the blues;
A church whose elders always speak,
And none is proud and all are meek.
Such perfect churches there may be,
But none of them are known to me.
But still, we'll work and pray and plan
To make our own the best we can.

19. APPROPRIATE CHURCH BEHAVIOR
In church last Sunday I noted a small child who was turning around smiling at everyone. He wasn't gurgling, spitting, humming, tearing the hymnbooks, or rummaging through his mother's handbag. He was just smiling. Suddenly his mother jerked him around, and in a stage whisper that everyone could hear, said, "Stop grinning. You're in church!" With that she gave him a slap on his hindside, and as the tears rolled down his cheeks she added, "That's better," and returned to her prayers. Here was a woman sitting next to the only life left in our civilization, the only hope, our only miracle, our only promise of infinity. If he couldn't smile in *church,* where was there left to go?

20. TIME TO BE NICE
A priest saw Robert Schuller's TV program "Hour of Power." One of the things that impressed him most was the practice of everyone turning around and shaking hands with and greeting the other worshipers seated nearby. The priest felt that their church was a bit stuffy and could use a bit of friendliness. So, one Sunday he announced that the following Sunday they were going to initiate this custom.

At the close of this same service a man turned around to the lady behind and said, "Good morning." She looked at him with shock at his boldness and said, "I beg your pardon! That friendliness business doesn't start until next Sunday."

21. THE CAR ANALOGY
Church members are like automobiles . . . they start missing before they quit.

22. HOW IT ALL BEGAN
In the Old Testament kings believed that God gave them direction in dreams. If they wanted to know what they were supposed to do in their administration, they would try to receive a direct word from God in their dreams. If they weren't getting any messages in their dreams while lying in their own beds, then they would sleep in the Temple, where they believed it would work better. This is the origin of the time-honored tradition of sleeping in church. I wanted to point that out even though those who would appreciate it most won't hear it.

23. LACK OF COURAGE
One of the bishops attending Vatican II later shared with a few colleagues a note from his personal journal: "Wisdom everywhere, courage nowhere. Dear Lord, we are dying of prudence."

24. MANDATORY BOREDOM
As the Sunday school class for seven-year-olds was well underway, one little boy suddenly exclaimed to the teacher, "Can we hurry up? This is boring!" Immediately the little girl to his left gave him a sharp elbow to the side and rebuked him. "Shut up. It's supposed to be boring!"

25. WHEAT AND TARES
God has some that the church doesn't. And the church has some that God doesn't. St. Augustine

26. NO EXCUSE SUNDAY
To encourage both the faithful and unfaithful to attend church this year, every Sunday will be a "No Excuse Sunday" and the following will be provided:

Cots will be placed in the vestibule for those who say, "Sunday is my only day to sleep."

Murine will be available for those with tired eyes—from watching TV too late on Saturday night.

There will be steel helmets for those who say, "The roof would cave in if I ever came to church."

Blankets will be furnished for those who think the church is too cold, and fans for those who say it is too hot.

We will have hearing aids for those who say, "The minister speaks too softly" and cotton for those who say, "The preacher's too loud."

Score cards will be available for those who wish to list the hypocrites present.

Some relatives will be in attendance for those who like to go visiting on Sundays.

There will be TV dinners for those who can't go to church and cook dinner also.

One section of the church will be devoted to trees and grass for those who like to seek God in nature.

Finally, the church will be decorated with both Christmas poinsettias and Easter lilies for those who have never seen it without them.

27. THE TATES IN YOUR CHURCH

Do you know how many members of the Tate family belong to your church? There is old man Dic Tate who wants to run everything, while Uncle Ro Tate tries to change everything. Their sister Agi Tate stirs up plenty of trouble, with help from her husband, Irri Tate.

Whenever new projects are suggested, Hesi Tate and his wife, Vege Tate, want to wait until next year. Then there is Aunt Imi Tate, who wants our church to be like all the others. Devas Tate provides the voice of doom, while Poten Tate wants to be a big shot.

But not all members of the family are bad. Brother Facili Tate is quite helpful in church matters. And a delightful, happy member of the family is Miss Felici Tate. Cousins Cogi Tate and Medi Tate always think things over and lend helpful, steady hands. And of course there is the black sheep of the family, Ampu Tate, who has completely cut himself off from the church.

28. THE PLAINTIVE CRY FOR RECOGNITION

A family had gone to the movies, and on the way in the young man of the family stopped by the refreshment stand to pick up some popcorn. By the time he got into the theater the lights were already dim. He scanned the theater and evidently couldn't find his family. The lady who tells the story says she watched him pace up and down the aisles searching the crowd in the near-darkness. As the lights began to go down even further he stopped and asked out loud, "Does anyone recognize me?"

I used the story to suggest that as visitors come into our church they are looking for family and companionship. And often, as they stand neglected in our church narthex, or on the front lawn after service—in the deepest recesses of their hearts they are crying out, "Does anyone recognize me?"

29. HOW DOES YOUR CHURCH SCORE?

A church newsletter mentioned a man who visited eighteen different churches on successive Sundays. He was trying to find out what the churches were really like. He said, "I sat near the front. After the service, I walked slowly to the rear, then returned to the front and went back to the foyer using another aisle. I smiled and was neatly dressed. I asked one person to direct me to a specific place: a fellowship hall, pastor's study, etc. I remained for coffee if served. I used a scale to rate the reception I received. I awarded points on the following basis:

   10 for a smile from a worshiper
   10 for a greeting from someone sitting nearby
   100 for an exchange of names
   200 for an invitation to have coffee
   200 for an invitation to return
   1000 for an introduction to another worshiper
   2000 for an invitation to meet the pastor

On this scale, eleven of the eighteen churches earned fewer than 100 points. Five actually received less than 20. The conclusion: The doctrine may be biblical, the singing inspirational, the sermon uplifting, but when a visitor finds nobody who cares whether he's here, he is not likely to come back."

30. A CHURCH WITHOUT WORKS

I was naked, and you questioned my lack of modesty in my appearance. I was imprisoned, and you debated the legal aspects of interference.

I was penniless, and you discussed tax-deductible donations from your wealth. I was sick, and you thanked the Lord for the blessings of your health.

I was hungry, and you formed a club to study malnutrition. I was homeless, and you said God's love was shelter under any condition.

I was lonely, and you left me by myself while you and your friends prayed. You seem so holy and close to God. Yet I'm still sick and alone and afraid!
RUTH M. WALSH

31. COOLER ATMOSPHERE

A church was having air-conditioning installed in the sanctuary and so the pastor was meeting with the contractor. The man asked the pastor a number of questions about the seating capacity, square footage, usual attendance, etc., all the while taking notes. Then in the midst of his calculations, he suddenly crumpled up the paper he was figuring on and started over.

"What's wrong?" asked the pastor.

"I was figuring for a theater instead of a church," replied the contractor.

"What's the difference? Wouldn't they be the same?"

"No, not really," answered the contractor. "You see, in a theater with all that's going on on the screen, there are certain biological changes that take place: heart rates are elevated, blood pressure increases, and body temperatures can begin to climb. In other words, there is a greater need for cooling when people get excited. On the other hand, in the church . . ."

TWENTY-ONE
Cleverness

1. GO WITH THE FLOW

A young couple who took their three-month-old baby to the movies was warned by the usher. He said, "If the baby cries, you'll have to leave. We'll give you your money back." After watching the show for a half hour, the husband asked his wife: "How do you like the movie?" She turned to him and whispered, "It's rotten." He agreed. "I think so, too. Pinch the baby."

2. KNOW YOUR CUSTOMER

A young salesman walked up to the receptionist and asked to see the company's sales manager. Ushered into the office, he said, "I don't suppose you want to buy any life insurance, do you?"

"No," replied the sales manager curtly.

"I didn't think so," said the salesman dejectedly, getting up to leave.

"Wait a minute," said the sales manager. "I want to talk to you." The salesman sat down again, obviously nervous and confused. "I train salesmen," said the sales manager, "and you're the worst I've seen yet. You'll never sell anything until you show a little confidence and accentuate the positive. Now, because you're obviously new at this, I'll help you out by signing up for a ten-thousand-dollar policy."

After the sales manager had signed on the dotted line, he said helpfully, "Young man, one thing you'll have to do is develop a few standard organized sales talks."

"Oh, but I have," replied the salesman, smiling. "This is my standard organized sales talk for sales managers."

3. SAY SOMETHING FUNNY

In the days before World War II, Frank Galen, who was to become a successful writer and producer of TV comedies, reported for his army physical when his draft notice came. When he finally reached the front of the long line, the sergeant looked over his papers and said, "So you're a comedy writer, huh? Say something funny." For a moment, the young man was speechless. Then, turning around to face the long line of recruits standing behind him in their underwear, he yelled, "The rest of you men can go home now. The position has been filled."

4. OUT OF THE BODY
When hit for a donation by a Hare Krishna at the airport, one man responded with the perfect answer: "I gave in a previous lifetime."

5. HUMOR IS SERIOUS
Jokes are no laughing matter to the brain. They are a type of release valve that enables us to think the unthinkable, accept the unacceptable, discover new relationships, adjust better, and maintain our mental health. They are also funny. Without them we probably would be a dull, dim-witted society, trapped in a harsh world too serious to bear.

6. WITHOUT MIRTH
A man without mirth is like a wagon without springs: He is jolted disagreeably by every pebble in the road. HENRY WARD BEECHER

TWENTY-TWO
Commitment

1. LOYAL TO THE END
What I call a good patient is one who, having found a good physician, sticks to him till he dies. OLIVER WENDELL HOLMES

2. TEMPORARY
Commitment means a willingness to be unhappy for awhile.

3. NO P.S.
A college man walked into a photography studio with a framed picture of his girlfriend. He wanted the picture duplicated. This involved removing it from the frame. In doing this, the studio owner noticed the inscription on the back of the photograph: "My dearest Tom, I love you with all my heart. I love you more and more each day. I will love you forever and ever. I am yours for all

eternity." It was signed "Diane," and it contained a P.S.: "If we ever break up, I want this picture back."

We who have been baptized have professed our love for God and for others. We belong to Christ. There can be no P.S. in our life given to God. We can never break up with Him. We are His. We belong to Him—forever. CHARLES KRIEG

4. LAZY CHRISTIANS
My single greatest concern is the growing inertia I see, inertia born out of our luxury and materialism. People are fooling themselves when they say the job is done. . . . The vast body of people in the world today have never been given enough information to know if they accept or reject Jesus. . . . Most people think what the gospel needs is more clever, skilled people, when what it needs is more people who are willing to bleed, suffer, and die in a passion to see people come to Christ. BOB PIERCE

5. I WANT TO BE USED LORD, BUT . . .
There was a pious old gentleman of an earlier generation who used to get up regularly at prayer meeting in his church to pray: "Use me, O Lord, use me—in some advisory capacity!"

6. TOTAL COMMITMENT
General William Booth, founder of the Salvation Army, was asked the secret of his amazing Christian life. Booth answered, "I told the Lord that he could have all that there is of William Booth."

7. THE SURRENDERED WILL
Laid on thine altar, O my Lord, Divine,
Accept my gift this day, for Jesus' sake;
I have no jewels to adorn thy shrine,
No world-famed sacrifice to make;
And here I bring within my trembling hands
This will of mine, a thing that seemeth small;
Yet thou alone canst understand
That when I yield Thee this, I yield Thee all!

8. HOW COMMITTED ARE YOU?
There is a story about two New York men who had never been out of the city. They decided that they had had it with city living, so they bought a ranch down in Texas in order to live off the land like their ancestors.

The first thing they decided they needed was a mule. So they went to a neighboring rancher and asked him if he had a mule to sell. The rancher answered, "No, I'm afraid not."

They were disappointed, but as they visited with the rancher for a few moments one of them saw some honeydew melons stacked against the barn and asked, "What are those?" The rancher, seeing that they were hopeless city slickers, decided to have some fun. "Oh," he answered, "those are mule eggs. You take one of those eggs home and wait for it to hatch, and you'll have a mule." The city slickers were overjoyed at this, so they bought one of the melons and headed down the bumpy country road toward their own ranch. Suddenly they hit an especially treacherous bump, and the honeydew melon bounced out the back of the pickup truck, hit the road, and burst open. Now, seeing in his rearview mirror what had happened, the driver turned his truck around and drove back to see if he could retrieve his mule egg.

Meanwhile a big old Texas jackrabbit came hopping by and saw this honeydew melon burst in the road. He hopped over to it and, standing in the middle of that mess, he began to eat. Now here came the two city slickers. They spied their mule egg burst open and this long-eared creature in the middle of it. One of the men shouted, "Our mule egg has hatched! Let's get our mule."

But seeing those two men coming toward it, the jackrabbit took off hopping in every direction with the two city fellows in hot pursuit. The two men from New York gave everything they had to catch him, but finally they could go no farther. Both men fell wearily onto the ground gasping for air while the jackrabbit hopped off into the distance. Raising up on his elbow, one of the men said to the other, "Well, I guess we lost our mule." The other man nodded grimly. "Yes, but you know," he said, "I'm not sure I wanted to plow that fast anyway."

9. INVOLVED OR COMMITTED?
Football coach Lou Holtz of Arkansas pointed out the difference between being merely involved and being truly committed to a cause. "The Kamikaze pilot that was able to fly missions was involved—but not committed."

TWENTY-THREE

Communication

1. WHAT'S IN A NAME?

A newspaper ad read: "Lost—one dog. Brown hair with several bald spots. Right leg broken due to auto accident. Left hip hurt. Right eye missing. Left ear bitten off in a dog fight. Answers to the name 'Lucky.'"

2. BREAKING THE BAD NEWS

A man was out of town on a trip and he asked his brother to take care of his cat for him while he was away. The cat was a beautiful Siamese and meant a great deal to the man, although the brother who was caring for the cat didn't like cats at all. When he got back from the trip he called his brother's house and asked about his cat. The brother was very curt, and replied, "Your cat died." And then he hung up. For days the man was inconsolable. Finally, he phoned his brother again to point out, "It was needlessly cruel and sadistic of you to tell me so bluntly that my poor cat had passed away." The brother demanded, "Well, what did you expect me to do?" He said, "Well, you could have broken the bad news to me gradually. First, you could have said the cat was playing on the roof. Later you could have called to say he fell off. The next morning you could have reported he had broken his leg. Then, when I came to get him, you could have told me he had passed away during the night. But you didn't have it in you to be that civilized. Now tell me—how's Mama?" The brother pondered momentarily, then announced, "She's playing on the roof."

3. OPENING LINE

I went to hear a lecture by Douglas Fairbanks, Jr. He started out by saying, "I feel like a mosquito in a nudist colony. I look around and I know it's wonderful to be here, but I don't know where to begin."

4. LIFE AND RISK

A newspaperman, visiting the Raiders' football camp a few years ago, had just come from the Jack London Historic Monument. He read a sample of London's prose to quarterback Ken Stabler:

"I would rather be ashes than dust! I would rather that my spark should burn out in a brilliant blaze than it should be stifled by dry rot.

"I would rather be a superb meteor, every atom of me in magnificent glow, than a sleepy and permanent planet. The proper function of man is to live, not to exist. I shall not waste my days in trying to prolong them. I shall use my time."

After reading this to the quarterback he asked, "What does that mean to you?"

Stabler replied: "Throw deep."

5. MIXED MESSAGE

A man came up to a fellow and said to him, "Sir, I don't know you, but I must ask you a question. It's kind of personal, but I'm dying to ask you. Would you be offended at a personal question?" The man was a bit taken aback but said, "Well, I guess not. What is it?" He said, "Well, I'm just so curious. Would you mind telling me if you are wearing a toupee?" The response came back immediately, "No, of course not!" But the man persisted. "Sir, you can be candid with me. I won't think any the less of you. Tell me honestly, are you wearing a toupee?" By now the man was getting a bit ticked off, and said, "Absolutely not" and started to leave. But the fellow would not be dismissed, he held on to his arm. "Please, sir, be patient with me. Honest, you are wearing toupee, aren't you?" By now the man was really uncomfortable and just wanted to get away from the pest. And simply to get rid of him said, "Well, if you insist, OK. Yes, I'm wearing a toupee."

"Really? You'd never know it."

6. QUESTIONS NOT TO ASK

A little girl was talking to her grandmother. She asked, "Grandma, how old are you?"

The grandmother replied, "Now dear, you shouldn't ask people that question. Most grown-ups don't like to tell their age."

The following day, the girl had another question. "Grandma, how much do you weigh?"

Once again the grandmother replied, "Oh, honey, you shouldn't ask grown-ups how much they weigh. It isn't polite."

The next day the little girl was back with a big smile on her face. She said, "Grandma, I know how old you are, You're sixty-two. And you weigh 140 pounds."

The grandmother was a bit surprised and said, "My goodness, how do you know?" The girl smiled and said, "You left your driver's license on the table, and I read it."

Grandmother said, "Oh, so that's how you found out."

The girl said, "That's right, and I also saw on your driver's license that you flunked sex."

7. CARE ABOUT TERMINOLOGY

The psychiatrist was concerned about his nurse's office procedure, so he said to her, "When you answer the phone, just say, 'We're terribly busy just now,' instead of 'It's a madhouse.'"

8. COMMUNICATION DETERIORATION

A school superintendent told his assistant superintendent the following: "Next Thursday morning at 10:30, Halley's Comet will appear over this area. This is an event which occurs only once every seventy-five years. Call the school principals and have them assemble their teachers and classes on their athletic fields and explain this phenomenon to them. If it rains, then cancel the day's observation and have the classes meet in the auditorium to see a film about the comet."

Assistant superintendent to school principals: "By order of the superintendent of schools, next Thursday at 10:30 Halley's Comet will appear over your athletic field. If it rains, then cancel the day's classes and report to the auditorium with your teachers and students where you will be shown films, a phenomenal event which occurs only once every seventy-five years."

Principals to teachers: "By order of the phenomenal superintendent of schools, at 10:30 next Thursday Halley's Comet will appear in the auditorium. In case of rain over the athletic field, the superintendent will give another order—something which occurs only once every seventy-five years."

Teachers to students: "Next Thursday at 10:30 the superintendent of schools will appear in our school auditorium with Halley's Comet; something which occurs once every seventy-five years. If it rains, the superintendent will cancel the comet and will order us out to our phenomenal athletic field."

Students to parents: "When it rains next Thursday at 10:30 over the school athletic field, the phenomenal seventy-five-year-old superintendent of schools will cancel all classes and appear before the school in the auditorium accompanied by Bill Haley and the Comets."

9. AWESOME OBEDIENCE

A few centuries before Christ a man named Alexander conquered almost all of the known world using military strength, cleverness and a bit of diplomacy. The story is told that Alexander and a small company of soldiers approached a strongly fortified walled city. Alexander, standing outside the walls, raised his voice and demanded to see the king. When the king arrived, Alexander insisted that the king surrender the city and its inhabitants to Alexander and his little band of fighting men.

The king laughed, "Why should I surrender to you? You can't do us any harm!" But Alexander offered to give the king a demonstration. He ordered his men to line up single file and start marching. He marched them straight toward a sheer cliff.

The townspeople gathered on the wall and watched in shocked silence as, one by one, Alexander's soldiers marched without hesitation right off the cliff to their deaths! After ten soldiers died, Alexander ordered the rest of the men to return to his side. The townspeople and the king immediately surrendered to Alexander the Great. They realized that if a few men were actually willing to commit suicide at the command of this dynamic leader, then nothing could stop his eventual victory.

Are you willing to be as obedient to the ruler of the universe, Jesus Christ, as those soldiers were to Alexander? Are you as dedicated and committed? Think how much power Christ could have in our area with just a portion of such commitment.

10. LOST CAUSE

I found New York City immense and confusing on my first trip there. One evening during the rush hour, I stopped at a newsstand in the heart of Times Square and asked the vendor which direction was north. "Look, buddy," he replied in a loud and annoyed voice. "We got uptown, we got downtown, and we got crosstown. We don't got north."

11. FORCEFUL ADVICE

At Washington National Airport a long line had formed at one of the airline ticket windows. Suddenly, a strange-looking character charged up to the front of the line, put ten dollars on the counter and said to the ticket agent, "I want to go to New York." The clerk said, "I'm sorry, sir, but you can't go to New York for ten dollars." The man asked, "Well, where can I go?" And fourteen people in the line told him where to go with great precision.

12. LOST IN TRANSLATION

I attended the Pastor's Conference at Mt. Hermon Conference Center and heard Chuck Swindoll of the Evangelical Free Church of Fullerton, California. He shared this story on the things that are sometimes lost in translation:

It seems that some years ago the people of Texas were being plagued by a Mexican bandit who continuously slipped across the border and robbed their banks. His name was Jorge Rodriguez. He had become bolder and more successful, and yet they could never capture him before he hightailed it back across the border to his hideout in the mountains of Mexico. Finally, they had had enough of this so they hired a well-known detective and sent him down into Mexico to get back their money. He set off for the small town reputed to be the hideout of Rodriquez.

The detective found the small Mexican town, walked into the saloon, and, lo and behold, there in the corner was the man he was after, Jorge Rodriquez. "A-ha!" he said, "I've found you!" and he pulled out his gun. "Where have you hidden the millions you have stolen from our banks in Texas? Tell me, or I'll blow you away!" At this point another man, Juan Garcia, who was also in the saloon, stepped up to the detective and said, "Sir, you are wasting your time talking to Jorge like this. He doesn't understand a word of English. He has no idea what you just said. Would you like me to translate for you.?" The detective said, "Yes, of course. Tell him to confess to me where the money is or I'll kill him." So Juan Garcia turned to Jorge and jabbered away at him for a few moments in Spanish. There was much gesturing and chattering, and Jorge told Juan in Spanish that if he would take the man to the well that was just a mile out of town, climb down into the well, and remove the third brick, there he would find more than $3 million in gold. When Jorge was finished speaking, Juan, the helpful translator, turned around to the detective and said, "Senõr, he says that he has absolutely no idea where the gold is. I'm sorry."

13. DID THE MESSAGE GET THROUGH?
An executive who had recently hired an English secretary had to go on a business trip to London. While he was away, a salesman who had never spoken to the new secretary made one of his periodic telephone calls to the executive's office. "Mr. Allen is in the United Kingdom," the secretary told him. The salesman was shocked. "I'm terribly sorry," he said. "Is it too late to send flowers?"

14. EMERGENCY
A man was filling out an application for a factory job, and was puzzled by the blank after "Person to notify in case of accidents." Finally he wrote, "Anybody in sight."

15. TRY AGAIN
A hobo knocked on the door of an English pub called "George and the Dragon." A woman opened the door. He asked, "Could I have a bit to eat?" The woman screamed at him and began to curse and malign him. Finally she slammed the door in his face. He knocked again and the woman opened the door. "Now," he said, "could I have a few words with George?"

16. GAPS IN COMMUNICATION
A grandmother was constantly trying to improve her little granddaughter's vocabulary. She taught her some new words to use and occasionally gave her advice on words *not* to use. On one occasion, the grandmother said, "My

dear, I want you to do something for me. Would you promise not to use two words? One is *swell* and the other is *lousy.* The girl said, "Sure, Granny. What are the two words?"

17. WHAT'S IN A TITLE?
There was once a difficulty in the Rev. Samuel West's congregation in old New England. The choir had declined to proceed with the music. So the shrewd clergyman introduced the services with the hymn "Come, We That Love the Lord," and asked the congregation to begin with the second verse: "Let those refuse to sing who never knew our God."

18. TECHNICAL JARGON
Maybe you saw the Wizard of Id comic strip the day the King came down to check with the Royal Technicians at work on the space project. The King says, "How's the Royal Space Project progressing?" And the technician replies, "We've run into a problem. There's been a major malfunction of the primary propulsion system in the first stage vehicle." The King asks, "What does that mean?" And the technician replies, "It means the rubber band broke."

19. A ROSE BY ANY OTHER NAME?
I'm always impressed with the human tendency to try to change reality by renaming things. You see it in academic papers where they often pour forth commonalities but disguise them in academic jargon and act as if they've said something profound. Part of the process of communication is exposing the several layers of truth—and putting it in varied language so that it comes across to any and all who are listening. All of which is to say I've always enjoyed stories that expose this nonsense. Take the business about titles. No one is a garbageman anymore—he's a Sanitation Engineer. No one is a janitor—he is called the Director of Custodial Services, or the Environmental Displacement Engineer.

It reminds me of the story of the man eating lunch in an organic natural food restaurant. When he looked into his soup, he was disturbed by what he saw. He called the waitress over and said, "Young lady, there's dirt in my soup."

She looked at it carefully and said, "No sir, that's earth."

20. MISTAKES IN COMMUNICATION
Two farmers were chatting in front of the bank. "I hear you made $60,000 in alfalfa," said the first. Not wishing to be impolite his friend replied, "Well, that isn't quite right. It wasn't me, it was my brother, it wasn't alfalfa, but oats; not $60,000 but $6,000; and he didn't make it, he lost it."

21. COMMUNICATION AND CRIME

Peter Drucker, often called the "father of American management," claims that 60 percent of all management problems are a result of faulty communications. A leading marriage counselor says that at least half of all divorces result from faulty communication between spouses. And criminologists tell us that upwards of 90 percent of all criminals have difficulty communicating with other people. NIDO QUBEIN

22. BABBLEJARGON

The following notice was sent home with some high school students: "Our school's cross-graded, multi-ethnic, individualized learning program is designed to enhance the concept of an open-ended learning program on the continuum of multi-ethnic, academically enriched learning, using the identified intellectually-gifted child as the agent of his own learning." One parent sent back a note which read, "I have a college degree, speak two foreign languages and four Indian dialects . . . but I haven't the faintest idea what you are talking about."

Christian, how about your communication of the gospel? Is it so loaded with babblespeak that no one understands what you are saying?

23. PUNCTUATION

It's important how you punctuate your writing. A woman who was concerned about her husband who had joined the navy, handed a prayer request to her pastor which read: "George Bowen, having gone to sea, his wife desires the prayers of the congregation for his safety." The pastor read the note to the congregation this way: "George Bowen, having gone to see his wife, desires the prayers of the congregation for his safety."

24. WHEN YOU REALLY DON'T NEED A CPA

Two men were in a hot-air balloon and were lost. They spotted a man on the ground so they descended within shouting distance hoping he could give them some direction. One man leaned over the edge of the basket and shouted: "Could you please tell us where we are?" The man said "Yes, you are in a balloon about fifty feet in the air." The man in the balloon said to his partner, "Let's ask someone who isn't a CPA." His friend said, "How do you know he's a CPA?" He said, "Because he gave us completely accurate information which was of absolutely no value to us!"

25. CLARITY IN COMMUNICATION

The following items are from letters for support received by a welfare department:

"I am writing the Welfare Department to say that my baby was born two years ago. When do I get my money?"

"I cannot get sick pay. I have six children. Can you tell me why?"

"I am glad to report that my husband who was reported missing is now dead."

"This is my eighth child. What are you going to do about it?"

"I am very much annoyed to find you have branded my son illiterate. This is a dirty lie as I married his father a week before he was born."

"I am forwarding my marriage certificate and three children. One is a mistake as you can see."

"Unless I get my husband's money pretty soon, I will be forced to live an immortal life."

"You have changed my little boy to a girl. Will this make a difference?"

"In accordance with your instructions, I have given birth to twins in the enclosed envelope."

26. TELL US A STORY
The intimate rapport of teller and audience is essential to modern storytelling, and perhaps the key to its newfound popularity. Ellin Greene, professor of the University of Chicago, says, "We're saying that television and other forms of entertainment aren't intimate enough and aren't giving us the kind of inner nourishment we need."

We so quickly get sidetracked from the simple story nature of our faith! We begin to think that theology saves us, that truth is somehow embodied in our theory of the atonement, or our mastery of eschatological charts. But when Jesus wanted to communicate the truth of God's kingdom, he left out the polysyllables and told a story about a woman who lost a coin or a man who dug for treasure. The kingdom of heaven is like this . . . he said. Dare we ask for a more "scholarly" explanation from the Son of God? Unless we become as children, he said, we cannot enter that kingdom. And children love stories. *The Bible Newsletter*

27. HOW'S THAT AGAIN
Psychologist James Dobson reports seeing a sign on a convent in southern California reading: Absolutely No Trespassing—Violators Will Be Prosecuted to the Full Extent of the Law. Signed, "The Sisters of Mercy."

28. SHOW THEM WHAT YOU MEAN
John McDonald is the author of seventy best-selling novels, including twenty about the "Salvage" expert, Travis McGee. McDonald was recently interviewed in *USA Today* by George Vasallo. One of the questions that was

put to him was: "What was the best piece of advice you were ever given?" His answer is a colorful illustration of the power of demonstration or example over mere theorizing. His answer was: "Don't tell 'em, show 'em." Bad version: "Fred was a man with a very bad case of body odor." Better version: "As Fred came walking down the country road, a herd of goats looked at him in consternation, then all ran off into a field gagging and coughing."

29. PREACHING OR CLEAVING?

The mother was waiting for the butcher, who was late. (This was back in the days when butchers made house calls.) She told Johnny, "I'm going upstairs, if the butcher comes, let me know. I want to talk to him." Johnny forgot who his mother wanted to see, so when the minister called, he shouted upstairs, "Ma, that man's here now." The mother answered, "I can't come now, give him the money out of my purse, and tell him we didn't like his tongue last week, and we're going to change!"

30. RETITLE IT

A seminarian turned in his typed-up sermon to his homiletics prof for grading. When he met with him for a conference the professor started out very positively. He said to the young man, "I like your exegesis. You have presented the meaning of the text in a helpful and clear fashion. Your three points make sense, they show balance and progression. Your introduction and your conclusion both show a great deal of thought. The illustrations you used seemed most appropriate. However, I am going to give you a *D* on the sermon." The seminarian was taken aback and said, "Why a *D* if it's all that good?"

The professor said, "Well, frankly, it's because of your sermon title. It is one of the worst I've ever seen. Nobody will want to come a hear a sermon entitled: 'The Pericopes of Jesus in Relationship to the Eschatology of the Apostle Paul.' I tell you what I'll do. You see if you can come up with a better sermon title and I'll reconsider the grade. What you want is a title that will reach out and grab people by the heart. A title that will compel them to come and hear what you have to say. Imagine that title out on the sign in front of a church with such impact that if a bus stopped in front of the church and the people on the bus saw the sign, it would be so powerful it would motivate them to immediately get off the bus and run into the church."

The young man said he would give it his best shot. So he went home and he wrestled with this task all night long, sweating bullets. The next morning he showed up at his prof's office and handed him his new sermon title, which read: "Your Bus Has a Bomb on It!"

31. NAVY JARGON

A newly commissioned ensign, at sea for the first time, was entering the wardroom when he bumped into a seaman carrying a mop and pail. The ensign asked him, "Where you going, sailor?" And he replied, "I'm going downstairs to mop the floor, sir." The ensign snorted. "You'd better learn naval terminology, sailor. You're not going downstairs to mop the floor, you're going below to swab the deck." The sailor replied, "I'll try to remember, sir." The ensign came back, "You'd better. If I ever hear you say 'downstairs' again, I'll throw you out that little round window over there."

32. COMPLETE BREAKDOWN

A mature-looking lady had an appointment with a marriage counsellor, and told him flat out: "I would like to divorce my husband." To this, the counselor replied, "Well, do you have any grounds?" She answered, "Why yes. We have almost an acre." The puzzled counselor asked her, "You don't understand. What I want to know is do you and your husband have a grudge?" The lady answered, "Actually, we don't, but we do have a nice carport." At this, the counselor shook his head and said, "Ma'am, I'm sorry, but I just don't see any reason why you should divorce your husband." The lady looked at the counselor and said to him, "It's just that the man can't carry on an intelligent conversation."

33. POWERFUL MESSAGE

Woman to neighbor: "I have a marvelous meat loaf recipe. All I do is mention it to my husband and he says, 'Let's eat out.'"

34. SYMPATHETIC ATTITUDE

A surgeon was discussing a case with a class of medical students: "The muscle in the patient's right leg has contracted until it is shorter than that in the left. Therefore, he limps. What would you do in such a circumstance?" One student raised his hand and said, "I'd limp too."

35. IDENTITY CRISIS

There is the story of a woman who, early one morning, made a mad dash out of the house when she heard the garbage truck pulling away. She was still in her bathrobe. Her hair was wrapped in big curlers. Her face was covered with sticky cream. She was wearing a chin-strap and a beat-up old pair of slippers. In short, she was a frightful picture. When she reached the sidewalk, she called out, "Am I too late for the garbage?" And the reply came back, "No, hop right in."

36. COMMUNICATION SNAFU

In the small town we lived in, the volunteer fire department's telephone was answered by the policeman on duty, who would in turn sound the fire whistle to rally the volunteers to duty. One Saturday morning my father, the town chief of police, had just come on duty when the fire department phone rang. He picked up the phone and said, "Fire Department." A voice on the other end of the line frantically said, "Send the fire truck!" Then the caller immediately slammed the phone down. My dad stood stunned, not knowing what to do. In a few minutes the phone rang again. Quickly he picked it up and said again, "Fire Department!" Again the voice cried, "Send the fire truck!" Again the caller immediately hung up. Realizing that someone's house was possibly at stake, he rushed outside and scanned the sky to see if he could see smoke and therefore send the fire trucks in that direction. While outside he also devised a plan as to how to keep the caller from hanging up so quickly if she called back. Sure enough the phone rang again and he went running inside. Picking up the phone he quickly asked, "Where's the fire?" The lady on the other end screamed, "In the kitchen," and slammed the phone down again.

37. FOUR SPEECHES IN ALL

William Lyon Phelps, the late Yale professor and lecturer, once said that he got credit for only one-fourth of his after-dinner speeches. "Every time I accept an invitation to speak, I really make four addresses. First is the speech I prepare in advance. That is pretty good. Second is the speech I really make. Third is the speech I make on my way home, which is the best of all; and the fourth is the speech the newspapers the next morning say I made, which bears no relation to any of the others."

TWENTY-FOUR

Communism

1. DIFFERING PERSPECTIVES

While working among Cuban Americans in Miami, I frequently heard the following story:

Shortly after the Communist revolution in Cuba, there were strong persuasive attempts at turning the people away from God. In grade schools, teachers would ask their students whether God could live up to His promises or not. Of course, the students said yes. The teacher would then illustrate how impotent God actually was. The teacher instructed the students to fervently pray for candy. After ten minutes, the teacher would ask if anyone received any candy. The students responded with a sad "No." Then the teacher would ask the students to ask the Communist state for candy. With expectant hearts, the students did so, and the teacher went around the room filling the students hands with sweets.

This truly is a differing perspective. Communism as a cure for social ills has no room for a loving God. The state's protection of the individual for the benefit of the state will never replace God's own Son dying for our sins on the cross.

2. RED ALERT

The story is told in Russia about the late Premier Leonid Brezhnev, who wanted to impress his old mother from the Ukraine. First he showed her through his sumptuous apartment in Moscow. She said nothing. Then he drove her in his chauffeured black limousine out to his dacha in Usovo, showed her the marble reception rooms, and treated her to a fine lunch of caviar and crab. She still appeared unimpressed. So he flew her in his private helicopter to his hunting lodge in Zavidovo, where a fire crackled in the huge fireplace of the banquet room. She seemed increasingly ill-at-ease. At last he burst out, "Well, Mama, what do you think?" She said with some hesitation, "It's nice, Leonid, but what if the Communists come back?"

TWENTY-FIVE

Compassion
(See also Love)

1. TELLING ABOUT GOD

Alice Lee Humphres, in her book *Angels in Pinafores,* tells about her experiences as a first grade teacher. She tells about one little girl who came to school one winter day wearing a beautiful white angora beret, white mittens, and a matching muff. As she was coming through the door, a mischievous little boy grabbed the white muff and threw it in the mud. After disciplining the little boy, the teacher sought to comfort the girl. Brushing the mud off of her soiled muff, the little girl looked up at the teacher and said in a quiet and responsible manner, "Sometime I must take a day off and tell him about God." As far as the girl was concerned, everything that was wrong with the boy could be made right if she could just tell him about God.

2. OUNCE OF PREVENTION

One of the most fascinating biographies I ever read was that of Irene Webster Smith by Russell Hitt. The title of the book is *Sensei* which means "teacher" in Japanese. Irene Smith was a Quaker and a missionary to Japan for some fifty years. Sensei became her name to the Japanese. She first went to Japan about 1915 under the Japan Evangelistic Band from her native Ireland. Her first assignment was to serve in the Tokyo Rescue Home, which sought to save prostitutes from their entrapment in the government-licensed brothels. In this early experience, Sensei learned how these young girls, who were unwanted by their parents, were sold into a life of prostitution and trained from their earliest years to know no other experience. These days in the Tokyo Rescue Home were very discouraging to Sensei, because these girls, no matter how they seemed to repent of their past, would so often revert to their life of immorality as soon as they regained their health.

In the midst of this frustrating job a thought came to Sensei. *It would be better to put a fence at the top of the precipice than an ambulance at the foot.* And with that thought a vision was born—a vision of a home for unwanted girls—a home warmed by love and bright with God's grace, a home where little girls, once destined for brothels and disease, could be brought up in happiness to lead full and useful Christian lives. And so for many years Sensei turned to the work of endeavoring to keep young girls from falling over this particular precipice.

Which is most important? Picking up the pieces in people's lives after calamity has struck (running an ambulance service), or catching a few, as it were, midair in a net, or building fences to keep people from trouble in the first place?

3. WE NEED EACH OTHER

A young woman was waiting for a bus in a slum area one evening when a rookie policeman approached her. "Want me to wait with you?" he asked. She replied, "Thank you, but that's not necessary. I'm not afraid." "Well, then," he said, grinning, "would you mind waiting with me?"

4. IT'S HARD TO HELP SOME PEOPLE

Two Cub Scouts, whose younger brother had fallen into the lake, rushed home to mother with tears in their eyes.

One of them sobbed, "We try to give him artificial respiration, but he keeps getting up and walking away."

5. REAL EMPATHY

A little girl was sent on an errand by her mother. She took much too long in coming back. Mother, therefore, demanded an explanation when she finally did return. The little girl explained that on her way she had met a little friend who was crying because she had broken her doll. "Oh," said the mother, "then you stopped to help her fix her doll?" "Oh, no," replied the little girl. "I stopped to help her cry."

6. STOP AND THINK FIRST

A professor at the UCLA Medical School asked his students this question: "Here is the family history: The father has syphilis. The mother has TB. They already have had four children. The first is blind. The second had died. The third is deaf. The fourth has TB. The mother is pregnant. The parents are willing to have an abortion if you decide they should. What do you think?" Most of the students decided on abortion. "Congratulations," said the professor. "You have just murdered Beethoven!" Nothing is so final as murder, even when it is done very early in a life. TERENCE PATTERSON

7. THE CHURCH'S MISSION—A PARABLE

Not long ago I visited my sister, a director of patient services for the children's unit of a large southern California hospital. She was conducting me on a tour through that unit. All the time—echoing through the halls—we could hear the cry of a baby coming from one of the rooms. Finally, we came to that room. It was a little child, about a year old, covered with terrible bruises, scratches, scars, from head to toe.

At first, I assumed the child must have been involved in a terrible accident. Then I looked closely at its legs. Written in ink all over them were obscenities. My sister told me that the child was the victim, not of an accident, but of its parents. Its internal injuries were so severe that it couldn't keep any food down. The scars on the bottom of its feet were burns caused by cigarettes.

If you've ever had trouble visualizing the consequences of human indifference—the perversion of life's basic relationships—what God himself is up against in this world of ours—I wish you could have looked with me at that battered, crying baby!

But I want to tell you what happened then. My sister leaned over the crib, and very carefully and tenderly lifted the child, and held it next to herself. At first the child screamed all the more, as if its innocent nature had come to be suspicious of every touch. But as she held it securely and warmly, the baby slowly began to quiet down. And finally, in spite of wounds and hurts and past experience, it felt the need to cry no more.

The baby remains in my memory as a living symbol of the choice we face in the mission of the church. Are we willing to let life's most precious values be battered and starved and crucified by default? Or will we reach out and pick them up and hold them close to our hearts? The time for commitment is not next year, next month, but now! PHILIP ANDERSON

8. INCARNATION IN THE MOUNTAINS

Years ago I remember seeing the news reports of a coal mining accident in the Allegheny mountains. Many miners escaped with their lives, but three men were still trapped somewhere deep within the earth's crust. Whether they were dead or alive, no one knew. What made the accident even more threatening to life was the presence of intense heat and noxious gases within the mine itself. If the men were not crushed by the rock, they well could have been asphyxiated by the fumes or killed by the heat. Two days went by before a search expedition was allowed to even enter the mine because of the heat and fumes. Even then, there was great danger in store for anyone who would dare descend into what could well be a deep, black grave.

I don't remember what happened to those three men. All I remember is a brief interview conducted with one of the members of the search party as he was preparing to enter the mine. A reporter asked him if he knew of the noxious gases and the extreme danger of the mine. The man said, "Yes."

"And you are still going down?"

And the man said, "Those men may still be alive." Without another word of explanation, he put on his gas mask, climbed into the elevator, and descended into the black inferno of the mine.

He put his life on the line that others might live. That is what Christ does.

9. YO HO HO AND A BOTTLE OF HOPE

On a cruise from Mexico to Hawaii in 1979, Los Angeles lawyer John Peckham and his wife, Dottie, put a note in a bottle and tossed it into the Pacific. Three years and nine thousand miles later, Vietnamese refugee Nguyen Van Hoa leaned down from a tiny, crowded boat and plucked the bottle from the South China Sea—amazed to find a name and address, a dollar for postage and the promise of a reward. "It gave me hope," said Hoa, who had escaped from a prison camp in Vietnam. Safe in a UN refugee camp in Thailand, Hoa wrote the surprised Peckhams. For two years they corresponded; Hoa married and had a son. Last year, the Peckhams agreed to sponsor the emigration of Hoa, now thirty-one, and his family. In April, they arrived for an emotional meeting with the Peckhams—and a new life from an old bottle.

10. RIGHTEOUS ANGER

Dr. David Swoap told the following at a commencement address at Westmont College this past year:

When I lived in Washington, D.C., I was privileged to meet Mother Teresa. I asked her, "Don't you ever become angry at the causes of social injustice that you see in India or in any of the places in which you work?"

Her response was, "Why should I expend energy in anger that I can expend in love?"

11. AT THE PLAYGROUND

While Penny and I were walking in the park the other day, a ten-year-old boy came racing around a tree, almost running into us and said, "Dad, where's Amy?" Instantly he realized his mistake and said, "Sir, I'm sorry. I thought you were my dad. I made a mistake."

I replied, "That's OK, everybody makes mistakes!"

As he began to walk away, I noticed he had a limp as well as the features of a child with Down's syndrome. After having walked about ten yards, as an afterthought, he turned around and started retracing his steps toward us.

"My name is Billy," he said. "You both were very nice to me, can I give you a hug?"

After giving each of us a tight hug he said, "I just wanted you to know that you're my friends and I am going to be praying for you. I have to go now and find my sister, Amy. Good-bye, and God bless you!"

Tears came to both Penny's and my eyes as we watched Billy, that child with Down's syndrome, limp to the playground to play with his little sister. After Billy went down the slide, his mother came over to him and gave him a big hug. It was obvious that he was a special child to her.

Sometimes God uses the Billys of the world to break down our walls of sophistication to show us what genuine kindness is all about. We must never underestimate the impact that a hug, smile, or encouraging word may have on a person's life. JIM SCHIBSTED

12. BONHOEFFER ON ABORTION

Destruction of the embryo in the mother's womb is a violation of the right to live which God has bestowed upon this nascent life. To raise the question whether we are here concerned already with a human being or not is merely to confuse the issue. The simple fact is that God certainly intended to create a human being and that this nascent human being has been deliberately deprived of his life. And that is nothing but murder. DIETRICH BONHOEFFER, *Ethics*

13. CALVIN ON ABORTION
The fetus carried in the mother's womb is already a man; and it is quite unnatural that a life be destroyed of one who has not yet seen its enjoyment. For it seems more unworthy that a man be killed in his home rather than in his field because for each man his home is his safest refuge. How much more abominable ought it to be considered to kill a fetus in the womb who has not yet been brought into the light. JOHN CALVIN, *Commentaries on the Last Four Books of Moses*

14. AM I MY BROTHER'S KEEPER?
In 1928, a very interesting case came before the courts in Massachusetts. It concerned a man who had been walking on a boat dock when suddenly he tripped over a rope and fell into the cold, deep water of an ocean bay. He came up sputtering and yelling for help and then sank again, obviously in trouble. His friends were too far away to get to him, but only a few yards away, on another dock, was a young man sprawled on a deck chair, sunbathing. The desperate man shouted, "Help, I can't swim!" The young man, an excellent swimmer, only turned his head to watch as the man floundered in the water, sank, came up sputtering in total panic, and then disappeared forever.

The family of the drowned man was so upset by that display of callous indifference that they sued the sunbather. They lost. The court reluctantly ruled that the man on the dock had no legal responsibility whatever to try and save the other man's life. In effect, the law agrees with Cain's presupposition: I am not my brother's keeper, and I have every legal right to mind my own business and to refuse to become involved. GARY INRIG

15. THE GUEST
A pious father always closed grace for the evening meal with these words: "Come, Lord Jesus, be our guest and bless what thou hast provided." "Papa," said the little son, "every evening you ask Jesus to come and be our guest, but he never comes." "My son," replied the father, "we can only wait. But we know that he will not despise our invitation." "Well, then," asked the little fellow, "if we expect him to come and have dinner with us, why don't we set a place for him at the table?" And so to save further embarrassing questions, the father permitted the boy to set a place at the table. Just then a knock

came at the door. When they opened it a poor helpless waif stood shivering in the cold. The son thought for a moment and finally said, "I guess Jesus couldn't come today, and so he sent this poor boy in his place." With little further conversation the little beggar boy was brought in and set at the empty place at the dinner table. JOHN W. WADE

16. DO UNTO OTHERS, ETC.
An Irishman was down on his luck and was panhandling on Fifth Avenue before the annual St. Patrick's Day parade got underway in New York City. As a couple strolled by, he called out: "May the blessing of the Lord, which brings love and joy and wealth and a fine family, follow you all the days of your life." There was a pause as the couple passed his outstretched hand without contributing. Then he shouted after them, "And never catch up to you!"

17. BEARING ONE ANOTHER'S BURDENS
In Booker T. Washington's autobiography, *Up from Slavery,* Mr. Washington recalled a beautiful incident of an older brother's love. He said the shirts worn on his plantation by the slaves were made of a rough, bristly, inexpensive flax fiber. As a young boy, the garment was so abrasive to his tender, sensitive skin that it caused him a great deal of pain and discomfort. His older brother, moved by his brother's suffering, would wear Booker's new shirts, until they were broken in and smoother to the touch. Booker said it was one of the most striking acts of kindness he had experienced among his fellow slaves. What a beautiful illustration of "bearing one another's burdens," which we are admonished to do in Galatians 6:20.

18. FEED MY SHEEP
A true story: A flight from Denver to Wichita was boarding. On an ambulance litter an attendant carried a 225-pound man as the last traveler to board. As they cradled him into a seat in front of us, it was evident he was totally paralyzed from his shoulders down. He was strapped in tightly, but as the pilot taxied to the runway the centrifugal force lunged him to the right causing him to fall toward the next seat. The stewardess again propped him up in an upright position. Hastily, we were airborne. Beverages were served, then a meal. As I finished the meal, I looked up to see the paralyzed gentleman, probably twenty-seven years old, with the meal before him with no one to feed him. My eyes filled with tears. The hostesses were busy serving food to all passengers, but here was a person traveling alone who could only look at the meal. It was beautifully prepared, tasty, and far above average for airline food.

Before I could wipe the tears from my eyes, I slipped from my seat to his side and inquired if the stewardess would be helping him eat. He did not know. I asked if I might help him. He responded with, "Oh, thank you, I would be so grateful for your help." As I cut the meal into bite sizes and placed them in his mouth, I felt awkward, conspicuous, but much needed. Before long I was coordinating bites as well as if they were entering my own mouth. He told me of his unfortunate accident, his lonesomeness, his joys, his struggles, his faith, his hope. His name was Bill. Our spirits blended—we experienced sacrament! Upon returning to my seat, my spirit was humbled as I thought of all the people who have had the Good News of the gospel set before them. It's available but no one to feed them, crippled with spiritual and psychological paralysis—and no one to feed them. My spirit flowed to the words Jesus asked Peter, "Do you love me?" Jesus responded, "Feed my sheep."

19. THE DEEPEST SYMPATHY
In 430 B.C. the historian Thucydides wrote, "It was in those who had recovered from the plague that the sick and the dying found most compassion." A preacher who has never needed comfort is not likely to be as concerned about giving comfort. CHARLES ALLEN, *What I Have Lived By*

20. MORE THAN WORDS
Kindness will influence more than eloquence.

21. THE POWER OF LOVE
Tears glistened in the eyes of the Salvation Army officer Shaw as he looked at the three men before him. Shaw was a medical missionary who had just arrived in India, and the Army was taking over this particular leper colony. These three men had manacles and fetters binding their hands and feet, cutting their diseased flesh. Captain Shaw turned to the guard and said, "Please unfasten the chains."

"It isn't safe," the guard replied, "these men are dangerous criminals as well as lepers!"

"I'll be responsible. They're suffering enough," Captain Shaw said, as he put out his hand and took the keys, then knelt and tenderly removed the shackles and treated their bleeding ankles and wrists.

About two weeks later Captain Shaw had his first misgivings about freeing these criminals; he had to make an overnight trip and dreaded leaving his wife and child alone. His wife insisted that she wasn't afraid with God being there. The next morning when she went to the front door, she was startled to see the three criminals lying on her steps. One explained, "We know the doctor go. We stay here all night so no harm come to you." That's how these dangerous men responded to an act of love. Christ came to set fettered people free.

22. FINDING HAPPINESS
Guard within yourself that treasure, kindness. Know how to give without hesitation, how to lose without regret, how to acquire without meanness. Know how to replace in your heart, by the happiness of those you love, the happiness that may be wanting to yourself. GEORGE SAND

23. DEALING WITH THE BLUES
Ten rules for getting rid of the blues: Go out and do something for someone else, and repeat it nine times.

24. CARRYING A BURDEN
Dr. Albert Schweitzer was eighty-five years old when I visited his jungle hospital at Lambarene, on the banks of the Ogowe River. You can imagine the deep and profound effect of that three-day visit, which included opportunity for some leisurely conversation with that great humanitarian, theologian, musician, and physician. But one event stands out in a special way.

It was about eleven in the morning. The equatorial sun was beating down mercilessly, and we were walking up a hill with Dr. Schweitzer. Suddenly he left us and strode across the slope of the hill to a place where an African woman was struggling upward with a huge armload of wood for the cookfires. I watched with both admiration and concern as the eighty-five-year-old man took the entire load of wood and carried it on up the hill for the relieved woman. When we all reached the top of the hill, one of the members of our group asked Dr. Schweitzer why he did things like that, implying that in that heat and at his age he should not. Albert Schweitzer, looking right at all of us and pointing to the woman, said simply, "No one should ever have to carry a burden like that alone." *From a letter from* ANDREW C. DAVISON, *Colgate Rochester Seminary*

25. SCARRED HANDS
A small orphaned boy lived with his grandmother. One night their house caught fire. The grandmother, trying to rescue the little boy asleep upstairs, perished in the smoke and flames. A crowd gathered around the burning house. The boy's cries for help were heard above the crackling of the blaze. No one seemed to know what to do, for the front of the house was a mass of flames.

Suddenly a stranger rushed from the crowd and circled to the back where he spotted an iron pipe that reached an upstairs window. He disappeared for a minute, then reappeared with the boy in his arms. Amid the cheers of the crowd, he climbed down the hot pipe as the boy hung around his neck.

Weeks later a public hearing was held in the town hall to determine in whose custody the boy would be placed. Each person wanting the boy was allowed to speak briefly. The first man said, "I have a big farm. Everybody needs the out-of-doors." The second man told of the advantages he could provide. "I'm a teacher. I have a large library. He would get a good education." Others spoke. Finally the richest man in the community said, "I'm wealthy. I could give the boy everything mentioned tonight: farm, education, and more, including money and travel. I'd like him in my home."

The chairman asked, "Anyone else like to say a word?" From the backseat rose a stranger who had slipped in unnoticed. As he walked toward the front, deep suffering showed on his face. Reaching the front of the room, he stood directly in front of the little boy. Slowly the stranger removed his hands from his pockets. A gasp went up from the crowd. The little boy, whose eyes had been focused on the floor until now, looked up. The man's hands were terribly scarred. Suddenly the boy emitted a cry of recognition. Here was the man who had saved his life. His hands were scarred from climbing up and down the hot pipe. With a leap the boy threw himself around the stranger's neck and held on for life. The farmer rose and left. The teacher, too. Then the rich man. Everyone departed, leaving the boy and his rescuer who had won him without a word. Those marred hands spoke more effectively than any words.

CONFESSION *(See Repentance)*

TWENTY-SIX

Conformity

1. FOLLOWING FADS
He who marries the spirit of the age will soon find himself a widower.
WILLIAM R. INGE

2. EVERYBODY'S DOING IT

We all hear the cry (from our teenagers, if not many others), "But everybody's doing it!" John Calvin called it "The Appeal to 'Custom' against Truth" in his Prefatory Address to King Francis when he wrote his *Institutes*:

"Even though the whole world may conspire in the same wickedness, he has taught us by experience what is the end of those who sin with the multitude. This he did when he destroyed all mankind by the Flood, but kept Noah with his little family; and Noah by his faith, the faith of one man, condemned the whole world (Gen. 7:1; Heb. 11:7). To sum up, evil custom is nothing but a kind of public pestilence in which men do not perish the less though they fall with the multitude."

3. BREAKAWAY

Richard Armstrong and Edward Watkin tell the story of a biologist's experiment with "processional caterpillars." On the rim of a clay pot that held a plant, he lined them up so that the leader was head-to-head with the last caterpillar. The tiny creatures circled the rim of the pot for a full week. Not once did any one of them break away to go over to the plant and eat. Eventually, all caterpillars died from exhaustion and starvation. The story of the processional caterpillars is a kind of parable of human behavior. People are reluctant to break away from the rhythmic pattern of daily life. They don't want to be different. We must break away from the crowd, however, if we are to accept Jesus' invitation to "go off alone" with him in prayer.

TWENTY-SEVEN
Confusion

1. LOSS OF NOTE

I write down everything I want to remember. That way, instead of spending a lot of time trying to remember what it is I wrote down, I spend the time looking for the paper I wrote it down on. BERYL PFIZER

2. COMPLETELY BEFUDDLED

A fellow bumped into his old friend whom he hadn't seen in many years. He asked, "How's your wife?" He replied, "She's in heaven." Without thinking, he responded, "Oh, I'm sorry." Then, realizing that was not the best phrase to use, he said, "I mean, I'm glad ... well, what I really mean is, I'm surprised."

3. BEDLAM
A middle-aged woman was sitting in her den when all of a sudden a small black snake crawled across the floor and under the couch. The women was deathly afraid of snakes, so she promptly ran to the bathroom to get her husband, who was taking a shower. The man of the house came running from the shower to the den with only a towel around his waist. The man took an old broom handle and began poking under the couch to retrieve the snake. At that point the family dog, who had been sleeping, awoke and became excited. In the dog's frenzy over the actions of the husband, the little terrier touched his cold nose to the back of the man's heel. Instead of realizing what had happened, the man surmised that the snake had outmaneuvered him and bitten him on the heel. He fainted dead away. The wife concluded that her husband, because of the physical exertion over trying to kill the snake, had had a heart attack. She ran from the house to a hospital emergency room that was one block away. The ambulance drivers arrived promptly and placed the man, who was now semiconscious, on a stretcher. As the attendants were carrying the man out of the den, the snake reappeared from beneath the couch. At this point one of the drivers became so excited that he dropped his end of the stretcher and broke the leg of the husband.

TWENTY-EIGHT
Conscience

1. ANTICIPATORY CONSCIENCE
Conscience is, in most men, an anticipation of the opinion of others.
HENRY TAYLOR

2. KEEPING IT CLEAN
It's easy enough to have a clear conscience—all it takes is a fuzzy memory.

3. WILLPOWER OR CONSCIENCE
A man consulted a psychiatrist. He complained, "I've been misbehaving, Doc, and my conscience is troubling me." The doctor asked, "And you want

something that will strengthen your willpower?" The fellow replied, "Well, no, I was thinking of something that would weaken my conscience."

TWENTY-NINE
Contentment

1. SELF-INVENTORY

The story is told of a farmer who had lived on the same farm all his life. It was a good farm, but with the passing years, the farmer began to tire of it. He longed for a change—for something "better." Every day he found a new reason for criticizing some feature of the old place. Finally, he decided to sell, and listed the farm with a real estate broker who promptly prepared a sales advertisement. As one might expect, it emphasized all the farm's advantages: ideal location, modern equipment, healthy stock, acres of fertile ground, etc. Before placing the ad in the newspaper, the realtor called the farmer and read the copy to him for his approval. When he had finished, the farmer cried out, "Hold everything! I've changed my mind. I am not going to sell. I've been looking for a place like that all my life."

CONVERSION *(See Change)*

THIRTY
Cooperation

1. WORKING AS A TEAM

Some missionaries in the Philippines set up a croquet game in their front yard. Several of their Agta Negrito neighbors became interested and wanted to join the fun. The missionaries explained the game and started them out, each with a mallet and ball. As the game progressed, opportunity came for one of the players to take advantage of another by knocking that person's ball

123

out of the court. A missionary explained the procedure, but his advice only puzzled the Negrito friend. "Why would I want to knock his ball out of the court?" he asked. "So you will be the one to win!" a missionary said. The short-statured man, clad only in a loincloth, shook his head in bewilderment. Competition is generally ruled out in a hunting and gathering society, where people survive not by competing but by sharing equally in every activity.

The game continued, but no one followed the missionaries' advice. When a player successfully got through all the wickets, the game was not over for him. He went back and gave aid and advice to his fellows. As the final player moved toward the last wicket, the affair was still very much a team effort. And finally, when the last wicket was played, the "team" shouted happily, "We won! We won!"

That is how the Church, the body of Christ, should be. We're a team. We all win together.

2. LET'S GET TOGETHER

In his book *Wind and Fire,* Bruce Larson tells of a friend of his who lives near Hoyt Park in Madison, Wisconsin, and who happens to be a great bird lover. Invariably, his yard is full of all kinds of birds in all seasons. However, the squirrels plague his bird feeders continually. Exasperated, he finally bought a pellet gun and began to shoot the squirrels, two and three a day, every day, week after week. In spite of these desperate measures, the squirrel population seemed undiminished. One day, he was discussing the irksome problem with his colleague at work. His friend said, "I solved that problem. I was troubled by squirrels, too. But now I trap them. I trap two or three a day and take them down to Hoyt Park and release them."

Larson comments, "That's an example of what can happen when we approach all of our problems individually, with no sense of the larger picture."

3. HONKING ENCOURAGEMENT

Maggie Kuhn, head of the Grey Panthers, tells of some interesting facts about sandhill cranes. It seems that these large birds, who commute great distances and traverse continents, have three remarkable qualities. First of all, they rotate leadership. No one bird stays out in front all the time. Second, they choose a leader that can handle turbulence. And then, all during the time one bird is leading, the rest are honking, signaling their affirmation. That's not a bad model for the church. Certainly we need leaders who welcome turbulence and who are aware that leadership ought to be rotated. But most of all, we need a church where we are all honking encouragement.
BRUCE LARSON

4. NO MAN IS AN ISLAND

Peter Goulding, in his book, *The Young Minister,* weaves into the pages of his plot a hermit who, on the outside, seems to have rejected society. As the story unfolds it can be seen that though he rejects society and the family of humanity, he is very dependent upon it. At one point, his large library is mentioned with no thought for the fact that without his fellow human beings this library would not have been a possibility. There was an implied dependence without even thinking about it. The hermit's very existence is dependent upon the society which he chooses to reject.

5. WORKING TOGETHER

Two men were riding a bicycle built for two when they came to a big steep hill. It took a great deal of struggle for the men to complete what proved to be a very stiff climb. When they got to the top the man in front turned to the other and said, "Boy, that sure was a hard climb." The fellow in back replied, "Yes, and if I hadn't kept the brakes on all the way we would certainly have rolled down backwards."

6. FOUR LESSONS FROM GEESE

We will never become a church that effectively reaches out to those who are missing out if we shoot our wounded and major on the minuses. Instead of being fishers of men, as Christ has called us, we will be keepers of an ever-shrinking aquarium. Next fall when you see geese heading south for the winter, flying along in V formation, you might be interested in knowing what science has discovered about why they fly that way. It has been learned that as each bird flaps its wings, it creates an uplift for the bird immediately following. By flying in a V formation, the whole flock adds at least 71 percent greater flying range than if each bird flew on its own. (Christians who share a common direction and a sense of community can get where they are going quicker and easier, because they are traveling on the thrust of one another.)

Whenever a goose falls out of formation, it suddenly feels the drag and resistance of trying to go it alone, and quickly gets back into formation to take advantage of the lifting power of the bird immediately in front. (If we have as much sense as a goose, we will stay in formation with those who are headed the same way we are going.) When the lead goose gets tired, he rotates back in the wing and another goose flies point. (It pays to take turns doing hard jobs—with people at church or with geese flying south.) The geese honk from behind to encourage those up front to keep up their speed. (What do we say when we honk from behind?) Finally, when a goose gets sick, or is wounded by a shot and falls out, two geese fall out of formation and follow him down to help and protect him. They stay with him until he is either able to fly, or until he is dead, and then they launch out on their own or with another formation to catch up with their original group. (If people knew we would stand by them like that in church, they would push down these walls to get in.) You see, all we have to do in order to attract those who are missing back to church is to demonstrate to the world that we have as much sense as geese here at church. That seems little enough price to pay to win the lost and minister to one another. Even geese have sense enough to know it works every time.

7. A DISCIPLINED TEAM

Several years ago, in England, Sir John Barbirolli was conducting a great symphony orchestra before a "standing room only" audience. The concert hall was unusual in that it was used for cultural events on weekdays and for religious services on Sundays. On this particular Saturday evening, one of the patrons of the orchestra noticed that the clergyman who was to preach there the next day was in the audience. He leaned over and said to him, cynically, "When are you going to fill this hall on Sunday the way Sir John Barbirolli has tonight?" The clergyman looked his antagonist straight in the eye and said with a steady voice, "I will fill this hall on Sunday morning when you give to me, as you gave to Sir John tonight, eighty-five disciplined men and women to be with him and to work with him."

THIRTY-ONE
Courage

1. COURAGE TO TAKE A STAND

When Honorius was emperor of Rome, about the year A.D. 400, the great Coliseum of Rome was often filled to overflowing with spectators. These had come from far and near to view the state games. Part of the sport consisted in watching as human beings battled with wild beasts or against one another until one or the other was killed. The assembled multitude made Roman holiday of such sport and found its highest delight in the death of a human being. It was on such a day when the vast crowd was watching the contest that a Syrian monk by the name of Telemachus stood up in the vast arena. Telemachus was torn by the utter disregard for the value of human life and so he leaped into the arena in the midst of the gladiatorial show and cried out, "This thing is not right! This thing must stop!" Because he was interfering with their pleasure, the authorities gave the command for Telemachus to be run through with a sword, which was done. Thus he died, but dying he kindled a flame in the hearts and consciences of thinking persons. History records that because of this within a few months the gladiatorial combats began to decline and very shortly they passed from history. Why? Because one man dared to speak out for what he felt was right.

2. REAL BRAVERY

If there is one thing upon earth that mankind loves and admires better than another, it is a brave man—a man who dares look the devil in the face and tell him he is the devil. JAMES GARFIELD

3. COURAGE TO RISK

Let come what will, I mean to bear it out,
And either live with glorious victory
Or die with fame, renowned in chivalry.
He is not worthy of the honeycomb
That shuns the hives because the bees have stings.

4. VARIOUS MOTIVATIONS FOR COURAGE

My cousin described an incident that happened to her son Buck in New York. A couple of weeks ago he was walking from the bus depot to his dad's apartment in upper Manhattan when he realized he was flanked by two young men.

"Give me your wallet."

"No."

"This is a gun. Give me your wallet or I'll shoot you."

"No."

"Hey, man. You don't understand. We're robbing you. Give me your wallet."

"No."

"Give me your wallet or I'll knife you."

"No."

"Give me your wallet or we'll beat you up."

By now the robber was whining.

"No." Buck had continued walking and after a while he noticed he was no longer accompanied. When he told me about it, I asked him, "Weren't you scared?"

127

"Of course. What else would I be?"

"Why didn't you give them your wallet?"

"My learner's permit's in it." DAVE MOTE

5. SPECTATORS VERSUS PARTICIPANTS

Just remember: Every baseball team could use a man who plays every position perfectly, never strikes out and never makes an error. The trouble is, there's no way to make him lay down his hot dog and come down out of the stands.

6. WANTED: A HUNDRED MEN

Give me a hundred men who fear nothing but sin, and desire nothing but God, and I will shake the world. I care not a straw whether they be clergymen or laymen; and such alone will overthrow the kingdom of Satan and build up the kingdom of God on earth.

7. IN HOT WATER

Courage in people is like a tea bag. You never know the strength until they're in hot water.

8. STAND UP AND BE COUNTED

Some years ago Premier Khrushchev was speaking before the Supreme Soviet and was severely critical of the late Premier Stalin. While he was speaking someone from the audience sent up a note: "What were you doing when Stalin committed all these atrocities?"

Khrushchev shouted, "Who sent up that note?" Not a person stirred.

"I'll give him one minute to stand up!" The seconds ticked off. Still no one moved.

"All right, I'll tell you what I was doing. I was doing exactly what the writer of this note was doing—exactly nothing! I was afraid to be counted!"

9. MOTTO OF THE FRENCH FOREIGN LEGION

If I falter, push me on. If I stumble, pick me up. If I retreat, shoot me.

10. COURAGE IN SPIRIT

The lady was small, old, and frail. She had lost the sight of her eye, and it had to be removed. When it was to be replaced with a false eye she said to the doctor, "Be sure and choose one with a twinkle in it."

11. HAVING THE NERVE

When I was a young writer with a very uncertain income, I went into a quiet park to contemplate a serious problem. For four years I had been engaged but didn't dare to marry. There was no way of foreseeing how little I might earn in the next year; moreover, we had long cherished a plan of living and

writing in Paris, Rome, Vienna, London—everywhere. But how could we go
three thousand miles away from everything that was familiar and secure,
without the certainty of some money now and then?

At that moment I looked up and saw a squirrel jump from one high tree
to another. He appeared to be aiming for a limb so far out of reach that the
leap looked like suicide. He missed—but landed, safe and unconcerned, on a
branch several feet lower. Then he climbed to his goal, and all was well. An
old man sitting on the bench said, "Funny, I've seen hundreds of 'em jump
like that, especially when there are dogs around and they can't come down to
the ground. A lot of 'em miss, but I've never seen any hurt in trying." Then
he chuckled. "I guess they've got to risk it if they don't want to spend their
lives in one tree." I thought, *A squirrel takes a chance—have I less nerve than a
squirrel?* We were married in two weeks, scraped up enough money for our
passage and sailed across the Atlantic—jumping off into space, not sure what
branch we'd land on. I began to write twice as fast and twice as hard as ever
before. And to our amazement we promptly soared into the realm of
respectable incomes. Since then, whenever I have to choose between risking a
new venture or hanging back, those five little words run through my
thoughts: "Once there was a squirrel. . . ." And sometimes I hear the old
man on the park bench saying, "They've got to risk it if they don't want to
spend their lives in one tree."

12. RISKING MUCH
To laugh is to risk appearing the fool.
To weep is to risk appearing sentimental.
To reach out for another is to risk involvement.
To expose feelings is to risk exposing our true self.
To place your ideas, your dreams, before the crowd is to risk loss.
To love is to risk not being loved in return.
To live is to risk dying.
To hope is to risk despair.
To try at all is to risk failure.
But risk we must, because the greatest hazard in life is to risk nothing. The
man, the woman, who risks nothing does nothing, has nothing, is nothing.

13. FIVE MINUTES MORE
A hero is no braver than anyone else; he only is brave five minutes longer.

14. EVEN THE BRAVE HAVE THEIR MOMENTS
Napoleon often referred to Marshall Ney as the bravest man he had ever
known. Yet Ney's knees trembled so badly one morning before a battle that

he had trouble mounting his horse. When he was finally in the saddle he shouted contemptuously, "Shake away, knees, you would shake worse than that if you knew where I am going to take you."

15. THE POWER OF A GREAT CHALLENGE

One of the most effective advertisements ever written appeared in a London newspaper earlier in this century. It read, "Men wanted for hazardous journey. Small wages, bitter cold, long months of complete darkness, constant danger, safe return doubtful."

The ad was written by Sir Ernest Shackleton, explorer of the South Pole. Regarding response, Shackleton said, "It seemed as though all the men in Great Britain were determined to accompany us."

16. OUT WHERE THE FRUIT IS

The story is told of Will Rogers who came to his friend Eddie Cantor for advice. Will wanted to make some important changes in his act—but was worried about the danger of such changes. He wasn't sure whether they would work. Eddie Cantor's response was, "Why not go out on a limb? That's where the fruit is!"

17. DESIGNED TO SAIL

A ship in harbor is safe, but that is not what ships are for. JOHN A. SHEDD

18. COURAGEOUS CONFRONTATIONS

Boris the Russian arrived at the Pearly Gates and was welcomed by St. Peter. Showing him around, the saint said, "You can go anywhere you want with one exception. You cannot go on the pink clouds!"

"Why not?" asked Boris.

"Because," answered St. Peter, "the pink clouds are reserved for people who have done something great."

"But I have done something great," said Boris. "I made a speech at the Kremlin against the Russian officials. Then I urged the people to revolt."

"Just when did this happen?" asked St. Peter.

Boris looked at his watch. "About two minutes ago."

19. VICTORY OR DEFEAT

Only by desertion can we be defeated. With Christ and for Christ victory is certain. We can lose the victory by flight but not by death. Happy are you if you die in battle, for after death you will be crowned. But woe to you if by forsaking the battle you forfeit at once both the victory and the crown. BERNARD OF CLAIRVAUX

20. GROWING IN COURAGE AND MIGHT

A man by the name of Mallory led an expedition to try to conquer Mt. Everest in the 1920s. The first expedition failed, as did the second. Then, with a team of the best quality and ability, Mallory made a third assault. But in spite of careful planning and extensive safety precautions, disaster struck. An avalanche hit and Mallory and most of his party were killed. When the few who did survive returned to England, they held a glorious banquet saluting the great people of Mallory's final expedition. As the leader of the survivors stood to acknowledge the applause, he looked around the hall at the framed pictures of Mallory and his comrades who had died. Then he turned his back to the crowds to face the huge picture of Mt. Everest which stood looming like a silent, unconquerable giant behind the banquet table. With tears streaming down his face, he addressed the mountain on behalf of Mallory and his dead friends. "I speak to you, Mt. Everest, in the name of all brave men living and those yet unborn. Mt. Everest, you defeated us once; you defeated us twice; you defeated us three times. But, Mt. Everest, we shall someday defeat you, because you can't get any bigger and we can."

21. DARING TO ACT

It is not the critic who counts, not the person who points out where the doer of deeds could have done better. The credit belongs to the person who is actually in the arena; whose face is marred by dust and sweat and blood; who strives valiantly; who errs and comes up short again and again; who knows the great enthusiasms, the devotions, and spends himself or herself in a worthy cause; who at best knows in the end the triumph of high achievement; and at the worst, at least fails while daring greatly; so that his or her place shall never be with those cold and timid souls who know neither victory or defeat. THEODORE ROOSEVELT

22. A BETTER KIND OF DUMB

Don't be afraid to ask dumb questions; they're easier to handle than dumb mistakes.

23. MEETING THE CRITICS

Nothing will ever be accomplished if every objection must be overcome. SAMUEL JOHNSON

24. COURAGE IN THE STORM

Do you remember Tom Dooley, that young doctor who organized hospitals, raised money, and literally poured out his life in the service of the afflicted peoples of Southeast Asia? Here was a man whose deep relationship with

God motivated him to abandon a soft career in the United States for a desperately difficult ministry overseas. In the end that relationship enabled him to die victoriously at the age of thirty-four. Here is the letter which on December 1, 1960, he wrote to the president of Notre Dame, his alma mater:

Dear Father Hesburgh: They've got me down. Flat on the back, with plaster, sand bags, and hot water bottles. I've contrived a way of pumping the bed up a bit so that, with a long reach, I can get to my typewriter. . . . Two things prompt this note to you. The first is that whenever my cancer acts up a bit, and it is certainly "acting up" now, I turn inward. Less do I think of my hospitals around the world, or of 94 doctors, fund-raisers, and the like. More do I think of one Divine Doctor and my personal fund of grace. It has become pretty definite that the cancer has spread to the lumbar vertebra, accounting for all the back problems over the last two months. I have monstrous phantoms; all men do. And inside and outside the wind blows. But when the time comes, like now, then the storm around me does not matter. The winds within me do not matter. Nothing human or earthly can touch me. A peace gathers in my heart. What seems unpossessable, I can possess. What seems unfathomable, I can fathom. What is unutterable, I can utter. Because I can pray. I can communicate. How do people endure anything on earth if they cannot have God?

25. STORMY SEA
Anyone can hold the helm when the sea is calm. PUBLILIUS SYRUS

Credibility

1. REPUTATION
He who is known to be an early riser can sleep 'til noon. ELIZABETH SLATER

2. REAL CREDIBILITY
If you tell a man that there are 300 billion stars in the universe, he'll believe you. But if you tell him a bench has just been painted, he has to touch it to be sure.

3. THE RIGHT TO REMAIN SILENT
Though everyone has an equal right to speak, not all have earned an equal right to be taken seriously. HUBERT HUMPHREY

4. A SURE SIGN
Never go to a doctor whose office plants have died. ERMA BOMBECK

5. CONFIDENCE IN THE EXPERT
Surgeon to patient: "I had to remove one of your livers, but you'll be up and around in no time, or I don't know my medicine." HOEST

6. LIFE CREDIBILITY
No one should pay attention to a man delivering a lecture or a sermon on his "philosophy of life" until he knows exactly how he treats his wife, his children, his neighbors, his friends, his subordinates, and his enemies. SYDNEY HARRIS

7. CLOPTON'S LAW
For every credibility gap there is a gullibility fill. RICHARD CLOPTON

8. MAKING IT PLAUSIBLE
People will accept your idea much more readily if you tell them Benjamin Franklin said it first. DAVID COMINS

9. HEAL THYSELF
Dr. Evan O'Neill Kane, chief surgeon of the Kane Summit Hospital in New York, had been a surgeon for almost four decades. He was fascinated by the possibility of the use of local anesthetics in areas that had always used a general anesthetic. He was concerned about the dangers of what he considered the overuse of general anesthesia. He wanted to find an appendectomy candidate who would be willing to do it with a local only. As Dr. Kane had performed nearly four thousand such operations he was confident this would be a good type of operation to do with such an approach. But it was tough to find someone who was willing to stay awake through such surgery. Finally, he found a willing candidate, and on February 15 he wheeled in the patient, prepped him, and prepared for the operation. The surgeon deftly cut into the patient, found the troublesome appendix, and took it out without a hitch. The operation was a rousing success, and the patient recovered nicely.

The date was 1921 and the patient was none other than Dr. Kane himself. He had succeeded in taking out his own appendix under local anesthetic. Dr. Kane gave new meaning to the expression "Physician, heal thyself!"

THIRTY-THREE
Criticism

1. IN NEON
How would you like a job where, if you make a mistake, a big red light goes on and eighteen thousand people boo? *Former hockey goalie* JACQUES PLANTE

2. MASS CRITICISM
If one person calls you an ass or a donkey, pay no attention to him. But if five people call you one, go out and buy yourself a saddle. *Arabian proverb*

3. RESPONSE TO CRANKS
Garry Moore once devised an answer to take care of crank letters. "The enclosed letter," he would write, "arrived on my desk a few days ago. I am sending it to you in the belief that as a responsible citizen you should know that some idiot is sending out letters over your signature."

4. PRAISE OR CRITICISM?
The trouble with most of us is that we would rather be ruined by praise than saved by criticism. NORMAN VINCENT PEALE

5. A CRITICAL SPIRIT
Then there's the story of the conscientious wife who tried very hard to please her ultracritical husband, but failed regularly. He always seemed the most cantankerous at breakfast. If the eggs were scrambled, he wanted them poached; if they were poached, he wanted them scrambled. One morning, with what she thought was a stroke of genius, the wife poached one egg and scrambled the other and placed the plate before him. Anxiously she awaited what surely this time would be his unqualified approval. He peered down at the plate and snorted, "Can't you do anything right, woman? You've scrambled the wrong one!"

6. ALTERNATIVES
An aspiring politician gave his speech his best shot. He felt that it was a stirring, fact-filled campaign speech. Then the candidate looked out on his audience and asked, "Are there any questions?" Someone in the back row called out, "Who else is running?"

7. COMMON GROUND
Nothing gives you more in common more quickly than finding out you dislike the same person.

8. PLAIN ENVY

A man and his dog were walking the beach when they come upon another visitor to the beach. The owner of the dog was proud of his dog's newly mastered feat, so he said to the visitor, "Watch this!" whereupon he tossed a piece of driftwood far out into the sea and the dog immediately ran on top of the ocean, fetched the wood, and ran back. The visitor just shook his head in disbelief. Whereupon the owner repeated the procedure twice. Finally he asked the visitor, "Did you notice anything unusual?" The visitor responded, "Your dog can't swim, can he?"

9. ONE-TRACK MIND

A boss commented to his secretary about one of his men: "Harry has such a bad memory, it's a wonder he remembers to breathe. I asked him to pick up a newspaper on his way back from lunch, but I'm not ever sure he'll remember his way back to the office." Just then Harry burst in the door, brimming with enthusiasm. He exclaimed, "Guess what, boss! At lunch I ran into old man Jones who hasn't given us an order in seven years. Before he left I talked him into a million-dollar contract!" The boss sighed and looked at his secretary, "What did I tell you? He forgot the newspaper."

10. SWEET CRITICISM

When someone says, "I hope you won't mind my telling you this," you can be sure you will.

11. EASY CRITICISM

Criticism comes more easily than craftsmanship.

12. A NOVEL REACTION TO CRITICISM

For a number of years, until her death in 1976, I worked off and on with Kathryn Kuhlman as a writer. Although Miss Kuhlman was very sensitive to criticism, she never let it deter her from her goal. Instead, she used it to help her get there—always seeming to make the very best out of even the harshest criticism.

Shortly after she went on nationwide television with her weekly program, she received a letter from a public school official in the little town of Iredell, Texas.

"I love you and love your program," he wrote. "It would have been much better, however, if you didn't have to spend so much time tugging at your skirt trying to pull it down over your knees. It was really distracting. Why don't you wear a long dress instead?"

Kathryn read the letter. "You know, he's right," she said to her secretary. She never wore another street-length dress on her TV program. A lesser

person would have responded with anger, or passed it off as just another senseless remark. But she was not that sort of lesser person. She heard. She coped. She let it help her toward her goal of communicating. All of which was possible because there was no root of bitterness to give a bad taste to everything that came into her life which presented another viewpoint.
JAMIE BUCKINGHAM, *Coping with Criticism*

13. MAKING LIFE SWEETER
Life itself would be impossible if it weren't for the imperfections of others.

14. EXPERTS
Too bad that all the people who know how to run the country are busy driving taxicabs and cutting hair. GEORGE BURNS

15. SURVIVING CRITICISM
Tom Wolfe is the well-known author of *The Right Stuff* (about the astronauts) and a number of other popular books. He has written articles that have assaulted our current culture. After one particularly strong satirical piece, he was attacked furiously by numerous critics. In a *West* magazine interview he spoke about his response to being so vilified:
Q. Were you scared the first time you saw their fury come at you?
A. I was. Walter Lippmann, a confidant of presidents who wrote on my very own paper, called me an ass. J. D. Salinger, who hadn't uttered a word to the press in a decade, sent a telegram calling my articles yellow journalism. E. B. White described me as a horseman riding very tall in the saddle, dragging an innocent victim on the ground behind him. . . . I thought the sky was falling. I wondered how I could possibly survive this. A week later, it gradually began to dawn on me nothing had happened except that people had become terribly interested in me. It was a valuable lesson.

It's part of the perversity of our times. If you are denounced enough, you become swell. Claus von Bulow walks into a restaurant, and people part like the Red Sea. You can't be denounced enough nowadays.

16. BLAME HUNTERS
Some people find fault as if it were buried treasure.

17. THE WAY IT WORKS
The probability of someone watching you is proportional to the stupidity of your actions.

18. THE CRITICAL SPIRIT
A salesman, visiting his barber for a haircut, mentioned that he was about to take a trip to Rome. The barber, who came from Italy, said, "Rome is a

terribly overrated city. What airline are you taking and what hotel are you staying at?"

When the salesman told him, the barber criticized the airline for being undependable and the hotel for having horrible service. He told him "You'd be better off to stay home."

But the salesman insisted: "I'm expecting to close a big deal, and then I'm going to see the pope."

The barber shook his head and said, "You'll be disappointed trying to do business in Italy and I wouldn't count on seeing the pope. He only grants audiences to very important people."

Two months later the salesman returned to the barber shop. The barber asked, "And how was your trip?"

The salesman replied, "Wonderful! The flight was perfect, the service at the hotel was excellent. I made a big sale, and I got to see the pope."

The barber was astounded. "You got to see the pope? What happened?"

"I bent down and kissed his ring."

"No kidding! And what did he say?"

"Well, he looked down at my head and then said to me, 'My son, where did you ever get such a lousy haircut?'"

19. MEDIOCRITY EVERY MORNING

A guest in a seaside hotel restaurant called over the head waiter one morning and said, "I want two boiled eggs, one of them so undercooked it's runny, and the other so overcooked that it's about as easy to eat as rubber. Also, grilled bacon that has been left on the plate to get cold, burnt toast that crumbles away as soon as you touch it with a knife, butter straight from the deep freeze so that it impossible to spread, and a pot of very weak coffee, lukewarm."

That's a complicated order, sir," said the bewildered waiter. "It might be a bit difficult."

The guest replied, "Oh, but that's exactly what you gave me yesterday!"

THIRTY-FOUR
Cruelty

1. THE RULES OF WAR
The rules, solemnly observed by sovereign nations, which make it illegal to hit below the toes. LEO ROSTEN, *Treasury of Jewish Quotations*

THIRTY-FIVE
Cynics
(See also Pessimism)

1. MARVELOUS DISCOVERY
The story is going around that up in the Stanford Research Laboratories they have made an important change in procedure recently. Instead of using rats in their experiments they are now using attorneys. When asked why this change was initiated, the head of the lab said: "Well, there are two reasons: there are more of them available, and besides, we find that the students don't get as emotionally attached to them."

THIRTY-SIX
Death
(See also Eternity, Grief)

1. NEW PERSPECTIVE
For centuries it appeared to human beings that the earth was stationary and that the sun moved around it. Then a man named Copernicus came along and proved that what seemed obvious on the surface was not, in fact, true. It was the earth that was moving around the sun, not the sun around the earth;

and that discovery has changed our understanding of our physical reality ever since. What Copernicus did to our perceptions of the earth and the sun, the risen Christ can do to our understanding of death. Those early conclusions we come to as children, about death, are not the deepest truth, although they appear to be from the surface observation. What we need here is a Copernican revolution at the image level, and I want to suggest that the risen Christ can effect such a change if we will open ourselves to the light and perspective He can shed at this point.

2. THE POWER OF LIFE

Before the second World War, there was a grave in Germany sealed with a granite slab and bound with strong chains. On it an atheist had inscribed, "Not to be opened throughout eternity." Yet somehow a little acorn had fallen into some crack, and its outer shell "died." Years after, everyone saw a huge oak tree which had completely broken up the slab, still having the inscribed arrogant words. The new life of the acorn had openly displayed the power of life. A. WETHERELL JOHNSON, *Created for Commitment*

3. CARRIED TO HIS ROOM

In a home of which I know, a little boy, the only son, was ill with an incurable disease. Month after month the mother had tenderly nursed him, read to him, and played with him, hoping to keep him from the dreadful finality of the doctor's diagnosis—the little boy was sure to die. But as the weeks went on he gradually began to understand that he would never be like the other boys he saw playing outside his window. Small as he was, he began to understand the meaning of the term *death,* and he too knew he was to die.

One day his mother had been reading to him the stirring tale of King Arthur and his knights of the Round Table, of Lancelot and Elaine the lily maid of Astelot, and about that last glorious battle where so many fair knights met their death.

She closed the book as her little son sat silent for an instant, deeply stirred. Then he asked the question weighing on his childish heart, "Mama, what is it like to die? Mama, does it hurt?" Quick tears sprang to her eyes and she fled to the kitchen, supposedly to tend to something on the stove. She knew it was a question with deep significance. She knew it must be answered satisfactorily. So she leaned for an instant against the smooth surface and breathed a hurried prayer that the Lord would keep her from breaking down before the boy and that she would be able to tell him the answer; the Lord did tell her. Immediately she knew how to explain it to him.

"Kenneth," she said to her son, "do you remember when you were a tiny boy how you used to play so hard all day that when night came you were too tired even to undress and you'd tumble into your mother's bed and fall asleep. That was not your bed, it was not where you belonged. You would only stay there a little while. Much to your surprise you would wake up and find yourself in your own bed in your own room. You were there because someone had loved you and taken care of you. Your father had come with big strong arms and carried you away.

"Kenneth, darling, death is just like that. We just wake up some morning to find ourselves in the other room. Our room where we belong, because the Lord Jesus loved us and died for us." The lad's shining face looking up into hers told her that the point had gone home and there would be no more fear, only love and trust in his little heart as he went to meet the Father in heaven. He never questioned again. Several weeks later he fell asleep just as she had said and Father's big, strong arms carried him to his own room.

PETER MARSHALL

4. THE ADVANCE MINER

The following story was told by Robert Hughes from the Lutheran Theological Seminary at Philadelphia.

Dr. Hughes' father was a coal-miner in northeastern Pennsylvania. His job was to check the mines for methane gas before the miners went down into the mines. Every morning he would descend alone into the mines, taking with him the safety light, and he would check out each of the tunnels and shafts of the mine to make sure that there was no deadly methane gas present. Of course, if the light of the safety lamp would so much as flicker, he would have to run for his life because it would detect the presence of methane gas. And then after checking the mine, he would rise up to the surface, and there would be all the miners gathered around expectantly waiting for him to announce, "It's OK; it's safe; you can now go down into the mine."

And as Dr. Hughes used the illustration, he said, "That's what Christ has done for us. Coming up out of the depths of death, he has announced to all who are gathered here in this life on earth: 'It's OK; it's safe. You can enter into death, into the darkness and the unknown. It's safe because I have been there and checked it out. It has not been victorious over me. I have overcome it, and I will be with you in death even as I have been with you in life.'"

5. I FEEL THE BOTTOM

Years ago, Dr. Arthur John Gossip preached a sermon entitled, "When Life Tumbles In, What Then?" He preached it the day after his beloved wife had suddenly died. He closed with these words:

"I don't think you need to be afraid of life. Our hearts are very frail, and there are places where the road is very steep and lonely, but we have a wonderful God. And as Paul puts it, 'What can separate us from His love? Not death,' he writes immediately. No, not death, for standing in the roaring Jordan, cold with its dreadful chill and, conscious of its terror, of its rushing, I, too, like Hopeful in *Pilgrim's Progress,* can call back to you who one day in your turn will have to cross it, 'Be of good cheer, my brother, for I feel the bottom and it is sound.'"

6. DEATH THE TRANSFORMER

I've learned something through all my experiences—that every exit is also an entrance. Every time you walk out of something, you walk into something. I got into this world by dying in the womb—and it must have been painful to get ripped out of that familiar place—but that was the prerequisite of my getting into time and space. You know at the end of my life in history there's going to be a similar kind of transition experience. And if we can get at the terror of death by saying it is a transformer rather than an annihilator, then also we can get rid of the idea that death is a thief and is taking something that is rightfully ours, which is the basis of all the rage that I know."
JOHN CLAYPOOL, *The Wittenburg Door*

7. MAKING A BUCK RIGHT UP TO THE END

In Fort Lauderdale, Florida, Ken McAvoy, a cancer patient who doctors say has only months to live, is doing a booming business with his offer to deliver a message to the deceased for twenty dollars. He placed two advertisements in a regional magazine offering to contact people on the other side and has fielded dozens of calls from people seeking his services. In the first week he had five requests. By the second, he had more than two dozen. Messages ranged from "I love you and will join you soon" to a simple "Why, Dad?" from a child cut out of a will.

8. HOLDING DEATH BACK

A woman became very ill. After a time of hospitalization she returned home, but was confined to bed. Her eight-year-old daughter was not aware of the terminal status of the illness.

This little girl stood outside the bedroom door one afternoon as the doctor, along with her father, visited her mother. She overheard the doctor say, "Yes, I will be frank with you. The time is not too far off. Before the last leaves have gone from the trees you will die." The little girl's presence was not detected.

Sometime later the father came to the breakfast table to find that his little girl was not there as he had expected. After searching for her he saw her out in the front yard. His heart was broken as he watched her picking up leaves that had begun to fall. She was using thread to tie them back onto the limbs of the tree. REX HUMBARD

9. WHAT MUST IT BE LIKE?

What must it be like to step on shore, and find it—heaven;
To take hold of a hand, and find it—God's;
To breathe a new air, and find it—celestial;
To feel invigorated, and find it—immortality;
To rise from the care, the loneliness, and turmoil of earth
Into one unbroken calm;
To wake up and find it—glory?

10. WILT THOU FORGIVE

Wilt Thou forgive that sin where I begun,
Which was my sin, though it were done before?
Wilt Thou forgive that sin, through which I run,
And do run still, though still I do deplore?
When Thou hast done, Thou hast not done, for I have more.
Wilt Thou forgive that sin which I have won
Others to sin, and made my sin their door?
Wilt Thou forgive that sin which I did shun
A year or two, but wallowed in, a score?
When Thou hast done, Thou hast not done, for I have more.
I have a sin of fear, that when I have spun
My last thread, I shall perish on the shore;
But swear by Thyself, that at my death Thy Son
Shall shine as He shines now, and heretofore;
And having done that, Thou hast done, I fear no more.
JOHN DONNE, "A Hymn to God the Father"

11. DEATH AS TRIUMPH

Sir Edward Jones attended the funeral of Robert Browning in Westminster Abbey, but he didn't like it. He knew this great poet, the virtues of his character, the abiding faith in his soul, the influence of his life, and he said the funeral was too sad and somber. "I would have given something," he wrote, "for a banner or two to wave, and much more I would have given if a chorister had come out of the triforium and rent the air with a trumpet."

12. JESUS' VICTORY

What death did to Jesus is nothing compared to what Jesus did to death.

13. MEDICAL JARGON

I recently visited a very seriously ill man in a local hospital. I was told that he was "pre-terminal" which evidently isn't quite terminal, but is expected to be so. I started thinking. Can't that really be said about everyone? Aren't we all "pre-terminal"?

14. THE LARGER PERSPECTIVE

Easter is God's everlasting "Yes" to humanity's troubled question: "If a man dies, shall he live again?" Not too long ago, James Gordon Gilkey, one of the Christian leaders in Portland, Oregon, was told by his physician that he had fallen victim to an incurable disease. There was no possible way by which death could be averted, or even long delayed. When this man heard the news, what did he do? Here is his own account of the hours which followed: "I walked out to my home five miles from the center of the city. There I looked at the river and the mountain that I loved, and then—as the twilight deepened—at the stars glimmering in the sky. I said to them, 'I may not see you many times more. But, river, I shall be alive when you have ceased your running to the sea. Mountain, I shall be alive when you have sunk down into the plain. Stars, I shall be alive when you have fallen to the sea.'"

15. CATCHING UP

When we physically die, in a sense we are just catching up with our baptism.
Evangelical Catechism: Christian Faith in the World Today

16. BIRTH AND DEATH

It seems to me that a good analogy for death is birth. The child, before birth, must certainly feel secure and safe. The environment, however limited, is warm and comfortable. The unborn infant knows what to count on in its existence. Birth must seem like death to the child, being thrust in such a traumatic way out of the comfortable and known. We would say to the child, if it were possible, that it is all a part of the plan. We would assure the child that there was even more love, and even grander existence awaiting him/her than could be imagined. We would say, "You can't believe the world that awaits!" But we cannot give those encouraging words. The child must pass through before finding out. Death is like that. We have to leave all that we have known. There has been security in our existence, in spite of its limitations. We know what we can count on. Death takes us from the comfort and safety, ending the only life we can imagine. For the person of God, however, there is awaiting an even greater existence. There is more love and the possibility of service and life than is beyond our imagination. It is all a part of the plan. God would say to us, "You can't believe the world that awaits!"

17. WHY BE AFRAID OF DEATH?

Why be afraid of death,
As though your life were breath?
Death but anoints your eyes
With clay. O glad surprise.
Why should ye be forlorn?
Death only husks the corn.
Why should you fear to meet
The thresher of the wheat?
Is sleep a thing to dread?
Yet sleeping you are dead
Till you awake and rise,
Here, or beyond the skies.
Why should it be a wrench
To leave your wooden bench!
Why not, with happy shout,
Run home when school is out!
The dear ones left behind?
Oh, foolish one and blind!
A day and you will meet—
A night and you will greet.
This is the death of death
To breathe away a breath
And know the end of strife,
And taste the deathless life,
And joy without a fear,
And smile without a tear;
And work, nor care to rest,
And find the last the best. MALTBIE D. BABCOCK

18. NOT LOST

A little girl whose baby brother had just died asked her mother where the baby had gone. "To be with Jesus," replied the mother. A few days later, talking with a friend, the mother said, "I am so grieved to have lost my baby." The little girl heard her, and, remembering what she had told her, asked, "Mother, is a thing lost when you know where it is?" "No, of course not." "Well, then, how can Baby be lost when he has gone to be with Jesus?" Her mother never forgot this. It was the truth.

19. HEAVEN'S DEMOGRAPHICS

I must not think it strange if God takes in youth those whom I would have kept on earth until they were older. God is peopling eternity, and I must not restrict Him to old men and women. JIM ELLIOT, *missionary*

20. EPITAPH

I am told that an Indiana cemetery has a tombstone (more than a hundred years old) which bears the following epitaph:

Pause Stranger, when you pass me by,
As you are now, so once was I.
As I am now, so you will be,
So prepare for death and follow me."

An unknown passerby read those words and underneath scratched this reply:

To follow you I'm not content,
Until I know which way you went.

21. THEN THEY WILL UNDERSTAND

Down below the surface of a quiet pond lived a little colony of water bugs. They were a happy colony, living far away from the sun. For many months they were very busy, scurrying over the soft mud on the bottom of the pond.

They did notice that every once in a while one of their colony seemed to lose interest in going about with his friends. Clinging to the stem of a pond lily, he gradually moved out of sight and was seen no more.

"Look!" said one of the water bugs to another. "One of our colony is climbing up the lily stalk. Where do you suppose he is going?"

Up, up, up he went slowly. Even as they watched him, the water bug disappeared from sight. His friends waited and waited but he didn't return.

"That's funny!" said one water bug to another.

"Wasn't he happy here?" asked a second water bug.

"Where do you suppose he went?" wondered a third.

No one had a answer. They were greatly puzzled.

Finally one of the water bugs, a leader in the colony, gathered his friends together. "I have an idea. The next one of us who climbs up the lily stalk must promise to come back and tell us where he went and why."

"We promise," they said solemnly.

One spring day, not long after, the very water bug who had suggested the plan found himself climbing up the lily stalk. Up, up, up he went. Before he knew what was happening, he had broken through the surface of the water, and fallen onto the broad, green lily pad above.

When he awoke, he looked about with surprise. He couldn't believe what he saw. A startling change had come to his old body. His movement revealed four silver wings and a long tail. Even as he struggled, he felt an impulse to move his wings. The warmth of the sun dried the moisture from the new body. He moved his wings again and suddenly found himself up above the water. He had become a dragonfly.

Swooping and dipping in great curves, he flew through the air. He felt exhilarated in the new atmosphere. By and by, he lighted happily on a lily pad to rest. Then it was that he chanced to look below to the bottom of the pond. Why, he was right above his old friends, the water bugs! There they were, scurrying about, just as he had been doing some time before.

Then he remembered the promise: "The next one of us who climbs up the lily stalk will come back and tell where he went and why."

Without thinking, he darted down. Suddenly he hit the surface of the water.

"I can't return!" he said in dismay. "At least I tried, but I can't keep my promise. Even if I could go back, not one of the water bugs would know me in my new body. I guess I'll just have to wait until they become dragonflies, too. Then they'll understand what happened to me, and where I went."

And the dragonfly winged off happily into his wonderful new world of sun and air. DORIS STICKNEY

22. HOUSING IN HEAVEN
A bus driver and a minister were standing in line to get into heaven. The bus driver approached the gate and St. Peter said, "Welcome, I understand you were a bus driver. Since I'm in charge of housing, I believe I have found the perfect place for you. See that mansion over the hilltop? It's yours."

The minister heard all this and began to stand a little taller. He said to himself, "If a bus driver got a place like that, just think what I'll get."

The minister approached the gate and St. Peter said, "Welcome, I understand you were a minister. See that shack in the valley?"

St. Peter had hardly gotten the words out of his mouth when the irate minister said, "I was a minister, I preached the gospel, I helped teach people about God. Why does that bus driver get a mansion, and I get a shack?"

Sadly St. Peter responded, "Well, it seems when you preached, people slept. When the bus driver drove, people prayed."

23. PLUTARCH'S CONSOLATORY LETTER TO HIS WIFE
The messenger you sent to tell me of the death of my little daughter missed his way. But I heard of it through another.

I pray you let all things be done without ceremony or timorous superstition. And let us bear our affliction with patience. I do know very well what a loss we have had; but, if you should grieve overmuch, it would trouble me still more. She was particularly dear to you; and when you call to mind how bright and innocent she was, how amiable and mild, then your grief must be particularly bitter. For not only was she kind and generous to other children, but even to her very playthings.

But should the sweet remembrance of those things which so delighted us when she was alive only afflict us now, when she is dead? Or is there danger that, if we cease to mourn, we shall forget her? But since she gave us so much pleasure while we had her, so ought we to cherish her memory, and make that memory a glad rather than a sorrowful one. And such reasons as we would use with others, let us try to make effective with ourselves. And as we put a limit to all riotous indulgence in our pleasures, so let us also check the excessive flow of our grief. It is well, both in action and dress, to shrink from an over-display of mourning, as well as to be modest and unassuming on festal occasions.

Let us call to mind the years before our little daughter was born. We are now in the same condition as then, except that the time she was with us is to be counted as an added blessing. Let us not ungratefully accuse Fortune for what was given us, because we could not also have all that we desired. What we had, and while we had it, was good, though now we have it no longer.

Remember also how much of good you still possess. Because one page of your book is blotted, do not forget all the other leaves whose reading is fair and whose pictures are beautiful. We should not be like misers, who never enjoy what they have, but only bewail what they lose.

And since she is gone where she feels no pain, let us not indulge in too much grief. The soul is incapable of death. And she, like a bird not long enough in her cage to become attached to it, is free to fly away to a purer air. For, when children die, their souls go at once to a better and a divine state. Since we cherish a trust like this, let our outward actions be in accord with it, and let us keep our hearts pure and our minds calm.

24. MIXED MESSAGE

A Philadelphia legal firm sent flowers to an associate in Baltimore upon the opening of its new offices. Through some mix-up the ribbon which bedecked the floral piece read "Deepest Sympathy." When the florist was duly informed of his mistake, he let out a cry of alarm. "Good heavens," he exclaimed, "then the flowers that went to the funeral said, 'Congratulations on Your New Location!'"

25. APPOINTMENT IN SAMARRA

Legend says that it happened in the streets of Damascus. A merchant sent his servant to the market. When the servant returned, trembling and agitated, he said, "While I was at the market, I was jostled by someone in the crowd. I turned to look and saw that Death had jostled me. She looked at me and made a threatening gesture. Master, please lend me your horse so I can escape. I want to ride to Samarra. There I will hide so that Death cannot find me." Later that same day the merchant himself was in the marketplace, and he also saw Death in the crowd. He said to her, "Why did you startle my servant this morning by making a threatening gesture?" Death replied, "That was no threatening gesture; it was simply a start of surprise. I was startled to see your servant in Damascus, for we have an appointment tonight in Samarra."

26. THE STING OF DEATH

The master preacher Donald Grey Barnhouse was widowed at a young age. The death of his wife left him and a six-year-old daughter in the home. He had real difficulty working through his own grief, but the hardest part was to comfort and explain the death to his daughter. He later recalled that all of his education and theological training left him at a loss.

One day he and the little girl were standing on a busy corner at a downtown intersection waiting for a light to change. Suddenly a very large truck sped by the corner, briefly blocking out the sun and frightening the little girl.

To comfort her, Dr. Barnhouse picked her up, and in a moment, the wisdom of God broke through and he was able to explain to his daughter:

"When you saw the truck pass it scared you, but let me ask you, had you rather be struck by the truck or the shadow of the truck?" She replied, "Of course, the shadow."

He went on to explain that when "your mother died, she was only hit by the shadow of death because Jesus was hit by the truck (death)." The Psalmist reminds us that God is with us even though we walk through the valley of the shadow of death.

27. WHAT DEATH IS NOT

Death is not extinguishing the light; it is only putting out the lamp because the Dawn has come." RABINDRANATH TAGORE

28. NOT TO FEAR

Though my soul may set in darkness, it will rise in perfect light; I have loved the stars too fondly to be fearful of the night. AN AGED ASTRONOMER

29. DEFINING TERMS
What the caterpillar calls the end, God calls a butterfly.

30. WAITING FOR DEATH
I am standing upon the seashore. A ship at my side spreads her white sails in the morning breeze and starts for the blue ocean. She is an object of beauty and strength, and I stand and watch her until at length she is only a ribbon or white cloud, just where the sea and sky come to mingle with each other. Then someone at my side says, "There, she's gone!" Gone where? Gone from my sight—that is all. She is just as large in mast and hull and spar as she was when she left my side and just as able to bear her load of living freight—to the place of destination. Her diminished size is in me, not in her; just at the moment when someone at my side says, "There! She's gone!" there are other voices ready to take up the glad shout, "There she comes!" And that, friends, is dying. MARY PICKFORD

31. SCAM OF THE MONTH CLUB
Recently *Psychology Today* had a contest they called Scamarama, asking their readers to send in a creative scam. In the March 1984 issue they printed their winners. This one took their Grand Prize:

Wish you were born rich? Now you can be! If you are one of the growing millions who are convinced of the reality of reincarnation, here's a once-in-a-lifetime offer!

First, leave us ten thousand dollars or more in your will. After you pass away, our professional medium will contact your spirit in the other world. Then you tell us when you're coming back and under what name. Upon your return, we regress you, at age twenty-one through hypnosis to this lifetime and ask you for your seven-digit account number.

Once you give us the number, we give you a check—on the spot—for your original investment plus interest! The longer you're gone, the more you will receive! You may come back to find yourself a billionaire!

Show your future self how much you care—leave a generous "welcome-back" present. We'll take care of the rest.

32. A LITTLE CHILD SHALL LEAD THEM
A nine-year-old who had leukemia was given six months to live. When the doctor broke the news to her parents outside her hospital room, the youngster overheard the doctor's words. But it did not become obvious until later that she knew about her condition. To everyone's surprise, her faith in Christ gave her an attitude of victory. She talked freely about her death with anticipation in her voice. As she grew weaker, it seemed that her joy became

more radiant. One day before she sank into a final coma, she said to her family, "I am going to be the first to see Jesus! What would you like me to tell Him for you?"

33. THE BINDING CORD
We free ourselves from the womb, but there is no knife sharp enough to cut the umbilical cord which binds us to our grave. PAUL ELDRIDGE

34. MEETING DEATH
So live that when thy summons comes to join
The innumerable caravan which moves
To that mysterious realm where each shall take
His chamber in the silent halls of death,
Thou goest not, like the quarry slave at night,
Scourged to his dungeon, but sustained and soothed
By an unfaltering trust, approach thy grave
Like one that wraps the drapery of his couch
About him, and lies down to pleasant dreams. WILLIAM CULLEN BRYANT

35. A GREAT RUN
As I sit in the study on a beautiful, cool August afternoon, I look back with many thanks. It has been a great run. I wouldn't have missed it for anything. Much could and should have been better, and I have, by no means, done what I should have done with all that I have been given. But the overall experience of being alive has been a thrilling experience. I believe that death is a doorway to more of it: clearer, cleaner, better, with more of the secret opened than locked. I do not feel much confidence in myself as regards all this, for very few have ever "deserved" eternal life. But with Christ's atonement and Him gone on before, I have neither doubt nor fear whether I am left here a brief time or a long one. I believe that I shall see Him and know Him, and that eternity will be an endless opportunity to consort with the great souls and the lesser ones who have entered into the freedom of the heavenly city. It is His forgiveness and grace that give confidence and not merits of our own. But again I say, it's been a great run. I'm thankful for it and for all the people who have helped to make it so, and especially those closest and dearest to me. SAMUEL MOOR SHOEMAKER

36. GOING THROUGH THE DOOR
Once a dying patient asked his doctor, who had come to make a house call on him, what death would be like. The doctor fumbled for a reply and then he heard his dog scratching at the door of the man's room. The answer came to him. The doctor looked at the patient and said, "Did you hear that noise?

That is my dog which I brought with me tonight, and I left him downstairs before I came up to your room. He climbed those stairs for he knows that I am in here. He has no other ideas about what is in this room for he has never been here. All he knows is that I am in here and that is good enough for him. You don't know what is on the other side of the door of death, but you do know that your Master is there."

That should be good enough for all of us. We will never walk through the door or through the valley of death alone. He will always be there to go with us through the door to the other side.

37. NEAR DEATH EXPERIENCES

The March 1985 issue of *Omni* magazine reported a study by Dr. Maurice Rawlings, cardiologist and professor of medicine at the University of Tennessee College of Medicine in Chattanooga. He and his emergency room colleagues are constantly treating such cases. It is now standard that those who have near death experiences later speak of having experiences of light, lush green meadows, rows of smiling relatives and tremendous peace.

However, in his study, also reported in his book *Beyond Death's Door,* Dr. Rawlings obtained new information by interviewing patients immediately after resuscitation while they are still too shaken to deny where they have been. Nearly 50 percent of the group of 300 interviewed reported lakes of fire and brimstone, devil-like figures and other sights hailing from the darkness of hell.

He says they later change their story because most people are simply ashamed to admit they have been to hell; they won't even admit it to their families. Concludes Dr. Rawlings, "Just listening to these patients has changed my whole life. There's a life after death, and if I don't know where I'm going, it's not safe to die."

38. GOING HOME

A ninety-year-old woman, a priest's mother, was taken to the hospital with a number of physical problems. Her son visited her and tried to cheer her up by saying, "Now, Mom, don't worry—you are going to be home in a few days." She replied brightly, "Oh, I know that. Just don't know *which* home."
Charles Krieg

39. HOMECOMING

Once there was an old man who everyday would take long walks with the Lord. On these walks, he and the Lord God would talk about all kinds of things—about the important times in the old man's life: when he met his wife, the birth of his children, special Christmases, etc. One day while they were out walking for an especially long time, the Lord looked at the old man and said: "We are closer to my house than we are to yours. Why don't you just come home with me." And that is what he did!

THIRTY-SEVEN

Decisions

1. PAINFUL DECISIONS

Right next to our cabin near Austin there was an oak tree that my son, Albert Jr., who had died in his twenties, had insisted on saving when the house was built a number of years ago. For years I had tried to steer the tree away from the house so that it would not damage it. For a while I was successful, but as the tree grew thicker and taller, I was no longer able to control it. It kept coming closer and closer to the house, and when the wind blew, the main trunk began to sway and strike at the vital structure of the house.

That oak tree had much sentimental value for me. I had made up my mind that I would steer it away from the house at whatever cost. But each time, after a few months, the tension lines came loose or snapped and broke. Nature was too determined, too forceful for me. There was nothing I could do to control the tree and pull it away from the house. Prospects for the future seemed even worse. Within a few years, at the rate it was growing, it would cause even more damage.

Last Tuesday I made up my mind. The tree had to come down. As I cut its upper branches, then the lower ones and finally the trunk itself, it was as if I was cutting my arms, my legs and finally my own heart. I had cut the tree that Albert Jr., wanted so much to save. When the last section of the trunk fell to the ground I sat down and wept.

Decisions such as these are difficult. Yet decisions must be made, not on the basis of what is evil and what is good, but on the basis of what is good and what is better. I cut down the tree that our son loved. But, more important, I spared the house that he helped build and loved, too. When the day was over, I felt that it had been a good one. Though hurtful, I had made the right choice. Many of our decisions are painful because we are faced with choosing between what is good and what is better. Yet we must make them.

2. WRONG CHOICES

This story is about a man named Fred who inherited $10 million, but the will provided that he had to accept it either in Chile or Brazil. He chose Brazil. Unhappily it turned out that in Chile he would have received his inheritance in land on which uranium, gold, and silver had just been discovered. Once in Brazil he had to choose between receiving his inheritance in coffee or nuts. He chose the nuts. Too bad! The bottom fell out of the nut market, and coffee went up to $1.30 a pound wholesale, unroasted. Poor Fred lost everything he had to his name. He went out and sold his solid gold watch for the money he needed to fly home. It seems that he had enough for a ticket to either New York or Boston. He chose Boston. When the plane for New York taxied up he noticed it was a brand-new super 747 jet with red carpets and chic people and wine-popping hostesses. The plane for Boston then arrived. It was a 1928 Ford trimotor with a sway back and it took a full day to get off the ground. It was filled with crying children and tethered goats. Over the Andes, one of the engines fell off. Our man Fred made his way up to the captain and said, "I'm a jinx on this plane. Let me out if you want to save your lives. Give me a parachute." The pilot agreed, but added, "On this plane, anybody who bails out must wear two chutes." So Fred jumped out of the plane, and as he fell dizzily through the air he tried to make up his mind which ripcord to pull. Finally he chose the one on the left. It was rusty and the wire pulled loose. So he then pulled the other handle. This chute opened, but its shroud lines snapped. In desperation, the poor fellow cried out, "St. Francis save me!" A great hand from heaven reached down and seized the poor fellow by the wrist and let him dangle in midair. Then a gentle but inquisitive voice asked, "St. Francis Xavier or St. Francis of Assisi?"

3. CRUCIAL DECISIONS

On the top of a hill in a Midwestern state stands a courthouse so situated that raindrops falling on one side of the roof travel by way of the Great Lakes into the Atlantic, while drops landing on the opposite side find their way through the Ohio and Mississippi to the Gulf. Just a breath of wind one way or the other may determine whether a single raindrop will end up either in the Gulf or in the Atlantic. Even so, one single decision is enough to determine man's destiny, either heaven or hell. Have you made the right decision?

THIRTY-EIGHT
Details

1. DETAILS MAKE THE DIFFERENCE

There must be detail in every great work. It is an element of effectiveness which no reach of plan, no enthusiasm of purpose, can dispense with. Thus, if a man conceives the idea of becoming eminent in learning, but cannot toil through the million of little drudgeries necessary to carry him on, his learning will be soon told. Or if a man undertakes to become rich, but despises the small and gradual advances by which wealth is ordinarily accumulated, his expectations will, of course, be the sum of his riches. Accurate and careful detail, the minding of common occasions and small things, combined with general scope and vigor, is the secret of all the efficiency and success in the world. HORACE BUSHNELL

THIRTY-NINE
Determination
(See also Ambition, Endurance)

1. BUILDING AND DESTROYING

To build may have to be the slow and laborious task of years. To destroy can be the thoughtless act of a single day. WINSTON CHURCHILL

2. SO, DO SOMETHING ABOUT IT

A young boy complained to his father that most of the church hymns were boring and old-fashioned, with tiresome words that meant little to his generation. His father challenged him with these words: "If you think you can write better hymns, why don't you?"

The boy accepted the challenge, went to his room, and wrote his first hymn. The year was 1690, and the young man was Isaac Watts. Among his 350 hymns are "Joy to the World," "When I Survey the Wondrous Cross," "I Sing the Almighty Power of God," and many other classics.

154

3. THE RESOLUTIONS OF JONATHAN EDWARDS
Resolved:

To live with all my might while I do live;

Never to lose one moment of time;

Never to do anything which I should despise or think meanly of in another;

Never to do anything out of revenge;

Never to do anything which I should be afraid to do if it were the last hour of my life.

4. HOW TO MAKE A FORTUNE
Make a bathroom scale that lies, convincingly. *Humorist* FRAN LEBOWITZ

5. GOALS REQUIRE PRELIMINARY STEPS
Ray Stedman of Peninsula Bible church in Palo Alto, California, once asked a nine-year-old boy what he wanted to be when he grew up, and he answered, "A returned missionary." The boy looked ahead not to the years of graduate study, not to the years of separation from home and loved ones, not to the months and years in steaming jungles or parched deserts—but to the final state of recognition and acclaim. It's hard to skip the preliminaries and still reach a final goal. The musician's finger exercises, the Olympic athlete's daily push-ups, and the Christian's daily stint in the prayer closet can't be bypassed.

6. ACTIVITY
It is better to wear out than to rust out. BISHOP CUMBERLAND

7. THINKING ON A GRAND SCALE
Decision of the builders of the cathedral in Seville, Spain, in 1401: "Let us build here a church so great that those who come after us will think us mad ever to have dreamed of it!"

8. REJECT REJECTION
Many of those who have risen from failure to real achievement have rejected the rejection of this world. In 1902, the poetry editor of *The Atlantic Monthly* returned a sheaf of poems to a twenty-eight-year-old poet with this curt note: "Our magazine has no room for your vigorous verse." The poet was Robert Frost, who rejected the rejection. In 1905, the University of Bern turned down a Ph.D. dissertation as being irrelevant and fanciful. The young physics student who wrote the dissertation was Albert Einstein, who rejected the rejection. In 1894, the rhetoric teacher at Harrow in England wrote on the sixteen-year-old's report card, "a conspicuous lack of success." The sixteen-year-old was Winston Churchill, who rejected the rejection.

9. AVERAGE MAN

I am only an average man, but I work harder at it than the average man. TEDDY ROOSEVELT

10. THINK BIG

Attempt something so great for God that it's doomed to failure unless God be in it.

11. HOW IMPOSSIBLE

Never tell anyone it can't be done ... God may have been waiting for centuries for somebody ignorant enough of the impossible to do that very thing. J. A. HOLMES

12. GOALS AND TARGETS

I like to think of a goal as a target. The bull's eye is 100. Concentric rings are 80, 60, 40, and 20. I aim for 100, but sometimes I hit 80 or even 20. But if I don't aim for 100, I will hit zero every time. Someone said, "I would rather attempt to do something great for God and fail, than to do nothing and succeed."

After Eisenhower won the Republican nomination for President from Robert Taft in 1952, a reporter asked Taft about his goals. He said, "My great goal was to become President of the United States in 1953." The reporter smirked. "Well, you didn't make it, did you?" He said, "No, but I became senator from Ohio!" MARK PORTER

13. GOALS, SHORT-TERM

Charlie Brown is at bat. STRIKE THREE. He has struck out again and slumps over to the bench. "Rats! I'll never be a big-league player. I just don't have it! All my life I've dreamed of playing in the big leagues, but I know I'll never make it."

Lucy turns to console him. "Charlie Brown, you're thinking too far ahead. What you need to do is set yourself more immediate goals."

He looks up. "Immediate goals?"

Lucy says, "Yes. Start with this next inning when you go out to pitch. See if you can walk out of the mound without falling down!"

14. SHORT-LIVED

Exhilaration is that feeling you get just after a great idea hits you, and before you realize what's wrong with it.

15. STEP ONE

The first step in solving any problem is to begin.

15. PERSISTENCE AND PRESENCE

In the first part of this century, Sir Ernest Shackleford began his voyage to the Antarctic. It was his dream to cross the twenty-one hundred miles of wasteland by dogsled. He didn't make it that far, however. On the way his ship was stopped by an ice pack and sank. He and his men had to trudge over drifting ice floes trying to reach the nearest land, nearly two hundred miles away, and the nearest human outpost nearly twelve hundred miles away. They towed behind them a lifeboat weighing nearly one ton. When they finally reached waters clear enough of ice to navigate, they faced waves as high as ninety feet. Finally they reached South Georgia Island, only to find that it had never been crossed before. When they finally reached their destination almost seven months after they began the journey, they were so bedraggled their friends did not recognize them. To a man, however, those who had completed the journey reported that they felt the presence of One unseen to guide them on their perilous trek. Somehow they knew they were not alone.

16. THE PLODDERS ARE CHRIST

When William Carey began thinking of going to India as a pioneer missionary, his father pointed out to him that he possessed no academic qualifications that would fit him for such a task. But Carey answered, "I can plod." How true it is that God accomplishes mighty things for his kingdom through those who are willing to persevere, who are willing to plod faithfully through one difficulty after another in the power of the Spirit.

17. THE DETERMINED LINCOLN

It comes as a shock to me to realize that the man who could write the Second Inaugural Address, regarded by many as the noblest of all political documents, and the Gettysburg Address, had no more than four months of formal education, and that in a one-room country schoolhouse where students ranged from age five to twenty-five, and the teacher probably had no more than an eighth-grade education, if that.

Lincoln is held up as an example of achievement in what we have come to know as "The American Dream." Where else but in America could this happen? One father, knowing the determination of Lincoln as a boy to achieve an education, said to his less than energetic son: "Do you know what Abe Lincoln was doing when he was your age? "No," replied the boy, "but I do know what he was doing when he was your age."

18. TRYING AGAIN AND AGAIN

Among other qualities of personal character, what makes a man great is his determination to keep going. Most sports buffs know that from 1960 to 1966 the record for the most stolen bases was held by the incredible Maury Wills. In 1962 he set the current club record for the Dodgers: 104 stolen bases in one regular season.

But Maury Wills set another record in those years. A record probably obscured by his other accomplishments. A rather dubious record, for in 1965, a year in which he again held high honors for the most stolen bases, he also took top billing for the most times caught stealing in a single season. He got thrown out (or "knocked down") thirty-one times that year. But . . . he got back up. And that's why we remember him. Proverbs 24:16: "For a righteous man falls seven times, and rises again."

19. REFUSAL TO CHANGE
A fanatic is someone who can't change his mind and won't change the subject. WINSTON CHURCHILL

20. PUT YOUR BODY WHERE YOUR MOUTH IS
A Nova Scotia insurance salesman had been told by his boss that he and the other agents were not assertive enough. They were not as outgoing as they needed to be. One salesman wanted to prove his boss wrong, and he didn't have to wait long for an opportunity.

Outside his seventeenth-floor window he noticed a scaffold with some workmen on it. He wrote a note asking them if they'd be interested in life, accident, or disability insurance, and he held the note up to the window.

They said they would listen to him if he would join them on the scaffold. He did, with the help of a cable from the roof, and he sold one of them fifty thousand dollars worth of life insurance.

21. STAY WITH IT
We read about people who sail around the world in a thirty-foot sailboat or overcome handicaps to win a gold medal at the Olympics, and we later find they're stories about persistence. I remember well the day I sat down to write the first of my radio programs. That was more than twenty years ago, more than fifty-two hundred programs ago, the equivalent of thirty-six full-length books. Certainly no world's record, but a good example of what persistence can do.

When we see the tired faces of commuters on the big city subway, and children climbing aboard the school bus, we see persistence at work. We see it in the expression of a housewife doing grocery shopping or the week's laundry. But everything we do contributes to the life we lead, the joys we experience, the satisfactions we realize from time to time. And persistence itself is a joy when we're doing what we enjoy and want to do. Not a very complicated formula, it is? EARL NIGHTINGALE

22. NEVER SAY DIE
Man who say it cannot be done should not interrupt man doing it!
Chinese proverb

23. BE SURE OF YOUR COURSE AND KEEP ON GOING
The setting was a cold January morning in a little town in Wisconsin, on the southern shore of Lake Superior. It happened to be the Saturday when they had their annual dog sled derby on the ice. A one-mile course had been staked out by sticking little fir trees in the ice. The whole course was easily visible because of the steep slope of the shore.

It was a youngsters' meet and the contenders ranged all the way from large boys with several dogs and big sleds to one little fellow who didn't seem over five with a little sled and one small dog. They took off at the signal and the little fellow with his one dog was quickly outdistanced—he was hardly in the race. All went well with the rest until, about halfway around, the team that was second started to pass the team then in the lead. They came too close and the dogs got in a fight. And as each team came up the dogs joined the fight. None seemed to be able to steer clear of it. Soon, from our position about a half mile away, there was just one big black seething mass of kids and sleds and dogs—all but the little fellow with his one that managed it, and the only one to finish the race.

As I reflect on the many vexing problems and the stresses of our times that complicate their solutions, this simple scene from long ago comes vividly to mind. And I draw the obvious moral: No matter how difficult the challenge or how impossible or hopeless the task may seem, if you are reasonably sure of your course, just keep on going!

24. CAN IT BE DONE?
The impossible is what nobody can do until somebody does.

25. WILL POWER UNLIMITED
Strength is the ability to break a chocolate bar into four pieces with your bare hands—and then eat just one of the pieces.

26. DETERMINATION IN USE
Jan Paderewski was asked by a fellow pianist if he could be ready to play a recital on short notice. The famous musician replied: "I am always ready. I have practiced eight hours daily for forty years." The other pianist said, "I

wish I had been born with such determination." Paderewski replied, "We are all born with it. I just used mine."

27. ONE STEP MORE

An explorer named Fridtjof Nansen was lost with one companion in the Arctic wastes. By miscalculation they ran out of all their supplies. They ate their dogs, the dog's harnesses, the whale oil for their lamps. Nansen's companion gave up and lay down to die. But Nansen did not give up. He told himself, "I can take one step more." As he plodded heavily through the bitter cold, step after step, suddenly across an ice hill he stumbled upon an American expedition that had been sent out to find him.

FORTY

Dignity

(See also Character, Integrity, Nobility)

1. BELIEFS MEN LIVE BY

Man is not on this earth merely to be happy, nor even to be simply honest. He is there to realize great things for humanity, to attain nobility and to surmount the vulgarity in which the existence of almost all individuals drags on. VINCENT VAN GOGH

2. CALLED TO BE EAGLES

A certain man went through a forest seeking any bird of interest he might find. He caught a young eagle, brought it home, and put it among the fowls and ducks and turkeys, and gave it chicken food to eat even though it was an eagle, the king of birds.

Five years later, a naturalist came to see him and, after passing through his garden, said: "That bird is an eagle, not a chicken."

"Yes," said the owner, "but I have trained it to be a chicken. It is no longer an eagle, it is a chicken, even though it measures fifteen feet from tip to tip of its wings."

"No," said the naturalist, "it is an eagle still; it has the heart of an eagle, and I will make it soar high up to the heavens."

"No," said the owner, "it is a chicken and it will never fly."

They agreed to test it. The naturalist picked up the eagle, held it up and said with great intensity: "Eagle, thou art an eagle; thou dost belong to the sky and not to this earth; stretch forth thy wings and fly."

The eagle turned this way and that, and then looking down, saw the chickens eating their food, and down he jumped.

The owner said: "I told you it was a chicken."

"No," said the naturalist, "it is an eagle. Give it another chance tomorrow."

So the next day he took it to the top of the house and said: "Eagle, thou art an eagle; stretch forth thy wings and fly." But again the eagle, seeing the chickens feeding, jumped down and fed with them.

Then the owner said: "I told you it was a chicken."

"No," asserted the naturalist," it is an eagle, and it has the heart of an eagle; only give it one more chance, and I will make it fly tomorrow."

The next morning he rose early and took the eagle outside the city and away from the houses, to the foot of a high mountain. The sun was just rising, gilding the top to the mountain with gold, and every crag was glistening in the joy of the beautiful morning.

He picked up the eagle and said to it: "Eagle, thou art an eagle; thou dost belong to the sky and not to the earth; stretch forth thy wings and fly."

The eagle looked around and trembled as if new life were coming to it. Yet it did not fly. The naturalist then made it look straight at the sun. Suddenly it stretched out its wings and, with the screech of an eagle, it mounted higher and higher and never returned. It was an eagle, though it had been kept and tamed as a chicken.

We have been created in the image of God, but men have made us think that we are chickens, and so we think we are; but we are eagles. Stretch forth your wings and fly! Don't be content with the food of chickens!
JAMES AGGREY

3. AIMING FOR EXCELLENCE
He who aims at excellence will be above mediocrity; he who aims at mediocrity will be far short of it. *Burmese proverb*

DISCOURAGEMENT
(See Adversity)

FORTY-ONE
Duty

1. ASPECTS OF DUTY
A duty is a task we look forward to with distaste, perform with reluctance, and brag about afterward.

FORTY-TWO
Easter
(See also Christ, Eternity)

1. EASTER TRUTH
The great Easter truth is not that we are to live newly after death—that is not the great thing—but that we are to be new here and now by the power of the Resurrection; not so much that we are to live forever, as that we are to, and may, live nobly now because we are to live forever. PHILLIPS BROOKS

2. A CHILD'S VERSION OF THE MEANING OF EASTER
Our three-year-old, Nicole, was as anxious for Easter to come as she had been for Christmas to come. Since my wife was expecting our third child in just a few weeks, many persons were giving us baby gifts since this was our first child in this church. Nicole had picked out a new dress and Mom had given her a new white bonnet. As we stopped at a store to buy her a new pair of shoes to go with her outfit, she once again said, "I can't wait for Easter, Daddy!" I asked her, "Do you know what Easter means, honey?" She replied, "Yes." "Well, what does Easter mean?" In her own sweet three-year-old way, with arms raised, a smile on her face, and at the top of her voice she said, "Surprise!" What better word could sum up the meaning of Easter! Surprise, death! Surprise, sin! Surprise, mourning disciples! Surprise, modern man! He's alive!

3. EASTER CROWN
Crowns have always been the sign of authority and Kingship. Charlemagne, whom historians say should deserve to be called "great" above all others,

wore an octagonal crown. Each of the eight sides was a plaque of gold, and each plaque was studded with emeralds, sapphires, and pearls. The cost was the price of a king's ransom. Richard the Lion Heart had a crown so heavy that two earls had to stand, one on either side, to hold his head. The crown that Queen Elizabeth wears is worth over $20 million. Edward II once owned nine crowns, something of a record. Put them all together, from all of Europe and from the archives of the East, all of them are but trinkets compared to Christ's crown. Revelation 19 says he had many diadems. He wears a crown of righteousness. He wears a crown of glory. He wears a crown of life. He wears a crown of peace and power. Among those crowns, one outshines the rest. It was not formed by the skilled fingers of a silversmith, nor created by the genius of a craftsman. It was put together hurriedly by the rough hands of Roman soldiers. It was not placed upon its wearer's head in pomp and ceremony, but in the hollow mockery of ridicule and blasphemy. It is a crown of thorns.

The amazing thing is that it belonged to me. I deserved to wear that crown. I deserved to feel the thrust of the thorns. I deserved to feel the warm trickle of blood upon my brow. I deserved the pain. He took my crown of thorns—but without compensation. He offers to me instead His crown of life, the crown that fadeth not away.

4. SPRING AND RESURRECTION
Green the grass. Ripe the bud. Yellow the flower. Blue the sky. Beautiful the butterfly. Risen the Lord!

5. READY FOR RESURRECTION MORNING
A true story is told about a distinguished man, the only white person buried in a Georgia cemetery reserved exclusively for blacks. He had lost his mother when he was just a baby. His father, who never married again, hired a black woman named Mandy to help raise his son. She was a Christian, and she took her task seriously. Seldom has a motherless boy received such warmhearted attention. One of his earliest memories was of Mandy bending tenderly over him in his upstairs bedroom each day and softly saying, "Wake up—God's mornin' is come."

As the years passed this devoted woman continued to serve as his surrogate mother. The young man went away to college, but when he would come home on holidays and in the summer she would still climb the stairs and call him in the same loving way. One day after he had become a successful statesman, the sad message came: "Mandy is dead. Can you attend her funeral?" As he stood by her grave in the cemetery, he turned to his friends and said, "If I die before Jesus comes, I want to be buried here beside Mandy. I like to think that on Resurrection Day she'll speak to me again and say, 'Wake up, my boy, God's mornin' is come!'"

6. LET LOOSE
In the drama *The Trial of Jesus,* John Masefield has the centurion Longinus report to Pilate after the crucifixion of Jesus. Longinus had been the officer in charge of the execution, and after his official report, Procula, Pilate's wife calls the centurion to come and tell her how the prisoner had died. Once the account is given, she asks, "Do you think he is dead?" Longinus answers, "No, lady, I don't." "Then where is he?" asks Procula. Longinus replies, "Let loose in the world, lady, where neither Roman nor Jew can stop his truth."

7. BEYOND THE CROSS
Every year thousands of people climb a mountain in the Italian Alps, passing the "stations of the cross" to stand at an outdoor crucifix. One tourist noticed a little trail that led beyond the cross. He fought through the rough thicket and, to his surprise, came upon another shrine, a shrine that symbolized the empty tomb. It was neglected. The brush had grown up around it. Almost everyone had gone as far as they cross, but there they stopped.

Far too many have gotten to the cross and have known the despair and the heartbreak. Far too few have moved beyond the cross to find the real message of Easter. That is the message of the empty tomb. LAVON BROWN

8. THE WEIGHTIER STONE
The heavy, ponderous stone that sealed Jesus in the confines of that rock-walled tomb was but a pebble compared to the Rock of Ages inside.

9. A BIBLE WITH A SAD ENDING
Thomas Jefferson, a great man, nevertheless could not accept the miraculous elements in Scripture. He edited his own special version of the Bible in which all references to the supernatural were deleted. Jefferson, in editing the Gospels, confined himself solely to the moral teachings of Jesus. The closing words of Jefferson's Bible are these: "There laid they Jesus and rolled a great stone at the mouth of the sepulchre and departed." Thank God that is not the way the story really ends!

10. THE MIRACLE OF EASTER BLOSSOMS
There is an old legend of a priest who found a branch of a thorn tree twisted around so that it resembled a crown of thorns. Thinking it a symbol of the crucifixion, he placed it on the altar in his chapel on Good Friday. Early on Easter morning he remembered what he had done. Feeling it was not appropriate for Easter Sunday, he hurried into the church to clear it away

before the congregation came. But when he went into the church, he found the thorn branches blossoming with beautiful roses.

11. RESURRECTED BUT SCARRED

If God raised Jesus from the dead, why didn't God fix him up? Why scars? Why the print of nails that you could feel with your fingers? Can it be that the gospel words is saying to us in our waiting: "You will not see Jesus Christ unless you see the wounds"? Somehow we must understand that the resurrected Christ is forever the wounded Christ. Living, but never fixed up. Not bound by death, yet scarred for eternity.

The deaf have a sign for Jesus. Quickly they make this sign many times during their worship: the middle finger of each hand is placed into the palm of the other. Jesus, the one with wounded hands. And when they touch the place, they remember. They hear the name in their own flesh.

JOHN VANNORSDALL

12. HE LIVES TODAY

I remember the witness of Bishop Lajos Ordass of the Lutheran Church in Hungary to a small group gathered at the Lutheran World Federation assembly in Minneapolis in 1957. As bishop, he protested the Communist regime's confiscation of church schools and was imprisoned for twenty months. Later he was under arrest for six years. He was a tall stately man, and I can still see his ashen face as he quietly told his story.

"They placed me in solitary confinement. It was a tiny cell, perhaps six feet by eight feet, with no windows, and soundproofed. They hoped to break down my resistance by isolating me from all sensory perceptions. They thought I was alone. They were wrong. The risen Christ was present in that room, and in communion with him I was able to prevail."

ANDREW WYERMANN

13. THE FOG LIFTED

It was June 18, 1815, the Battle of Waterloo. The French under the command of Napoleon were fighting the Allies (British, Dutch, and Germans) under the command of Wellington. The people of England depended on a system of semaphore signals to find out how the battle was going. One of these signal stations was on the tower of Winchester Cathedral.

Late in the day it flashed the signal: "W-E-L-L-I-N-G-T-O-N- - -D-E-F-E-A-T-E-D- -." Just at that moment one of those sudden English fog clouds made it impossible to read the message. The news of defeat quickly spread throughout the city. The whole countryside was sad and gloomy when they heard the news that their country had lost the war. Suddenly the fog lifted, and the remainder of the message could be read. The message had four words, not two. The complete message was: "W-E-L-L-I-N-G-T-O-N- - -D-E-F-E-A-T-E-D- - -T-H-E- - -E-N-E-M-Y!" It took only a few minutes for the good news to spread. Sorrow was turned into joy, defeat was turned into victory!

So it was when Jesus was laid in the tomb on the first Good Friday afternoon. Hope had died even in the hearts of Jesus' most loyal friends. After the frightful crucifixion, the fog of disappointment and misunderstanding had crept in on the friends of Jesus. They had "read" only part of the divine message. "Christ defeated" was all that they knew. But then on the third day—Easter Sunday—the fog of disappointment and misunderstanding lifted, and the world received the complete message: "Christ defeated death!" Defeat was turned into victory; death was turned to life!

14. GOD'S MARVELOUS EASTER CHEMISTRY
A workman of the great chemist Michael Faraday accidentally knocked a silver cup into a solution of acid. It was promptly dissolved, eaten up by the acid. The workman was terribly disturbed by the accident. The chemist came in and put a chemical into the jar, and shortly all the silver was precipitated to the bottom. The shapeless mass was lifted out and sent to the silversmith, and the cup was restored to its original shape. If a human genius can do a things like this, why should we doubt that God can raise the dead?

15. THE LAST WORD
The simplest meaning of Easter is that we are living in a world in which God has the last word. On Friday night it appeared as if evil were the master of life. The holiest and most lovable One who had ever lived was dead and in His tomb, crucified by the order of a tyrant without either scruples or regrets. He who had raised the highest hopes among men had died by the most shameful means. A cross, two nails, a jeering mob of debauched souls, and a quick thrust of a spear had ended it all. Those hours when His voice was stilled and His hands were quiet were the blackest through which the race has ever lived. If Caesar could put an end to Jesus, then no man could ever dare aspire or hope again. Hope, in such a world, could be nothing better than a mockery. Then came Easter morning and the glorious word: "He is risen!" And evil's triumph was at an end. Since that hour when Mary in the garden first discovered the staggering fact of victory, no man whose heart was pure and whose labors were honest has ever had reason to fear or despair if he believed in the Resurrection. PAUL HOVEY

16. A VOICE TO SHOUT

On the Easter just before he died, D. William Sangster painfully printed a short note to his daughter. A deeply spiritual Methodist, he had been spearheading a renewal movement in the British Isles after World War II. Then his ministry, except for prayer, was ended by a disease which progressively paralyzed his body, even his vocal chords. But the last Resurrection Sunday he spent on earth, still able to move his fingers, he wrote: "How terrible to wake up on Easter and have no voice to shout, 'He is risen!' Far worse, to have a voice and not want to shout."

17. EASTER AFFIRMATION

About 1930, the Communist leader Bukharin journeyed from Moscow to Kiev. His mission was to address a huge assembly. His subject, atheism. For a solid hour he aimed his heavy artillery at Christianity, hurling argument and ridicule. At last he was finished and viewed what seemed to be the smoldering ashes of men's faith. "Are there any questions?" Bukharin demanded. A solitary man arose and asked permission to speak. He mounted the platform and moved close to the Communist. The audience was breathlessly silent as the man surveyed them first to the right, then to the left. At last he shouted the ancient Orthodox greeting, "CHRIST IS RISEN!" The vast assembly arose as one man and the response came crashing like the sound of an avalanche, "HE IS RISEN INDEED!"

18. I'VE TAKEN YOUR STING

A little boy and his father were driving down a country road on a beautiful spring afternoon. Suddenly out of nowhere a bumblebee flew in the car window. Since the little boy was deathly allergic to bee stings, he became petrified. But the father quickly reached out, grabbed the bee, squeezed it in his hand, and then released it. But as soon as he let it go, the young son became frantic once again as it buzzed by the little boy. His father saw his panic-stricken face. Once again the father reached out his hand, but this time he pointed to his hand. There still stuck in his skin was the stinger of the bee. "Do you see this?" he said. "You don't need to be afraid anymore. I've taken the sting for you." And this is the message of Easter. We do not need to be afraid of death anymore. Christ faced death for us. And by His victory, we are saved from sin. Christ has taken the sting! First Corinthians 15:22 asks: "Where, oh death, is your sting?" Christ has taken the stinger for us. He has risen! Fear is gone. New life is ours.

19. WHICH IS MORE DIFFICULT?

What reason have atheists for saying that we cannot rise again? Which is the more difficult—to be born or to rise again? Is it more difficult to come into being than to return to it? BLAISE PASCAL

20. IF EASTER MEANS ANYTHING

If Easter means anything to modern man, it means that eternal truth is eternal. You may nail it to the tree, wrap it up in grave clothes, and seal it in a tomb. But truth crushed to earth shall rise again. Truth does not perish. It cannot be destroyed. It may be distorted. It has been silenced temporarily. It has been compelled to carry its cross to Calvary's brow or to drink the cup of poisoned hemlock in a Grecian jail, but with an inevitable certainty after every Black Friday dawns truth's Easter morn. DONALD HARVEY TIPPET

21. NO MORE FEAR

The Easter message tells us that our enemies, sin, the curse, and death, are beaten. Ultimately they can no longer start mischief. They still behave as though the game were not decided, the battle not fought; we must still reckon with them, but fundamentally we must cease to fear them any more. KARL BARTH, *Dogmatics in Outline*

EDUCATION *(See Learning)*

FORTY-THREE
Endurance
(See also Determination)

1. PRESSING ON

In a far country lived a band of minstrels who traveled from town to town presenting music to make a living. They had not been doing well. Times were hard; there was little money for common folk to come to hear the minstrels, even though their fee was small. Attendance had been falling off, so early one evening the group met to discuss their plight. "I see no reason for opening tonight," one said. "To make things even worse than they may have been, it is starting to snow. Who will venture out on a night like this?" "I agree," another disheartened singer said. "Last night we performed for just a handful. Fewer will come tonight. Why not give back their meager fees and cancel the concert? No one can expect us to go on when just a few are in the audience." "How can anyone do his best for so few?" a third inquired. Then he turned to another sitting beside him. "What do you think?" The man appealed to was older than the others. He looked straight at his troupe. "I know you are discouraged. I am too. But we have a responsibility to those who might come. We will go on. And we will do the best job of which we are capable. It is not the fault of those who come that others do not. They should not be punished with less than the best we can give." Heartened by his words, the minstrels went ahead with their show. They never performed better. When the show was over and the small audience gone, the old man called his troupe to him. In his hand was a note, handed to him by one of the audience just before the doors closed behind him. "Listen to this, my friends!" Something electrifying in his tone of voice made them turn to him in anticipation. Slowly the old man read: "Thank you for a beautiful performance." It was signed very simply—"Your King."

2. ALL IS ATTAINABLE
I hold a doctrine to which I owe much, indeed, but all the little I ever had, namely, that with ordinary talent and extraordinary perseverance, all things are attainable. T. F. BUXTON

3. THE PATIENCE OF THE SCRIBES
Although we do not possess the original manuscripts of the New Testament, we do have over 99.9 percent of the original text, and this is because of the faithful work of manuscript copyists over the centuries. Yet the copying of the New Testament was a long and arduous process. Though it seems strange to us today, in antiquity, it was not customary to sit at a table or a desk while writing. Rather, it was customary for scribes to stand while making brief notes or to sit on a stool or bench (or even on the ground), holding their scroll on their knees. Something of the drudgery of copying manuscripts can be gleaned from the notes they often placed at the close of their books. The following are some examples:

"He who does not know how to write supposes it to be no labor; but though only three fingers write, the whole body labors."

"Writing bows one's back, thrusts the ribs into one's stomach, and fosters a general debility of the body."

In an Armenian manuscript of the Gospels, there is a note that complains that a heavy snowstorm was raging outside and that the scribe's ink froze, his hand became numb, and the pen fell from his fingers.

"As travelers rejoice to see their home country, so also is the end of a book to those who toil [in writing]."

"The end of the book; thanks be to God!"

"There is no scribe who will not pass away, but what his hands have written will remain forever."

FORTY-FOUR

Enthusiasm

(See also Zeal)

1. GIVING UP ON ENTHUSIASM

To give up enthusiasm wrinkles the soul. SAMUEL ULLMAN

2. TOUGH TO HIDE FEELINGS

An easterner who walked into a western saloon was amazed to see a dog sitting at a table playing poker with three men. He asked, "Can that dog really play cards?" One of the men answered, "Yeah, but he ain't much of a player. Whenever he gets a good hand he wags his tail."

FORTY-FIVE

Eternity

(See also Death)

1. I SHALL RISE

I shall rise from the dead, from the prostration, from the prosternation of death, and never miss the sun, which shall be put out, for I shall see the Son of God, the Sun of Glory, and shine myself as that sun shines. I shall rise from the grave, and never miss this city, which shall be nowhere, for I shall see the city of God, the new Jerusalem. I shall look up and never wonder when it shall be day, for the angel will tell me that time shall be no more, and I shall see and see cheerfully that last day of judgment, which shall have no night, never end, and be united to the Ancient of Days, to God Himself, who had no morning, never began. JOHN DONNE

2. FATHER AT THE GAME

Some years ago Columbia University had a great football coach by the name of Lou Little. One day Lou had a boy try out for the varsity team who wasn't really very good. But Lou noticed that there was something unique about him—while he wasn't nearly good enough to make the team, he had such irrepressible spirit and contagious enthusiasm that Lou thought, *This boy would be a great inspiration on the bench. He'll never be able to play, but I'll leave him on the team to encourage the others.*

As the season went on, Lou began to develop a tremendous admiration and love for this boy. One of the things that especially impressed him was the manner with which the boy obviously cared for his father. Whenever the father would come for a visit to the campus the boy and his father would always be seen walking together, arm in arm, an obvious indication of an exceptional bond of love between them. They could always be seen on Sunday going to and from the university chapel. It was obvious that theirs was a deep and mutually shared Christian faith. Then, one day, a telephone call came to Coach Little. He was informed that the boy's father had just died—would he be the one to tell the boy? With a heavy heart Lou informed the boy of his father's death, and he immediately left to go home for the funeral.

A few days later the boy returned to the campus, only two days before the biggest game of the season. Lou went to him and said, "Is there anything I can do for you? Anything at all?" And to the coach's astonishment the boy said, "Let me start the game on Saturday!" Lou was taken aback. He thought, *I can't let him start—he's not good enough.* But he remembered his promise to help and said, "All right—you can start the game," but he thought to himself, *I'll leave him in for a few plays and then take him out.* The day of the big game arrived. To everyone's surprise the coach started this boy who had never played in a game all season. But imagine even the coach's surprise when, on the very first play from scrimmage, that boy was the one who single-handedly made a tackle that threw the opposing team for a loss. The boy went on to play inspired football play after play. In fact, he played so exceptionally that Lou left him in for the entire game; the boy led his team to victory and he was voted the outstanding player of the game.

When the game was finally over Lou approached the boy and said, "Son, what got into you today?" And the boy replied, "You remember when my father would visit me here at school and we would spend a lot of time

171

together walking arm in arm around the campus? My father and I shared a secret that nobody around here knew anything about. You see, my father was blind—and today was the first time he ever saw me play!"

It is because of resurrection vision that we are able to "play above our heads" in the game of life and "see" the purposes and power and love of God.

3. WELL DONE, GOOD AND FAITHFUL SERVANT

A veteran missionary was returning home to the U.S. after several terms on the field. Aboard a ship bound for New York harbor, a secularist challenged him by pointing out the futility of giving one's life in missionary service. He continued by noting that no one on board ship was paying any attention to the veteran missionary, a sign they apparently considered his efforts quite wasted.

The servant of God responded, "I'm not home yet."

The agnostic assumed the missionary was referring to a large crowd that would meet the ship, and he scoffed again when they disembarked—not a solitary person welcomed the missionary. Once again, the missionary said, "I'm not home yet."

A lonely train ride lay ahead as he made his trek from New York City to his small Midwestern hometown. Reaching his destination, the missionary could no longer fight back the tears as the train pulled off. Again, he stood alone. It was then that the inner voice of God's Spirit brought comfort by reminding the faithful servant, "You're not home yet."

4. EVIDENCES OF GOD

This life were brutish did we not sometimes
Have intimations clear of wider scope,
Hints of occasion infinite, to keep
The soul alert with noble discontent
And onward yearnings of unstilled desire;
Fruitless, except we now and then divined
A mystery of purpose, gleaning through
The secular confusion of the world,
Whose will we darkly accomplish, doing ours.
JAMES RUSSELL LOWELL, "The Cathedral"

5. ANOTHER WORLD

If I find in myself a desire which no experience in this world can satisfy, the most probable explanation is that I was made for another world. C. S. LEWIS

6. TRAVELING LIGHT

In the last century, an American tourist paid a visit to a renowned Polish rabbi, Hofetz Chaim. He was astonished to see that the rabbi's home was only a simple room filled with books, plus a table and a cot.

The tourist asked, "Rabbi, where is your furniture?" Hofetz Chaim replied, "Where is yours?"

The puzzled American asked, "Mine? But I'm only a visitor here. I'm only passing through." The rabbi replied, "So am I."

7. OPENING THE DAWN

I feel within me that future life. I am like a forest that has been razed; the new shoots are stronger and brighter. I shall most certainly rise toward the heavens ... the nearer my approach to the end, the plainer is the sound of immortal symphonies of worlds which invite me. For half a century I have been translating my thoughts into prose and verse: history, philosophy, drama, romance, tradition, satire, ode, and song; all of these I have tried. But I feel I haven't given utterance to the thousandth part of what lies with me. When I go to the grave I can say, as others have said, "My day's work is done." But I cannot say, "My life is done." My work will recommence the next morning. The tomb is not a blind alley; it is a thoroughfare. It closes upon the twilight but opens upon the dawn. VICTOR HUGO

8. THE RUMOR OF RESURRECTION

At present we are on the outside of the world, the wrong side of the door. We discern the freshness and purity of morning, but they do not make us fresh and pure. We cannot mingle with the splendors we see. But all of the leaves of the New Testament are rustling with the rumor that it will not always be so. Some day, God willing, we shall get in. C. S. LEWIS, *The Weight of Glory*

9. HEAVEN AND HELL BY CHOICE

Arthur J. Schlesinger, Jr., reminisced about Edward F. Prichard, Jr., politician, sometime crook, interesting character from Kentucky: "He had a diverting fancy about Judgment Day. When the last trumpet sounded, he would say, the Lord isn't going to send people to heaven or to hell, 'He's going to take away their inhibitions, and everybody's going to go where he belongs.'"

10. THINKING BACK

When Fred arrived at the Pearly Gates there was hardly any line and he didn't have to wait more than a minute before his interview. Naturally, he was a little nervous about getting through the gates and into the heavenly city. Very quickly he found himself standing before an impressive angelic being with a clipboard who started getting his entry data down. After name, address, and a few other particulars, the angelic being said, "Fred, it would help the process if you could share with me some experience from your life on earth when you did a purely unselfish, kindly deed." Well, Fred thought about it for a minute and then said, "Oh, yes. I think I have something you might be interested in. One day I was walking along and I came upon a little old lady who was being mercilessly beaten up by a huge motorcycle gang type of fellow. He was smacking her back and forth. Well, I just stepped right up and first I pushed over his motorcycle—just to distract his attention. And then I kicked him real hard in the shins and told the old lady to run for help. And then I hauled off and gave the guy a great shot right to the gut with my fist."

The being looked at Fred with a great deal of interest and said, "Wow, that's quite a story. I'm very impressed. Could you tell me just when this happened?" Fred looked at his watch and said, "Oh, about two or three minutes ago."

11. HOME IN ETERNITY
A prominent citizen in town was dying. As he lay in his lovely home, the best doctors surrounding him, he whispered, with a note of despair, "I'm leaving home, I'm leaving home." Across town there lay a solitary figure in surroundings bare. Her modest home contained only the most threadbare of life's essentials. In her eye was a gleam. Before she died she was heard to say, "I'm going home, I'm going home."

12. THE SURE SIGN
Early in my career as a doctor, I went to see a patient who was just coming out of anesthesia. Far off church chimes were sounding. The woman murmured, "I must be in heaven." Then she saw me. She said, "No, I can't be, there's Dr. Campbell."

13. TIMING IS EVERYTHING
The pastor was speaking about heaven, about eternal bliss and the joys that are awaiting each person on "the other side." He paused for effect and asked, "How many of you here want to go to heaven?" All hands were raised except for an eight-year-old boy sitting in the front pew. The minister asked, "Don't you want to go to heaven, too, Son?"

The boy replied, "Yes, but I thought you were making up a load to go right now."

14. THOSE GREATER MOUNTS

These small and perishable bodies we now have were given to us as ponies are given to schoolboys. We must learn to manage: not that we may some day be free of horses altogether but that some day we may ride bareback, confident and rejoicing, those greater mounts, those winged, shining and world-shaking horses which perhaps even now expect us with impatience, pawing and snorting in the king's stables. C. S. LEWIS

15. THINKING OF THE NEXT WORLD

If you read history you will find that the Christians who did most for the present world were precisely those who thought most of the next. It is since Christians have largely ceased to think of the other world that they have become so ineffective in this. C. S. LEWIS

16. HEAVEN AND EARTH

Heaven or *heavenly* in the New.Testament bear little relation to the meanings we have so unscripturally attached to them. For us, heaven is an unearthly, humanly irrelevant condition in which bed-sheeted, paper-winged spirits sit on clouds and play tinkly music until their pipe-cleaner halos drop off from boredom. . . . But in Scripture, it is a city with boys and girls playing in the streets; it is buildings put up by a Department of Public Works that uses amethysts for cinder blocks and pearls as big as the Ritz for gates; and indoors, it is a dinner party to end all dinner parties at the marriage supper of the Lamb. It is, in short, earth wedded, not earth jilted. It is the world as the irremovable apple of God's eyes. ROBERT CAPON, *The Parables of the Kingdom*

17. WHERE IS HEAVEN?

What is heaven going to be like? Just as there is a mystery to hell, so there is a mystery to heaven. Yet I believe the Bible teaches that heaven is a literal place. Is it one of the stars? I don't know. I can't even speculate. The Bible doesn't inform us. I believe that out there in space where there are one thousand million galaxies, each a hundred thousand light years or more in diameter, God can find some place to put us in heaven. I'm not worried about where it is. I know it is going to be where Jesus is. Christians don't have to go around discouraged and despondent with their shoulders bent. Think of it—the joy, the peace, the sense of forgiveness that He gives you, and then heaven, too. BILLY GRAHAM

18. WATCH YOUR AIM

Aim at heaven and you will get earth thrown in. Aim at earth you will get neither. C. S. LEWIS

19. THE UNDERWATER GOD

In the Hebrides Islands they have a lovely legend about a god who lived beneath the sea. And the great desire of this god who lived beneath the sea was to have a little baby boy—a human baby. So he was always trying to catch little babies that might be in boats passing along the surface of the sea from island to island. And so the people always clutched their children close when in their boats.

On one occasion, he almost got a boat. He was surging behind it, this sea-god, when the boat reached shore. And they lifted the little boy who was in it out onto the shore just as this god approached in a great wave. And they hurried away with the boy. At least they thought they'd gotten away except the sea-god managed to send just one little wavelet into the heart of that little child. And as that god, momentarily frustrated, settled back down to his palace beneath the waves, he was heard to say, "He will return to me for I have put a part of myself into his heart."

Years later, the people of the village were astonished one day to see a strong, young man go down to the beach and get in a rowboat and begin to row out into the sea—but not toward another island. And they called out to him, "There is no island that way." But on he rowed. And as they watched, when he had gotten a good distance, he stood up and dived into the sea to the god who had put a part of himself into that boy's heart.

When we were made, God put a bit of himself, a bit of eternity, a bit of the Kingdom of Heaven right inside of us and it cries out for him.

BRUCE THEILEMAN

20. A VISION OF HEAVEN

In recent years there have been a number of stories in the "Life After Life" vein. One of the most moving that I have read is the story that is told by singer Johnny Cash about the death of his brother, Jack, in 1944. Jack was two years older than Johnny and had always been his hero and model. On Saturday, May 12, 1944, Jack went to work at a workshop, cutting fence posts. Johnny had tried to talk Jack into going to a movie with him that day but funds were low and the family needed the money.

While at the workshop Jack fell across the table saw and was badly injured. He was rushed to the hospital, but they didn't expect him to live through the day. He lingered for a week, in and out of consciousness, sometimes hallucinating, then back into a coma. After a week of his condition worsening, it was obvious that he was going to die. The family gathered in the hospital room. Jack was swollen from the ravages of the traumatic injury. Johnny Cash tells the story:

"I remember standing in line to tell him good-bye. He was still unconscious. I bent over his bed and put my cheek against his and said, 'Good-bye, Jack.' That's all I could get out.

"My mother and daddy were on their knees. At 6:30 A.M. he woke up. He opened his eyes and looked around and said, 'Why is everybody crying over me? Mama, don't cry over me. Did you see the river?'

"And she said, 'No, I didn't, Son.'

"'Well, I thought I was going toward the fire, but I'm headed in the other direction now, Mama. I was going down a river, and there was fire on one side and heaven on the other. I was crying, 'God, I'm supposed to go to heaven. Don't You remember? Don't take me to the fire.' All of a sudden I turned, and now, Mama, can you hear the angels singing?'

"She said, 'No, Son, I can't hear it.'

"And he squeezed her hand and shook her arm, saying, 'But Mama, you've got to hear it.' Tears started rolling off his cheeks and he said, 'Mama, listen to the angels. I'm going there, Mama.'

"We listened with astonishment.

"'What a beautiful city,' he said. 'And the angels singing. Oh Mama, I wish you could hear the angels singing.' Those were his last words. And he died.

"The memory of Jack's death, his vision of heaven, the effect his life had on the lives of others, and the image of Christ he projected have been more of an inspiration to me, I suppose, than anything else that has ever come to me through any man." JOHNNY CASH, *Man in Black*

21. A SCIENTIFIC REPORT
Thomas Edison was a scientific genius and an exacting and practical man who didn't casually say anything he didn't believe. Mrs. Edison told about the night Edison was at death's door. Suddenly it was evident that he wanted to say something, so she and the doctor bent down close. This great scientist, with a smile on his face, said, "It is very beautiful over there!"

FORTY-SIX
Evangelism
(See also Missions, Witnessing)

1. SPREADING THE WORD
The story is told of a small dog which had been struck by a car and was lying by the side of the road. A doctor, driving by, noticed that the dog was still alive, stopped his car, picked up the dog, and took him home with him. There he discovered that the dog had been stunned, had suffered a few minor cuts and abrasions, but was otherwise all right. He revived the dog, cleaned up the wounds and was carrying the animal from the house to the garage when suddenly it jumped from his arms and scampered off. "What an ungrateful little dog," the doctor said to himself. He thought no more about the incident until the next evening when he heard a scratching at the door. When he opened it, there was the little dog he had treated with another hurt dog.

2. WHAT KIND OF METHOD?
One day a lady criticized D. L. Moody for his methods of evangelism in attempting to win people to the Lord. Moody's reply was "I agree with you. I don't like the way I do it either. Tell me, how do you do it?" The lady replied, "I don't do it." Moody retorted, "Then I like my way of doing it better than your way of not doing it."

3. THE SNOWBALL EFFECT
"How can I ever repay you?" asked a person of a friend who had done him a great favor. "I shall forever be indebted to you for your kindness." "Not necessarily," answered the friend. "If you really want to repay me, keep your eye open for somebody who needs help as badly as you did, and help him. If you are willing to do this, I shall be fully repaid for I shall enjoy the warm feeling that someday—through you—I shall have helped a fellow I didn't even know."

4. OUR TASK IN THE DARKNESS
At age twelve, Robert Louis Stevenson was looking out into the dark from his upstairs window watching a man light the streetlamps. Stevenson's governess came into the room and asked what he was doing. He replied, "I am watching a man cut holes in the darkness." I see this as a marvelous picture

of what our task should be as sharers of God's light—people who are busy cutting holes in the spiritual darkness of our world.

5. TELL SOMEONE ELSE, MY BROTHERS

A monastery in Germany trained Christian brothers for various responsibilities within the Roman Catholic church. One Christian brother in training lived in mortal fear of being called upon to preach the sermon in the daily chapel exercises. As this young man thought about his apprehension, he decided to head it off by going to the monitor of the monastery and discussing the problem with him. In the course of the conversation he said, "Sir, I am willing to do any menial job that you assign me. I would be delighted to go out into the fields and plow, fertilize, and irrigate them by hand to increase the productivity. If you would care for me to do so, I would be happy to get down on my hands and knees and scrub the floors here in the monastery. It would be a privilege for me to polish the silverware. Any menial job that you call upon me to do I shall be happy to do. However, please don't ask me to preach a sermon in the chapel."

The monitor, looking at the young man and recognizing that an assignment to preach was exactly what he needed, replied, "Tomorrow you are to conduct the chapel and preach the sermon." The next day as this young brother stood behind the pulpit and looked out into the eyes of his peers who had assembled in the sanctuary, he was greatly apprehensive. He was so nervous he hardly knew what to do. He started his sermon by asking, "Brothers, do you know what I am going to say?" They all shook their heads in the negative. He continued, "Neither do I. Let's stand for the benediction. *Pax vobiscum.*"

Naturally, the monitor was infuriated by this. He said to the young man, "I am going to give you a second chance. Tomorrow you are to conduct the service in the chapel, and this time I want you to preach a message."

The next day the scene was the same. And the young man began as he had the day before, "Brothers, do you know what I am going to say?" When they all nodded their heads in the affirmative, he said, "Since you already know, there is no point in my saying it. Let's stand for the benediction. *Pax vobiscum.*"

The monitor was livid with anger. Once again he went to the young brother and literally roared at him, "I am tired of your chicanery. Tomorrow I am going to give you a third chance. If you don't come through, I am going to put you in solitary confinement on bread and water."

The third day the scene was the same. The brother began as he had the two previous days, "Brothers, do you know what I am going to say?" Some nodded their heads in the affirmative. Some shook their heads in the negative. He then said, "Let those who know tell those who don't. Let's stand for the benediction. *Pax vobiscum.*"

6. WHY RUSH?

An ancient story recalls how Satan once summoned his top three aides to plan how to stop a group of dedicated Christians from effective missionary work.

One of the lieutenants, Rancor, said to Satan, "We should convince them that there is no God." Satan sneered at Rancor and replied, "That would never work. They know that there is a God."

Another of Satan's aides, Bitterness, spoke up. "We'll convince them that God does not really care about right or wrong." Satan toyed with the notion for a few moments, but rejected it because he knew that too many Christians know that God does care.

Malice, the third satanic helper, came up with his idea. "We'll let them go on thinking that there is a God and that He cares about right and wrong. But we will keep whispering that there is no hurry, there is no hurry."

Satan howled with glee. He advanced Malice higher in his malevolent organization. Satan knew that he would find this stratagem successful with many, many Christians. FRANK S. MEAD

7. BETRAYING THE SECRET

A group of prospectors set out from Bannock, Montana (then capital of the state), in search of gold. They went through many hardships and several of their little company died en route. Finally they were overtaken by the Indians who took their good horses, leaving them with only a few limping old ponies. Then they threatened them, telling them to get back to Bannock and stay there, for if they overtook them again, they would murder the lot of them. Defeated, discouraged, and downhearted, the prospectors sought to make their way back to the capital city. On one occasion as they tethered out the limping ponies on a creekside, one of the men casually picked up a little stone from the creek bed. He called to his buddy for a hammer and upon cracking the rock, he said, "It looks as though there may be gold here." The two of them panned gold the rest of the afternoon and managed to realize twelve dollars' worth. The entire little company panned gold the next day in the same creek and realized fifty dollars, a great sum in those days. They said to one another: "We have struck it!" They made their way back to Bannock and vowed not to breathe a word concerning this gold strike. They secretively set about re-equipping themselves with supplies for another prospecting trip. But when they got ready to go back, three hundred men followed them. Who had told on them? No one! Their beaming faces betrayed the secret!

If we have been enamored with Him, whom having not seen we love, we should be unable to conceal the treasure: Our beaming faces should betray the secret! L. E. MAXWELL

FORTY-SEVEN

Excuses

1. THE STORY OF NOAH RETOLD

And the Lord said unto Noah: "Where is the ark which I commanded thee to build?"

And Noah said unto the Lord: "Verily, I have had three carpenters off ill. The gopherwood supplier hath let me down—yea, even though the gopherwood hath been on order for nigh upon twelve months. What can I do, O Lord?"

And the Lord said unto Noah: "I want that ark finished even after seven days and seven nights."

And Noah said: "It will be so."

And it was not so. And the Lord said unto Noah: "What seemeth to be the trouble this time?"

And Noah said unto the Lord: "Mine subcontractor hath gone bankrupt. The pitch which Thou commandest me to put on the outside and on the inside of the ark hath not arrived. The plumber hath gone on strike. Shem, my son who helpeth me on the ark side of the business, hath formed a pop group with his brothers Ham and Japheth. Lord, I am undone."

And the Lord grew angry and said: "And what about the animals, the male and female of every sort that I ordered to come unto thee to keep their seed alive upon the face of the earth?"

And Noah said: "They have been delivered unto the wrong address but should arrive on Friday."

And the Lord said: "How about the unicorns, and the fowls of the air by sevens?"

And Noah wrung his hands and wept, saying: "Lord, unicorns are a discontinued line; thou canst not get them for love nor money. And fowls of the air are sold only in half-dozens. Lord, Lord, Thou knowest how it is."

And the Lord in His wisdom said: "Noah, my son, I knowest. Why else dost thou think I have caused a flood to descend upon the earth?"

2. REASONS TO AVOID CHURCH

A husband and his wife arose one Sunday morning and the wife dressed for church. It was just about time for the service when she noticed her husband hadn't moved a finger toward getting dressed. Perplexed, she asked, "Why aren't you getting dressed for church?" He said, "Cause I don't want to go." She asked, "Do you have any reasons?" He said, "Yes, I have three good reasons. First, the congregation is cold. Second, no one likes me. And third, I just don't want to go."

The wife replied, wisely, "Well, honey, I have three reasons why you should go. First, the congregation is warm. Second, there are a few people there who like you. And third, you're the pastor! So get dressed!"

3. EXCUSES FOR STINGINESSS

Horace Bushnell made this list of those excused from benevolence giving.

Those who believe "every man for himself."

Those who believe that Christ made a mistake when he said: "Go into all the world and preach the gospel."

Those who regret that missionaries ever came to our ancestors.

Those who believe that the gospel will not save anybody.

Those who want no share in the final victory.

Those who believe they are not accountable to anybody for the trust they enjoy.

Those who are prepared to accept the final sentence. "Inasmuch as ye did it not to one of these, you did not to me."

4. DOGGONE EXCUSES

A class of high school sophomores had been assigned a term paper. Now the day of reckoning had come, the papers were due to be handed in. The teacher knew that a particular student, named Gene, had not been working steadily on his paper as others had in the class. He was prepared for some sort of excuse. When the teacher went to collect the papers Gene said, "My dog ate it." The teacher, who had heard them all, gave Gene a hard stare of unbelief. But Gene insisted and persisted, "It's true. I had to force him, but he ate it."

5. BEST ALIBI

When the Police League of Indiana sponsored a Best Speeding Alibi contest, one honorable mention award went to an exasperated father who was stopped with a load of fighting, squalling children in his backseat. He told the officer, "I was trying to get away from all the noise behind me."

6. WORST ALIBI
George Shamblin insisted to police that he was trying to save his wife from drowning when he threw rocks at her as she struggled in the Kanawha River. "I was trying to drive her back to shore," he said.

7. LATE DATE
As the young boy was trying to sneak his date back into her home—very late—the couple was met by a very angry father at the head of the stairs. He boomed out, "Young man, didn't I hear the clock strike four when you brought my daughter home?" The clever boy replied, "Yes sir, you did. It was going to strike eleven, but I grabbed it and held the gong so it wouldn't disturb you." The father muttered, "Doggone it! Why didn't I think of that in my day?"

8. CREATIVITY
A farmer asked his neighbor if he might borrow a rope.

"Sorry," said the neighbor, "I'm using the rope to tie up my milk."

"Milk?" exclaimed the first farmer. "Rope can't tie up milk."

"I know," replied the neighbor, "but when a man doesn't want to do something, one reason is as good as another."

FORTY-EIGHT

Experience

1. EACH LEARNS ANEW
Each generation has to find out for itself that the stove is hot.

2. THE FINE PRINT
The difference between education and experience: Education is what you get from reading the small print. Experience is what you get from not reading it.

3. EXPERIENCE ONLY ONCE
If at first you don't succeed, so much for skydiving.

4. THE REAL MEANING OF SKILL

The essence of skill is extracting meaning from everyday experience.

5. THE LIMITS OF OUR OWN EXPERIENCE

We ought not permit the term *experience* to be confined within the brackets of one's own existence. The meaning of experience is a poor and haggard thing if it only refers to what has happened to me. The meaning of education and of culture is that we live vicariously a thousand other lives, and all that has happened to human beings, things that have been recorded not by my experience but by the experience of others, become a second life, and a third, and so on. I'm annoyed by those who defy experience by saying, "Well, I haven't met it yet; it hasn't happened to me. Therefore, it has no authority." I would be a poor person if the only things I knew were what I have found out for myself. . . . There is today a general religious bias toward a galloping subjectivity. But our first obligation to a text is to let it hang there in celestial objectivity—not to ask what it means to us. A good sermon or a good teaching job must begin with angelic objectivity. . . . The text had a particular meaning before I saw it, and it will continue to mean that after I have seen it. JOSEPH SITTLER

6. THE BEST TEACHER

A good scare teaches more than good advice.

7. HELP FROM EXPERIENCE

Two nimrods flew deep into remote Canada for elk hunting. Their pilot, seeing that they had bagged six elk, told them the plane could carry only four out.

"But the plane that carried us out last year was exactly like this one," the hunters protested. "The horsepower was the same, the weather was similar, and we had six elk then."

Hearing this, the pilot reluctantly agreed to try. They loaded up and took off, but sure enough there was insufficient power to climb out of the valley with all that weight, and they crashed. As they stumbled from the wreckage, one hunter asked the other if he knew where they were.

"Well, I'm not sure," replied the second, "but I think we are about two miles from where we crashed last year."

8. SECOND TIME

Don't underestimate the importance of experience. It'll help you recognize a mistake when you make it again.

FORTY-NINE

Failure

(See also Adversity, Success)

1. HOW YOU RESPOND

Failure doesn't consist in stumbling and falling. The failure is in staying there on the floor. Success is in finding something while you're down there to pick up with you. After his butcher shop in Brooklyn was robbed four times in one month, William Levine bought a bulletproof vest in 1980. Other business proprietors asked him where they could get a vest like his. Mr. Levine began taking orders as a sideline. Today Levine is out of the butcher business and full-time president of Body Armor, International. He supplies forty sales representatives across the country and is selling five hundred to six hundred vests a month.

2. FREE CHOICES

No one learns to make right decisions without being free to make wrong ones.

3. THE FAILURE TO FEAR

You've failed many times, although you may not remember. You fell down the first time you tried to walk. You almost drowned the first time you tried to swim, didn't you? Did you hit the ball the first time you swung a bat? Heavy hitters, the ones who hit the most home runs, also strike out a lot. R. H. Macy failed seven times before his store in New York caught on. English novelist John Creasey got 753 rejection slips before he published 564 books. Babe Ruth struck out 1,330 times, but he also hit 714 home runs. Don't worry about failure. Worry about the chances you miss when you don't even try!

4. HANDLING FAILURE

The real legacy of my life was my biggest failure—that I was an ex-convict. My greatest humiliation—being sent to prison—was the beginning of God's greatest use of my life; He chose the one experience in which I could not glory for His glory. CHARLES COLSON, *Loving God*

5. PROFITING FROM FAILURE

A young man of thirty-two had been appointed president of the bank. He'd never dreamed he'd be president, much less at such a young age. So he approached the venerable chairman of the board and said, "You know, I've just been appointed president. I was wondering if you could give me some advice." The old man came back with just two words: "Right decisions!" The young man had hoped for a bit more than this, so he said, "That's really helpful, and I appreciate it, but can you be more specific? How do I make right decisions?" The wise old man simply responded, "Experience." The young man said, "Well, that's just the point of my being here. I don't have the kind of experience I need. How do I get it?" Came the terse reply, "Wrong decisions!"

6. FEAR OF FAILURE
An essential aspect of creativity is not being afraid to fail. Scientists made a great invention by calling their activities hypotheses and experiments. They made it permissible to fail repeatedly until in the end they got the results they wanted. In politics or government, if you made a hypothesis and it didn't work out, you had your head cut off.

7. EVERY CLOUD HAS A SILVER LINING
The youngster brought home a report card heavy with poor grades. His mother asked, "What have you to say about this?" The boy replied, "One thing is for sure, you know I ain't cheating!"

8. REAL INSECURITY
That's finding on your new job that your name is written on the door in chalk—and there's a wet sponge hanging next to it.

FIFTY
Faith

1. FAITH IN THE WORST OF TIMES
Sweeping across Germany at the end of World War II, Allied forces searched farms and houses looking for snipers. At one abandoned house, almost a heap of rubble, searchers with flashlights found their way to the basement. There, on the crumbling wall, a victim of the Holocaust had scratched a Star of David. And beneath it, in rough lettering, the message:
I believe in the sun—even when it does not shine;
I believe in love—even when it is not shown;
I believe in God—even when he does not speak. ROBERT SCHULLER

2. THEORIES ABOUT GOD'S EXISTENCE

Imagine a family of mice who lived all their lives in a large piano. To them in their piano-world came the music of the instrument, filling all the dark spaces with sound and harmony. At first the mice were impressed by it. They drew comfort and wonder from the thought that there was Someone who made the music—though invisible to them—above, yet close to them. They loved to think of the Great Player whom they could not see. Then one day a daring mouse climbed up part of the piano and returned very thoughtful. He had found out how the music was made. Wires were the secret; tightly stretched wires of graduated lengths which trembled and vibrated. They must revise all their old beliefs; none but the most conservative could any longer believe in the Unseen Player. Later, another explorer carried the explanation further. Hammers were now the secret, numbers of hammers dancing and leaping on the wires. This was a more complicated theory, but it all went to show that they lived in a purely mechanical and mathematical world. The Unseen Player came to be thought of as a myth. . . . But the pianist continued to play.
Leadership

3. THE SINGING BIRD

Faith is the bird that feels the light and sings to greet the dawn while it is still dark.

4. CYNICAL VIEW OF FAITH

For one of the more acerbic definitions, consider Ambrose Bierce's definition of faith with these cynical words: "Faith—belief without evidence in what is told by one who speaks without knowledge of things without parallel."

5. CANDID PRAYER

There was a farmer who had three sons: Jim, John, and Sam. No one in the family ever attended church or had time for God. The pastor and the others in the church tried for years to interest the family in the things of God to no avail. Then one day Sam was bitten by a rattlesnake. The doctor was called and he did all he could to help Sam, but the outlook for Sam's recovery was very dim indeed. So the pastor was called and appraised of the situation. The pastor arrived, and began to pray as follows:

"O wise and righteous Father, we thank Thee that in Thine wisdom thou didst send this rattlesnake to bite Sam. He has never been inside the church and it is doubtful that he has, in all this time, ever prayed or even acknowledged Thine existence. Now we trust that this experience will be a valuable lesson to him and will lead to his genuine repentance.

"And now, O Father, wilt thou send another rattlesnake to bite Jim, and another to bite John, and another really big one to bite the old man. For years we have done everything we know to get them to turn to Thee, but all in vain. It seems, therefore, that what all our combined efforts could not do, this rattlesnake has done. We thus conclude that the only thing that will do this family any real good is rattlesnakes; so, Lord, send us bigger and better rattlesnakes. Amen."

6. READY FOR RAIN
The drought of the past winter threatened the crop in a village of Crete. The priest told his flock: "There isn't anything that will save us, except a special litany for rain. Go to your homes, fast during the week, believe and come on Sunday for the litany of rain." The villagers heard him, fasted during the week and went to the church on Sunday morning, but as soon as the priest saw them, he was furious. He said, "Go away, I will not do the litany. You do not believe." "But Father," they protested, "we fasted and we believe." "Believe? And where are your umbrellas?"

7. CLINGING TO CHRIST
I will stick to Christ as a burr to a topcoat! *Last words of* KATHERINE VON BORA, *wife of Martin Luther*

8. HOW YOU KNOW
A twelve-year-old boy became a Christian during a revival. The next week at school his friends questioned him about the experience. "Did you see a vision?" asked one friend. "Did you hear God speak?" asked another. The youngster answered no to all these questions. "Well, how did you know you were saved?" they asked. The boy searched for an answer and finally he said: "It's like when you catch a fish, you can't see the fish or hear the fish; you just feel him tugging on your line. I just felt God tugging on my heart."

9. BELIEVING IN THE UNSEEN
It seems the pastor's small son was told by his mother that he should wash his hands because there were germs living in all that dirt. He refused and complained: "Germs and Jesus! Germs and Jesus! That's all I ever hear around this house and I've never seen either one."

10. BECOMING SPIRITUAL
We never become truly spiritual by sitting down and wishing to become so. You must undertake something so great that you cannot accomplish it unaided. PHILLIPS BROOKS

11. WISDOM FROM HELEN KELLER

I believe that we can live on earth according to the teachings of Jesus, and that the greatest happiness will come to the world when man obeys His commandment "Love one another."

I believe that we can live on earth according to the fulfillment of God's will, and that when the will of God is done on earth as it is done in heaven, every man will love his fellowmen, and act toward them as he desires they should act toward him. I believe that the welfare of each is bound up in the welfare of all.

I believe that life is given us so we may grow in love, and I believe that God is in me as the sun is in the color and fragrance of a flower—the Light in my darkness, the Voice in my silence.

I believe that only in broken gleams has the Sun of Truth yet shone upon men. I believe that love will finally establish the kingdom of God on earth, and that the cornerstones of that kingdom will be liberty, truth, brotherhood, and service. HELEN KELLER

12. THE BOTTOM LINE

It's not what men eat, but what they digest that makes them strong;
Not what we gain, but what we save that makes us rich;
Not what we read, but what we remember that makes us learned;
Not what we preach or pray, but what we practice and believe that makes us Christians. FRANCIS BACON

13. WAIT AND TREAD WATER

A few years ago I almost drowned in a storm at sea in the Gulf of Mexico when I found myself swimming far from shore, having tried to reach my drifting boat. I got into that predicament through my own stupidity, something not unusual at all. I can remember saying, "Well, this is it." The waves were seven or eight feet high, and the sky was dark with gale force winds and lightning. I was drifting out to sea when the Word of the Lord came to me and saved my life. What I thought He said was, "I'm here, Larson, and you're not coming home as soon as you think. Can you tread water?" Somehow that had never occurred to me. Had I continued my frantic effort to swim back to shore, I would have exhausted my strength and gone down.

In all sorts of situations we can make matters worse by our frantic efforts to save ourselves when God is trying to tell us, "Stand still." We have gotten ourselves into a hopeless situation and the more we do the worse it gets.
BRUCE LARSON, *Wind and Fire*

14. FAITH ON THE WIRE

Imagine, if you will, a wire stretched between the bank building and the city hall on the square in our town. A lone individual stands atop the bank building and announces his intent to walk across the wire to the other building. Of course, a crowd has gathered below because what he intends is a bit strange (needless to say). The tightrope walker asks the crowd if they believe he can make it across. They nod in assent (who would be dumb enough to try without a reasonable chance?). Carefully, slowly he teeters his way across almost falling. Reaching the other side he holds up a wheelbarrow and asks the crowd if they think he could push it across before him. Some nod in assent. Some shrug their shoulders in response. The tightrope walker then singles out a man and yells down to him, "Sir, do you think I can make it?" The response is affirmative so the walker says, "Then prove your faith by riding in the wheelbarrow." Christ calls to us personally, saying He will guide us over life with its dangers. Would you ride in the wheelbarrow?

15. THE EVIDENCE OF PERSONAL EXPERIENCE

A bold unbeliever was lecturing a group on the folly of religious faith in general and the Christian faith in particular. At the close of the presentation the speaker invited people to propound any questions they might have. In the audience was the town drunkard, who had been converted to Christ. In response to the invitation the converted alcoholic came up front, took out an orange, peeled it, and ate it without comment.

The speaker asked if he had a question for him. After downing the last segment of orange the convert turned to the infidel and asked, "Was the orange I just ate sweet or sour?" Angrily, the speaker replied, "You idiot, how can I know whether it was sweet or sour when I never tasted it?" To this the converted drunkard retorted, "And how can you know anything about Christ if you have not tried Him?"

16. FINANCIAL BELIEF

There are no atheists among people called in for an IRS tax audit.

17. BELIEF IN THE VISIBLE

Some things have to be believed to be seen.

FIFTY-ONE
Family
*(See also Children, Fathers,
Mothers, Parents, Youth)*

1. GENETIC POVERTY
Poverty is hereditary. You can get it from your children (also true of insanity).

2. GENETIC MIRACLE
One of the great mysteries of life is how the idiot that your daughter married can be the father of the smartest grandchildren in the whole wide world.

3. ASK ME
Don't be annoyed when your children ask impossible questions. Be proud that they think you know the answers.

4. THE PROPER GRIP
Rearing kids is like holding a wet bar of soap—too firm a grasp and it shoots from your hand, too loose a grasp and it slides away. A gentle but firm grasp keeps it in your control.

5. THE STORK
A little boy asked his mother where he came from, and also where she had come from as a baby. His mother gave him a tall tale about a beautiful white-feathered bird. The boy ran into the next room and asked his grandmother the same question and received a variation on the bird story. He then scampered outside to his playmate with the comment, "You know, there hasn't been a normal birth in our family for three generations."
HOWARD HENDRICKS, *Heaven Help the Home*

6. A CHILD IS LISTENING
One day a young mother and her kindergarten-age son were driving down the street. The inquisitive little boy asked, "Mommy, why do the idiots only come out when Daddy drives?"

7. TODAY, TODAY
Now is the time to love. Tomorrow the baby won't be rocked, the toddler won't be asking why, the schoolboy won't need help with his lesson, nor will he bring his school friends home for some fun. Tomorrow the teenager will have made his major decision. Love today. JOHN DRESCHES

8. LOVE ADDS THE CHOCOLATE

A house is a house is a house—until love comes through the door, that is. And love intuitively goes around sprinkling that special brand of angel dust that transforms a house into a very special home for very special people: your family.

Money, of course, can build a charming house, but only love can furnish it with a feeling of home.

Duty can pack an adequate sack lunch, but love may decide to tuck a little love note inside.

Money can provide a television set, but love controls it and cares enough to say no and take the guff that comes with it.

Obligation sends the children to bed on time, but love tucks the covers in around their necks and passes out kisses and hugs (even to teenagers!).

Obligation can cook a meal, but love embellishes the table with a potted ivy trailing around slender candles.

Duty writes many letters, but love tucks a joke or a picture or a fresh stick of gum inside.

Compulsion keeps a sparkling house. But love and prayer stand a better chance of producing a happy family.

Duty gets offended quickly if it isn't appreciated. But love learns to laugh a lot and to work for the sheer joy of doing it.

Obligation can pour a glass of milk, but quite often love will add a little chocolate.

9. TIME SPENT

Paul Tsongas was a young and rising member of the U.S. Senate. Learning he had cancer made him reevaluate the time he had been spending with his wife and children, compared with the time he spent at work. After spending a rare evening at home with them, he realized that with the schedule he was keeping, the next night like this would probably be several years in the future. After this sobering realization he made this observation: "Nobody on his deathbed ever said, 'I wish I had spent more time on my job.'"

10. THE GIFT OF IMAGINATION

In Berkeley, near the campus of the University of California, there's a place where the ramp goes up the freeway. Just about the time vacations begin that ramp is loaded with college kids hitching rides. They have signs saying SACRAMENTO or L.A. and other destinations which they hold up for the passing motorist to see and respond to. But one man was particularly impressed when he saw a young man with a sign saying simply, MOM IS WAITING. How could you resist?

11. VACATION OVERLOAD

There were four couples who rented a summer house for two months. Each couple took their two week vacation there and took the combined thirteen children of the four families with them. One couple was bragging on this clever plan to a friend when the friend said, "I don't think of two weeks in a cabin with thirteen kids to be much of a vacation." "Oh no," they replied. "Those two weeks were absolutely terrible. The vacation was the six weeks at home without the children."

12. ANYONE THERE?

Home is the place where you can say whatever you want to. No one will be listening to you anyway.

13. SURE-FIRE OBEDIENCE

A mother had a particularly trying day with her young son. Finally she flung up her hands and shouted, "All right, Billy. Do anything you darn well please! Now let me see you disobey THAT!"

14. MEETING THE REQUIREMENTS TO DRIVE

On his sixteenth birthday the son approached his father and asked, "Dad, I'm sixteen now. When I get my license can I drive the family car?"

His dad looked at him and said, "Son, driving the car takes maturity, and first, you must prove you are responsible enough. And one way you must do that is to bring up your grades. They are not acceptable. Secondly, you must read the Bible everyday. And finally, I want you to get that haircut—it looks outrageous."

The son began the task of fulfilling his father's requirements, knowing that the last might be impossible. When his grades came out he came to his dad with a big smile. "Look, Dad, all A's and B's on my report card. Now can I drive the family car?"

"Very good, Son. You are one-third the way there, but have you been reading the Bible?" the father asked.

"Yes, Dad, everyday," said the son.

"Very good, Son. You are two-thirds of the way there. Now when are you going to get that hair cut?"

The son, thinking he could outsmart his dad, responded, "Well, I don't see why I should get my hair cut to drive the car. Jesus had long hair, didn't he?" The father looked at his boy and said, "That's right, Son, and Jesus walked everywhere he went."

15. AN EDUCATION IN ITSELF
Family life teaches you loyalty, patience, understanding, perseverance, and a lot of other things you wouldn't need if you'd stayed single.

16. GENERATION GAP
It's hard to know just where one generation ends and the next one begins, but it's somewhere around 9:00 P.M.

17. FAMILIES PASS ON THE FAITH
May I share with you some reasons why I believe? All good reasons, none of them the really real reason. There's my family. I believe because I was brought up in a believing family. I don't make any bones about that. I don't know what would have happened to me if I had been born in the depths of Manchuria of a Chinese family. I just don't know. I do know that I was led to believe in the love of God as soon as I learned I should eat my oatmeal. We did a lot of believing in our house. We didn't have much else to do, as a matter of fact. Other kids sang "Jesus loves me this I know 'cause the Bible tells me so." I sang, "Jesus loves me this I know, 'cause my ma told me so."

I wasn't alone. You probably heard about a reporter asking the great German theologian, Karl Barth, toward the end of his career: "Sir, you've written these great volumes about God, great learned tomes about all the difficult problems of God. How do you know they're all true?" And the great theologian smiled and said, "'Cause my mother said so!"

Families are God's primary missionary society. LEWIS SMEDES, *Fuller Theological Seminary*

18. KEEPING IN TOUCH
Money isn't everything, but it's a surefire way not to lose touch with your kids.

19. LITERACY'S LIABILITIES
Nobody who can read is ever successful at cleaning out the attic.

20. HOW NOT TO DO IT
The sheriff's office in a Texas city once distributed a list of rules titled "How to Raise a Juvenile Delinquent in Your Own Family":

Begin with infancy to give the child everything he wants. This will insure his believing that the world owes him a living.

Pick up everything he leaves lying around. This will teach him he can always throw off responsibility on others.

Take his part against neighbors, teachers, policemen. They are all prejudiced against your child. He is a "free spirit" and never wrong.

Finally, prepare yourself for a life of grief. You're going to have it.

21. GENETIC FACT

Parenting is hereditary. If your parents didn't have any children, you're not likely to have any either.

22. THE GUILTY PARTY EXPOSED

The father was brushing his teeth when his seven-year-old daughter barged into the bathroom without knocking. "Aha," she rebuked, "so you're the one who keeps putting the cap back on the toothpaste!"

23. TO THE THIRD AND FOURTH GENERATION

Max Jukes lived in New York. He did not believe in Christ or in Christian training. He refused to take his children to church, even when they asked to go. He has had 1,026 descendants; 300 were sent to prison for an average term of thirteen years; 190 were public prostitutes; 680 were admitted alcoholics. His family, thus far, has cost the state in excess of $420,000. They made no contribution to society.

Jonathan Edwards lived in the same state, at the same time as Jukes. He loved the Lord and saw that his children were in church every Sunday, as he served the Lord to the best of his ability. He has had 929 descendants, and of these 430 were ministers; 86 became university professors; 13 became university presidents; 75 authored good books; 7 were elected to the United States Congress. One was vice president of his nation. His family never cost the state one cent but has contributed immeasurably to the life of plenty in this land today.

24. THE BOOK'S DEDICATION

John Drakeford dedicated one of his books: "To my two sons, Warwick and Brenton, teachers in the art of family living, who in the process have put gray hairs in my head, bills in my pocket, illustrations in my sermons, happiness in my home, and pride in my heart."

25. PARENTAL INFLUENCE

The biography, *Norma,* is the story of well-known singer for Lawrence Welk, Norma Zimmer. One of the more poignant aspects of her story is that of her teen years. Her parents were a source of great pain to her because of their drinking. Though these years were difficult for her, she began to find an escape into a better world through singing. As a senior in high school, Norma was invited to become a featured church soloist by Carl A. Pitzer of the University Christian Church in Seattle. When her parents heard she was to sing a solo in church they both insisted they wanted to hear her, though they did not normally attend. She tells the story of that morning:

"I was excited and elated at the prospect of singing again. The choir processed down the middle aisle, and as we walked I stole glances at the congregation, trying to find my parents. . . . I couldn't spot Mom and Dad.

"Then in horror I saw them—weaving down the aisle in a state of disheveled intoxication. They were late. Few empty seats were left. My parents stumbled over the feet of other people to reach a place in the middle of the row. The whole congregation stared. I don't know how I ever got through that morning. The invocation, the congregational hymn, the prayer, the offering—and then I stood up to sing. 'How beautiful upon the mountains are the feet of him that bringeth good tidings.' The song seemed interminable. I tried to think only of the words and kept my eyes from turning to the row where my parents sat.

"I took my seat, my heart pounding, my cheeks burning. Dr. Hastings started to preach. At first I hardly heard him. Then his words reached me, 'God is our refuge and strength, a tested help in time of trouble.'

"My own trouble seemed to bear down on me with tremendous weight that morning. I felt I had more than my share of grief, and I knew I needed help. I realized how desperate life in our family was without God, and that day I recommitted my life to Him. As Dr. Hastings preached that morning, Jesus came into my life not only as Savior but for daily strength and direction."

26. DON'T LET THEM GET AWAY
"I'm really worried," said one little boy to a friend. "Dad slaves away at his job so I'll never want for anything, so I'll be able to go to university if I want to. Mom works hard every day washing and ironing, cleaning up after me, taking care of me when I get sick. They spend every day of their lives working just on my behalf. I'm worried. . . ." His friend asked, "What have you got to worry about?" And he replied, "I'm afraid they might try to escape."

27. CAN FAMILY LIFE BE FUN?
A family in the East was planning a month's vacation to the West Coast. At the last minute the father's work responsibilities prevented him from going, but Mom insisted that she was capable of driving and that she and the kids would go ahead. Dad got out the maps and planned the route and where the family should stop each night. A couple of weeks later, the father completed his extra work responsibilities. He decided to surprise the family, so he flew to a West Coast city without calling them. Then he took a taxi out into the country on a highway that, according to his travel plan, the family should be driving on later that day. The taxi driver dropped him off on the side of the road. Dad waited there until he saw the family car coming, then stuck out his

thumb as a hitchhiker. As Mom and the kids drove past, they did a double take. One of the kids said, "Hey wasn't that Dad?" Mom screeched to a stop, backed up to the hitchhiker and the family had a joyful reunion. Later, when a newspaper reporter asked the man why he would do such a crazy thing, he responded, "After I die, I want my kids to be able to say, 'Dad sure was fun, wasn't he?'"

28. THE IMPORTANCE OF PRESENCE
The importance of parental presence as a support for children's achievements should not be underestimated. It is a clear sign that the parents care when they take the time to come to see their children perform, particularly when the children know that the parents are not there for their own pleasure or enjoyment. This awareness of parental presence is even true among preschool children although in a somewhat muted form. I remember visiting my middle son's nursery school class, at the request of his teacher, so that I could observe a "problem child" in the class.

It so happened that I was sitting and observing a group of boys, including my son, who sat in a circle nearby.

Their conversation went like this: Child A: "My daddy is a doctor and he makes a lot of money and we have a swimming pool." Child B: "My daddy is a lawyer and he flies to Washington and talks to the president. Child C: "My daddy owns a company and we have our own airplane."

Then my son (with aplomb, of course): "My daddy is here!" with a proud look in my direction. Children regard the public presence of their parents as a visible symbol of caring and connectedness that is far more significant than any material support could ever be. DAVID ELKIND

29. WHITEWASHING THE BLACK SHEEP
The children in a prominent family decided to give their father a book of the family's history for a birthday present. They commissioned a professional biographer to do the work, carefully warning him of the family's "black sheep" problem: Uncle George had been executed in the electric chair for murder. The biographer assured the children, "I can handle that situation so that there will be no embarrassment. I'll merely say that Uncle George occupied a chair of applied electronics at an important government institution. He was attached to his position by the strongest of ties and his death came as a real shock."

30. HOME OR HOUSE
A reporter came to a fire one day where a house was steadily burning down to the ground. He noticed that there was a little lad standing by with his

mom and dad. The reporter said, "Son, it looks like you don't have a home any more." The little boy answered courageously, "We have a home—we just don't have a house to put it in."

31. WHEN LIFE BEGINS
Martha Tippin of our church in Saratoga tells me she heard a Roman Catholic priest discussing the important theological topic of "When Does Life Begin?" on the radio. He pointed out that some feel it begins at the moment of conception, while others are convinced it starts when the baby takes the first breath. But, he pointed out, there is an increasing number who feel that life doesn't really begin until the last kid leaves home and the dog dies.

32. TEAMWORK IN FINANCES
The wife had been poring over the family's financial figures and finally said to her husband, "Well, I've worked out a budget—now you'll have to work out a raise!" GODDARD SHERMAN

33. RELATING TO ONE ANOTHER
Sixteen-year-old daughter: "Has anyone seen my new sweater?"
Her father: "You mean the one that cost thirty dollars?"
Her sister: "You mean the one you won't let me wear?"
Her brother: "You mean the stupid one that makes you look fat?"
Her grandma: "You mean the one with the low neckline?"
Her mother: "You mean the one that has to be washed by hand in cold water?"
Everyone was talking about the same sweater, but no one answered her question.

34. FAMILY ENCOURAGEMENT
Mary was having a tough day and had stretched herself out on the couch to do a bit of what she thought to be well-deserved complaining and self-pitying. She moaned to her mom and brother, "Nobody loves me . . . the whole world hates me!" Her brother, busily occupied playing a game, hardly looked up at her and passed on this encouraging word: "That's not true, Mary. Some people don't even know you." What a lift!

35. MOMMA AND COURTSHIP
One of my most fruitful sources of illustrative material on family life is the comic strip "Momma" by Mel Lazarus. Momma is always trying to straighten out her three grown children. One of the continuing themes is the proper courtship and marriage of her daughter, Mary Lou. One day Momma asks Mary Lou why she isn't married yet. Mary Lou responds: "Nobody's proposed, Momma, although I am very popular with the boys." Momma

retorts: "Well, whatever is making you popular with the boys—STOP IT until one of them proposes." In another strip Mary Lou is on the front porch saying good night to her boyfriend and he is whispering sweet nothings in her ear. Momma is trying to eavesdrop from the window but can't hear what's going on. When Mary Lou finally gets inside, Momma asks, "Mary Lou, what did he whisper to you?" Mary Lou answers "Ah, just 'love stuff,' Momma." Momma replies, "Decent 'love stuff' can be spoken freely, out loud. . . . Decent 'love stuff' can be shouted from rooftops." Finally, her voice reaches a crescendo: "DECENT 'LOVE STUFF' CAN BE EMBROIDERED ON SAMPLERS!"

36. A NOVEL PROGRAM FOR KIDS
The parent-teacher group was involved in a serious discussion about what the school's students could do after dismissal each day. Among the many suggestions made were: playgrounds, youth huts, bicycle trails, canteens and even a student center with a paid supervisor. Finally, a practical grandmother quietly said, "Couldn't they just go home?"

37. OBSERVATION ON MOBILITY
Nothing keeps a family together like having one car in the shop.

FIFTY-TWO
Fathers

1. THE AGONY OF FATHERHOOD
A young father-to-be was pacing back and forth, wringing his hands in the hospital corridor while his wife was in labor. He was tied up in knots of fear and anxiety, and beads of perspiration dropping from his brow revealed the agony of his suffering. Finally, at 4:00 A.M. a nurse popped out of a door and said, "Well, sir, you have a little girl." He dropped his hands, became limp, and said, "Oh, how I thank God it's a girl. She'll never have to go through the awful agony I've had tonight!"

2. THE IDEAL FATHER
The father of five children had won a toy at a raffle. He called his kids together to ask which one should have the present. "Who is the most obedient?" he asked. "Who never talks back to mother? Who does

everything she says?" Five small voices answered in unison. "You play with it, Daddy!"

3. DEFINITION OF A FATHER
A father is a man who carries photographs where his money used to be.

4. MY SON, MY SON
A fine Scottish Christian man, who was a successful businessman, had one son. He was proud of his boy for he was for all outward purposes a splendid, well-educated, and respected young fellow—until one day he was arrested for embezzlement. At the trial he was found guilty. And all through the trial, and even up through the rendering of the verdict, the young man appeared essentially unconcerned and proud and nonchalant. Certainly he was not humbled or broken by the experience thus far.

But then the verdict was brought in. The judge told the young man to stand for the sentence. He stood, still somewhat cocky and proud. And he glanced around the courtroom, only to notice that over at his attorney's table his father too was standing. His father had recognized that he was involved with the problem of what his boy had become.

He looked and saw his father—who once had walked and stood erect with head and shoulders straight, as those of an honest man with a clear conscience. And now those same shoulders were bowed low with sorrow and shame as he stood to receive, as though it were for himself, his son's sentence from the judge. At the sight of his father, bent and humiliated, the son finally began to weep bitterly and for the first time repented of his crime.

5. A WISH FOR CLOSENESS
A letter written during World War II by a father to his soldier son:
Dear Son,
I wish I had the power to write
The thoughts wedged in my heart tonight
As I sit watching that small star
And wondering where and how you are.
You know, Son, it's a funny thing
How close a war can really bring
A father, who for years with pride,
Has kept emotions deep inside.
I'm sorry, Son, when you were small
I let reserve build up that wall;
I told you real men never cried,
And it was Mom who always dried

Your tears and smoothed your hurts away
So that you soon went back to play.
But, Son, deep down within my heart
I longed to have some little part
In drying that small tear-stained face,
But we were men—men don't embrace.
And suddenly I found my son
A full-grown man, with childhood done.
Tonight you're far across the sea,
Fighting a way for men like me.
Well, somehow pride and what is right
Have changed places here tonight
I find my eyes won't stay quite dry
And that men sometimes really cry.
And if we stood here, face to face,
I'm sure, my Son, we would embrace.

6. YOUR FATHER KNOWS THE WAY

When I was a small boy growing up in Pennsylvania we would often visit my grandparents who lived nine miles away. One night a thick fog settled over the hilly countryside before we started home. I remember being terrified, and asking if we shouldn't be going even slower than we were. Mother said gently, "Don't worry. Your father knows the way."

You see, Dad had walked that road when there was no gasoline during the war. He had ridden that blacktop on his bicycle to court Mother. And for years he had made those weekly trips back to visit his own parents.

How often when I can't see the road of life, and have felt that familiar panic rising in my heart I have heard the echo of my mother's voice: "Don't worry. Your Father knows the way."

7. A FATHER'S LOVE

On a cold winter evening a man suffered a heart attack and after being admitted to the hospital, asked the nurse to call his daughter. He explained, "You see, I live alone and she is the only family I have." The nurse went to phone the daughter. The daughter was quite upset and shouted, "You must not let him die! You see, Dad and I had a terrible argument almost a year ago. I haven't seen him since. All these months I've wanted to go to him for forgiveness. The last thing I said to him was 'I hate you.'" The daughter cried and then said, "I'm coming now. I'll be there in thirty minutes."

The patient went into cardiac arrest, and code 99 was alerted. The nurse prayed, "O God, his daughter is coming. Don't let it end this way." The efforts of the medical team to revive the patient were fruitless. The nurse observed one of the doctors talking to the daughter outside the room. She could see the pathetic hurt in her face. The nurse took the daughter aside and said, "I'm sorry." The daughter responded, "I never hated him, you know. I loved him, And now I want to go see him." The nurse took her to the room, and the daughter went to the bed and buried her face in the sheets as she said good-bye to her deceased father. The nurse, as she tried not to look at this sad good-bye, noticed a scrap of paper on the bed table. She picked it up and read: "My dearest Janie, I forgive you. I pray you will also forgive me. I know that you love me. I love you, too. Daddy."

8. FATHER'S ROLE
The most important thing a father can do for his children is to love their mother. THEODORE HESBURGH

9. PARENTAL PERSPECTIVE
It is said of Boswell, the famous biographer of Samuel Johnson, that he often referred to a special day in his childhood when his father took him fishing. The day was fixed in his adult mind, and he often reflected upon many of the things his father had taught him in the course of their fishing experience together. After having heard of that particular excursion so often, it occurred to someone much later to check the journal that Boswell's father kept and determine what had been said about the fishing trip from the parental perspective. Turning to that date, the reader found only one sentence entered: "Gone fishing today with my son; a day wasted."

10. RIGHT BEHIND FATHER
A man and his young son were climbing a mountain. They came to a place where the climbing was difficult and even dangerous. The father stopped to consider which way he should go. He heard the boy behind him say, "Choose the good path, Dad; I'm coming right behind you!" *Author unknown*

11. LUTHER THE TENDER FATHER
Martin Luther was a good father, knowing as if by instinct the right mixture of discipline and love. "Punish if you must, but let the sugar-plum go with the rod." He composed songs for his children, and sang these songs with them while he played the lute. His letters to his children are among the jewels of German literature. His sturdy spirit, which could face an emperor in war, was almost broken by the death of his favorite daughter Magdalena at the age of fourteen. "God," he said, "has given no bishop so great a gift in a thousand years as He has given me in her." He prayed night and day for her recovery. "I love her very much, but, dear God, if it is Thy holy will to take

her, I would gladly leave her with Thee." And he said to her: "Lena dear, my little daughter, thou wouldst love to remain here with thy father; art thou willing to go to that other Father?" "Yes, dear Father," Lena answered, "just as God wills." When she died he wept long and bitterly. As she was laid in the earth he spoke to her as to a living soul: "Du liebes Lenichen, you will rise and shine like the stars and the sun. How strange it is to know that she is at peace and all is well, and yet be so sorrowful!"

12. COLLECT CALLS
Illinois Bell reported not long ago that the volume of long-distance calls made on Father's Day was growing faster than the number on Mother's Day. The company apologized for the delay in compiling the statistics, but explained that the extra billing of calls to fathers slowed things down. Most of them were collect.

13. JUSTICE AND LOVE
At dinner one evening Tommy misbehaved. His father, always a strict disciplinarian, reprimanded him saying, "Tommy, if you do not behave you will be sent to your room!" Tommy did not listen. Ordered from the room, he heard his father's last words: "And there will be no more food for you tonight!"

Later, in bed, Tommy's thoughts of his behavior began to bother him. He was hungry. He couldn't remember ever having felt more alone or alienated. He began to cry. Then he heard a noise on the stairs. Footsteps came closer to his room. His door opened and his father came in. Closing the door he came over to Tommy's bed and said, "I love you, Son, and I've come to spend the night with you."

14. THE QUAKER FATHER
A Quaker family lived in Pennsylvania. Against the father's wishes, the son Jonathan ran off and enlisted in the cause of the North during the Civil War.

Time passed and no word from Jonathan. One night the father had a dream that his son had been wounded in action, was in distress, and needed the care of a father.

So the father left the farm, and discovered where the troops might be. He made his way by horse-drawn buggy until he came to the scene of action. He inquired until he found the commander and asked about his son. The commander replied that there had been heavy action earlier in the day and many had fallen wounded. Some had been cared for, but others were still left out in the trenches. But he gave permission to the father to go and try to find his son. He told him where the action had taken place.

It was now about dark, so the father lit a lantern, and the light fell across wounded young men, some calling for help, many too seriously wounded to cry for assistance.

The task seem impossible. How could he find his son among all those wounded and dying?

He devised a little plan, methodically he would comb the scene of action with his lantern. But that wasn't fruitful. As he stumbled over body after body he almost despaired.

Then he began calling loudly, "Jonathan Smythe, thy father seeketh after thee." Then he would walk a little ways and call again, "Jonathan Smythe, thy father seeketh after thee."

A groan could be heard here and there. "I wish that were my father."

He kept diligently at his search. Then he heard a very faint, barely audible reply, "Father, over here." And then, "I knew you would come."

The father knelt down and took him in his arms, comforting him with his presence. He dressed the wound, carried him to the buggy, took him to a place of seclusion and nursed him back to health.

FIFTY-THREE

Fear

1. SUMMER SCENE
When little Jimmy returned home from summer camp, his parents asked him if he had been homesick. He replied, "Not me, but some of the kids were who had dogs."

2. CAUTIOUS INVESTMENT
One day in July, a farmer sat in front of his shack, smoking his corncob pipe. Along came a stranger who asked, "How's your cotton coming?"

"Ain't got none," was the answer. "Didn't plant none. 'Fraid of the boll weevil."

"Well, how's your corn?"

"Didn't plant none. 'Fraid o' drouth."

"How about your potatoes?"

"Ain't got none. Scairt o' tater bugs."

The stranger finally asked, "Well, what did you plant?"

"Nothin'," answered the farmer. "I just played it safe."

3. TIGERS IN THE DARK

Several years ago there was a well-known television circus show that developed a Bengal tiger act. Like the rest of the show, it was done "live" before a large audience. One evening, the tiger trainer went into the cage with several tigers to do a routine performance. The door was locked behind him. The spotlights highlighted the cage, the television cameras moved in close, and the audience watched in suspense as the trainer skillfully put the tigers through their paces. In the middle of the performance, the worst possible fate befell the act: the lights went out! For twenty or thirty long, dark seconds the trainer was locked in with the tigers. In the darkness they could see him, but he could not see them. A whip and a small kitchen chair seemed meager protection under the circumstances, but he survived, and when the lights came on, he calmly finished the performance. In an interview afterward, he was asked how he felt knowing that the tigers could see him but that he could not see them. He first admitted the chilling fear of the situation, but pointed out that the tigers did not know that he could not see them. He said, "I just kept cracking my whip and talking to them until the lights came on. And they never knew I could not see them as well as they could see me."

This experience gives us a vivid parable of human life. At some point in our lives, all of us face the terrifying task of fighting tigers in the dark. Some face it constantly. Many people cope daily with internal problems that are capable of destroying them. They cannot visualize their problems or understand them, but their problems seem to have them zeroed in.

THOMAS LANE BUTTS, *Tigers in the Dark*

4. ANTICIPATING THE WORST

When you fear that the worst will happen, your own thoughts may help to bring it about. Someone once wrote, "Fear is the wrong use of imagination. It is anticipating the worst, not the best that can happen." A salesman, driving on a lonely country road one dark and rainy night, had a flat. He opened the trunk—no lug wrench. The light from a farmhouse could be seen dimly up the road. He set out on foot through the driving rain. Surely the farmer would have a lug wrench he could borrow, he thought. Of course, it was late at night—the farmer would be asleep in his warm, dry bed. Maybe he wouldn't answer the door. And even if he did, he'd be angry at being awakened in the middle of the night. The salesman, picking his way blindly in the dark, stumbled on. By now his shoes and clothing were soaked. Even if the farmer did answer his knock, he would probably shout something like, "What's the big idea waking me up at this hour?" This thought made the salesman angry. What right did that farmer have to refuse him the loan of a lug wrench? After all, here he was stranded in the middle of nowhere, soaked to the skin. The farmer was a selfish clod—no doubt about that! The salesman finally reached the house and banged loudly on the door. A light went on inside, and a window opened above. A voice called out, "Who is it?" His face white with anger, the salesman called out, "You know darn well who it is. It's me! And you can keep your blasted lug wrench. I wouldn't borrow it now if you had the last one on earth!"

FINANCES *(See Money, Stewardship)*

FIFTY-FOUR

Flattery
(See also Talk)

1. THE CERTAIN CURE
Flattery is the best cure for deafness. PAUL ELDRIDGE

2. FINDING OUT THE TRUTH
Rule number two in public speaking: After a flattering introduction, never tell the audience you don't deserve it. They'll find out soon enough.

3. FLATTERY OF A TYRANT
In ancient Greece, the politically crafty philosopher Aristippus had learned to get along in court by flattering the tyrant Denys. Aristippus looked down his nose at some of his less prosperous fellow philosophers and wise men who would not stoop that low. One day he saw his colleague Diogenes washing some vegetables and he said to him disdainfully: "If you would only learn to flatter King Denys you would not have to be washing lentils."

Diogenes looked up slowly and in the same tone replied, "And you, if you had only learned to live on lentils, would not have to flatter King Denys."

4. TRUTH HIDDEN BY FLATTERY
We hate the hypocrite more keenly than the mere liar because the hypocrite adds to his lie the lacquer of flattery, which we are gullible enough to accept as tribute to our merit. PAUL ELDRIDGE

5. NOT TO BE CONSUMED
Flattery is like chewing gum—enjoy it briefly, but don't swallow it!

6. THE HEART OF FLATTERY
Flatterer: One who extremely exaggerates in his opinion of your qualities, so that it may come nearer to your opinion of them. OSCAR WILDE

FIFTY-FIVE

Flexibility

1. GOING WITH THE FLOW
The winds and waves are always on the side of the ablest navigators. EDWARD GIBBON

2. BOOKER T.'S FLEXIBILITY
Booker T. Washington arrived in a city to make a speech. His train was late and he was in a hurry. He dashed out of the station to the cabstand, but the cabby growled, "I don't drive niggers." Washington said, "All right, I'll drive you. Get in the back."

3. FLEXIBLE PLAN
A man stopped to chat with a farmer who was erecting a new building. He asked, "What are you putting up?" The farmer replied, "Well, if I can rent it, it's a rustic cottage. If I can't, it's a cow shed."

4. MR. VANDERBILT AND MR. GOULD
Cornelius Vanderbilt, who controlled the New York Central, regarded Jay Gould, who headed the lesser Erie Railroad, as an upstart. At one time, he made an attempt to force Gould out of the railroad business. This was during the period when cattle from the West were shipped to Buffalo, then reshipped over one of these two lines to New York city. The prevailing rate for a carload was $100. Vanderbilt cut the price to $75. As anticipated, Gould reduced it to $50. Vanderbilt went to $25. Gould made it $10.

Determined to prevail, Vanderbilt slashed the price to $1 a carload. That was enough for Gould. He refused to meet this last price, and the business went to the New York Central. Although it had been expensive, Vanderbilt felt that it had been worth it to bring Gould to his knees.

But his triumph was short-lived. After a few weeks had passed, he learned that Gould had bought all the cattle coming into Buffalo and had shipped them to New York City via the Central at $1 a carload, cleaning up a fortune at Vanderbilt's expense. The price went back to $100.

5. ADJUSTING YOUR GOALS TO REALITY

One bitterly cold winter night a young man plodded through knee-high snow to the home of the girl he had been dating regularly. Tonight was the night. He asked her to marry him. Being very practical, the young woman replied, "When you have several thousand dollars, I will seriously consider it."

Six months later, the two strolled hand in hand through a park along the river. He stopped to kiss her and asked, "When are we going to get married?"

She inquired, "Well, you remember my condition. Just how much money have you saved?"

He responded, "Exactly seventy-five dollars.

She sighed and smiled, "Oh well, I guess that's close enough!"

6. PLAN B

I have a very fine doctor. If you can't afford the operation, he touches up the X rays. HENNY YOUNGMAN

7. ALTERING TO FIT THE SURE REALITIES

There was an officer in the navy who had always dreamed of commanding a battleship. He finally achieved that dream and was given commission of the newest and proudest ship in the fleet. One stormy night, as the ship plowed through the seas, the captain was on duty on the bridge when off to the port he spotted a strange light rapidly closing with his own vessel. Immediately he ordered the signalman to flash the message to the unidentified craft, "Alter your course ten degrees to the south." Only a moment had passed before the reply came: "Alter your course ten degrees to the north." Determined that *his* ship would take a backseat to no other, the captain snapped out the order to be sent: "Alter course ten degrees—I am the CAPTAIN!" The response beamed back, "Alter your course ten degrees—I am Seaman Third Class Jones." Now infuriated, the captain grabbed the signal light with his own hands and fired off: "Alter course, I am a battleship." The reply came back. "Alter your course, I am a lighthouse."

No matter how big or important any of us think we are, God's Word stands forth as an unchanging beacon. All other courses must be altered to His.

8. THE CULTURALLY POLITE FACADE

A wonderful Chinese meal was set out for us on a small table under the trees. The food was covered by big blue flies, which the Chinese kept swatting away. Finally we sat down in Chinese fashion, with the wife of the host serving us. We were just three missionaries with the Chinese host, who was the only man. By this time we were well used to chopsticks, rice, sweet and sour pork, and fish. At this table there was a huge codfish complete with head and big eyes.

We were able to enjoy the conversation. For some unknown reason, I happened to be seated next to the host. Suddenly he used his own chopsticks to place in my bowl of rice the greatest delicacy of the feast; namely, one of that cod's huge eyes! He smiled, thinking how honored I would feel. Honored! Looking longingly at the chickens feeding underneath the table, I smiled at my host and I looked at Miss McQueen and knew what I had to do. I thanked God I possessed a large throat—one swallow and it was over. Never again did I have such a "treat," for this delicacy belonged to that region only! A true missionary always eats what is put before her like the Chinese; she is supposed to "become Chinese." God helped me to keep down that ugly cod's eye. WETHERELL JOHNSON, *Created for Commitment*

FIFTY-SIX

Folly

1. ALWAYS READ THE INSTRUCTIONS

A man was at a banquet listening to an well-known and much-admired political leader making a speech. He was seated next to the speaker's wife. He had noticed that the speaker was immaculately attired—he even had fancy monograms on his socks. But when he looked a little closer he saw that the monogram was not your usual two or three letters—but rather four letters. And they didn't seem to have any relationship to his initials. Rather, on closer inspection he noticed that the monogram was TGIF. Puzzled by these familiar initials being on the man's socks he turned to the politician's wife and asked why he had TGIF on his socks, which everyone knew meant "Thank Goodness It's Friday." She nodded her head negatively and said, "Oh no, that's not what the letters are for. The monograms are there to help him get dressed. They stand for 'Toes Go In First!'"

2. PRIORITIES

A cartoon in "The Wizard of Id" showed a poor bedraggled peasant coming up behind Rodney, the foot soldier, pointing his finger in his back and saying, "This is a stick-up! Hand over your money!" Rodney turns around with his hands up and then notices the crook is just using his finger and comments, "You don't even have a weapon!" The thief agrees and says: "It's the first thing I'm going to buy!"

3. APPROPRIATE FEAR

I'm scared! I don't know whether the world is full of smart men bluffing or imbeciles who mean it. MORRIE BRICKMAN

4. THE DULL OF UNDERSTANDING

A certain man was troubled with dizzy spells. He went from one doctor to another and none could tell him what the problem was. He tried everything, it seemed. Finally, it was bothering him so much he started to lose weight, and he couldn't sleep at night. He became a nervous wreck and his health began to deteriorate. He had lost hope that he would ever recover. So he decided to prepare for the worst. He made out his will, bought a cemetery plot, and even made arrangements with the local undertaker for what he was convinced was his soon demise. He even decided to buy a new suit of clothes to be buried in. When he went into the haberdasher's he was measured for everything and picked out shoes, socks, coat, pants—and he asked for a size 15 shirt as well. The clerk said, "But, sir, you need a size 16½ shirt, not 15." But the man insisted we wore a size 15. Finally, in exasperation the clerk said, "But if you wear a size 15 you'll get dizzy spells."

5. SHAME OR PLEASURE

When I was a child of seven years old, my friends, on a holiday, filled my pockets with coppers. I went directly to a shop where they sold toys for children, and, being charmed with the sound of a whistle that I met by the way in the hands of another boy, I voluntarily offered and gave all my money for one. I then came home and went whistling all over the house, much pleased with my whistle, but disturbing all the family. My brothers and sisters and cousins, understanding the bargain I had made, told me I had given four times as much for it as it was worth; put me in mind of what good things I might have bought with the rest of the money; and laughed at me so much for my folly that I cried with vexation; and the reflection gave me more chagrin than the whistle gave me pleasure. BENJAMIN FRANKLIN

6. PREPARING FOR A NEW VOCATION
A man became disenchanted with the city life he was living. He decided to move to the country and start a chicken farm. He bought a farmhouse with some land around it and, after he had moved in, he bought 200 baby chicks. But they all quickly died. He bought 200 more baby chicks but, again, they all died a short time later. Puzzled and distressed, the man wrote to the county agricultural agent and described everything that had happened. He concluded his letter, "I want very much to be a successful chicken farmer. Therefore, can you tell me: Have I been planting the chicks too close together or too deep?" Whereupon the county agent wrote back and said, "I can't answer your question until you send me a soil sample."

7. THE GAMBLER'S ILLUSION
A gambling nut bet on twelve football games over the weekend and lost on all of them. The next weekend he bet on twelve more football games and lost again. The following week he called his bookie, who told him there were no football games scheduled. However, the bookie explained he could have his pick of either team in eight hockey games. The big plunger sneered, "Hockey? What the blazes do I know about hockey?"

8. SHORTSIGHTED SWINE
A pig ate his fill of acorns under an oak tree and then started to root around the tree. A crow remarked, "You should not do this. If you lay bare the roots, the tree will wither and die." "Let it die," said the pig. "Who cares as long as there are acorns?"

9. THE RIGHT TO BE STUPID
Everyone has a constitutional right to be a jackass as long as he knows when the statute of limitations run out.

10. THE SIN OF GOVERNMENT WASTE
Senator William Proxmire reported to the Senate that the Department of Transportation had squandered $225,000 on a study forecasting transportation needs in the year 2025. Proxmire pointed out that this study took the entire federal tax payments of more than 120 of his Wisconsin constituents. And for what? To produce findings like these: (1) If there is a new Ice Age, a lot of people will have to move to the South or Southwest; (2) if people start having a lot of kids again, there will be increased demand for transportation services for them; (3) it will be risky using automobiles in regions where urban guerilla warfare breaks out.

11. I DON'T BELONG HERE

A preacher was addressing the people one Sunday, trying to impress upon them the importance of religion. "All you people of this congregation," he cried from the pulpit, "One day you're going to die. Do you hear me? All you people of this congregation, one day you're going to die." One little man sitting in the front pew started to laugh, so the preacher asked him, "What's so funny?" The man answered: "I don't belong to this congregation."

12. DEAD, YET NOT REALLY

After he was defeated for the Presidency, Thomas E. Dewey said the best analogy of his feelings the day after—when he saw defeat snatched from the jaws of victory—was of the mourner who had passed out from too much drinking at a wake and was laid in a spare coffin in the funeral parlor to sleep it off. When he came to and realized where he was lying, he asked himself, "If I'm alive, why am I in this coffin? And if I'm dead, why do I have to go to the bathroom?"

FIFTY-SEVEN

Forgiveness
(See also Mercy)

1. LIMITED FORGIVENESS

A pastor's son and his mom had been to a shopping mall and the boy had acted badly, wanting this and that, running off, etc. As they were driving home, he could sense her displeasure and said, "When we ask God to forgive us when we are bad, He does, doesn't He?" His mother replied, "Yes, He does." The boy continued, "And when he forgives us, He buries our sins in the deepest sea, doesn't He?" The mom replied, "Yes, that's what the Bible says." The boy was silent for awhile and then said, "I've asked God to forgive me, but I bet when we get home, you're going to go fishing for those sins, aren't you?"

Too often, we do "go fishing" for other people's sins that God has already buried.

2. OUR ONENESS IN CHRIST

I was speaking at the Indiana State Prison. Only weeks earlier, Stephen Judy had been electrocuted there. An execution always creates a special tension in a prison, and I could sense it that day. It was in the air, in the voices of the guards, in the faces of the men.

After my talk, the warden walked us through the maze of cell blocks to that most dreaded of places—an isolated wing where five men awaited their final decree and death. Nancy Honeytree, the talented young gospel singer who is part of our team, was with me; several of our volunteers came along as well. Finally, we were ushered through two massive steel gates into the secure area. The inmates were allowed out of their cells, and we joined in a circle in the walkway while Nancy strummed the guitar and sang. It was a beautiful moment for those condemned men—and for us—as we closed by singing together "Amazing Grace."

Two of the men, I knew from their correspondence with me, were believers. One of them, James Brewer, had the most radiant expression during our visit, and he sang at the top of his lungs.

As we were shaking hands and saying good-bye, I noticed that Brewer walked back into his cell with one of our volunteers. The others began filing out, but this volunteer remained in Brewer's cell; the two were standing shoulder to shoulder, together reading the Bible. I was expected in two hours in Indianapolis for a meeting with the governor, so I walked back into the cell. "We've got to go," I called out, beckoning to our volunteer.

"Just a minute, please," he replied. I shook my head and repeated, "Sorry, time's up, the plane is waiting."

"Please, please, this is very important," the volunteer replied. "You see, I am Judge Clement. I sentenced this man to die. But now he is born again. He is my brother and we want a minute to pray together."

I stood in the entrance to that solitary, dimly lit cell, frozen in place. Here were two men—one black, one white; one powerful, one powerless; one who had sentenced the other to die. Yet there they stood grasping a Bible together, Brewer smiling so genuinely, the judge so filled with love for the prisoner at his side.

Impossible in human terms! Brewer should despise this man, I thought. Only in Christ could this happen. The sight of those men standing together as brothers in that dingy cell will remain vivid in my mind forever.

3. THE SCANDAL OF THE CROSS

On the evening of April 25, 1958, a young Korean exchange student, a leader in student Christian affairs in the University of Pennsylvania, left his flat and went to the corner to post a letter to his parents in Pusan. Turning from the mailbox he stepped into the path of eleven leather-jacketed teenage boys. Without a word they attacked him, beating him with a blackjack, a lead pipe and with their shoes and fists. Later, when the police found him in the gutter, he was dead. All Philadelphia cried out for vengeance. The district attorney secured legal authority to try the boys as adults so that those found guilty could be given the death penalty. Then a letter arrived from Korea that made everyone stop and think. It was signed by the parents and by twenty other relatives of the murdered boy. It read in part:

"Our family has met together and we have decided to petition that the most generous treatment possible within the laws of your government be given to those who have committed this criminal action. . . . In order to give evidence of our sincere hope contained in this petition, we have decided to save money to start a fund to be used for the religious, educational, vocational, and social guidance of the boys when they are released. . . . We have dared to express our hope with a spirit received from the gospel of our Savior Jesus Christ who died for our sins." A. LEONARD GRIFFITH, *Beneath the Cross of Jesus*

4. TIME FOR FORGIVENESS
Some years ago, after a vigorous brotherly and sisterly disagreement, our three children retired only to be aroused at two o'clock in the morning by a terrific thunderstorm. Hearing an unusual noise upstairs I called in to find out what was going on. A little voice answered, "We are all in the closet forgiving each other." ROBERT C. TUTTLE

5. FORGIVING AND FORGETTING
Several years ago, Coach Joe Paterno and his Penn State football team were playing for the national championship against Alabama in the Sugar Bowl. They probably would have won, but they had a touchdown called back because there was a twelfth man on the field. After the game, Paterno was asked to identify the player. "It's only a game," he said. "I have no intention of ever identifying the boy. He just made a mistake."

6. LIMITED FORGIVENESS
I was assisting another pastor in a revival meeting when we visited a man who had been active in the church, but, due to a dispute with a fellow member, he had quit attending church. We reasoned with him at length about the need for forgiveness and returning to church. Reluctantly, he agreed, and we had prayer together. When we were leaving, he followed us to the car and said, "Now, I'll forgive him, but all I want is for him to stay on his side of the road, and I'll stay on mine." M. B. WEBB

7. THE COORS TRIUMPH

On February 9, 1960, Adolph Coors III was kidnapped and held for ransom. Seven months later his body was found on a remote hillside. He had been shot to death. Adolph Coors IV, then fifteen years old, lost not only his father but his best friend. For years young Coors hated Joseph Corbett, the man who was sentenced to life for the slaying.

Then in 1975 Ad Coors became a Christian. While he divested himself of his interest in the family beer business, he could not divest himself of the hatred that consumed him. Resentment seethed within him and blighted his growth in faith. He prayed to God for help because he realized how his hatred for Corbett was alienating him from God and other persons. The day came, however, when claiming the Spirit's presence, Ad Coors visited the maximum security unit of Colorado's Canon City penitentiary and tried to talk with Corbett. Corbett refused to see him. Coors left a Bible inscribed with this message: "I'm here to see you today and I'm sorry that we could not meet. As a Christian I am summoned by our Lord and Savior, Jesus Christ, to forgive. I do forgive you, and I ask you to forgive me for the hatred I've held in my heart for you." Later Coors confessed, "I have a love for that man that only Jesus Christ could have put in my heart."

8. THE CRUCIAL WORD

Dwight Moody's father died when Dwight was only four. A month later Mrs. Moody gave birth to twins; she now had nine mouths to feed and no income. Merciless creditors dogged the widow, claiming everything they could get their hands on.

As if Mrs. Moody didn't have enough troubles, her eldest boy later ran away from home. Certain that her son would return, Mrs. Moody placed a light for him in the window each night. Young Dwight was inspired by her faith and prayers. He wrote: "I can remember how eagerly she used to look for tidings of that boy; how she used to send us to the post office to see if there was a letter from him . . . some night when the wind was very high, and the house would tremble at every gust, the voice of my mother was raised in prayer for that wanderer."

Her prayers were answered. Her prodigal son did eventually return. Dwight remembered: "While my mother was sitting at the door, a stranger was seen coming toward the house, and when he came to the door he stopped. My mother didn't know her boy. He stood there with folded arms and a great beard flowing down his breast, his tears trickling down his face. When my mother saw those tears she cried, 'Oh, it's my lost son!' and entreated him to come in. But he stood still! 'No mother,' he answered, 'I will not come in until I hear first that you have forgiven me.'"

Mrs. Moody was only too willing to forgive. She rushed to the door, threw her arms around him, and there the prodigal found forgiveness.

9. FORGIVENESS AND FORGOTTENNESS
Bruce Larson tells the true story of a Catholic priest living in the Philippines, a much-loved man of God who once carried a secret burden of long-past sin buried deep in his heart. He had committed that sin once, many years before, during his time in seminary. No one else knew of this sin. He had repented of it and he had suffered years of remorse for it, but he still had no peace, no inner joy, no sense of God's forgiveness.

There was a woman in this priest's parish who deeply loved God, and who claimed to have visions in which she spoke with Christ, and He with her. The priest, however, was skeptical of her claims, so to test her visions he said to her, "You say you actually speak directly with Christ in your visions. Let me ask you a favor. The next time you have one of these visions, I want you to ask Him what sin your priest committed while he was in seminary."

The woman agreed and went home. When she returned to the church a few days later, the priest said, "Well, did Christ visit you in your dreams?"

She replied, "Yes, He did."

"And did you ask Him what sin I committed in seminary?"

"Yes, I asked Him."

"Well, what did He say?"

"He said, 'I don't remember.'"

This is what God wants you to know about the forgiveness He freely offers you. When your sins are forgiven, they are forgotten. The past—with its sins, hurts brokenness, and self-recrimination—is gone, dead, crucified, remembered no more. What God forgives, He forgets.

10. CONDITIONAL FORGIVENESS
A man lay on his deathbed, harassed by fear because he had harbored hatred against another. He sent for the individual with whom he had had a disagreement years before; he then made overtures of peace. The two of them shook hands in friendship. But as the visitor left the room, the sick man roused himself and said, "Remember, if I get over this, the old quarrel stands." G. RAY JORDAN

11. CONSCIOUS ACT OF FORGETTING
Clara Barton was never known to hold resentment against anyone. One time a friend recalled to her a cruel thing that had happened to her some years previously, but Clara seemed not to remember the incident. "Don't you

remember the wrong that was done you?" the friend asked Clara. She answered calmly, "No, I distinctly remember forgetting that."

12. FORGIVEN AND GONE

Corrie ten Boom, in her book *Tramp for the Lord* had these words to say regarding forgiveness:

"It was 1947. . . . I had come from Holland to defeated Germany with the message that God forgives. It was the truth they needed most to hear in that bitter, bombed-out land, and I gave them my favorite mental picture. Maybe because the sea is never far from a Hollander's mind, I like to think that that's where forgiven sins are thrown. 'When we confess our sins,' I said, 'God casts them into the deepest ocean, gone forever. . . . Then God places a sign out there that says No Fishing Allowed!'"

13. THE DEEP NEED TO FORGIVE

When Leonardo da Vinci was painting "The Last Supper," he became angry with a man and lashed out at him. He even threatened him. Then he went back to his fresco and tried to paint the face of Jesus. He couldn't for there was too much evil stirring inside him. The lack of peace forced him to put down his brushes, go find the man, and ask his forgiveness. Only then did he have the inner calm needed to do the face of his Master.

14. ACTIVE FORGIVENESS

A small boy at a summer camp received a large package of cookies in the mail from his mother. He ate a few, then placed the remainder under his bed. The next day, after lunch, he went to his tent to get a cookie. The box was gone.

That afternoon a camp counselor, who had been told of the theft, saw another boy sitting behind a tree eating the stolen cookies. He said to himself, "That young man must be taught not to steal."

He returned to the group and sought out the boy whose cookies had been stolen. He said, "Billy, I know who stole your cookies. Will you help me teach him a lesson?" The puzzled boy replied, "Well, yes—but aren't you going to punish him?"

The counselor explained, "No, that would only make him resent and hate you. No, I want you to call your mother and ask her to send you another box of cookies."

The boy did as the counselor asked and a few days later received another box of cookies in the mail.

The counselor said, "Now, the boy who stole your cookies is down by the lake. Go down there and share your cookies with him."

The boy protested, "But he's the thief."

"I know. But try it—see what happens."

Half an hour later the camp counselor saw the two come up the hill, arm and arm. The boy who had stolen the cookies was earnestly trying to get the other to accept his jackknife in payment for the stolen cookies, and the victim was just as earnestly refusing the gift from his new friend, saying that a few old cookies weren't that important anyway.

15. THE GREAT HUNGER FOR FORGIVENESS

The story is told in Spain of a father and his teenage son who had a relationship that had become strained. So the son ran away from home. His father, however, began a journey in search of his rebellious son. Finally, in Madrid, in a last desperate effort to find him, the father put an ad in the newspaper. The ad read: "Dear Paco, meet me in front of the newspaper office at noon. All is forgiven. I love you. Your father."

The next day at noon in front of the newspaper office 800 "Pacos" showed up. They were all seeking forgiveness and love from their fathers.

16. A GLORIOUS MIXTURE

Years after her concentration camp experiences in Nazi Germany, Corrie ten Boom met face to face one of the most cruel and heartless German guards that she had ever contacted. He had humiliated and degraded her and her sister. He had jeered and visually raped them as they stood in the delousing shower. Now he stood before her with hand outstretched and said, "Will you forgive me?" She writes: "I stood there with coldness clutching at my heart, but I know that the will can function regardless of the temperature of the heart. I prayed, Jesus, help me! Woodenly, mechanically I thrust my hand into the one stretched out to me and I experienced an incredible thing. The current started in my shoulder, raced down into my arms and sprang into our clutched hands. Then this warm reconciliation seemed to flood my whole being, bringing tears to my eyes. 'I forgive you, brother,' I cried with my whole heart. For a long moment we grasped each other's hands, the former guard, the former prisoner. I have never known the love of God so intensely as I did in that moment!" To forgive is to set a prisoner free and discover the prisoner was you.

17. GOD'S ACHIEVEMENT

Forgiveness is man's deepest need and God's highest achievement.
HORACE BUSHNELL

18. YOU CAN'T BUY FORGIVENESS

A little boy came to the Washington Monument and noticed a guard standing by it. The little boy looked up at the guard and said, "I want to buy it." The guard stooped down and says, "How much do you have?" The boy reached into his pocket and pulled out a quarter. The guard said, "That's not enough." The boy replied, "I thought you would say that." So he pulled out nine cents more. The guard looked down at the boy and said, "You need to understand three things. First, thirty-four cents is not enough. In fact, $34 million is not enough to buy the Washington Monument. Second, the Washington Monument is not for sale. And third, if you are an American citizen, the Washington Monument already belongs to you."

We need to understand three things about forgiveness. First, we can not earn it. Second, it is not for sale. And third, if we accept Christ, we already have it.

19. LOVE AND THE ENEMY

We found ourselves on the same track with several carloads of Japanese wounded after we were freed from the Kwai prison camp. These unfortunates were on their own without medical care. No longer fit for action in Burma, they had been packed into railway cars which were being returned to Bangkok.

They were in a shocking state. I have never seen men filthier. Uniforms were encrusted with mud, blood, and excrement. Their wounds, sorely inflamed and full of pus, crawled with maggots. The maggots, however, in eating the putrefying flesh, probably prevented gangrene.

It was apparent why the Japanese were so cruel to their prisoners. If they didn't care for their own, why should they care for us?

The wounded looked at us forlornly as they sat with their heads resting against the carriages, waiting for death. They had been discarded as expendable, the refuse of war. These were the enemy. They were more cowed and defeated that we had ever been.

Without a word most of the officers in my section unbuckled their packs, took out part of their ration and a rag or two, and, with water canteens in their hands, went over to the Japanese train.

Our guards tried to prevent us, bawling, "No goodka! No goodka!" But we ignored them and knelt down by the enemy to give water and food, to clean and bind up their wounds. Grateful cries of "Aragatto!" ("Thank you") followed us when we left. . . .

I regarded my comrades with wonder. Eighteen months ago they would have joined readily in the destruction of our captors had they fallen into their hands. Now these same officers were dressing the enemy's wounds.

We had experienced a moment of grace, there in those bloodstained railway cars. God had broken through the barriers of our prejudice and had given us the will to obey His command, "Thou shalt love." ERNEST GORDON, *Through the Valley of the Kwai*

20. FORGIVENESS IS FREEDOM

My six-year-old son used one of those super adhesive glues on an airplane he was building. In less than three minutes, his right index finger was bonded to a shiny blue wing of his DC-10. He tried to free it. He tugged it, pulled it, waved it frantically; but he couldn't budge his finger free. Soon, we located a solvent that did the job and ended our little crisis.

Last night I remembered that scene when I visited a new family in our neighborhood. The father of the family introduced his children:

"This is Pete. He's the clumsy one of the lot."

"That's Kathy coming in with mud on her shoes. She's the sloppy one."

"As always, Mike's last. He'll be late for his own funeral, I promise you."

The dad did a thorough job of gluing his children to their faults and mistakes.

People do it to us and to those we love all the time. They remind us of our failures, our errors, our sins, and they won't let us live them down. Like my son trying frantically to free his finger from the plane, there are people who try, sometimes desperately, to free themselves from their past. They would love a chance to begin again.

When we don't let people forget their past, when we don't forgive, we glue them to their mistakes and refuse to see them as more than something they have done. However, when we forgive, we gently pry the doer of the hurtful deed from the deed itself, and we say that the past is just that—past—over and done with.

God does what we are unable to do or what those around us don't want to do or are unable to do for us. When we accept his forgiveness, he separates us from our sins. "As far as the east is from the west," the psalmist says, which means as far as you can imagine, that offense will be wiped away, blotted out.

The good news—the very good news—of the gospel is that we don't have to remain in bondage, glued to our sins. The healing power of God is ours for the asking, promising freedom and the loving embrace of a Father who forgets our past and clothes us for a new life.

21. THE STRUGGLE WITHIN

A young soldier was going off to fight in World War II against the Japanese. As his father put him on the train and waved good-bye, he turned with bitter tears and said, "If my son is killed, I hope every Jap in the world is killed!" Yet the fact that the father was a Christian made it difficult to feel that way in reality. He had a fierce struggle with himself and finally realized that it was not Christian to hate, whether his son lived or died. He declared rather, "I will not hate. I refuse to be destroyed by hate!"

A year later the son was killed. Soon life insurance money arrived. The father did not really need the ten thousand dollars so he sent it to the Southern Baptist Foreign Mission Board and designated it for missions to the Japanese.

How could the father do that? Only by the miracle of Calvary. Only God can change bitterness and hate into love.

22. FORGIVENESS IS . . .

Forgiveness is the windblown bud which blooms in placid beauty at Verdun.

Forgiveness is the tiny slate-gray sparrow which has built its nest of twigs and string among the shards of glass upon the wall of shame.

Forgiveness is the child who laughs in merry ecstasy beneath the toothed fence that closes DaNang.

Forgiveness is the fragrance of the violet which still clings fast to the heel that crushed it.

Forgiveness is the broken dream which hides itself within the corner of the mind oft called forgetfulness, so that it will not bring pain to the dreamer.

Forgiveness is the reed which stands up straight and green when nature's mighty rampage halts, full spent.

Forgiveness is a God who will not leave us after all we've done.

GEORGE ROEMISCH

23. THE GREAT PRIVILEGE

"Forgiveness to the injured doth belong." These are the words of the poet, John Dryden. Simon Wiesenthal, a prisoner and survivor of the Nazi concentration camps, tells the story of a Nazi who made him listen while he confessed the atrocities he had committed. The SS trooper, tormented by guilt, begged Wiesenthal, as a Jew, to forgive him. Wiesenthal turned and walked away. Later, he wrote, "Forgetting is something that time alone takes care of, but forgiveness is an act of volition, and only the sufferer is qualified to make decision." Wiesenthal wondered, had he done the right thing in refusing to forgive the SS troops. Reflection: What do you think? Are there some crimes that simply cannot be forgiven?

24. THE TRANSFORMING LOOK

A man came back to work in a place from which he had been fired several months previously. His work was superior. A fellow worker remembered how inconsistent he had been in the past and asked, "What happened to make such a difference in you?" The man told this story: When I was in college I was part of a fraternity initiation committee. We placed the new members in the middle of a long stretch of a country road. I was to drive my car at as great a speed as possible straight at them. The challenge was for them to stand firm until a signal was given to jump out of the way. It was a dark night. I had reached one hundred miles an hour and saw their looks of terror in the headlights. The signal was given and everyone jumped clear—except one boy. I left college after that. I later married and have two children. The look on that boy's face as I passed over him at a hundred miles an hour stayed in my mind all the time. I became hopelessly inconsistent, moody, and finally became a problem drinker. My wife had to work to bring in the only income we had. I was drinking at home one morning when someone rang the doorbell. I opened to find myself facing a woman who seemed strangely familiar. She sat down in our living room and told me she was the mother of the boy I had killed years before. She said that she had hated me and spent agonizing nights rehearsing ways to get revenge. I then listened as she told me of the love and forgiveness that had come when she gave her heart to Christ. She said, "I have come to let you know that I forgive you and I want you to forgive me." I looked into her eyes that morning and I saw deep in her eyes the permission to be the kind of man I might have been had I never killed that boy. That forgiveness changed my whole life.

25. GENERAL LEE AND FORGIVENESS

In Charles Bracelen Flood's book *Lee: The Last Years,* he tells of a time after the Civil War when Robert E. Lee visited a Kentucky woman who took him to the remains of a grand old tree in front of her home. There she cried bitterly that its limbs and trunk had been destroyed by Union artillery fire. She waited for Lee to condemn the North or at least sympathize with her loss. Lee paused, and then said, "Cut it down, my dear madam, and forget it."

26. THE TESTIMONY DID NOT LIE

In *Loving God,* Charles Colson tells of a quiet act of forgiveness that began a chain of events that still survives. Deep in one of Siberia's prison camps a Jew by the name of Dr. Boris Kornfeld was imprisoned. As a medical doctor he worked in surgery and otherwise helped both the staff and the prisoners. He met a Christian, whose name is unknown, whose quiet faith and his frequent reciting of the Lord's Prayer moved Dr. Kornfeld.

One day, while repairing a guard's artery which had been cut in a knifing, he seriously considered suturing it in such a way that he would bleed to death a little while later. Then, appalled by the hatred and violence he saw in his own heart, he found himself repeating the words of the nameless prisoner: "Forgive us our sins as we forgive those who sin against us."

Shortly after that prayer Dr. Kornfeld began to refuse to go along with some of the standard practices of the prison camp, including one day turning in an orderly who had stolen food from a dying patient. After that he knew his life was in danger, so he began to spend as much time as possible in the relative safety of the hospital.

One afternoon he examined a patient who had just been operated on for cancer of the intestines, a man whose eyes and face reflected a depth of spiritual misery and emptiness that moved Kornfeld. So the doctor began to talk to the patient, telling him the entire story, an incredible confession of secret faith.

That night someone snuck in and smashed Dr. Kornfeld's head while he was asleep—he died a few hours later.

But Kornfeld's testimony did not die. For the patient who had heard his confession, became, as a result, a Christian. And he survived that prison camp and went on to tell the world what he had learned there. The patient was the great writer—Aleksandr Solzhenitsyn.

27. TRANSIENT FORGIVENESS
Two little brothers, Harry and James, had finished supper and were playing until bedtime. Somehow, Harry hit James with a stick, and tears and bitter words followed. Charges and accusations were still being exchanged as mother prepared them for bed. The mother instructed, "Now James, before you go to bed you're going to have to forgive your brother." James was thoughtful for a few moments, and then he replied, "Well OK, I'll forgive him tonight, but if I don't die in the night, he'd better look out in the morning."

28. A CURE FOR HATRED
A woman testified to the transformation in her life that had resulted through her experience in conversion. She declared, "I'm so glad I got religion. I have an uncle I used to hate so much I vowed I'd never go to his funeral. But now, why, I'd be happy to go to it any time."

29. BREAKING THE BRIDGE
He who cannot forgive others breaks the bridge over which he must pass himself. GEORGE HERBERT

30. COMPLETING THE ACT OF FORGIVENESS
About the year 1830, a man named George Wilson killed a government employee who caught him in the act of robbing the mails. He was tried and

sentenced to be hanged. However, President Andrew Jackson sent him a pardon. But Wilson did a strange thing. He refused to accept the pardon, and no one knew what to do. So the case was carried to the Supreme Court.

Chief Justice Marshall, perhaps one of the greatest justices ever, wrote the court's opinion. In it he said, "A pardon is a slip of paper, the value of which is determined by the acceptance of the person to be pardoned. If it is refused, it is no pardon. George Wilson must be hanged." And so he was.

31. RADICAL, FORGIVING LOVE

During the Korean War a South Korean Christian civilian was arrested by the Communists and ordered shot. But when the young Communist leader learned that the prisoner was in charge of an orphanage, caring for small children, he decided to spare him and kill his son instead. So they took his nineteen-year-old son and shot him right there in front of the Christian man. Later, the fortunes of war changed and that same young Communist leader was captured by the UN forces, tried, and condemned to death. But before the sentence could be carried out, the Christian whose boy had been killed came and pleaded for the life of the killer. He declared that this Communist was young, that he really did not know what he was doing. The Christian said, "Give him to me and I will train him." The UN forces granted the request and the father took the murderer of his boy into his own home and cared for him. And today, that young man, formerly a Communist, is a Christian pastor, serving Christ. This is the power of forgiving love that can only be described as superabundant, the kind of love the dying Stephen reflected in the Book of Acts.

32. LOVE IS EVERYWHERE

After eighteen months in the ministry, a pastor went to his file cabinet to pull out the "Love" file. He discovered he didn't have one. Impossible! It must be misfiled. He searched among Faith and Fasting, between Healing and Heaven. Perhaps it was sandwiched by Christology and Christian Ed. After all, these have to do with Love don't they? But it wasn't there, nor was it found after Money or ahead of Missions.

When he stopped to reflect, the Holy Spirit solved the mystery. The Love file was scattered, yet not misfiled. Parts of it were found under Patience, Kindness, Humility, Trust, Hope, Loyalty, and Perseverance. But the pastor found the greatest part of the Love file, squarely-centered and deeply-seated, in Forgiveness.

33. THE DEGREE OF FORGIVENESS

We pardon in the degree that we love. FRANCOIS DE LA ROCHEFOUCAULD

224

FIFTY-EIGHT

Freedom

1. BONDAGE, REAL OR IMAGINED

Harry Houdini, the famed escape artist from a few years back, issued a challenge wherever he went. He could be locked in any jail cell in the country, he claimed, and set himself free in short order. Always he kept his promise, but one time something went wrong. Houdini entered the jail in his street clothes; the heavy, metal doors clanged shut behind him. He took from his belt a concealed piece of metal, strong and flexible. He set to work immediately, but something seemed to be unusual about this lock. For thirty minutes he worked and got nowhere. An hour passed, and still he had not opened the door. By now he was bathed in sweat and panting in exasperation, but he still could not pick the lock. Finally, after laboring for two hours, Harry Houdini collapsed in frustration and failure against the door he could not unlock. But when he fell against the door, it swung open! *It had never been locked at all!* But in his mind it was locked, and that was all it took to keep him from opening the door and walking out of the jail cell.
ZIG ZIGLAR

2. THE MASADA MENTALITY

Archibald Rutledge tells the story that as a young boy he was always catching and caging wild things. He particularly loved the sound of the mockingbird, so he decided to catch one and keep it so he could hear it sing any time.

He found a very young mockingbird and placed it in a cage outside his home. On the second day he saw a mother bird fly to the cage and feed the young bird through the bars. This pleased young Archibald. But then the following morning he found the little bird was dead.

Later young Arch was talking to the renowned ornithologist Arthur Wayne, who told him, "A mother mockingbird, finding her young in a cage, will sometimes take it poisonous berries. She evidently thinks it better for one she loves to die rather than live in captivity."

3. SYMBOLS OF SLAVERY

In 1838, after a strong emancipation movement among blacks, slavery was abolished in Jamaica, to take effect on August 1. On the evening of the last day in July a large company of former slaves gathered on the beach for a solemn, yet joyous, occasion. A large mahogany coffin had been constructed

225

and placed on the sand next to an accommodating hole in the beach. All evening the soon-to-be-emancipated slaves placed, with some ceremony, symbols of their enslavement. There were chains, leg-irons, whips, padlocks, and other similar symbols of slavery. A few minutes before midnight came the box was lowered into the hole in the beach. Pushing sand into the hole to cover the coffin, all joined their voices with one accord to sing: "Praise God from whom all blessings flow, praise him all creatures here below, praise him above ye heavenly host, praise Father, Son and Holy Ghost." They were free from their slavery. How much they were like Christians, who, through Christ's death are free from their slavery to sin. And how like them are Christians, who in heaven shall be free from the very reminder and presence of sin.

FIFTY-NINE

Friends

1. THE BUSINESS OF FRIENDSHIP
The main business of friendship is to sustain and make bearable each other's burdens. We may do more of that as friends than we do anything else.
EUGENE KENNEDY

2. THE DEPTH OF FRIENDSHIP
One could not but be moved by the story of the soldier who asked his officer if he might go out into the "No Man's Land" between the trenches in World War I to bring in one of his comrades who lay grievously wounded. "You can go," said the officer, "but it's not worth it. Your friend is probably killed, and you will throw your own life away." But the man went. Somehow he managed to get to his friend, hoist him onto his shoulder, and bring him back to the trenches. The two of them tumbled in together and lay in the trench bottom. The officer looked very tenderly on the would-be rescuer, and then he said, "I told you it wouldn't be worth it. Your friend is dead and you are mortally wounded." "It was worth it, though, sir," he said. "How do you mean, 'worth it'? I tell you your friend is dead." "Yes, sir," the boy answered, "but it was worth it, because when I got to him he was still alive, and he said to me, 'Jim, I knew you'd come.'"

3. DEEP REJECTION
A few years back Pepper Rodgers was in the middle of a terrible season as football coach at UCLA. It even got so bad that it upset his home life. He recalls, "My dog was my only friend. I told my wife that a man needs at least two friends and she bought me another dog."

4. PEACE TOGETHER
Ah, the beauty of being at peace with another, neither having to weigh thoughts or measure words, but spilling them out just as they are, chaff and grain together, certain that a faithful hand will keep what is worth keeping, and with a breath of kindness blow the rest away. *Arab proverb*

5. FALSE FRIENDS
False friends are like a shadow, keeping close to us while we walk in the sunshine, but leaving us when we cross into the shade. CHRISTIAN BOVEE

6. BITTER DEFINITION
A true friend always stabs you in the front. OSCAR WILDE

7. DAMAGED MEMORY
Lending money to a friend is dangerous—it could damage his memory.

8. CONFIDENTIALITY
Cheri, a first grader, was having trouble adjusting to school. I called her into my office for a chat, confident that my many years of training as a guidance counselor had more than prepared me to handle the situation. "Cheri," I said, "I want to be your friend. I will never tell your mommy or your daddy or your teacher anything we talk about if you don't want me to. I want you to know that you can always trust me." With tearful eyes, she looked up and replied, "Gee, Mrs. Edwards, you're just like my dog."

9. THE GIFT OF ENCOURAGING WORDS
A great place to glean some profound insights into life is from children's stories. On a Winnie the Pooh record, for instance, there is a scene that is a delightful illustration of our desire to hear words that are friendly and warm, rather than harsh or hard:

One day Pooh Bear is about to go for a walk in the Hundred Acre wood. It's about 11:30 in the morning. It is a fine time to go calling—just before lunch. So Pooh sets out across the stream, stepping on the stones, and when he gets right in the middle of the stream he sits down on a warm stone and thinks about just where would be the best place of all to make a call. He says to himself, "I think I'll go see Tigger." No, he dismisses that. Then he says, "Owl!" Then, "No, Owl uses big words, hard-to-understand words." At last

227

he brightens up! "I know! I think I'll go see Rabbit. I like Rabbit. Rabbit uses encouraging words like, 'How's about lunch?' and 'Help yourself, Pooh!' Yes, I think I'll go see Rabbit."

10. TRUTH THAT MAY HURT

When a stranger identifies you from a friend's description, it's best that you don't hear the description.

11. THE TRANSFORMING POWER OF FRIENDSHIP

As a part of an assignment for a doctoral thesis, a college student spent a year with a group of Navajo Indians on a reservation in the Southwest. As he did his research he lived with one family, sleeping in their hut, eating their food, working with them, and generally living the life of a twentieth-century Indian. The old grandmother of the family spoke no English at all, yet a very close friendship formed between the two. They spent a great deal of time sharing a friendship that was meaningful to each, yet unexplainable to anyone else. In spite of the language difference, they shared the common language of love and understood each other. Over the months he learned a few phrases of Navajo, and she picked up a little of the English language. When it was time for him to return to the campus and write his thesis, the tribe held a going-away celebration. It was marked by sadness since the young man had become close to the whole village and all would miss him. As he prepared to get up into the pickup truck and leave, the old grandmother came to tell him good-bye. With tears streaming from her eyes, she placed her hands on either side of his face, looked directly into his eyes and said, "I like me best when I'm with you." Isn't that the way we feel in the presence of Jesus? He brings out the best in us. We learn to see ourselves as worthy and valuable when we are in His presence. The hurts, the cares, the disappointments of our lives are behind us when we look in His eyes and realize the depth of His love. Our self-esteem no longer depends on what we have done or failed to do; it depends only on the value that He places on us. To be conformed to the image of Jesus Christ is to generate in other people the Indian grandmother's simple statement: "I like me best when I'm with you."

12. A WISE STRATEGY FOR LIFE

When we bought our new television set, the neighbors gathered one Saturday to help us put up the antenna. Since we had only the simplest tools, we weren't making much progress . . . until a man who was new on the block appeared with an elaborate tool box, with everything we needed to get the antenna up in record time. As we stood around congratulating ourselves on this piece of good luck, we asked our new neighbor what he made with such fancy tools. Looking at us all, he smiled and answered, "Friends, mostly."

13. THE OTHER GUY
You can make more friends in two months by becoming interested in other people than you can in two years by trying to get people interested in you. DALE CARNEGIE

14. ONLY TEMPORARY
Real friends are those who, when you make a fool of yourself, don't think you've done a permanent job.

15. HOW TO WIN FRIENDS
The whole art of pleasing lies in never speaking of oneself, always persuading others to speak of themselves. Everyone knows this and everyone forgets it. EDMOND AND JULES GONCOURT

SIXTY
Frustration

1. WORK UNDONE
What the reason of the ant laboriously drags into a heap, the wind of accident will collect in one breath. FRIEDRICH VON SCHILLER

2. PITHY WORDS
On an office poster: "One day I shall burst my buds of calm and blossom fully into hysteria."

3. FREE, INDEED!
The warranty on a new color TV set had no sooner run out than the set started having trouble. The lady of the house called the company and they sent a man to fix it. When he found that the warranty had expired he tried to talk her into signing a contract for repair insurance.

The woman was told that, if she signed it, there would be no charge for the present call. The lady, however, didn't want to commit herself yet: she hadn't studied the plan and its cost closely enough. She said she wanted to think it over.

The repairman sighed with resignation and said, "Well, ma'am, if you want free service, don't forget, you have to pay for it."

4. READING OR THINKING

A man bought a new gadget—unassembled, of course—and after reading and rereading the instructions couldn't figure out how it went together. Finally, he sought the help of an old handyman who was working in the backyard. The old fellow picked up the pieces, studied them, then began assembling the gadget. In a short time he had it all put together. "That's amazing," said the man. "And you did it without even looking at the instructions!" "Fact is," said the old man, "I can't read, and when a fellow can't read he's got to think."

5. PROBLEM SOLVING

A woman in Terre Haute, Indiana, called the police station to report a skunk in her cellar. The police told the woman to make a trail of bread crumbs from the basement to the yard and to wait for the skunk to follow it outside. A little later the woman called back and said, "I did what you told me. Now, I've got two skunks in my cellar."

SIXTY-ONE

Gifts

1. YOUR GIFTS ARE NOT YOUR OWN

You have your gifts not so much for your own sake as for the sake of others. You are like an apple tree that produces fruit not for its own consumption but for the consumption of others. Your gifts are given so you can bless others by ministering to them. If you have the gift of teaching, you have it so others in the body will be taught. If you have the gift of hospitality, it is because others need the gracious welcome they receive from you. If even one gifted person fails to function, the body of Christ is deprived of a ministry it needs to function well.

2. WE'RE ALL PRESENTS

During the Christmas season when our daughter was three years old, the number of presents under the tree slowly increased as the day approached. Caught up in the spirit and excitement of gifts and giving as only three-year-olds can be, one morning she was picking up, examining, shaking, and guessing what was inside of every package. Then, in a burst of inspiration, she picked up a big red bow that had fallen off one present and held it on top of her head. She looked up at me with twinkling eyes and beamed a smile as bright as the Star as she said, "Look at me, Daddy! I'm a present!"

Her words were more true than she realized! Our children are indeed the most wonderful gifts God gives us, at Christmas or any time. We may appreciate the gifts of talents and skills, either God-given or acquired; but do we consider our children as divine gifts—presents from God? What is more unique and special than our children?

To help us understand the kind of God we have, the Lord went so far as to send us God's own Son . . . the most remarkable present of all!

3. DIFFERENT SONGS TO SING
The woods would be silent if no birds sang except those that sang best.
HENRY VAN DYKE

4. TRAINING FOR GIFTS
Whenever you start talking about gifts (Romans 12)—you get into one of those exotic medieval arguments about the line between gifts and talents. And can you develop gifts? A reporter once said to George Bernard Shaw: "You have a marvelous gift for oratory. How did you develop it?" Shaw retorted, "I learned to speak as men learn to skate or cycle, by doggedly making a fool of myself until I got used to it."

5. A GOD OF VARIETY
Someone has imagined the carpenter's tools holding a conference. Brother Hammer presided. Several suggested he leave the meeting because he was too noisy. Replied the Hammer, "If I have to leave this shop, Brother Screw must go also. You have to turn him around again and again to get him to accomplish anything."

Brother Screw then spoke up. "If you wish, I will leave. But Brother Plane must leave too. All his work is on the surface. His efforts have no depth."

To this Brother Plane responded, "Brother Rule will also have to withdraw, for he is always measuring folks as though he were the only one who is right."

Brother Rule then complained against Brother Sandpaper, "You ought to leave too because you're so rough and always rubbing people the wrong way."

In the midst of all this discussion, in walked the Carpenter of Nazareth. He had arrived to start His day's work. Putting on His apron, He went to the bench to make a pulpit from which to proclaim the gospel. He employed the hammer, screw, plane, rule, sandpaper, and all the other tools. After the day's work when the pulpit was finished, Brother Saw arose and remarked, "Brethren, I observe that all of us are workers together with the Lord."

God is a God of variety. In nature, what a diversity of animals! Every snowflake is different, every fingerprint, every face. Likewise, God is a God of variety in His church. What a diversity of gifts He has bestowed on believers to equip them for service! LESLIE B. FLYNN, *Nineteen Gifts of the Spirit*

6. GIFT AND THE GIVER
For the real good of every gift it is essential, first, that the giver be in the gift—as God always is, for He is love—and next, that the receiver know and receive the giver in the gift. Every gift of God is but a harbinger of His greatest and only sufficing gift—that of Himself. No gift unrecognized as coming from God is at its own best: therefore many things that God would gladly give us must wait until we ask for them, that we may know whence they come. When in all gifts we find Him, then in Him we shall find all things. GEORGE MACDONALD, *Second Series,* "The Word of Jesus on Prayer"

7. LAUGHTER IS A GIFT
A thirty-eight-year-old scrubwoman would go to the movies and sigh, "If only I had her looks." She would listen to a singer and moan, "If only I had her voice." Then one day someone gave her a copy of the book, *The Magic of Believing.* She stopped comparing herself with actresses and singers. She stopped crying about what she didn't have and started concentrating on what she did have. She took inventory of herself and remembered that in high school she had a reputation for being the funniest girl around. She began to turn her liabilities into assets. A few years ago Phyllis Diller made over $1 million in one year. She wasn't good-looking and she had a scratchy voice, but she could make people laugh.

8. DEVELOPING YOUR GIFTS
One of Ripley's "Believe It or Not" items pictured a plain bar of iron worth $5. The same bar of iron if made into horse shoes would be worth $50. If it were made into needles, it would be worth $5,000. If it were made into balance springs for fine Swiss watches, it would be worth $500,000. The raw material is not as important as how it's developed. God says we have spiritual gifts, but their worth to Him will be dependent on how we develop them.

9. ONLY A PEBBLE?
Some of you remember Aesop's great fable about an old crow who was out in the wilderness and very thirsty. He had not had anything to drink in a

long time. He came to a jug that had a little water in the bottom of it. The old crow reached his beak into the jug to get some of that water, but his beak wouldn't quite touch the water. So what did he do? He started picking up pebbles one at a time and dropping them into the jug. And as more and more pebbles accumulated in the bottom of the jug the water rose in the bottle until finally the old crow was able to drink all that he desired.

That's a parable of the way God has chosen to work out his plan in our world. Each of us dropping in our own little pebble—teaching that Sunday school class, serving on a committee, providing transportation for the youth, visiting our lonely neighbor. Utilizing the gifts that are ours to serve in the ways we can may not seem all that important at the time, but as the pebbles accumulate in the bottom of the jug, and the water rises, God builds His kingdom and brings his plan to fruition. You are important!

SIXTY-TWO

Giving
(See also Stewardship)

1. THE SPIRIT OF CHRISTMAS GIVING
Several years ago a thirteen-year-old boy who attended Mohawk Central School at Paines Hollow in New York heard an appeal for contributions to Santa Claus Anonymous, a group that provides gifts for unfortunate children that otherwise would go without Christmas presents. The boy struggled to save a few pennies for this purpose. On the Friday before Christmas vacation he had fifteen cents and planned to turn in this small treasure at the school that day. But a furious blizzard blasted the area that Friday and the school buses could not run. So the boy waded a considerable distance through deep snow to give his fifteen cents to the school principal. The principal found it difficult to control his emotions as he accepted the gift, for the youngster was one of the destitute children listed to receive a Christmas present from Santa Claus Anonymous.

2. LONG WALK, MUCH LOVE
The African boy listened carefully as the teacher explained why it is that Christians give presents to each other on Christmas Day. "The gift is an expression of our joy over the birth of Jesus and our friendship for each other," she said.

When Christmas Day came, the boy brought the teacher a sea shell of lustrous beauty. "Where did you ever find such a beautiful shell?" the teacher asked.

The youth told her that there was only one spot where such extraordinary shells could be found—a certain bay several miles away.

"Why . . . why, it's gorgeous," said the teacher. "But you shouldn't have gone all that way to get a gift for me."

His eyes brightening, the boy answered, "Long walk part of gift."

3. THE CHRISTMAS WE WILL NEVER FORGET

When our son Pete was six, it was a Depression year and the bare essentials were all we could afford. We felt we were richer than most people, though, in things of the mind and imagination and spirit. That was a comfort of sorts to us, but nothing a six-year-old could understand.

With Christmas a week off, we told Pete that there could not be any store-bought presents this year—for any of us. "But I'll tell you what we can do," said his father with an inspiration born of heartbreak. "We can make pictures of the presents we'd like to give each other."

For the next few days each of us worked secretly, with smirks and giggles. Somehow we did scrape together enough to buy a small tree. But we had pitifully few decorations to trim it with. Yet, on Christmas morning, never was a tree heaped with such riches! The gifts were only pictures of gifts, to be sure, cut out or drawn and colored and painted, nailed and hammered and pasted and sewed. But they were presents, luxurious beyond our dreams: A slinky black limousine and a red motor boat for Daddy. A diamond bracelet and a fur coat for me. Pete's presents were the most expensive toys cut from advertisements. Our best present to him was a picture of a fabulous camping tent, complete with Indian designs, painted, of course, by Daddy, and magnificent pictures of a swimming pool, with funny remarks by me. Daddy's best present to me was a watercolor he had painted of our dream house, white with green shutters and forsythia bushes on the lawn.

Naturally we didn't expect any "best present" from Pete. But with squeals of delight, he gave us a crayon drawing of flashy colors and the most modernistic technique. But it was unmistakably the picture of three people laughing—a man, a woman, and a little boy. They had their arms around one another and were, in a sense, one person. Under the picture he had printed just one word: US. For many years we have looked back at that day as the richest, most satisfying Christmas we have ever had.

MARGERY TALLCOTT

4. A BROTHER LIKE THAT

A college friend of mine named Paul received a new automobile from his brother as a pre-Christmas present. On Christmas Eve, when Paul came out of his office, a street urchin was walking around the shiny new car, admiring it. "Is this your car, mister?" he asked.

Paul nodded. "My brother gave it to me for Christmas."

The boy looked astounded. "You mean your brother gave it to you, and it didn't cost you nothing? Boy, I wish . . ."

He hesitated, and Paul knew what he was going to wish. He was going to wish he had a brother like that. But what the lad said jarred Paul all the way down to his heels, "I wish," the boy went on, "that I could be a brother like that."

Paul looked at the boy in astonishment, then impulsively asked, "Would you like to ride in my automobile?"

"Oh, yes! I'd love that!"

After a short ride the urchin turned, and with his eyes aglow said, "Mister, would you mind driving in front of my house?"

Paul smiled a little. He thought he knew what the lad wanted. He wanted to show his neighbors that he could ride in a big automobile.

But Paul was wrong again.

"Will you stop right where those two steps are?" the boy asked.

He ran up the steps. Then, in a little while, Paul heard him coming back, but he was not coming fast.

He was carrying his little polio-crippled brother. He sat him down on the bottom step, then sort of squeezed up against him and pointed to the car.

"There she is, Buddy, just like I told you upstairs. His brother gave it to him for Christmas, and it didn't cost him a cent. And someday I'm gonna give you one just like it. Then you can see for yourself all the pretty things in the Christmas windows that I've been trying to tell you about."

Paul got out and lifted the little lad to the front seat of his car. The shining-eyed older brother climbed in beside him and the three of them began a memorable holiday ride.

That Christmas Eve Paul learned what Jesus meant when He said: "There is more happiness in giving." C. ROY ANGELL

5. MIXED MOTIVES

Sometimes our generosity comes from mixed motives. It seems that some vandals had cut down six royal palms along Miami's Flagler Street. Since the palms were very expensive, Dade County authorities weren't sure if they could replace them very soon. But then someone donated six more and even had them planted. The old ones had been about fifteen feet tall and provided a nice foreground for a "Fly Delta" billboard. The new palms are thirty-five feet tall—completely hiding the sign. The new donor: Eastern Airlines.

6. SPECIAL SALE PRICE

One afternoon three children, two boys and a girl, entered a flower shop. They were about nine or ten years old, raggedly dressed, but at this moment well-scrubbed. One of the boys took off his cap and gazed around the store somewhat doubtfully, then came up to the person who owned the store and said, "Sir, we'd like something in yellow flowers."

There was something in their tense nervous manner that made the man think that this was a very special occasion. He showed them some inexpensive yellow spring flowers. The boy who was the spokesman for the group shook his head. "I think we'd like something better than that."

The man asked, "Do they have to be yellow?" The boy answered, "Yes, sir. You see, Mickey would like 'em better if they were yellow. He had a yellow sweater. I guess he'd like yellow better than any other color."

The man asked, "Are they for his funeral?"

The boy nodded, suddenly choking up. The little girl was desperately struggling to keep back the tears. "She's his sister," the boy said. "He was a swell kid. A truck hit him while he was playing in the street." His lips were trembling now. The other boy entered the conversation. "Us kids in his block took up a collection. We got eighteen cents. Would roses cost an awful lot, sir—yellow roses, I mean?"

The man smiled. "It just happens that I have some nice yellow roses here that I'm offering special today for eighteen cents a dozen." The man pointed to the flower case.

"Gee, those would be swell! Yes, Mickey'd sure like those."

The man said, "I'll make up a nice spray with ferns and ribbons. Where do you want me to send them?"

One of the boys responded, "Would it be all right, mister, if we took them with us? We'd kind of like to—you know—give 'em to Mickey ourselves. He'd like it better that way."

The florist fixed the spray of flowers and accepted the eighteen cents gravely and watched the youngsters trudge out of the store. And he felt within his heart the warm glow of the presence of God, for he had remembered anew the meaning of the words of Jesus: "Even as you have done it unto one of these little ones, you have done it unto me."

7. REAL POWER

Giving is the highest expression of potency. ERICH FROMM

8. THE GIFT OF CHRISTMAS

I was visiting an elderly woman recently. While there she asked me to get a box of letters from her dresser. As I was getting the letters, I saw a beautiful quilt in the drawer. When I asked about the quilt she said I could take it out and look at it. What a masterpiece! She told me her grandmother had made the quilt as a wedding gift years before. When I asked her why she did not have it on her bed, she said, "Oh, it's too beautiful to use." I thought it sad that she felt her gift was better hidden in a drawer—preserved—rather than used. God gave humanity a beautiful gift, the most beautiful gift in the world. Do we consider this gift something that should be tucked away in a drawer, "too beautiful to use"?

9. AN ASSORTMENT OF GIVERS

There are three kinds of givers—the flint, the sponge, and the honeycomb. To get anything out of a flint you must hammer it. And then you get only chips and sparks. To get water out of a sponge you must squeeze it, and the more you use pressure, the more you will get. But the honeycomb just overflows with its own sweetness. Which kind of giver are you?

10. THE SURROUNDING MASTER

A mother, wishing to encourage her young son's progress at the piano, bought tickets for a Paderewski performance. When the night arrived, they found their seats near the front of the concert hall and eyed the majestic Steinway waiting on stage. Soon the mother found a friend to talk to, and the boy slipped away. When eight o'clock arrived, the spotlights came on, the audience quieted, and only then did they notice the boy up on the bench, innocently picking out, "Twinkle, Twinkle, Little Star." His mother gasped, but before she could retrieve her son, the master appeared on the stage and quickly moved to the keyboard. He whispered to the boy, "Don't quit—keep playing." Leaning over, Paderewski reached down with his left hand and began filling in a bass part. Soon his right arm reached around the other side, encircling the child, to add a running obbligato. Together, the old master and the young novice held the crowd mesmerized. In our lives, unpolished though we may be, it is the Master who surrounds us and whispers in our ear, time and again, "Don't quit—keep playing." And as we do, he augments and supplements until a work of amazing beauty is created.
DARREL L. ANDERSON, *Leadership*

11. ENOUGH IS ENOUGH

It had been a hard winter in the Appalachian area. The snow had piled up deeper and deeper, the mercury dropped, rivers froze, people suffered. The

Red Cross used helicopters to fly in supplies. One crew had been working day after day—long hours. They were on their way home late in the afternoon when they saw a little cabin submerged in the snow. There was a thin whisper of smoke coming from the chimney. The rescue team figured they were probably about out of food, fuel, perhaps medicine. Because of the trees they had to put the helicopter down a mile away. They put on heavy packs with emergency supplies, trudged through heavy snow, waist deep, reached the cabin exhausted, panting, perspiring. They pounded on the door. A thin, gaunt mountain woman opened the door and the lead man gasped, "We're from the Red Cross." She was silent for a moment and then she said, "It's been a hard winter, Sonny, I just don't think we can give anything this year."

12. THE SEVEN LEVELS OF GIVING

1. Giving to the poor, but with bad grace
2. Giving with a good grace, but not enough
3. Giving enough, but only after being asked
4. Giving without being asked
5. Giving without knowing who will benefit from the gift
6. Giving without the beneficiary of the gift knowing who is helping him
7. Fighting poverty by giving the poor person the means to escape from his condition

13. CHEAP GIVING

The world's stingiest man went Christmas shopping, but everything he saw was too expensive except a $50 vase that was on sale for $2 because the handle had been broken off. He bought it and had the salesman ship it by mail so that his friend would think he had paid $50 for it and that it had been broken in shipment. A week after Christmas he received a thank you note from his friend. "Thank you for the lovely vase," his letter said. "It was so nice of you to wrap each piece separately."

14. WHO'S SHARING WHAT WITH WHOM?

A woman was out shopping one day and decided to stop for a cup of coffee. She bought a bag of cookies, put them into her purse, and then entered a coffee shop. All the tables were filled, except for one at which a man sat reading a newspaper. Seating herself in the opposite chair, she opened her purse, took out a magazine, and began reading.

After a while, she looked up and reached for a cookie, only to see the man across from her also taking a cookie. She glared at him; he just smiled at her, and she resumed her reading.

Moments later she reached for another cookie, just as the man also took one. Now feeling quite angry, she stared at the one remaining cookie—whereupon the man reached over, broke the cookie in half and offered her a piece. She grabbed it and stuffed it into her mouth as the man smiled at her again, rose, and left.

The woman was really steaming as she angrily opened her purse, her coffee break now ruined, and put her magazine away. And there was her bag of cookies, unopened. All along she'd unknowingly been helping herself to the cookies belonging to the man she had shared the table with.

15. MAKING A LIFE
We make a living by what we get out of life, but we make a life by what we give.

16. THE GIFT IS IN YOUR HAND
Anthony Campolo, sociology professor at Eastern Baptist College and popular speaker, told of his experience one year at a Women's Conference where he was making a major address. At the point in the program when the women were being challenged with a several thousand dollar goal for their mission projects, the chairperson for the day turned to Dr. Campolo and asked him if he would pray for God's blessing upon the women as they considered what they might do to achieve the goal. To her utter surprise, Dr. Campolo came to the podium and graciously declined her invitation. "You already have the resources necessary to complete this mission project right here within this room," he continued. "It would be inappropriate to ask for God's blessing, when God has already blessed you with abundance and the means to achieve this goal. The necessary gifts are in your hands. As soon as we take the offering and underwrite this mission project, we will thank God for freeing us to be the generous, responsible and accountable stewards that we are called to be as Christian disciples." When the offering was taken, the mission challenge was oversubscribed, and Dr. Campolo led a joyous prayer of thanksgiving for God's abundant blessings and for the faithful stewardship of God's people.

17. WHAT YOU DON'T KNOW
A favorite story is of a man of substance approached to contribute to a major financial campaign. The urgent need and compelling case were stated, and the call was made for his support. The man responded: "I understand why you think I can give fifty thousand dollars. I am a man with my own business and, it is true, I have all the signs of affluence. But there are some things you don't know. Did you know that my mother is in an expensive nursing

home?" Well, no, we didn't know. "Did you know also that my brother died, and left a family of five and had almost no insurance?" No, we didn't. "Did you know my son is deeply religious, has gone into social work, and makes less than the national poverty level to meet the needs of his family?" No, we hadn't realized. "Well, then, if I don't give any of them a penny, why do you think I'll give it to you?" DONALD E. MESSER

18. A DIAMOND AND THE FULLNESS OF STRENGTH

The Koh-i-noor diamond is among the most spectacular in the world. Queen Victoria received it as a gift from a maharajah when he was a lad. Later as a grown man this maharajah visited Queen Victoria again. He requested that the stone be brought from the Tower of London to Buckingham Palace. The maharajah took the diamond and, kneeling before the Queen, gave it back to her, saying, "Your Majesty, I gave this jewel when I was a child, too young to know what I was doing. I want to give it to you again in the fullness of my strength, with all of my heart and affection, and gratitude, now and forever, fully realizing all that I do."

As believers in Jesus Christ, we need to reiterate those words offering again our lives to Jesus Christ: "I want to give You back my life, Lord Jesus, that I gave You several years ago. I want to give it again to You with gratitude, fully cognizant of all that I am doing."

19. HEART DISEASE

If you haven't got any charity in your heart, you have the worst kind of heart trouble. BOB HOPE

20. HELPING YOURSELF

It is one of the most beautiful compensations of this life that no man can sincerely try to help another without helping himself.
RALPH WALDO EMERSON

21. JOY OF GIVING

Author Thomas Carlyle tells how, when he was a boy, a beggar came to the door. His parents were out and he was alone in the house. On a boyish impulse, he broke into his own savings bank and gave the beggar all that was in it, and he tells us that never before or since did he know such sheer happiness as came to him in that moment. There is indeed joy in giving.

22. SEVEN WAYS TO GIVE

1. The Careless Way: To give something to every cause that is presented, without inquiring into its merits.
2. The Impulsive Way: To give from impulse—as much and as often as love and pity and sensibility prompt.

3. The Lazy Way: To make a special offer to earn money for worthy projects by fairs, bazaars, etc.

4. The Self-Denying Way: To save the cost of luxuries and apply them to purposes of religion and charity. This may lead to asceticism and self-complacence.

5. The Systematic Way: To lay aside as an offering to God a definite portion of our gains—one tenth, one fifth, one third, or one half (rich or poor can follow this plan).

6. The Equal Way: To give God and the needy just as much as we spend on ourselves.

7. The Heroic Way: To limit our own expenditures to a certain sum and give all the rest of our income.

23. RECEIVING HONOR

No man was ever honored for what he received. Honor is the reward for what he gave.

SIXTY-THREE

God, Nature of

1. THE EXTRAVAGANCE OF GOD

More sky than man can see,
More seas than he can sail,
More sun than he can bear to watch,
More stars than he can scale.
More breath than he can breathe,
More yield than he can sow,
More grace than he can comprehend,
More love than he can know. RALPH W. SEAGER

2. GOD'S UNCHANGING CHARACTER

It fortifies my soul to know
That though I perish, truth is so;
That howsoever I stray and range
Whate'er I do, Thou dost not change.
I steadier step when I recall
That if I slip, Thou dost not fall. ARTHUR HUGH CLOUGH

3. FINDING GOD'S RESOURCES

The Amazon River is the largest river in the world. The mouth is 90 miles across. There is enough water to exceed the combined flow of the Yangtze, Mississippi, and Nile Rivers. So much water comes from the Amazon that they can detect its currents 200 miles out in the Atlantic Ocean. One irony of ancient navigation is that sailors in ancient times died for lack of water . . . caught in windless waters of the South Atlantic. They were adrift, helpless, dying of thirst. Sometimes other ships from South America who knew the area would come alongside and call out, "What is your problem?" And they would exclaim, "Can you spare us some water? Our sailors are dying of thirst!" And from the other ship would come the cry, "Just lower your buckets. You are in the mouth of the mighty Amazon River." The irony of ancient Israel and the tragedy around us today is that God, the fountain of living water, is right here and people don't recognize Him! EARL PALMER

SIXTY-FOUR

God's Care and Guidance

1. CATCH AN EYE

On a summer day I took my three-year-old daughter to a kiddy park in Dallas to ride the rides. I put her on a small ride which she insisted on trying even though it was the "scariest." As she whipped around the corners in the kiddy car, she wrinkled up her face into a terrified cry. I tried to catch her attention, and finally she caught my eye, and I was smiling and shouting, "Hey, this is fun!" When she saw that I was not terrified, but smiling, she also began to laugh. What was once terrifying, became enjoyable—even fun! I thought how our Heavenly Father will "put us on some scary rides" in life, not really to terrify us, but to cause us to catch His eye, to teach us that He is in control and we can trust Him.

2. FACING REALITY

Anyone who doesn't believe in miracles isn't a realist. DAVID BEN-GURION, *late prime minister of Israel*

3. THE ULTIMATE ANSWER TO LOSTNESS

An elderly gentleman was out walking with his young grandson. "How far are we from home?" he asked the grandson. The boy answered, "Grandpa, I don't know." The grandfather asked, "Well, where are you?" Again the boy answered, "I don't know." Then the grandfather said good-naturedly, "Sounds to me as if you are lost." The young boy looked up at his grandfather and said, "Nope, I can't be lost. I'm with you." Ultimately, that is the answer to our lostness, too. We can't be lost if He is with us.
KING DUNCAN

4. SAVED ALONE

In the year 1873, Horatio Spafford, a Christian lawyer from Chicago, placed his wife and four children on the luxury liner *Ville de Havre* sailing from New York to France. Spafford expected to join them in about three or four weeks after finishing up some business, but with the exception of his wife he never saw them again. The trip started out beautifully. But on the evening of November 21, 1873, as the *Ville de Havre* proceeded peacefully across the Atlantic, the ship was suddenly struck by another vessel, the *Lochearn,* and sank a mere thirty minutes later, with the loss of nearly all on board.

On being told that the ship was sinking Mrs. Spafford knelt with her children and prayed that they might be saved or be made willing to die, if such was God's will. A few minutes later, in the confusion, three of the children were swept away by the waves while she stood clutching the youngest. Suddenly the youngest child was swept from her arms. Mrs. Spafford became unconscious and awoke later to find that she had been rescued by sailors from the *Lochearn.* But the four children were gone.

Back in the United States, Horatio Spafford was waiting for news of his family, and at last, ten days later (after the rescue ship had reached Cardiff), it came. "Saved alone" was his wife's message. That night Spafford walked the floor of his rooms in anguish, as anyone would have done. But this was not all. For as he shared his loss with His Lord, a loss which could not be reversed in this life, he found, as many have, that peace which indeed passes all understanding. Toward morning he told a friend named Major Whittle, "I am glad to be able to trust my Lord when it costs me something." Then, sometime later, as he reflected on the disaster at sea, he wrote this hymn:
When peace, like a river, attendeth my way,
When sorrows like sea-billows roll;
Whatever my lot, Thou hast taught me to say,
It is well, it is well with my soul.

Though Satan should buffet, though trials should come,
   Let this blest assurance control,
That Christ has regarded my helpless estate,
   And hath shed His own blood for my soul.
My sin—Oh, the bliss of this glorious thought,
   My sin—not in part, but the whole,
Is nailed to the cross and I bear it no more,
   Praise the Lord, praise the Lord, O my soul!
And, Lord, haste the day when the faith shall be sight,
   The clouds be rolled back as a scroll,
The trump shall resound and the Lord shall descend,
   "Even so"—it is well with my soul.

5. I KNOW WHO HOLDS TOMORROW

A few days before I left home to prepare for the ministry my gray-haired pastor, Rev. Temple, told me this story. I have told it many, many times since, especially in connection with the song, "I Know Who Holds Tomorrow."

"When my son was small, we often walked together out through the fields and neighboring pasture behind the parsonage. At first the little fellow would hold onto my little finger, but he found that when he stepped into a hoof-print or stumbled over something, his grip would fail and down he'd go in the dust or snow. Not giving it much thought, my mind on other matters, I'd stop and he'd get up, brush himself off, and grab my little finger again, gripping a little harder this time.

"Needless to say, this occurred frequently until one day as he was brushing himself off, he looked at me and said, 'Daddy?' I replied, 'Yes, Son, what is it?' He said, 'I think if you would hold *my* hand, I wouldn't fall.'

Pastor Temple then turned to me and with a tear in his eye he said, "You know, he still stumbled many times after that, but he never hit the ground. Now, as you walk with God, don't try to hold on to Him, let Him hold on to you. You may stumble but He'll never let you fall." FRED MUSSER, *The Tabernacle*

6. FOLLOWING

Do not follow where the path may lead. Follow God, instead, where there is no path and leave a trail.

7. AN INSIDE JOB

In a remote Swiss village stood a beautiful church. It was so beautiful, in fact, that it was known as the Mountain Valley Cathedral. The church was not only beautiful to look at—with its high pillars and magnificent stained glass windows—but it had the most beautiful pipe organ in the whole region. People would come from miles away—from far off lands—to hear the lovely tones of this organ.

But there was a problem. The columns were still there—the windows still dazzled with the sunlight—but there was an eerie silence. The mountain valley no longer echoed the glorious fine-tuned music of the pipe organ.

Something had gone wrong with the pipe organ. Musicians and experts from around the world had tried to repair it. Every time a new person would try to fix it the villagers were subjected to sounds of disharmony—awful penetrating noises which polluted the air.

One day an old man appeared at the church door. He spoke with the sexton and after a time the sexton reluctantly agreed to let the old man try his hand at repairing the organ. For two days the old man worked in almost total silence. The sexton was, in fact, getting a bit nervous. Then on the third day—at high noon—the mountain valley once again was filled with glorious music. Farmers dropped their plows, merchants closed their stores—everyone in town stopped what they were doing and headed for the church. Even the bushes and trees of the mountain tops seemed to respond as the glorious music echoed from ridge to ridge.

After the old man finished his playing, a brave soul asked him how he could have fixed the organ, how could he restore this magnificent instrument when even the world's experts could not. The old man merely said it was an inside job. "It was I who built this organ fifty years ago. I created it—and now I have restored it."

That is what God is like. It is He who created the universe, and it is He who can, and will, and is in the process of restoring it.

8. EMPTY OR FULL

I gave them to Him,
All the things I'd valued so
Until I stood there empty-handed.
Every glittering toy did go.
And I walked earth's lonely highways
In my rags and poverty;
Till I heard His voice entreating,
"Lift your empty hands to Me."
Empty hands I lifted to Him,
And He filled them with a store
Of His own transcendent riches
Till my hands could hold no more.

And at last I comprehended,
With my mind so slow and dull,
That God could not pour His riches
Into hands already full.

9. DIFFERENT STRATEGY
God gently leads His children along. Me, He yanks! BOB PIERCE

10. WHERE HE LEADS ME
In "pastures green?"
Not always.
Sometimes He
Who knoweth best, in kindness leadeth me
In weary ways, where heavy shadows be.
And by "still waters"?
No, not always so;
Ofttimes the heavy tempests round me blow,
And o'er my soul the waves and billows go.
But when the storm beats loudest,
And I cry
Aloud for help, the Master standeth by,
And whispers to my soul, "Lo, 'tis I."
So, where He leads me, I can safely go,
And in the blest hereafter I shall know,
Why in His wisdom He hath led me so.

11. CREEPING ON THE PROMISES
In the early days of our country a weary traveler came to the banks of the Mississippi River for the first time. There was no bridge. It was early winter, and the surface of the mighty stream was covered with ice. Could he dare cross over? Would the uncertain ice be able to bear his weight?

Night was falling, and it was urgent that he reach the other side. Finally, after much hesitation and with many fears, he began to creep cautiously across the surface of the ice on his hands and knees. He thought that he might distribute his weight as much as possible and keep the ice from breaking beneath him.

About halfway over he heard the sound of singing behind him. Out of the dusk there came a man, driving a horse-drawn load of coal across the ice and singing merrily as he went his way.

Here he was—on his hands and knees, trembling lest the ice be not strong enough to bear him up! And there, as if whisked away by the winter's wind, went the man, his horses, his sleigh, and his load of coal, upheld by the same ice on which he was creeping!

Like this weary traveler, some of us have learned only to creep upon the promises of God. Cautiously, timidly, tremblingly we venture forth upon His promises, as though the lightness of our step might make His promises more secure. As though we could contribute even in the slightest to the strength of His assurances!

He has promised to be with us. Let us believe that promise! He has promised to uphold us. Let us believe Him when He says so. He has promised to grant us victory over all our spiritual enemies. Let us trust His truthfulness. Above all, He has promised to grant us full and free forgiveness of all our sins because of Jesus Christ, our Savior. And He has promised to come and take us to His heavenly home. Let us take Him at His word.

We are not to creep upon these promises as though they were too fragile to uphold us. We are to stand upon them—confident that God is as good as His word and that He will do what He has pledged.

The Bread Line, NEWSLETTER OF THE COLBY PRESBYTERIAN CHURCH, COLBY, KANSAS

12. HOW DO YOU THINK OF GOD?

At first I saw God as my observer, my judge, keeping track of the things I did wrong, so as to know whether I merited heaven or hell when I die. He was out there sort of like the president. I recognized His picture when I saw it, but I didn't really know Him.

But later on when I recognized this Higher Power, it seemed as though life was rather like a bike ride, but it was a tandem bike, and I noticed that God was in the back helping me pedal.

I don't know just when it was that he suggested we change places, but life has not been the same since—life with my Higher Power, that is. God makes life exciting!

But when He took the lead, it was all I could do to hang on! He knew delightful paths, up mountains and through rocky places—and at breakneck speeds. Even though it looked like madness, he said, "Pedal!"

I worried and was anxious and asked, "Where are you taking me?" He laughed and didn't answer, and I started to learn trust.

I forgot my boring life and entered into adventure. When I'd say, "I'm scared," He'd lean back and touch my hand.

He took me to people with gifts that I needed, gifts of healing, acceptance, and joy. They gave me their gifts to take on my journey, our journey, God's and mine.

And we were off again. He said, "Give the gifts away; they're extra baggage, too much weight." So I did, to the people we met, and I found that in giving I received, and our burden became light.

At first I did not trust Him in control of my life. I thought He'd wreck it. but He knows bike secrets—knows how to make it lean to take sharp corners, dodge large rocks, and speed through scary passages.

And I am learning to shut up and pedal in the strangest places. I'm beginning to enjoy the view and the cool breeze on my face with my delightful constant Companion.

And when I'm sure I just can't do any more, He just smiles and says, "Pedal!"

SIXTY-FIVE
God's Love

1. THE LOST CHILD

A lady told of taking her grandsons, ages four and six, to spend the day at Disneyland. During the course of the day she bought each of them a little flag. On several occasions they stopped to watch the marching band of "toy" soldiers and each time the boys would be spellbound as the band marched by. All at once, the grandmother realized that the four-year-old was gone. She searched all about, calling his name, and making her way through the crowd. As she sat down to catch her breath and try to determine what to do, she looked up to see the marching band of toy soldiers. There, at the end of the line, smiling merrily, and waving his flag, was little Mikey, having the time of his life, completely unaware that he was lost! How like the world, going on its merry way, unaware of a loving Father's concern for its lostness. But someday the band will stop playing. Then and only then will those unreached realize that they are lost.

2. A STONE IN THE SUN

We were hiking in the mountains out West when I saw the stone—a small one, about the size of a half-dollar, with smooth rounded edges. Ordinarily I would have passed it by, not being a rock hound. It would have remained there for another thousand years perhaps, a mere pebble among the larger stones on the trail. But this one instantly caught my eye. It was special. Glinting in the sunlight, it seemed to reflect all the surrounding colors, as though trying to mirror nature. Into my pocket went the rare find. All the way home to the East Coast I thought about where I should display it so its beauty could be most enjoyed. I finally placed it in a curio cabinet, next to some jade and carved ivory. I forgot it for a while. Then one day, while dusting, I was surprised to see that the stone had completely lost its luster. It sat on the shelf among the other lovely objects, a hard, gray chunk of nothing, downright ugly. I was shocked. What had happened to the prize I had so carefully brought back with me across the continent? Where was the sparkle and the colors that had attracted me so much? Disgusted, I snatched it up and started for the trash can in the backyard. Then, just as I opened the kitchen door, a beam of light struck the stone. As though by magic, it began to shimmer, to glow again. In an instant the beautiful jewel tones shone brilliantly. Had they returned? Or had they always been there, dormant, waiting to be released? Wondering, I glanced up at the sky. Sunlight? That was the answer. The rays from the sun were all my stone needed to come alive. How much like each of us! Of ourselves our lives are empty, colorless, without meaning. Only when we are touched by the glory of God is our inner beauty revealed.

3. INCLUSIVE LOVE
During the war a man died and his two friends desperately wanted to give him a decent burial. They found a cemetery in a nearby village. It happened to be a Roman Catholic cemetery and the dead man had been a Protestant. When the two friends found the priest in charge of the burial grounds, they requested permission to bury their friend, but the priest refused because the man had not been a Catholic. When the priest saw their disappointment, he explained that they could bury their friend outside the fence. This was done. Later, they returned to visit the grave but couldn't find it. Their search led them back to the priest and, of course, they asked him what had happened to the grave. The priest told them that during the night he was unable to sleep because he had made them bury their friend outside the fence. So he got up and moved the fence to include the dead soldier. In Christ, God has "moved the fence" to include the undeserving.

4. THE CHILD ON THE FREEWAY
It was just a couple of weeks before Christmas in southern California a number of years back. A friend of mine, then assistant pastor in a large local church, shared with me this true story that happened in his own family. His wife and her sister had been Christmas shopping and were speeding along

the freeway on their way home. It was a cold, blustery night, dark and rainy. His wife and her sister were busily chatting in the front seat of the car. My friend's three-year-old daughter was in the backseat by herself.

Suddenly the two adults were aware of a strange, unnatural, and horrifying set of sounds as they heard the back door of the car open, the whistle of wind, and a sickening muffled sound. Quickly they turned and saw the child had fallen out of the car and was tumbling along the freeway.

Panic! The mother slammed on the brakes and pulled the car to a wrenching stop, jumped out and ran full speed back toward the child. When they arrived at her motionless body, they noticed something strange. All of the traffic was stopped, lined up like a parking lot just behind her body. The child had not been hit by a car. In fact, the car that would have hit her was stopped just a few feet short of her prone form. Wonder number one.

A truck driver jumped down out of his cab and was bending over the girl as they arrived at the scene. He said, "She's still alive. Let's get her to a hospital quickly. There's one nearby." He picked up the child, they all got into his large truck, and sped off to a nearby hospital. The child was unconscious but still breathing. Wonder number two.

When they arrived at the hospital, they rushed into the emergency room and the doctors immediately began to check her vital signs. The room was hushed. Finally the doctor spoke. "Well, other than the fact that she is unconscious and scraped, she appears to be in good shape. I don't see any broken bones. Her blood pressure is good. Her heart is fine. So far, so good." No apparent gross damage. She was only bruised and skinned from her vicious tumble along the freeway. Wonder number three.

The mother bent over her child. Her eyes were full of tears and her heart was filled with gratitude for such a miracle. Suddenly, without warning, the child's eyes opened, she looked up at her mother and said, "Mommy, you know, I wasn't afraid." Startled, the mother said, "Oh, what do you mean?"

"Well," she said, "while I was lying on the road waiting for you to get back to me—I wasn't afraid, because I looked up, and right there I saw Jesus holding back the traffic with his arms outstretched."

Wonder after wonder—and every wonder true.

5. GOD'S CHILDREN

Our Sunday school superintendent had two new boys in Sunday school. In order to register them she had to ask their ages and birthdays. The bolder of the two said, "We're both seven. My birthday is April 8, 1976, and my brother's is April 20, 1976." "But that's impossible!" answered the superintendent. "No, it's not," answered the quieter brother. "One of us is adopted." "Which one?" asked the superintendent before she could curb her tongue. The boys looked at each other and smiled, and the bolder one said to the superintendent, "We asked Dad awhile ago, but he just said he loved us both, and he couldn't remember any more which one was adopted."

In Romans 8:17, Paul writes: "Now if we are [God's] children, then we are heirs—heirs of God and co-heirs with Christ . . ." (NIV) Paul's comparison is to adoption. By our faith in Christ we become his adopted brothers and sisters—adopted sons and daughters of God. As fully adopted and accepted children, we share the same inheritance as the begotten Son, Jesus. No wonder all creation waits eagerly for the full revealing and adoption to happen!

6. ONLY ONE CHILD TO LOVE

A young woman had been seeing a psychiatrist. The doctor had established that she was a wife and mother of three children, and he asked, "Which of your three children do you love the most?" She answered instantly, "I love all three of my children the same." He paused. The answer was almost too quick, too glib. He decided to probe a bit. "Come, now, you love all three of your children the same?" "Yes, that's right," she said, "I love all of them the same." He said, "Come off it now! It is psychologically impossible for anyone to regard any three human beings exactly the same. If you're not willing to level with me, we'll have to terminate this session." With this the young woman broke down, cried a bit, and said, "All right, I do not love all three of my children the same. When one of my three children is sick, I love that child more. When one of my three children is in pain, or lost, I love that child more. When one of my children is confused, I love that child more. And when one of my children is bad—I don't mean naughty, I mean really bad—I love that child more." Then she added, "Except for those exceptions I do love all three of my children about the same." The Christian faith represents a God who knows and loves you just as He knows and loves all other human beings on this planet—but with this addition: when you are sick or hurting or lost or confused or in pain or depraved—He loves you even more. So, we personalize the message that "God loves each one of us as if there were only one of us to love."

7. THE UNIQUE CHILD OF GOD

Nearly a year ago Peg and I had a very hard week. Wednesday night—Mike slept downstairs in his room—where children belong—and we slept upstairs in ours where moms and dads belong. Thursday night—we were 350 miles away and he was in Ramada 325 and we were in 323—connecting rooms and we left the door open and talked and laughed together. Friday night—

700 miles from home and he was in 247 and we were in 239, but it was just down the balcony and somehow we seemed together. Saturday night—he was in the freshman dorm, and we were back in 239. Monday night—we were home and he was 700 miles away in Chapman 309.

Now we had been through this before. Bob, Jr., had gone away to college and we had gathered ourselves together until we had gotten over it—mainly because he's married now and he only lives ten miles away and comes to visit often with Deb and Robert III. So we thought we knew how to handle separation pretty well, but we came away lonely and blue.

Oh, our hearts were filled with pride for our fine young man, and our minds were filled with memories from tricycles to commencements, but deep down inside somewhere we just ached with loneliness and pain.

Somebody said you still have three at home—three fine kids and there is still plenty of noise, plenty of ball games to go to, plenty of responsibilities, plenty of laughter, plenty of everything . . . except Mike. And in parental math five minus one just doesn't equal plenty.

And I was thinking about God. He sure has plenty of children—plenty of artists, plenty of singers, and carpenters, and candlestick makers, and preachers, plenty of everybody . . . except you, and all of them together can never take your place. And there will always be an empty spot in His heart—and a vacant chair at His table when you're not home.

And if once in a while it seems He's crowding you a bit—try to forgive Him. It may be one of those nights when He misses you so much He can hardly stand it. BOB BENSON, *Come Share the Being*

8. PROVIDENTIAL CARE OR FLUKE?

Two books that offer a number of excellent stories that can be used as illustrations are those by Paul Aurandt: *Paul Harvey's the Rest of the Story* (Bantam) and *More of Paul Harvey's The Rest of the Story* (Morrow). Compiled originally for Harvey's nationally syndicated radio series, the stories are built around the surprise ending format.

One of my favorites is the one about West Side Baptist Church in Beatrice, Nebraska. Normally all of the good choir people came to church on Wednesday night to practice, and they tended to be early, well before the 7:30 starting time. But one night, March 1, 1950, one by one, two by two, they all had excuses for being late.

Marilyn, the church pianist overslept on her after-dinner nap, so she and her mother were late. One girl, a high school sophomore, was having trouble with her homework. That delayed her, so she was late. One couple couldn't get their car started. They, and those they were to pick up, were subsequently late. All eighteen choir members, including the pastor and his wife, were late. All had good excuses. At 7:30, the time the choir rehearsal was to begin, not one soul was in the choir loft. This had never happened before.

But that night, the only night in the history of the church that the choir wasn't starting to practice at 7:30, was the night that there was a gas leak in the basement of the West Side Baptist Church. At precisely the time at which the choir would have been singing, the gas leak was ignited by the church furnace and the whole church blew up. The furnace room was right below the choir loft!

9. PROFIT AND LOSS

I counted all my dollars while God counted crosses;
I counted gains while he counted losses;
I counted my worth by the things gained in store,
But He sized me up by the scars that I bore.
I coveted honors and sought for degrees;
He wept as He counted the hours on my knees.
I never knew till one day by a grave
How vain are the things that we spend life to save.
I did not know till a friend went above
That richest is he who is rich in God's love.

10. THE NAMED AND THE NAMELESS

God has a name. The misery on the earth is nameless, the evil among men is nameless, for the powers of darkness love to be without a name. Nameless, anonymous letters, letters without signatures are usually vulgar. But God is no writer of anonymous letters; God puts His name on everything that He does, affects, and says; God has no need to fear the light of day.
WALTER LUTHI, *The Lord's Prayer*

11. LOVE IN EVERYTHING

We call it mercy—it is God's forgiving love.
We call it providence—it is God's caring love.
We call it kindness—it is God's understanding love.
We call it Christ's passion and death—it is God's proven love.
We call it happiness—it is God's encouraging love.
We call it the will of God—it is God's unerring love.
We call it heaven—it is God's rewarding love.
We call it eternity—it is God's unending love.
Pulpit Helps

12. DISCOVERING GOD IN THE PACIFIC

During World War II the famous American pilot, Captain Eddie Rickenbacker, was flying on a special mission to the Pacific Islands. The plane crashed, and Rickenbacker and his crew were lost at sea for twenty-one days. Rickenbacker wrote of that experience: "In the beginning many of the men were atheists or agnostics, but at the end of the terrible ordeal each, in his own way, discovered God. Each man found God in the vast, empty loneliness of the ocean. Each man found salvation and strength in prayer, and a community of feeling developed which created a liveliness of human fellowship and worship, and a sense of gentle peace."

13. QUICK STUDY

A young soldier who was fighting in Italy during World War II jumped into a foxhole just ahead of some bullets. He immediately tried to deepen the hole for more protection and was frantically scraping away the dirt with his hands. He unearthed something metal and brought up a silver crucifix, left by a former resident of the foxhole. A moment later another leaping figure landed beside him as the shells screamed overhead. When the soldier got a chance to look, he saw that his new companion was an army chaplain. Holding out the crucifix, the soldier gasped, "Am I glad to see you! How do you work this thing?"

14. THE DEEPER MEANING OF POISON IVY

At a summer religious camp for children one of the counselors was leading a discussion on the purpose God had for everything He created. They began to find good reasons for clouds and trees and rocks and rivers and animals and just about everything else in nature. Finally, one of the children said, "If God had a good purpose for everything, then why did He create poison ivy?" The discussion leader gulped and, as he struggled with the question, one of the other children came to his rescue, saying, "The reason God made poison ivy is because He wanted us to know there are certain things we should keep our cotton-pickin' hands off."

15. RELATED TO THE CAPTAIN

A young boy happened upon an old man who was fishing in the mighty Mississippi River. Immediately the lad began to ply the aged fisherman with a myriad of questions as only young boys can do. With the patience of the ages, the old man answered each query.

Suddenly their conversation was interrupted by the shrill whistle of the majestic *River Queen* paddling relentlessly down river. The sight of the ship gleaming and splashing spray in the sunlight caused the surprised spectators to stare in awe and appreciation.

Then above the noise of the paddle wheel was heard a small boy's voice calling across the water; "Let me ride! Let me ride!"

The old man turned to the boy and tried to calm him down explaining that the *River Queen* was too important a ship to stop and give rides to little boys.

The young child cried all the more, "Let me ride!"

Old eyes bulged in disbelief as that great ship pulled for shore and a gangplank was lowered. In a flash two young feet scampered up and onto the deck. The ship with its new cargo safely on board began to pull back into the main stream. The old man continued to stare after the ship.

Then a shock of yellow hair appeared above the rail. It was quickly followed by two blue eyes, button nose, and cherub lips. "Mister, I knew this ship would stop for me. The captain is my father!"

16. GOD'S MYSTERY

I have observed the power of the watermelon seed. It has the power of drawing from the ground and through itself two hundred thousand times its weight. When you can tell me how it takes this material and out of it colors an outside surface beyond the imagination of art, and then forms inside of it a white rind and within that again a red heart, thickly inlaid with black seed, each one of which is capable of drawing through itself two hundred thousand times its weight—when you can explain to me the mystery of a watermelon, you can ask me to explain the mystery of God.

17. GOOD INTENTIONS

It's always easy the night before to get up early the next morning.

SIXTY-SIX

Gossip
(See also Talk*)*

1. BUT IS IT TRUE?

The more interesting the gossip, the more likely it is to be untrue.

2. MOTIVATION FOR BREVITY

Nothing makes a long story short like the arrival of the person you happen to be talking about.

3. GOSSIP AND NOISE
The difference between noise and gossip is whether you raise your voice or lower it. FRANKLIN P. JONES

4. JUMBLED GOSSIP
It isn't the things that go in one ear and out the other that hurt as much as the things that go in one ear, get all mixed up, and then slip out the mouth.

5. ENLARGING THE FLOW
The small streams of gossip poured into the ears emerge as mighty cataracts out of the mouths. PAUL ELDRIDGE

SIXTY-SEVEN
Grace

1. THE WAY GRACE WORKS
Grace does not make everything right. Grace's trick is to show us that it is right for us to live; that it is truly good, wonderful even, for us to be breathing and feeling at the same time that everything clustering around us is wholly wretched. Grace is not a ticket to Fantasy Island; Fantasy Island is dreamy fiction. Grace is not a potion to charm life to our liking; charms are magic. Grace does not cure all our cancers, transform all our kids into winners, or send us all soaring into the high skies of sex and success. Grace is rather an amazing power to look earthy reality full in the face, see its sad and tragic edges, feel its cruel cuts, join in the primeval chorus against its outrageous unfairness, and yet feel in your deepest being that it is good and right for you to be alive on God's good earth. Grace is power, I say, to see life very clearly, admit it is sometimes all wrong, and still know that somehow, in the center of your life, "It's all right." This is one reason we call it amazing grace. . . . Grace is the one word for all that God is for us in the form of Jesus Christ. LEWIS B. SMEDES, *How Can It Be All Right When Everything Is Wrong?*

2. A SIXTH GRADER'S DEFINITION
A miracle is something extraordinary that happens without any strings attached.

3. GRACE AT COMMUNION

A large prosperous downtown church had three mission churches under its care that it had started. On the first Sunday of the New Year all the members of the mission churches came to the city church for a combined Communion service. In those mission churches, which were located in the slums of the city, were some outstanding cases of conversions—thieves, burglars, and so on—but all knelt side by side at the Communion rail.

On one such occasion the pastor saw a former burglar kneeling beside a judge of the Supreme Court of England—the judge who had sent him to jail where he had served seven years. After his release this burglar had been converted and become a Christian worker. Yet, as they knelt there, the judge and the former convict, neither one seemed to be aware of the other.

After the service, the judge was walking home with the pastor and said to the pastor, "Did you notice who was kneeling beside me at the Communion rail this morning?"

The pastor replied, "Yes, but I didn't know that you noticed." The two walked along in silence for a few more moments, and then the judge said, "What a miracle of grace." The pastor nodded in agreement. "Yes, what a marvelous miracle of grace." Then the judge said "But to whom do you refer?" And the pastor said, "Why, to the conversion of that convict." The judge said, "But I was not referring to him. I was thinking of myself." The pastor, surprised, replied: "You were thinking of yourself? I don't understand." "Yes," the judge replied, "it did not cost that burglar much to get converted when he came out of jail. He had nothing but a history of crime behind him, and when he saw Jesus as his Savior he knew there was salvation and hope and joy for him. And he knew how much he needed that help. But look at me. I was taught from earliest infancy to live as a gentleman; that my word was to be my bond; that I was to say my prayers, go to church, take Communion and so on. I went through Oxford, took my degrees, was called to the bar and eventually became a judge. Pastor, nothing but the grace of God could have caused me to admit that I was a sinner on a level with that burglar. It took much more grace to forgive me for all my pride and self-deception, to get me to admit that I was no better in the eyes of God than that convict that I had sent to prison.

4. LOOKING FOR THE LIGHT

G. Campbell Morgan was once approached by a soldier who said he would give anything to believe that God would forgive sins, "but I cannot believe He will forgive me if I just turn to Him. It is too cheap." Dr. Morgan said to him: "You were working in the mine today. How did you get out of the pit?"

He answered, "The way I usually do; I got into the cage and was pulled to the top." "How much did you pay to come out of the pit?" "I didn't pay anything." "Weren't you afraid to trust yourself to that cage? Was it not too cheap?" The man replied, "Oh, no! It was cheap for me, but it cost the company a lot of money to sink that shaft." The man saw the light, that it was the infinite price paid by the Son of God for our salvation, which comes to us by faith and not by anything that we can do.

SIXTY-EIGHT

Gratitude

1. CONSIDER THE POSSIBILITIES

When Robinson Crusoe was wrecked on his lonely island, he drew up in two columns what he called the evil and the good. He was cast on a desolate island, but he was still alive—not drowned, as his ship's company was. He was apart from human society, but he was not starving. He had no clothes, but he was in a hot climate where he did not need them. He was without means of defense, but he saw no wild beasts such as he had seen on the coast of Africa. He had no one to whom he could speak, but God had sent the ship so near to the shore that he could get out of it all the things necessary for his basic wants. So he concluded that there was not any condition in the world so miserable but that one could find something for which to be grateful. DON EMMITTEE

2. TALLEST TALES DEPARTMENT

A man was being chased by a ferocious tiger. He ran until he came to a sheer cliff. As the tiger came bearing down on him, he grabbed a rope hanging over the cliff and climbed down out of the tiger's reach. The man looked up and saw the tiger leering at him, waiting to devour him. Then he looked down below the cliff. There was a deadly drop to the rocks of over five hundred feet. Then he looked up and saw two mice beginning to chew the rope. What should he do? The tiger above, the rocks below, and the rope about to break! Just then he saw a bright red strawberry growing out of the side of the cliff. He stretched out his hand, plucked the strawberry and popped it into his mouth. The juices of the strawberry were so sweet that as he ate he couldn't contain himself. "Delicious, that's the best strawberry I ever tasted!"

Had the man been preoccupied with the tiger (the past) or preoccupied with the future (the rocks below), he would never have enjoyed the strawberry, which we could call "the gift of the present."

3. SEEKING IN THE LIGHT

Use your eyes as if tomorrow you would be stricken blind. If I had three days to see, this is what I would want to see. On the first day I would want to see the people whose kindness and companionship have made my life worth living. I would call in my friends and look for a long time into their faces. I would also look into the face of a new baby. I would like to see the many books which have been read to me.

The next day I would get up early to see the dawn. I would visit a museum to learn of man's upward progress in the making of things. I would go to an art museum to probe the human souls by studying paintings and sculpture.

The third morning I would again greet the dawn, eager to discover new beauties in nature. I would spend this last day in the haunts of persons, where they work. I would stand at a busy street corner, trying to understand something of the daily lives of persons by looking into their faces and reading what is written there.

On the last evening I would go to a theater and see a hilariously funny play, so as to appreciate the overtones of humor in the human spirit. Yes, by God's light in Christ, seeing what matters and beholding the extraordinary in the commonplace. HELEN KELLER

4. FROM ONE GENERATION TO THE NEXT

A man was watching his eighty-year-old neighbor planting a small peach tree. He inquired of him as follows: "You don't expect to eat peaches from that tree, do you?" The old man rested on his spade. He said, "No, at my age I know I won't. But all my life I've enjoyed peaches—never from a tree I planted myself. I'm just trying to pay the other fellows who planted the trees for me."

5. THE RIGHT PERSPECTIVE

If you haven't all the things you want, be grateful for all you don't have that you don't want. MARTY RADCLIFF

6. THANKS FOR FAMILIAR THINGS

I offer thanks for just familiar things—
The ruddy glory of the sunset sky,

The shine of firelight as the dusk draws nigh,
The cheery song my little kettle sings,
The woodland music of my giant pine,
The last sweet tokens that my garden yields,
The mellow tints upon the autumn fields,
The far-off misty mountains' purple line,
The sense of rest that home so surely brings,
The books that wait my pleasure, true and fine,
Old friendships that I joy to feel are mine.
I offer thanks for just familiar things.

7. FOR THIS OUR BOUNTY

We thank thee for this smiling land of ours,
For all the beauty and the grandeur here;
We thank Thee most for freedom dearly bought
By Pilgrim band and sturdy pioneer.
Had they not bravely lived and so endured,
This priceless gift could never have been gained.
In thanks and solemn praise we raise our hearts,
And vow to keep our honor still unstained.
For this our bounty, Lord, we give Thee thanks
With grateful hearts as brimming as our store.
Our flocks are fed, our fields have yielded well.
Dear Lord, we could not rightly ask for more.
Pray, make us humble for our harvest's yield
And mindful of our neighbors in distress;
Unless in our abundance he may share,
Then empty is our show of thankfulness.

8. PRAISE AND THANKSGIVING

Heap high the board with plenteous cheer
And gather to the feast
And toast the sturdy pilgrim band
Whose courage never ceased.
Give praise to that All-Gracious One
By whom their steps were led;
And thanks unto the harvest's Lord
Who sends our daily bread. ALICE WILLIAMS BROTHERTON

9. RADICAL GRATITUDE

The following is an excerpt from the diary of George Muller, who founded orphanages in Victorian England.

August 18, 1838: I have not one penny in hand for the orphans. In a day or two again many pounds will be needed. My eyes are up to the Lord. Evening. Before this day is over, I have received from a sister five pounds. She had some time since put away her trinkets, to be sold for the benefit of the orphans. This morning, whilst in prayer, it came to her mind, I have this five pounds, and owe no man anything, therefore it would be better to give this money at once, as it may be some time before I can dispose of the trinkets. She therefore brought it, little knowing that there was not a penny in hand, and that I had been able to advance only four pounds, fifteen shillings and five pence for housekeeping in the Boys' Orphan-House, instead of the usual ten pounds.

August 23: Today I was again without one single penny, when three pounds was sent from Clapham, with a box of new clothes for the orphans.

Muller was later to look back on the period from September 1838 to the end of 1846 as the time when the greatest trials of faith were experienced in the orphan work. They were not years of continuous difficulty: rather there tended to be a pattern of a few months of trial, followed by some months of comparative plenty. During the whole period, according to Muller, the children knew nothing of the trial. In the midst of one of the darkest periods, he recorded, "These dear little ones know nothing about it, because their tables are as well supplied as when there was eight hundred pounds in the bank, and they have lack of nothing." At another time he wrote, "The orphans have never lacked anything. Had I had thousands of pounds in hand, they would have fared no better than they have; for they have always had good nourishing food, the necessary articles of clothing, etc." In other words, the periods of trial were so in the sense that there was no excess of funds: God supplied the need by the day, even by the hour. Enough was sent, but no more than enough.

10. THE ATTITUDE OF GRATITUDE

In some parts of Mexico hot springs and cold springs are found side by side—and because of the convenience of this natural phenomenon the women often bring their laundry and boil their clothes in the hot springs and then rinse them in the cold ones. A tourist, who was watching this procedure commented to his Mexican friend and guide: "I imagine that they think old Mother Nature is pretty generous to supply such ample, clean hot and cold water here side by side for their free use." The guide replied, "No senõr, there is much grumbling because she supplies no soap."

11. MOST PRECIOUS POSSESSION
Pastor Rittenhouse and his family were on vacation traveling down the highway when they saw a suitcase fly off the top of a car going the opposite direction. They stopped to pick it up, but the driver of the other car never stopped. The only clue to the driver's identity was a twenty dollar gold piece inscribed: "Given to Otis Sampson at his retirement by Portland Cement Company." After extensive correspondence, Otis Sampson was located and contacted. He wrote a letter telling them to discard the suitcase and all its contents, and send only the gold piece. Mr. Sampson used the phrase "my most precious possession," several times to describe the gold piece. Pastor Rittenhouse sent the gold piece, and wrote a cover letter telling Otis Sampson about his most prized possession, Jesus Christ. A year later, the pastor received a Christmas package. In it was the twenty dollar gold piece. Mr. Sampson wrote, "You will be happy to know we have become active members of a church. We want you to have this gold piece. I am seventy-four; my wife is seventy-two. You were the first one to tell us about Jesus. Now He is our most prized possession."

12. THE GREATEST VIRTUE
Thankfulness leaves no room for discouragement. I once read a legend of a man who found the barn where Satan kept his seeds ready to be sown in the human heart, and on finding the seeds of discouragement more numerous than others, he learned that those seeds could be made to grow almost anywhere. When Satan was questioned, he reluctantly admitted that there was one place in which he could never get them to thrive. "And where is that?" asked the man. Satan replied sadly, "In the heart of a grateful man." V. Norskov Olsen, president, loma linda university

13. BECAUSE HE WASN'T KILLED
We heard of a man and woman who gave a sizeable contribution to the church to honor the memory of their son who lost his life in the war. When the announcement was made of the generous donation, a woman whispered to her husband, "Let's give the same amount for our boy!" Her husband said, "What are you talking about? Our son wasn't killed." "That's just the point," she said. "Let's give it as an expression of our gratitude to God for sparing his life!"

14. THANKS FOR LITTLE THINGS

It was Thanksgiving season in the nursing home. The small resident population was gathered about their humble Thanksgiving table, and the director asked each in turn to express one thing for which they were thankful. Thanks were expressed for a home in which to stay, families, etc. One little old lady in her turn said: "I thank the Lord for two perfectly good teeth, one in my upper jaw and one in my lower jaw that match so that I can chew my food."

15. THE HEART'S GRATITUDE

As flowers carry dewdrops, trembling on the edges of the petals, and ready to fall at the first waft of the wind or brush of bird, so the heart should carry its beaded words of thanksgiving. At the first breath of heavenly flavor, let down the shower, perfumed with the heart's gratitude. HENRY WARD BEECHER

16. ALMOST EXPRESSED THANKS

In Vermont a farmer was sitting on the porch with his wife. He was beginning to realize how much she meant to him. It was about time—for they had lived together forty-two years, and she had been such a help, a very willing worker. One day as they sat together, he said, "Wife, you've been such a wonderful woman that there are times I can hardly keep from telling you." LESLIE FLYNN

17. THANKS FOR THE WEEVIL

In southern Alabama is the town of Enterprise, in Coffee County. There they have erected a monument to an insect, honoring the Mexican boll weevil. In 1895 the boll weevil began to destroy the major crop of the county, cotton. In desperation to survive the farmers had to diversify, and by 1919 the county's peanut crop was many times what cotton had been at its height. In that year of prosperity a fountain and monument were built. The inscription reads: "In profound appreciation of the boll weevil and what it has done as the herald of prosperity this monument was erected by the citizens of Enterprise, Coffee County, Alabama." Out of a time of struggle and crisis had come new growth and success. Out of adversity had come blessing.

18. THE PILGRIM PROCLAMATION

Inasmuch as the great Father has given us this year an abundant harvest of Indian corn, wheat, beans, squashes, and garden vegetables, and has made the forests to abound with game and the sea with fish and clams, and inasmuch as He has protected us from the ravages of the savages, has spared us from pestilence and disease, has granted us freedom to worship God according to the dictates of our own conscience; now, I, your magistrate, do proclaim that all ye Pilgrims, with your wives and little ones, do gather at ye meeting house, on ye hill, between the hours of 9 and 12 in the day time, on Thursday, November ye 29th of the year of our Lord one thousand six hundred and twenty-three, and the third year since ye Pilgrims landed on ye Pilgrim Rock, there to listen to ye pastor, and render thanksgiving to ye Almighty God for all His blessings. WILLIAM BRADFORD, *governor of the Plymouth Colony, 1623*

19. A SCHOLAR'S PERSPECTIVE
Matthew Henry, the famous Bible scholar, was once accosted by thieves and robbed of his purse. He wrote these words in his diary:

"Let me be thankful first because I was never robbed before; second, although they took my purse, they did not take my life; third, because, although they took my all, it was not much; and fourth, because it was I who was robbed, and not someone else."

20. FOREVER THANKFUL
On the tombstone of her husband's grave, a Southern mountain woman had chiseled in rough and uneven letters this epitaph: "He always appreciated." J. KENNETH MORRIS

21. IN PRAISE OF THANKSGIVING
Would you know who is the greatest saint in the world? It is not he who prays most or fasts most; it is not he who gives most alms, or is more eminent for temperance, chastity, or justice; but it is he who is always thankful to God who wills everything that God willeth, who receives everything as an instance of God's goodness, and has a heart always ready to praise God for it. WILLIAM LAW, *A Serious Call to a Devout and Holy Life*

22. THE MAGNETIC HEART
If one should give me a dish of sand and tell me there were particles of iron in it, I might look for them with my eyes and search for them with my clumsy fingers and be unable to detect them; but let me take a magnet and sweep through it and now would it draw to itself the almost invisible particles by the mere power of attraction.

The unthankful heart, like my finger in the sand, discovers no mercies; but let the thankful heart sweep through the day and as the magnet finds the iron, so it will find, in every hour, some heavenly blessings, only the iron in God's sand is gold! HENRY WARD BEECHER

23. SAY THANK YOU
Thou hast given so much to me,
Give one thing more—a grateful heart.
Not thankful when it pleases me,
As if Thy blessings had spare days,
But such a heart, whose pulse may be Thy praise. GEORGE HERBERT

24. THE SALT OF LIFE
Fulton Oursler tells of his old nurse, who was born a slave on the eastern shore of Maryland and who attended the birth of his mother and his own birth. She taught him the greatest lesson in giving thanks and finding contentment. "I remember her as she sat at the kitchen table in our house; the hard, old, brown hands folded across her starched apron, the glistening eyes, and the husky old whispering voice, saying, 'Much obliged, Lord, for my vittles.' 'Anna,' I asked, 'what's a vittle?' 'It's what I've got to eat and drink, that's vittles.' 'But you'd get your vittles whether you thanked the Lord or not.' 'Sure, but it makes everything taste better to be thankful.'"

25. THANK GOD
The roar of the world in my ears,
Thank God for the roar of the world!
Thank God for the mighty tide of fears
Against me always hurled!
Thank God for the bitter and ceaseless strife,
Thank God for the stress and the pain of life,
And oh, thank God for God! JOYCE KILMER

SIXTY-NINE
Grief
(See also Death)

1. CREATING SOMETHING NEW OUT OF ASHES
Some years ago Alexander Woolcott described a scene in a New York hospital where a grief-stricken mother sat in the hospital lounge in stunned silence, tears streaming down her cheeks. She had just lost her only child and she was gazing blindly into space while the head nurse talked to her, simply

because it was the duty of the head nurse to talk in such circumstances.

"Did Mrs. Norris notice the shabby little boy sitting in the hall just next to her daughter's room?"

No, Mrs. Norris had not noticed him.

"There," continued the head nurse, "there is a case. That little boy's mother is a young French woman who was brought in a week ago by ambulance from their shabby one-room apartment to which they had gravitated when they came to this country scarcely three months ago. They had lost all their people in the old country and knew nobody here. The two had only each other. Every day that lad has come and sat there from sunup to sundown in the vain hope that she would awaken and speak to him. Now, he has no home at all!"

Mrs. Norris was listening now. So the nurse went on, "Fifteen minutes ago that little mother died, dropped off like a pebble in the boundless ocean, and now it is my duty to go out and tell that little fellow that, at the age of seven, he is all alone in the world." The head nurse paused, then turned plaintively to Mrs. Norris. "I don't suppose," she said hesitantly, "I don't suppose that you would go out and tell him for me?"

What happened in the next few moments is something that you remember forever. Mrs. Norris stood up, dried her tears, went out and put her arms around the lad and led that homeless child off to her childless home, and in the darkness they both knew they had become lights to each other!

2. SORROW, THE TEACHER
I walked a mile with Pleasure;
She chatted all the way;
But left me none the wiser
For all she had to say.
I walked a mile with Sorrow,
And ne'er a word said she;
But, oh! the things I learned from her,
When Sorrow walked with me. ROBERT HAMILTON

3. TRUE GRIEF
A visitor at a zoo noticed an attendant crying quietly over in a corner. The visitor asked another attendant what the man was crying about, and he was told that one of the elephants had died. Touched by this, the visitor then asked, "I assume he must have been particularly fond of that elephant?" And the reply came back, "No, it's not that. What he's crying for is that he's the one who has to dig the grave."

4. HIDDEN JOY

A gifted public speaker was asked to recall his most difficult speaking assignment. He said, "That's easy. It was an address I gave to the National Conference of Undertakers. The topic they gave me was 'How to Look Sad at a Ten Thousand Dollar Funeral.'"

5. SORROWS IN PERSPECTIVE

Sorrows are often like clouds, which though black when they are passing over us, when they are past become as if they were the garments of God thrown off in purple and gold along the sky. HENRY WARD BEECHER

6. THE NIGHT OF SORROW

Blessed to us is the night, for it reveals the stars.

SEVENTY

Guidance

1. SEARCHING FOR THE RIGHT WAY

Once a Hasidic teacher told this parable: A man had been wandering about in a forest for several days, unable to find the way out. Finally he saw a man approaching him in the distance. His heart was filled with joy. *Now I shall surely find out which is the right way out of this forest,* he thought to himself. When they neared each other, he asked the man, "Brother, will you please tell me the way out of the forest? I have been wandering about in here for several days and I am unable to find my way out." Said the other to him, "Brother, I do not know the way out either, for I, too, have been wandering about in here for many days. But this much I can tell you. Do not go the way that I have gone, for I know that it is not the way. Now come, let us search for the way out together." The teacher added: "So it is with us. The one thing that each one of us knows is that the way we have been going until now is not the way. Now come, let us join hands and look for the way together."

2. ASKING FOR HELP

Sign on the back of a trailer: "If I'm not headed west, stop me and turn me around."

SEVENTY-ONE

Habit

1. RUSH, RUSH

I heard recently about a man who prided himself on being exceedingly punctual. He followed a very precise routine every morning. His alarm went off at 6:30. He rose briskly, shaved, showered, ate his breakfast, brushed his teeth, picked up his briefcase, got into his car, drove to the nearby ferry landing, parked his car, rode the ferry across to the downtown business area, got off the ferry, walked smartly to his building, marched to the elevator, rode to the seventeenth floor, hung up his coat, opened his briefcase, spread his papers out on his desk, and sat down in his chair at precisely 8:00. Not 8:01, not even 7:59. Always at 8:00 A.M. He followed this same routine without variation for eight years.

Until one morning his alarm did not go off and he slept fifteen minutes late. When he did awake, he was panic-stricken. He rushed through his shower, nicked himself when he shaved, gulped down his breakfast, only halfway brushed his teeth, grabbed up his briefcase, jumped into his car, sped to the ferry landing, jumped out of his car, and looked for the ferry. There it was, out in the water a few feet from the dock. He said to himself, "I think I can make it," and he ran down the dock toward the ferry at full speed. Reaching the edge of the pier he gave an enormous leap out over the water and miraculously landed with a loud thud on the deck of the ferry.

The captain rushed down to make sure he was all right and said, "Man, that was a tremendous leap, but if you would have just waited another minute, we would have reached the dock, and you could have walked on."

2. SHORT MEMORY

A man who flew his own plane got tired of the long auto trip from the airport to his country place which was situated on a lovely lake. So he had the idea of equipping his plane with pontoons so he could land right in front of his cottage. However, on his first trip up to the country with his newly-equipped plane, he headed for a landing at the airport just as he always had done in the past. Old habits are hard to break. But as he was going in for the landing it dawned on his wife what was happening and she hollered, "What do you think you're doing? You can't land this thing on the runway. You don't have any wheels, you've got pontoons on it!"

Fortunately, her warning shout was in time and he pulled up from his landing pattern and swung the airplane around and headed the plane for a landing on the lake.

After the plane landed safely on the lake, he heaved a really big sigh of relief and turned to his wife and said, "That's about the stupidest thing I've ever done!" Then he turned, opened the door, stepped out, and fell directly into the lake.

3. FOLLOWING ORDERS

There is an ancient story of a sentry standing day after day at his post with no apparent reason for his being there. One day, a passerby asked him why he was standing in that particular place. "I don't know," the sentry replied, "I'm just following orders." The passerby then went to the captain of the guard and asked him why the sentry was posted in that place. "I don't know," the captain replied. "We're just following orders." This prompted the captain of the guard to pose the question to higher authority. "Why do we post a sentry at that particular spot?" he asked the king. But the king didn't know. So he summoned his wise men and asked them the question. The answer came back that one hundred years before, Catherine the Great had planted a rosebush and had ordered a sentry placed there to protect it. The rosebush had been dead for eighty years, but the sentry still stood guard.

4. CONDITIONED

Years ago the Denver Zoo had a difficult decision to make. They were offered the gift of a beautiful, large polar bear, but the problem was that there was no existing room for the bear. At the time of the gift the board of directors was in the middle of a fund-raising campaign to renovate the zoo. They changed the strategy to include a magnificent habitat for the polar bear in their renovation plans.

In the meantime the bear was put in a small temporary cage. The space was so small that it could only take three steps, turnaround, and walk three steps back.

Because of unforeseen delays the construction took three years, but the bear's new home was grand—waterfalls, caves, and lots of space. The bear entered its new home, looked around, took three steps, turned around, took three steps back, and turned around.

5. PAY AS YOU GO

A conductor on the Santa Fe was converted and united with the church. After he had been faithful in his religious duties for some weeks, he was asked one Sunday morning to help take the offering. He started down the aisle, and all went well until he came to a richly dressed woman. She allowed the plate to go past her, whereupon the conductor unconsciously reached up for the bell rope to stop the train, and said, "Madam, if you don't pay, you'll have to get off."

6. THE NATURE OF HABITS
All habits gather by unseen degrees—
As brooks make rivers, rivers run to seas. JOHN DRYDEN

7. RUTS AREN'T SO BAD
Why this passion for shaking people out of ruts? I am devoted to ruts. Moreover, most of the people who are in ruts are much nicer, and much happier, than the people who are not. Ruts are the wise old wrinkles that civilization has traced on the earth's ancient face. BEVERLY NICHOLS, *The Gift of a Home*

8. THE POWERFUL MOTIVATION OF HABITS
Farmer Brown and farmer Green were neighbors. Farmer Brown had a dog that loved to chase cats. Farmer Green had a cat that hated dogs. Whenever Brown came to visit Green, his dog would come along. As soon as the dog got into Green's yard the dog and the cat would be off, and the cat would fly at top speed around the house with the dog in hot pursuit. As they came out from behind the house, the cat would take a flying leap and make his escape up the big maple tree. This happened every time Brown came to visit Green. After a few years Green cut down the tree. A couple of days later Brown and his dog came to visit. The dog and the cat took off. Out from around the house came the cat with the dog right on his tail. The cat was thirty feet in the air before he realized that something was different.

SEVENTY-TWO
Handicaps
(See also Adversity)

1. HANDICAP'S TRIUMPHS
John Bartel was a healthy, athletic, twenty-year-old young man who was gradually taking full charge of the family dairy farm with all its multiple duties.

It was a beautiful spring day in the lusciously green Fraser Valley, British Columbia. The grass was just right for filling the huge silos for winter feed. John was busily unloading the heavy fodder into the silage cutter and blower when a large bunch momentarily stopped the conveyer belt. By sheer habit, John stepped on the guilty bunch to get it moving again while his eyes selected the next place to insert his pitchfork, when he felt a tug on his right leg and he watched in horror as his foot and then his leg were shredded and sent up into the silo.

When he finally extracted himself, all he had left was a three-inch stub. Praying earnestly all the while, he undid his pant belt and used it as a tourniquet to stop the profuse bleeding. Painfully, he dragged himself into the milk parlor of the dairy and called for an ambulance.

A few days after the operation and cleanup, he sat in his wheelchair in the hospital sun room, feeling sorry for himself and wishing himself dead rather than handicapped for the rest of his life. He noticed another wheelchair enter the room. A middle-aged man sat there with a blanket around him and looked at John with some disdain and said, "Young man, shame on you whining away like that here. You should be thankful that you are alive and healthy!" John replied a bit tersely, "You don't understand. . . . My leg is gone forever!" "Well, then, look at this," replied the man as he threw off the blanket and revealed two stubs about as long as John's. He then continued, "Young man, get well; then go out there and prove to the world that you can do as much with one leg as anyone else who has his two legs."

John went back to the farm and after a number of fittings, had a mechanical leg and foot made to suit his needs. He milks up to seventy cows at a time for his livelihood. He has taken over full possession of the family farm. John swims and water-skis (he always slaloms), he was featured in a sports magazine a few years ago as an ardent downhill skier. John Bartel married my niece. When I officiated at the wedding, I suggested they could remain standing for the prayer of blessing, but John said, "No way, I can kneel down and get up like everyone else on my own when the prayer is over."

They have a fine family of three children. John takes the oldest boy, now eight, to the top of the five thousand foot Mount Cheam as they both ride their trail motor bikes along that mountain trail. John and his wife Margaret were the youth leaders in their church for a number of years. He is now about thirty-three and has proven that he can do everything with only one leg and more than others can do with two, at least nearly everything . . . he can't stand only on his mechanical leg. He has a good sense of humor and a living, practical faith in the determination to succeed. And he is successful in so many ways and an encouragement and example to everyone. John would say, "I can do all things through Christ, which strengthens me."

2. SPORTING OBSTACLES

On November 8, 1970, there was a hard-fought game between the New Orleans Saints and the Detroit Lions. The game was nip and tuck, and it came down to the last final seconds to see who would win. The crowd gasped as they realized that the Saints were going to try a field goal of sixty-three yards. To try something that had never been done before in the history of man would certainly take a Goliath of a person. The crowd looked for a man with a size 45 shoe and a chest as big as the back of a semi. But instead they saw a man run out onto the field who had no fingers on his right hand, no toes on his right foot, and only half of his kicking foot. When Tom Dempsey kicked that ball he set history for professional football and set a world record that had never been done before. The beautiful thought about Tom Dempsey is not that he won a football game, but that he saw an obstacle and refused to be handicapped.

3. IGNORING HANDICAPS

In a small town in the midwest where I spent six years of my early youth, there lived a mentally retarded adult named Myron. It was during Depression years and there was no place for Myron to be "kept" but at home. He lived there with his mother and they survived on the work that Myron did as a gardener.

He had a proverbial "green thumb," and the places where he did the gardening were easy to identify. The lawns, shrubs, hedges, flowers—all showed care, skill, and loving attention. Myron also did "volunteer" work. He cut grass, raked leaves, and planted flowers in what would otherwise have been unsightly vacant lots. He was probably best known for his "oil can." He always carried a small can of lubricating oil in his hip pocket. A squeaky door or hinge or gate always got a "free" dose from Myron's oil can.

Never a Sunday went by that Myron was not in church with his mother.

Yes, we boys tried to "tease" him. But he always got the better of us because he refused to be anything but cheerful, full of good humor, and totally unflappable.

Myron died a few years after I left town to attend college. It was not easy to arrange, but I went back for the funeral. I was not prepared for what I saw. It seemed that everyone in town had decided to attend the funeral and there were scores of others, like myself, who had traveled from distant places to be there.

Without consciously attempting to do so, Myron had patterned for us the kind of life that really matters. No, he had not achieved fame, fortune, or honor. But he had been a worker, an optimist, an "easer of tensions" and a faithful churchman. He was a man who "overcame" a handicap that he didn't even know he had.

4. WHAT DO YOU WALK ON?
When William Pitt was prime minister of Great Britain, he moved about painfully on crutches. A man came to him one day complaining that he had been given an impossible task. In response, Pitt picked up his crutches and shook them at the man. "Impossible, sir?" he shouted. "I walk on impossibilities."

5. DEMOSTHENES ON THE PODIUM
When Demosthenes, the famed Greek orator, first spoke in public, he was hissed off the platform. His voice was harsh and weak and his appearance unimpressive. He determined that his fellow citizens would yet appreciate his words, so he practiced day and night. He shaved half his head so no one would want to invite him to social events. To overcome a stammer, he recited with pebbles in his mouth and yelled against the thunders of the Aegean Sea so his voice would get louder. He stood beneath a suspended sword to train himself not to favor a shoulder that kept hitching. He practiced facial expressions in front of a mirror. It's not surprising that when he next appeared in public he moved the Greek nation.

He and another orator spoke on a matter of national concern. When his companion concluded his speech, the crowd said, "What marvelous oratory!" But when Demosthenes finished, they cried with one voice, "Let us go and fight Philip!" JAY OSWALD SANDERS

6. GOD'S ATTENTION GETTERS
Happinessce Jones is a renowned concert organist and teacher at Baylor University. Several years ago she played the first full concert on the new pipe organ at the Crystal Cathedral in California, which cost over $1 million. At the age of sixteen she was a piano major at the University of Texas. A sprained wrist interrupted her promising career as a pianist. For six weeks she could not touch a keyboard. Not wanting to waste the time, she decided to learn to play organ pedals with her feet, and a new career was born. "God has a way," she relates, "to get your attention and say, 'Hey, I have something better for you to do.'"

7. DESPITE BLINDNESS
George Matheson was born in Glasgow, Scotland, in 1842. Before he reached the age of two, it was discovered that his eyesight was defective. He, his

parents, and the specialists fought a heroic fight, but before George had finished his course at Glasgow University he was completely blind. With courage and faith he graduated with honors in philosophy, studied for the ministry, and in a few years' time became the minister of one of the largest churches in Edinburgh, where he carried on a memorable ministry. In addition to his laborious preparation of his services he did a great deal of parish visitation, wrote numerous articles and twelve books, and continued his own studies throughout his life.

It must have been heartbreaking for George Matheson's parents to have a strange infection in their baby's eyes lead to his blindness. Yet, in that tragic situation George Matheson found God's resources available for him. God poured into his heart the courage, resourcefulness, and grim perseverance that gave him victory over his handicap. Through it all his faith grew stronger, and after twenty years of blindness he wrote:

O Love that will not let me go,
I rest my weary soul in Thee!
I give Thee back the life I owe,
That in Thine ocean depths its flow
May richer, fuller be.

8. AND HE DID

Born on a Kansas farm and educated in a one-room school, he lived a tough and difficult existence as a boy. Glenn and his brother kept the school's fire going, and one morning when the boys poured kerosene on live coals, the stove blew sky high. Glenn would have escaped, but his brother had been left behind. Rushing back to help, he suffered terrible burns as did his brother. His brother died, and Glenn's legs sustained severe damage.

The story does not end here, however. Glenn had long dreamed of making a track record. Through a period of discouragement, disappointment, and threatened meaninglessness, he somehow kept going . More, he made up his mind that he would walk again—and he did! That he would run—and he did! That he would discipline himself—and he did! That he would master the mile—and he did! That he would break the international record—and he did!

Glenn Cunningham purposed in his heart. The purpose in a person's heart captures the soul and has power to transform the ugliest circumstances into the richest blessings.

9. HANDICAPPED AND SPORTING

The late singer and actor Gordon MacRae told this story:

It seems that Arnold Palmer was invited to come to a convention of blind golfers. He asked the golfers how they were able to know what direction to hit the ball. One blind golfer explained that the caddy went out ahead of him with a little bell which he would ring as he stood near the hole. The blind golfer would then hit the ball toward the sound of the bell. Arnold asked how well it worked, and the blind golfer said that it worked so well he was willing to take on Arnold Palmer for a round of golf; and just to make it interesting, was willing to bet Palmer ten thousand dollars he could beat him. Well, this just blew Palmer's mind. He pressed him, but the man insisted he was willing to bet that amount on his ability to beat Palmer. So, the deal was struck. Palmer said, "OK. What time do we tee off?" And the blind man said, "10:30 . . . tonight!"

10. A PARABLE OF UNITY
During Vacation Bible School last week my wife had an experience with her primary class that she says she will never forget. Her class was interrupted on Wednesday about an hour before dismissal when a new student was brought in. The little boy had one arm missing, and since the class was almost over, she had no opportunity to learn any of the details about the cause or his state of adjustment. She was very nervous and afraid that one of the other children would comment on his handicap and embarrass him. There was no opportunity to caution them, so she proceeded as carefully as possible. As the class time came to a close, she began to relax. She asked the class to join her in their usual closing ceremony. "Let's make our churches," she said. "Here's the church and here's the steeple, open the doors and there's . . ." The awful truth of her own actions struck her. The very thing she had feared that the children would do, she had done. As she stood there speechless, the little girl sitting next to the boy reached over with her left hand and placed it up to his right hand and said, "Davey, let's make the church together." This story may be seen as a parable of our search for oneness in Christ: to put our inadequate, handicapped lives alongside the lives of others and to pray, "Let's make the church together."

11. WIZARD OF ELECTRICITY
Charles Steinmetz, the electrical genius, and one of the founding fathers of the colossal General Electric, was crippled from birth. His body was grotesque; he was so short in stature that he looked like a dwarf; he was a hunchback.

His mother died before he was one year old. His father was comparatively poor, but was determined that as far as possible, young Charles would have a thorough education. Charles couldn't run and play games as normal boys did, so he made up his mind that he would devote himself to science. He set this goal: "I will make discoveries that will help other people."

When he immigrated to the U.S., he could not speak a word of English. The port authorities were tempted to return him to his native Switzerland. His face was swollen from the cold he had endured on the boat passage across the Atlantic. He was dwarfed and misshapen in body. His sight was defective. His clothes were shabby.

But Charles stayed, and even found a job that paid him twelve dollars a week. And he showed amazing abilities. The infant company, General Electric, quickly realized that in Charles Steinmetz they had one of the greatest experts in the world in the field of electricity. His career was marked by unparalleled research and development.

When Steinmetz died in 1923, one writer said, "This deformed hunchback had the mind of an angel and the soul of a seer." Though he was twisted and dwarfed in body, Charles Steinmetz was a giant in mind and spirit.

12. TWO WAYS OF RESPONDING

Two paraplegics were in the news recently. One was Kenneth Wright, a high school football star and later, an avid wrestler, boxer, hunter, and skin diver. A broken neck sustained in a wrestling match in 1979 left him paralyzed from the chest down. He underwent therapy, and his doctors were hopeful that one day he would be able to walk with the help of braces and crutches. But, apparently, the former athlete could not reconcile himself to his physical disability. He prevailed upon two of his best friends to take him in his wheelchair to a wooded area, where they left him alone with a twelve-gauge shotgun. After they left, he held the shotgun to his abdomen and pulled the trigger. Kenneth Wright, twenty-four, committed suicide. The second paraplegic in the news was Jim McGowan. Thirty years ago, at the age of nineteen, Jim was stabbed and left paralyzed from the middle of his chest down. He is now confined to a wheelchair. But he made the news recently when he made a successful parachute jump, landing on his target in the middle of Lake Wallenpaupack in the Poconos. Newspeople learned a number of things about Jim. He lives alone, cooks his meals, washes his clothes, and cleans his house. He drives himself in his specially equipped automobile. He has written three books, and he did the photography for our country's first book on the history of wheelchair sports. Two men with handicaps: one chose life and the other one didn't. As Robert Frost wrote: "Two roads diverged in a yellow wood, and I took the one less traveled by . . . and that has made all the difference."

13. I WAS THERE

I have a dear friend, Bill Mann, who has one of the great singing voices in the Christian church in this nation. I remember some years ago he told me about the most special concert in his life. It was after the concert was over and he returned to his dressing room. Waiting for him there was a woman who was blind, deaf, and mute. Through the lady who was with her, she asked if he would sing for her the last song he sang in the concert. "Surely," he said.

And standing only five inches from his face . . . and placing her fingers on his lips and on his vocal cords, he sang again, "Were You There When They Crucified My Lord?" As he finished singing, a tear trickled down the face of Helen Keller. Indistinctly, she said, as the words were repeated by the lady with her: "I was there!"

"Deaf, blind, mute from birth?" you say. "Isn't that too much for one individual to bear?"

No, as a matter of fact, of all the women in this nation there was probably no contemporary who gave others more insight into the meaning of suffering than Helen Keller . . . or more insight into the love of God.

SEVENTY-THREE
Happiness and Joy

1. IN THE LONG RUN

If you wish to be happy for one hour, get intoxicated. If you wish to be happy for three days, get married. If you wish to be happy for eight days, kill your pig and eat it. If you wish to be happy forever, learn to fish.
Chinese proverb

2. LIMITS

A man had just had his annual physical exam and was waiting for the doctor's initial report. After a few minutes the doctor came in with his charts in his hand and said: "There's no reason why you can't live a completely normal life as long as you don't try to enjoy it."

3. SOFT AND GENTLE
Happiness is a butterfly, which, when pursued, is always just beyond your grasp, but which, if you will sit down quietly, may alight upon you.
NATHANIEL HAWTHORNE

4. THE THREE ESSENTIALS
The grand essentials to happiness in this life are something to do, someone to love, and something to hope for. JOSEPH ADDISON

5. CHOOSING HAPPINESS
It's so important to know you can choose to feel good. Most people don't think they have that choice. NEIL SIMON

6. INDIRECT JOY
How happy are the pessimists! What joy is theirs when they have proved there is no joy. MARIE EBNER-ESCHENBACH

7. A SMILE
A smile costs nothing, but gives much. It enriches those who receive, without making poorer those who give. It takes but a moment, but the memory of it sometimes lasts forever. None is so rich or mighty that they can get along without it, and none is so poor but that they can be made rich by it. A smile creates happiness in the home, fosters good will in business, and is the countersign of friendship. It brings rest to the weary, cheer to the discouraged, sunshine to the sad, and it is nature's best antidote for trouble. Yet it cannot be bought, begged, borrowed, or stolen, for it is something that is of no value to anyone until it is given away. Some people are too tired to give you a smile. Give them one of yours, as none needs a smile so much as the one who has no more to give.

8. SHARED JOY
A sorrow shared is half the sorrow, while a joy shared is twice the joy.

9. STRATEGY FOR HAPPINESS
I have learned to seek my happiness by limiting my desires, rather than in attempting to satisfy them. JOHN STUART MILL

10. LEARNING TO LET GO
The joy is not always in getting what we want but in letting go of what we don't need.

11. TRAGEDY TO TRIUMPH
Dr. Viktor Frankl, author of the book *Man's Search for Meaning,* was imprisoned by the Nazis in World War II because he was a Jew. His wife, his

children, and his parents were all killed in the holocaust.

The Gestapo made him strip. He stood there totally naked. As they cut away his wedding band, Viktor said to himself, "You can take away my wife, you can take away my children, you can strip me of my clothes and my freedom, but there is one thing no person can *ever* take away from me—and that is my freedom to choose how I will react to what happens to me!" Even under the most difficult of circumstances, happiness is a choice which transforms our tragedies into triumph.

12. LEARNING IT EARLY

The art of happiness, like that of bicycling, should be learned as early as possible. The balance, the unconscious poise, the effortless adjustment, do not come naturally to those who have never known them in childhood. MARGARET KENNEDY

13. REALISTIC HAPPINESS

Who could speak more realistically about the illusion of a yuppie value system than Alexander Solzhenitsyn, who suffered deprivation of all that money can buy. In "The Prison Chronicle" he says, as few of us can, "Don't be afraid of misfortune and do not yearn after happiness. It is, after all, all the same. The bitter doesn't last forever, and the sweet never fills the cup to overflowing. It is enough if you don't freeze in the cold and if hunger and thirst don't claw at your sides. If your back isn't broken, if your feet can walk, if both arms work, if both eyes can see, and if both ears can hear, then whom should you envy? And why? Our envy of others devours us most of all. Rub your eyes and purify your heart and prize above all else in the world those who love you and wish you well."

14. C. S. LEWIS ON JOY

Happiness is never in our power and pleasure is. I doubt whether anyone who has tasted joy would ever, if both were in his power, exchange it for all the pleasure in the world. C. S. LEWIS, *Surprised by Happiness*

15. DR. GEORGE BURNS

If you were to go around asking people what would make them happier, you'd get answers like a new car, a bigger house, a raise in pay, winning a lottery, a face-lift, more kids, less kids, a new restaurant to go to—probably not one in a hundred would say a chance to help people. And yet that may bring the most happiness of all.

I don't know Dr. Jonas Salk, but after what he's done for us with his polio vaccine, if he isn't happy, he should have that brilliant head of his examined. Of course, not all of us can do what he did. I know I can't do what he did; he beat me to it.

But the point is, it doesn't have to be anything that extraordinary. It can be working for a worthy cause, performing a needed service, or just doing something that helps another person. GEORGE BURNS

16. GOOD DAYS
An older member of our parish taught me a beautiful lesson one day when I casually wished him a good day. He remarked, "They're all good days. It's what we put in them that changes them." In Genesis 1 we read that as God made the world day by day, he pronounced that creation process good—day by day.

17. FULL LIFE
If you observe a really happy man you will find him building a boat, writing a symphony, educating his son, growing double dahlias in his garden, or looking for dinosaur eggs in the Gobi desert. He will not be searching for happiness as if it were a collar button that has rolled under the radiator. He will not be striving for it as a goal in itself. He will have become aware that he is happy in the course of living life twenty-four crowded hours of the day. W. BERAN WOLFE

18. A SIMPLE FORMULA
You should do something every day to make other people happy, even if it's only to leave them alone.

19. HELEN KELLER ON HAPPINESS
Many persons have a wrong idea about what constitutes true happiness. It is not attained through self-gratifications, but through fidelity to a worthy purpose.

20. THE LIGHT OF HAPPINESS
Happiness has no reason. It is not to be found in the facts of our lives, but in the color of the light by which we look at the facts.

21. KEATS ON JOY
A thing of beauty is a joy for ever:
Its loveliness increases; it will never
Pass into nothingness; but still will keep
A bower quiet for us, and a sleep
Full of sweet dreams, and health and quiet breathing. JOHN KEATS, *Endymion*

22. WHO IS HAPPY?

An English newspaper asked this question: "Who are the happiest people on earth?" These were the four prize-winning answers:

- A craftsman or artist whistling over a job well done.
- A little child building sand castles.
- A mother, after a busy day, bathing her baby.
- A doctor who has finished a difficult and dangerous operation, and saved a human life.

No millionaires among these, one notices. No kings or emperors. Riches and rank, no matter how the world strives for them, do not make happy lives.

23. PRESCRIPTION FOR UNHAPPINESS

1. Make little things bother you: don't just let them, *make* them!
2. Lose your perspective of things, and keep it lost. Don't put first things first.
3. Get yourself a good worry—one about which you cannot do anything but worry.
4. Be a perfectionist: condemn yourself and others for not achieving perfection.
5. Be right, always right, perfectly right all the time. Be the only one who is right, and be rigid about your rightness.
6. Don't trust or believe people, or accept them at anything but their worst and weakest. Be suspicious. Impute ulterior motives to them.
7. Always compare yourself unfavorably to others, which is the guarantee of instant misery.
8. Take personally, with a chip on your shoulder, everything that happens to you that you don't like.
9. Don't give yourself wholeheartedly or enthusiastically to anyone or to anything.
10. Make happiness the aim of your life instead of bracing for life's barbs through a "bitter with the sweet" philosophy.

Use this prescription regularly for awhile and you will be guaranteed unhappiness.

24. TOP OF THE LINE

The supreme happiness of life is the conviction that we are loved.
Victor Hugo

25. SHORT BUT SWEET

Happiness makes up in height for what it lacks in length. Robert Frost

26. GOETHE'S VIEW

Who is the happiest of men? He who values the merits of others, and in their pleasure takes joy, even as though t'were his own.
JOHANN WOLFGANG VON GOETHE

27. FINDING JOY

It is not easy to find happiness in ourselves, and it is not possible to find it elsewhere. AGNES REPPLIER

28. THE SOURCE OF HAPPINESS

Happiness grows at our own firesides, and is not to be picked in strangers' gardens. DOUGLAS JERROLD

29. ON A ROADSIDE SIGN

The road to happiness is always under construction.

30. DIVIDED JOY

Grief can take care of itself, but to get the full value of joy, we must have somebody to divide it with. MARK TWAIN

31. IT FOLLOWS

Those who bring sunshine into the lives of others cannot keep it from themselves. J. M. BARRIE

32. SACRIFICAL LOVE AND HEDONISM

Jesus said: "If any man will come after me, let him deny himself and take up his cross daily and follow me." A few years ago college president William Banowski interviewed Hugh Hefner. He wrote of this encounter:

I was made keenly aware of the universal appeal of Jesus during one of my conversations with Hugh Hefner in Chicago. As we talked, Mr. Hefner surprised me by saying, "If Christ were here today and had to choose between being on the staff of one of the joy-killing, pleasure-denying churches, he would, of course, immediately join us." What most offended Jesus' contemporaries, and what modern men find even harder to accept, is His insistence that to find life we must first lose it. Hugh Hefner writes: "We reject any philosophy which holds that a man must deny himself for others." The playboy cult holds that every man ought to love himself preeminently and pursue his own pleasure constantly. Nowhere is the clash between popular playboyism and the ethical realism of Jesus any sharper than over how the good life is to be achieved. Hugh Hefner tells us to get all we can. Jesus tells us to give all we can. Because the clash is total, there is no way to gloss over it. The popular philosophy teaches that to get life you must grab it;

Jesus taught that to win we must surrender. The conflict is absolute and irrevocable.

33. THE ALTERNATIVES
Some pursue happiness . . . others create it.

34. THE PHILOSOPHICAL APPROACH TO TAIL CHASING
A big dog saw a little dog chasing its tail and asked, "Why are you chasing your tail so?" Said the puppy, "I have mastered philosophy; I have solved the problems of the universe which no dog before me has rightly solved; I have learned that the best thing for a dog is happiness, and that happiness is my tail. Therefore I am chasing it; and when I catch it, I shall have happiness."

Said the old dog, "My son, I, too, have paid attention to the problems of the universe in my weak way, and I have formed some opinions. I, too, have judged that happiness is a fine thing for a dog, and that happiness is in my tail. But I have noticed that when I chase after it, it keeps running away from me, but when I go about my business, it comes after me." C. L. JAMES

35. THE TRIAL
One is never more on trial than in the moment of excessive good fortune. LEW WALLACE

36. WHO HELPS THE HELPER?
The story is told of a young man who come to a renowned doctor in Paris complaining of depression. He asked what he could do to get well. The doctor thought of a well-known young man named Grimaldi, a leader of café society who cut a wide and lighthearted swath through Paris nightlife. The doctor told the young man, "Introduce yourself to Grimaldi. Let him show you how to enjoy yourself and you will get well." The downcast young patient looked up with a sardonic smile and said, "I am Grimaldi." LANCE WEBB, *How Bad Are Your Sins?*

37. FEELING THROUGH OTHERS
Helen Keller was deaf and blind from an incurable childhood disease. Anne Sullivan taught her to read through her senses of touch, smell, and taste. At the end of her autobiography Helen Keller says:

"Fate—silent, pitiless—bars the way. Fain would I question his imperious decree; for my heart is undisciplined and passionate, but my tongue will not utter the bitter, futile words that rise to my lips, and they fall back into my heart like unshed tears. Silence sits immense upon my soul. Then comes hope with a smile and whispers, 'There is joy in self-forgetfulness.' So I try to make the light in other people's eyes my sun, the music in others' ears my symphony, the smile on others' lips my happiness."

38. TRUE JOY

This is the true joy in life: being used for a purpose recognized by yourself as a mighty one. The being thoroughly worn out before you are thrown on the scrap heap; the being a force of nature instead of a feverish selfish little clod of ailments and grievances complaining that the world will not devote itself to making you happy. GEORGE BERNARD SHAW

39. PACKAGES FROM HELL

Every package from hell comes disguised as ecstasy. JIM MURRAY

40. BABE ZAHARIAS ON HAPPINESS

George Zaharias, the husband of the great golfer Babe Didrikson Zaharias once told Bob Richards this story:

Babe was dying of cancer, and he stood by her bed, crying like a baby. She said, "Now, honey, don't take on so. While I've been in the hospital, I have learned one thing. A moment of happiness is a lifetime, and I have had a lot of happiness. I have a lot of it."

Richards wrote about this later, in his book *Heart of a Champion:* "That's courage . . . to stress the quality of life rather than just the quantity, to meet life's greatest tragedy with a smile. . . . That's what makes courage."

41. THE WATCH TICKS ON

Many years ago, a little boy was given a priceless possession: his deceased grandfather's gold pocket watch. How he treasured it! But one day, while playing at his father's ice plant, he lost the watch amid all the ice and sawdust.

He searched and scratched, becoming frantic, but no watch. Then he suddenly realized what to do. He stopped scurrying around and became very still. In the silence, he heard the watch ticking.

God has given each of us a priceless gift of joy in Jesus. How easy it is to lose our joy in the scurrying around of life. Yet it is always there to find, if we will but pause and listen to the beautiful presence of Jesus in our hearts.

HEAVEN AND HELL *(See Eternity)*

SEVENTY-FOUR

Honesty

(See also Truth)

1. BENDING THE TRUTH

A young mother encountered her son on the street when he should have been in school. When the boy finished explaining why he was not where he was supposed to be, the mother replied, "I'm not accusing you of telling a lie. I'm just saying that I have never before heard of a school that gives time off for good behavior."

2. WHOOPS, TOO LATE

Employees in a Midwestern company recently found this message printed on their pay envelopes: "If the amount in this envelope does not agree with the amount on your pay slip, please return the envelope unopened to the cashier."

3. SUMMER ETHICS

A young lady was soaking up the sun's rays on a Florida beach when a little boy in his swimming trunks, carrying a towel, came up to her and asked her, "Do you believe in God?" She was surprised by the question but replied, "Why, yes, I do." Then he asked her: "Do you go to church every Sunday?" Again, her answer was "Yes!" Then he asked: "Do you read your Bible and pray every day?" Again she said, "Yes!" But by now her curiosity was very much aroused. At last the lad sighed and said, with obvious relief, "Will you hold my quarter while I go in swimming?"

4. DON'T LET IT HAPPEN AGAIN

One day Sam Jones got fifty cents too much in his pay envelope, but he didn't say a word. During the week the paymaster found out his mistake, and on the next payday deducted fifty cents.

Jones said, "Excuse me, sir, but I'm fifty cents short this week."

"You didn't complain last week," replied the paymaster.

Sam came back, "No, sir, I don't mind overlooking one mistake. But when it happens twice, then it's time to say something."

5. INSOMNIA AND INCOMPLETE REPENTANCE

An honest letter was sent to the Internal Revenue Service. It stated: "Dear Sirs: I cannot sleep. Last year, when I filed my income tax return, I deliberately misrepresented my income. Now I cannot sleep. Enclosed is a check for $150 for taxes. If I still cannot sleep, I will send you the rest!"

6. DEEP CANDOR
Dentist is overheard speaking to his patient as he bends over him with a hypodermic needle in hand: "You might feel a little sting. On the other hand, it might feel as though you've been kicked in the mouth by a mule."

7. SIN FOUND OUT
A certain woman, preparing to entertain guests, went to a small grocery store to buy food. She stopped at the meat counter and asked the attendant for a large chicken. He reached down into the cold storage compartment, grabbed the last chicken he had, and placed it on the scale. "This one weighs four pounds, ma'am," he said. "I'm not sure that will be enough," the woman replied. "Don't you have a bigger one?" The attendant put the chicken back into the compartment, pretended to search through the melting ice for another one, and then brought out the same bird, discreetly applying some finger pressure to the scale. "Ah," he said with a smile, "this one weighs six pounds." "I'm just not sure," the woman said with a frown. "I'll tell you what—wrap them both up for me!"

8. BE SURE TO GET THE WHOLE STORY
A farmer in Bloomington bought a horse and was told, honestly, by the seller that there was only one thing wrong with the horse: He liked to sit on avocados. The farmer said, "Well, that's fine with me. There aren't any avocados around here." So he put down his money, mounted the horse and started home. On the way they had to cross a stream, and right in the middle the horse sat down and wouldn't budge. The farmer walked back to the horse dealer and explained what happened. "Well, now you never said nothin' about water, so I didn't tell you . . . " The farmer said, "Didn't tell me what?" The horseman explained, "If he can't get avocados he likes to sit on fish."

9. CHILDISH DECEPTION
This true story takes place in the kindergarten class in an experimental school. The august superintendent of schools walked into the library unannounced. All the staff members were terribly flustered. The superintendent just smiled and seated himself beside a cute little girl. She was looking at a pre-primer. It consisted of single items on a page. He asked the little tyke to identify the items. She responded with, "That's a boy and that's a girl and that's a house. That's a car, that's a top, and that's a truck." When she came to a picture of a hatchet, she said, "That's a hammer." He

said nothing. She turned the page and there was a hammer. She turned back and looked again at the hatchet, then back at the hammer. She quickly closed the book and, smiling sweetly, she said, "We are in the library and we really shouldn't be talking." What a perfect picture of our quickly learned ability to hide our sin.

10. THE LITTLE VOICE INSIDE

When I was a boy, I was walking along a street and happened to spy a cart full of watermelons. I was fond of watermelon, so I sneaked quietly up to the cart and snitched one. Then I ran into a nearby alley and sank my teeth into the melon. No sooner had I done so, however, than a strange feeling came over me. Without a moment's hesitation, I made my decision. I walked back to the cart, replaced the melon—and took a ripe one. MARK TWAIN

11. TO TELL A LIE

In Boston a minister noticed a group of boys standing around a small stray dog. "What are you doing, boys?"

"Telling lies," said one of the boys. "The one who tells the biggest lie gets the dog."

"Why, when I was your age," the shocked minister said, "I never ever thought of telling a lie."

The boys looked at one another, a little crestfallen. Finally one of them shrugged and said, "I guess he wins the dog."

12. GOING OUT OF BUSINESS

This notice appeared in the window of a store in New York City: "Don't be fooled by imitators who claim to be going out of business. We have been going out of business longer than anyone on this block."

13. DRIVING WITHOUT THE NECESSARY PAPERS

Nothing improves a person's driving skills like the sudden discovery that his license has expired.

14. A PERSISTENT PROBLEM WITH THE TRUTH

A little girl had developed a bad habit. She was always lying. Once when she was given a St. Bernard dog for her birthday, she went out and told all the neighbors that she had been given a lion. The mother took her aside and said, "I told you not to lie. You go upstairs and tell God you are sorry. Promise God you will not lie again." The little girl went upstairs, said her prayers, then came down again. Her mother asked, "Did you tell God you are sorry?" The little girl replied, "Yes, I did. And God said sometimes He finds it hard to tell my dog from a lion, too."

15. HONEST DEALINGS

A client went to his attorney and said: "I am going into a business deal with a man I do not trust. I want you to frame an airtight contract that he can't break, which will protect me from any sort of mischief he may have on his mind." The attorney replied: "Listen, my friend. There is no group of words in the English language that will take the place of plain honesty between men, which will fully protect either of you if you plan to deceive each other."

16. STRATEGIC TIMING OF THE TRUTH

A New Hampshire farmer took his horse to see the veterinarian. He complained about the horse: "One day he limps, the next day he doesn't. What should I do?" The vet advised him, "On the day he doesn't limp, sell him!"

17. PLAN AHEAD

A favorite joke among San Francisco lawyers concerns the phony who fakes an injury in an auto accident, comes to court in a wheel chair, and is awarded two hundred thousand dollars. When the verdict is announced, the insurance company lawyer snaps, "You're going to be tailed by a private eye wherever you go from now on, and as soon as you take one step out of that wheelchair, we'll throw you in jail." The phony smiles and advises the lawyer pleasantly, "Don't go to all that trouble. I'm going from here to the Waldorf in New York, then to the Savoy in London, then to the Ritz in Paris, then on to the French Riviera . . . and after that to Lourdes for the miracle."

18. GRAVE EXCUSES

A young man arrested for stealing a car, had the year's most novel excuse. He'd found the automobile in front of a cemetery, he explained, and thought the owner was dead.

19. PARTIAL LYING

A school principal received a phone call. The voice said, "Thomas Bradley won't be in school today." The principal was a bit suspicious of the voice. He asked, "Who is speaking?" The voice came back, "My father."

20. CHICKENS COMING TO ROOST

John Smith was a loyal carpenter, working for a very successful building contractor who called him into his office one day and said, "John, I'm putting you in charge of the next house we build. I want you to order all the materials and oversee the whole job from the ground up."

John accepted the assignment with great enthusiasm and excitement. For ten days before ground was broken at the building site, John studied the blueprints. He checked every measurement, every specification. Suddenly he had a thought. "If I am really in charge," he said to himself, "why couldn't I cut a few corners, use less expensive materials, and put the extra money in my pocket? Who would know the difference? Once the house is painted, it will look just great."

So John set about his scheme. He ordered second-grade lumber, but his reports indicated that it was top-grade. He ordered inexpensive concrete for the foundation, put in cheap wiring, and cut every corner he could, yet he reported the purchase of much better materials. When the home was completed and fully painted, he asked the contractor to come and see it.

"John," said the contractor, "what a magnificent job you have done! You have been such a good and faithful carpenter all these years that I have decided to show my gratitude by giving you this house you have built, as a gift!"

21. HONESTY AS A POLICY
The editor of a small-town newspaper grew tired of being called a liar, and announced that he would tell the truth in the future. The next issue contained the following item:

"Married—Miss Sylvan Rhodes and James Collins, last Saturday at the Baptist parsonage, by the Rev. J. Gordon. The bride is a very ordinary town girl, who doesn't know any more about cooking than a jackrabbit, and never helped her mother three days in her life. She is not a beauty by any means and has a gait like a duck. The groom is an up-to-date loafer. He has been living off the old folks at home all his life and is now worth shucks. It will be a hard life."

SEVENTY-FIVE
Hope
(See also Optimism)

1. START WITH A BROWNIE
A number of years ago, in a mental institution outside Boston, a young girl known as "Little Annie" was locked in the dungeon. The dungeon was the only place, said the doctors, for those who were hopelessly insane. In Little Annie's case, they saw no hope for her, so she was consigned to a living

death in that small cage which received little light and even less hope. About that time, an elderly nurse was nearing retirement. She felt there was hope for all of God's children, so she started taking her lunch into the dungeon and eating outside Little Annie's cage. She felt perhaps she should communicate some love and hope to the little girl.

In many ways, Little Annie was like an animal. On occasions, she would violently attack the person who came into her cage. At other times, she would completely ignore them. When the elderly nurse started visiting her, Little Annie gave no indication that she was even aware of her presence. One day, the elderly nurse brought some brownies to the dungeon and left them outside the cage. Little Annie gave no hint she knew they were there, but when the nurse returned the next day, the brownies were gone. From that time on, the nurse would bring brownies when she made her Thursday visit. Soon after, the doctors in the institution noticed a change was taking place. After a period of time they decided to move Little Annie upstairs. Finally, the day came when the "hopeless case" was told she could return home. But Little Annie did not wish to leave. She chose to stay, to help others. She it was who cared for, taught, and nurtured Helen Keller, for Little Annie's name was Anne Sullivan.

2. PLANNING THE NEXT WEDDING

A man in his middle years was on a Caribbean cruise. On the first day out he noticed an attractive woman about his age who smiled at him in a friendly way as he passed her on the deck, which pleased him. That night he managed to get seated at the same table with her for dinner. As the conversation developed, he commented that he had seen her on the deck that day and he had appreciated her friendly smile. When she heard this she smiled and commented, "Well, the reason I smiled was that when I saw you I was immediately struck by your strong resemblance to my third husband."

At this he perked up his ears and said, "Oh, how many times have you been married?"

She looked down at her plate, smiled demurely, and answered, "Twice."

3. HOPE AND DESPAIR

Hope is a projection of the imagination; so is despair. Despair all too readily embraces the ills it foresees; hope is an energy and arouses the mind to explore every possibility to combat them. . . . In response to hope the imagination is aroused to picture every possible issue, to try every door, to fit together even the most heterogeneous pieces in the puzzle. After the solution has been found it is difficult to recall the steps taken—so many of them are just below the level of consciousness. THORNTON WILDER

4. THE CYNICAL VIEW
Hope, deceitful as it is, serves at least to lead us to the end of life along an agreeable road. LA ROCHEFOUCAULD

5. FEAR AND HOPE
We promise according to our hopes, and perform according to our fears. LA ROCHEFOUCAULD

6. THE DESPAIR OF THE WORLD'S WISDOM
I just finished a study of the Book of Revelation, ending on the high note of the triumph of the last two chapters. What a glorious denouement is painted for us in the Apocalypse! I was reminded of the opposite view of the eschaton in the well-known quote from Bertrand Russell in *A Free Man's Worship*. His description of the bottom line is this: "All the labor of the ages, all the devotion, all the inspiration, all the noonday brightness of human genius, are destined to extinction in the vast death of the solar system . . . the whole temple of man's achievement must inevitably be buried beneath the debris of a universe in ruins. Only within the scaffolding of these truths, only on the firm foundation of unyielding despair can the soul's habitation henceforth be safely built."

Somehow, that doesn't come across to me as a "firm foundation."

So also this assessment by Will Durant, well-known historian: "Life has become, in that total perspective which is philosophy, a fitful pollution of human insects on the earth, a planetary eczema that may soon be cured; nothing is certain in it but defeat and death."

Contrast these visions of the future with the sure word of Scripture as found in Matthew 28. Jesus said, "Lo, I am with you always, even to the end of the world."

7. IN FLIGHT
The natural flights of the human mind are not from pleasure to pleasure but from hope to hope. SAMUEL JOHNSON

8. COLERIDGE ON HOPE
Work without hope draws nectar in a sieve,
And hope without an object cannot live. SAMUEL TAYLOR COLERIDGE

9. TOMORROW'S HOPE
Psychologist William Marston asked three thousand people, "What have you to live for?" He was shocked to discover that 94 percent were simply enduring the present while they waited for the future . . . waited for something to happen . . . waited for "next year" . . . waited for a "better time" . . . waited for "someone to die " . . . waited "for tomorrow," unable

to see that all anyone ever has is today, because yesterday is gone and tomorrow exists only in hope.

10. KEEP YOUR HOPE ALIVE

The world is full of hopes and expectations that motivate men and women. Some of these hopes prove illusory and empty when time has passed. Some men put their hopes in fading realities. I am reminded of the dramatic speech of Douglas McArthur over thirty years ago when he addressed Congress after returning from Korea (at Harry Truman's sudden behest). His memorable speech included these sad lines: "I am closing my fifty-two years of military service. When I joined the army, even before the turn of the century, it was the fulfillment of all my boyish hopes and dreams. The world has turned over many times since I took the oath on the plain at West Point, and the hopes and dreams have long since vanished."

11. HOPE THE MOTIVATOR

An examination was being held in little Emma's class at school and the question was asked: "Upon what do hibernating animals subsist during the winter?" Emma thought for a few minutes and then wrote: "All winter long, hibernating animals subsist on the hope of a coming spring!"

12. HOPE ON THE HIGH SEAS

You may remember the story of the long and rough Atlantic crossing where the seasick passenger was leaning over the rail of the ocean liner and had turned several shades of green. A steward came along and tried to cheer him up by saying, "Don't be discouraged, sir! You know, no one's ever died of seasickness yet!" The nauseous passenger looked up at the steward with baleful eyes and replied: "Oh, don't say that! It's only the hope of dying that's kept me alive this long!"

13. A BOY'S HOPE

Several years ago a teacher assigned to visit children in a large city hospital received a routine call requesting that she visit a particular child. She took the boy's name and room number and was told by the teacher on the other end of the line, "We're studying nouns and adverbs in his class now. I'd be grateful if you could help him with his homework so he doesn't fall behind the others." It wasn't until the visiting teacher got outside the boy's room that she realized it was located in the hospital's burn unit. No one had prepared her to find a young boy horribly burned and in great pain. She felt that she couldn't just turn and walk out, so she awkwardly stammered, "I'm the hospital teacher, and your teacher sent me to help you with nouns and adverbs." The next morning a nurse on the burn unit asked her, "What did you do to that boy?" Before she could finish a profusion of apologies, the nurse interrupted her: "You don't understand. We've been very worried about him, but ever since you were here yesterday, his whole attitude has changed. He's fighting back, responding to treatment. . . . It's as though he's decided to live." The boy later explained that he had completely given up hope until he saw that teacher. It all changed when he came to a simple realization. With joyful tears he expressed it this way: "They wouldn't send a teacher to work on nouns and adverbs with a dying boy, would they?"

14. KEEPING HOPE ALIVE

At the university there was a piano teacher that was simply and affectionately known as "Herman." One night at a university concert, a distinguished piano player suddenly became ill while performing an extremely difficult piece. No sooner had the artist retired from the stage when Herman rose from his seat in the audience, walked onstage, sat down at the piano and with great mastery completed the performance. Later that evening, at a party, one of the students asked Herman how he was able to perform such a demanding piece so beautifully without notice and with no rehearsal. He replied, "In 1939, when I was a budding young concert pianist, I was arrested and placed in a Nazi concentration camp. Putting it mildly, the future looked bleak. But I knew that in order to keep the flicker of hope alive that I might someday play again, I needed to practice every day. I began by fingering a piece from my repertoire on my bare board bed late one night. The next night I added a second piece and soon I was running through my entire repertoire. I did this every night for five years. It so happens that the piece I played tonight at the concert hall was part of that repertoire. That constant practice is what kept my hope alive. Everyday I renewed my hope that I would one day be able to play my music again on a real piano, and in freedom.

SEVENTY-SIX

Hospitality

1. HOSPITALITY TIPS

Someone once asked Perle Mesta, the great Washington hostess, the secret of her success in getting so many rich and famous people to attend her parties. She said it was all in the greetings and the good-byes. As each guest arrived

she met him or her with "At last you're here!" And as each left she
expressed her regrets with: "I'm sorry you have to leave so soon!"

SEVENTY-SEVEN
Humility

1. REAL HUMILITY
A college girl visited the home of Beethoven. She slipped under the rope and
began playing Beethoven's piano. She said to the one in charge, "I suppose
every musician who comes here wants to play this piano." He explained to
her that recently the great Paderewski was visiting there and someone asked
him to play that piano. He replied, "No, I do not feel worthy to play the
great master's piano."

2. TO APPEAR HUMBLE
Thomas More was ambitious, but he did not want people to know that he
was. He loved the praise of the crowd and worked hard to create a public
image of himself as a man who took no care for what people thought of him.
Yet he hated criticism and responded furiously whenever attacked. He was
gregarious, but he felt a contrary pull to solitude, loving isolation and
serenity, and he never overcame his early longing for the unambitious, remote
life of the cloistered monk, the monk he always thought he should have been.
He worked hard to seem humble. But he always wanted to be somebody, and
he always tried to make the public imagine that high position had been thrust
upon him only because great and wise men insisted that his talents were too
large to be hidden. Few people have enjoyed greater success in advertising
their humility. RICHARD MARIUS, *Thomas More*

3. A PERSPECTIVE ON SUCCESS
A newspaper reporter was interviewing an old rancher and asked him to
what he would attribute his success as a rancher. With a twinkle in his eye
the man replied, "It's been about 50 percent weather, 50 percent good luck,
and the rest is brains."

4. APPLAUSE

The late Bishop Fulton J. Sheen was greeted by a burst of applause when he made his appearance as a speaker at a meeting in Minneapolis. He responded by saying: "Applause before a speaker begins is an act of faith. Applause during the speech is an act of hope. Applause after he has concluded is an act of charity."

5. LEWIS ON HUMILITY

C. S. Lewis recounts that when he first started going to church he disliked the hymns, which he considered to be fifth-rate poems set to sixth-rate music. But as he continued, he said, "I realized that the hymns (which were just sixth-rate music) were, nevertheless, being sung with devotion and benefit by an old saint in elastic-side boots in the opposite pew, and then you realize that you aren't fit to clean those boots. It gets you out of your solitary conceit." PAUL BRAND, *Fearfully and Wonderfully Made*

6. THE GIFT OF STANDING BY

Donald Grey Barnhouse told the story (supposedly true) about Chief Justice Charles Evans Hughes. When he moved to Washington, D.C., to take up his duties as chief justice, he transferred his membership letter to a Baptist church in the area. His father had been a Baptist minister and he also made a profession of faith in Christ. It was the custom for all new members to come to the front of the sanctuary at the close of the worship service. The first to be called that morning was Ah Sing, a Chinese laundryman who had moved to the capital from the West coast. He took his place at the far side of the church. As the dozen or so other people were called forward they stood at the opposite side of the church, leaving Ah Sing standing alone. But when Chief Justice Hughes was called, he took his place beside the laundryman. When the minister had welcomed the group into the church fellowship he turned to the congregation and said, "I do not want this congregation to miss this remarkable illustration of the fact that at the cross of Jesus Christ the ground is level." Barnhouse commented: "Mr. Hughes behaved like a true Christian. He took his place beside the laundryman, and by his act he prevented embarrassment to the humble Chinese; he showed, too, the love of Christ—he had this gift of standing by."

7. A WORD FOR HUMILITY

Muhammad Ali was in his prime, and as he was about to take off on an airplane flight, the stewardess reminded him to fasten his seat belt. He came back brashly, "Superman don't need no seat belt." The stewardess quickly came back, "Superman don't need no airplane, either." Ali fastened his belt.

8. BROKAW THE CELEBRITY

Success can sometimes dazzle you in the achieving, but there's usually someone around to help you keep perspective. TV newsman Tom Brokaw has a story about that:

Brokaw was wandering through Bloomingdale's in New York one day, shortly after he was promoted to cohost on the "Today" show. That show was a pinnacle of sorts for Brokaw after years of work, first in Omaha, then for NBC in Los Angeles and Washington, and he was feeling good about himself. He noticed a man watching him closely. The man kept staring at him and finally, when the man approached him, Brokaw was sure he was about to reap the first fruits of being a New York television celebrity.

The man pointed his finger and said, "Tom Brokaw, right?"

"Right," said Brokaw.

"You used to do the morning news on KMTV in Omaha, right?"

"That's right," said Brokaw, getting set for the accolades to follow.

"I knew it the minute I spotted you," the fellow said. Then he paused and added, "Whatever happened to you?"

9. MORE HUMILITY

A pastor was asked to speak for a certain charitable organization. After the meeting the program chairman handed the pastor a check. "Oh, I couldn't take this," the pastor said with some embarrassment. "I appreciate the honor of being asked to speak. You have better uses for this money. You apply it to one of those uses." The program chairman asked, "Well, do you mind if we put it into our Special Fund?" The pastor replied, "Of course not. What is the special fund for?" The chairman answered, "It's so we can get a better speaker next year."

10. COMMENCEMENT

I remember when I got my diploma several years ago—it was an exciting day, with all the processionals, the ceremony, the talks by the speakers who told us about our responsibility to save the world. I remember after I got my diploma in my hand, as the crowd began to disperse, I looked around me past the stadium to the city beyond and then began to think of the size of the world that lay even beyond the city. I looked down at my diploma again, then back at the city and the world, and as I turned again to the diploma, from out of nowhere, those famous words by Tallulah Bankhead suddenly came into my mind, "Truly, there is less here than meets the eye."

From a baccalaureate address given by the Rev. Peter Gomes at the Stanford Chapel in 1977

11. A DECISIVE MOMENT

Former Secretary of Labor Raymond Donovan tells the story of being on Air Force One. He was in the back compartment of the jet while President Reagan was in the front of the compartment.

The phone rang in the back compartment and the voice said, "Mr. Donovan, the president would like for you to join him for lunch." Secretary Donovan straightened his tie and thought to himself how important he was to have the president ask him to lunch.

Just as Donovan walked through the doorway into the president's compartment, the red phone rang, the Presidential Hot Line. Wow—what a moment to be present! Reagan picked up the phone and said, "Yes—uh-huh. Yes—what are my options?" Donovan's heart almost stopped. His mind raced. Then President Reagan continued, "OK. I'll have the iced tea!" Donovan's ego was deflated.

12. INTIMIDATION OF THE GREAT

Christian Herter was running hard for reelection as governor of Massachusetts, and one day he arrived late at a barbecue. He'd had no breakfast or lunch, and he was famished. As he moved down the serving line, he held out his plate and received one piece of chicken. The governor said to the serving lady, "Excuse me, do you mind if I get another piece of chicken. I'm very hungry." The woman replied, "Sorry, I'm supposed to give one piece to each person." He repeated, "But I'm starved," and again she said: "Only one to a customer." Herter was normally a modest man, but he decided this was the time to use the weight of his office and said, "Madam, do you know who I am? I am the governor of this state." She answered, "Do you know who I am? I'm the lady in charge of chicken. Move along, mister." This is a woman who knew her position and wasn't about to be intimidated. Do we as Christians recognize the significant position in which we stand because of Christ?

13. THE IRREPLACEABLE YOU

Dick Jones lived as if everything in the whole community depended upon him. One morning he woke up early with a high fever. His wife called next door to a doctor friend. When he diagnosed that Jones had viral pneumonia, he suggested that Dick stay in bed for several days but Dick complained, "No! I've got a breakfast meeting at the school, I'm president of the PTA board, then I've got crucial business at the office, a luncheon date, and three very important dates this afternoon, and then the Building Committee at church this evening. There's no way I can be sick today doctor."

"I'm sorry," says his doctor friend, "but Dick, I don't know anyone who's indispensable, and I suggest you stay in bed." But at that very moment, as the story goes, Dick's high fever sent him into a trance. And there in that trance, he saw himself looking in on heaven. The angels were gathering around God and His holy throne. But everything seemed to be in disarray; some papers were being passed around, and finally after some discussion, the angels passed a significant-looking paper to God, He read it and God was obviously upset. God got up off His throne and said "Oh, no! Oh, no! What will I do today? What will I do?" The angels in chorus said, "What is it, God? What is it?" And God replied, "What will I do today? Dick Jones is sick!"

14. THE OCEAN OF TRUTH

I seem to have been only like a boy playing on the seashore and diverting myself in now and then finding the smoother pebble or a prettier shell than ordinary whilst the great ocean of truth lay all undiscovered before me.
ISAAC NEWTON

SEVENTY-EIGHT

Identity

1. AUTHENTICITY—THE REAL ME

A woman got on an elevator in a tall office building. There was just one other person in the elevator, a handsome man. She pushed the button for her floor and then casually looked over at the man and suddenly had one of those moments of recognition shock. Could it be? The man looked exactly like Robert Redford, the movie star. Her gaze was almost involuntarily riveted on him. Finally, she blurted out, "Are you the *real* Robert Redford?" He smiled and said, "Only when I'm alone!"

2. NO NEED FOR WORDS

When you know who you are, you don't have to impress anyone. When Jesus was taken before the high priest, who asked, "What do you have to say for yourself?" Jesus was silent. Wrong question.

When the high priest then asked Him if He was the Son of God, Jesus said, "I am." Right question.

Before Pilate, who asked, "Are you the King of the Jews?" Jesus replied, "Yes, it is as you say." Right question.

In the Luke account, Herod asked Jesus question after question, but there was no reply. Wrong questions.

When you have discovered your identity, you need to say little else. Toyohiko Kagawa, the Japanese Christian who spent his life working with and for the poor, was speaking at Princeton. When he finished his talk, one student said to another, "He didn't say much, did he?"

A woman sitting nearby leaned over and murmured, "When you're hanging on a cross, you don't have to say anything." STANLEY MOONEYHAM

3. PASSING THE TEST

It seems that this college student needed a small two-hour course to fill out his schedule. The only one that fit was in Wildlife Zoology. He had some reservations as he heard the course was tough and the teacher a bit different. But, it seemed like the only choice so he signed up.

After one week and one chapter the professor had a test for the class. He passed it out and it was a sheet of paper divided into squares and in each square was a carefully drawn picture of some bird legs. Not bodies, not feet—just different birds' legs. The test simply asked them to identify the birds from the pictures of their legs.

Well, he was absolutely floored. He didn't have a clue. The student sat and stared at the test and got madder and madder. Finally, reaching the boiling point, he stomped up to the front of the classroom and threw the test on the teacher's desk and exclaimed, "This is the worst test I have ever seen and this is the dumbest course I have ever taken." The teacher looked up at him and said, "Young man, you just flunked the test." Then the teacher picked up the paper, saw that the student hadn't even put his name on the paper, and said, "By the way, young man, what's your name?" At this the student bent over, pulled up his pants, revealed his legs and said, "You identify me."

4. THE NAME IDENTIFIES

Several centuries before Christ, Alexander the Great came out of Macedonia and Greece to conquer the Mediterranean world. He didn't know it, but God was using him to prepare the way for the coming of the Messiah—for it was as a result of Alexander's conquests that Greek was established as the common language of the Grecian and later even Roman Empire. On one of his campaigns, Alexander received a message that one of his soldiers had been continually, and seriously, misbehaving and thereby shedding a bad light on the character of all the Greek troops. And what made it even worse was that this soldier's name was also Alexander. When the commander learned this, he sent word that he wanted to talk to the errant soldier in person. When the young man arrived at the tent of Alexander the Great, the commander asked him, "What is your name?" The reply came back, "Alexander, sir." The commander looked him straight in the eye and said forcefully, "Soldier, either change your behavior or change your name." This story has a lesson for each of us. When we call ourselves Christians, we are identifying with Jesus Christ. When we wear a cross, or ICHTHUS, or put Christian stickers on our cars, we are being a witness for Him. We are being identified with the name of Christ. Is your behavior compatible with that name and with the symbol that shows that you are a Christian?

SEVENTY-NINE

Incarnation—
God in Christ

(See also Christ, Christmas)

1. THE COMMUNION OF LIFE WITH LIFE

"The best way to send an idea," said scientist J. Robert Oppenheimer, "is to wrap it up in a person." The theological word for all of that is *incarnation,* meaning "in the flesh." Jesus was the incarnation of God. Jesus was the way that God sent His "idea" to humanity; there was and is no better way! One of the early church fathers whose name was Ignatius explained that "by the Incarnation, God broke His silence." Less scholarly as an explanation but equally to the point was the remark of a little girl who said, "Some people couldn't hear God's inside whisper and so He sent Jesus to tell them out loud." The Gospel of John declares dramatically, "The Word became flesh and dwelt among us." The Word, that living expression of God, tells out loud His truth and sees to it that we are in touch with the power and glory at the heart of Creation. We are brought into the personal presence of the lover of our souls. How great that blessing! How wonderful that gift!
GENE BARTLETT

2. SOMEONE WITH SKIN

There is a small voice that penetrated the stillness of the night. It comes from the bedroom across the hall. "Daddy, I'm scared!" Out of your groggy, fuzzy state, you respond with, "Honey, don't be afraid, Daddy's right across the hall." After a very brief pause the little voice is heard again, "I'm still scared." Always quick with an insight you respond, "You don't need to be afraid. God is with you. God loves you." This time the pause is longer . . . but the voice returns, "I don't care about God, Daddy; I want someone with skin on!"

It seems like the logic used by the little child is precisely the reason for the Incarnation. After thousands of years of being unsuccessful in being able to convince his people that he really loved them, our Creator realized that the best way to demonstrate his love for us was to send "someone with skin on."

3. HE CLIMBED IN WITH US

I read about a grandfather who found his grandson jumping up and down in his playpen, crying at the top of his voice. When Johnnie saw his grandfather, he reached up his little chubby hands and said, "Out, Gramps, out."

It was only natural for the grandfather to reach down to lift him out of his predicament, but as he did the mother of the child stepped up and said "No, Johnnie, you are being punished—so you must stay in."

The grandfather was at a loss to know what to do. The child's tears and chubby hands reached deep into his heart. But the mother's firmness in correcting her son must not be taken lightly. But love found a way. The grandfather could not take the grandson out of the playpen, so he climbed in with him. Beloved that is what our Lord Jesus Christ did for us at the cross (or at Christmas). In leaving heaven for earth He climbed in with us. The Bible says, "The Word was made flesh, and dwelt among us."

4. I COULD HELP THEM IF . . .

Father and son were taking a nature hike through the woods when they came upon some ants working furiously to clear a path. The ants were scurrying here and there trying desperately to provide a clear path for ant travel. They worked individually as well as a team, but to no avail. Father and son watched a long time in silence. Finally the boy looked at his dad and said, "I wish I could help the ants."

Father responded by telling his son that his presence would send them to hide for safety. After some more silence and some more observation the son spoke with much intent. "You know, Dad, if I could become an ant, become one of them for a short time, I could help them."

5. GOD LEADS A PRETTY SHELTERED LIFE

Billions of people were scattered on a great plain before God's throne. Some of the groups near the front talked heatedly—not with cringing shame, but with belligerence. "How can God judge us?" said one. "What does He know about suffering?" snapped a brunette. She jerked back a sleeve to reveal a tattooed number from a Nazi concentration camp. "We endured terror, beatings, torture, death!" In another group a black man lowered his collar. "What about this?" he demanded, showing an ugly rope burn. "Lynched for no crime but being black! We have suffocated in slave ships, been wrenched from loved ones, toiled till death gave release." Far out across the plain were hundreds of such groups. Each had a complaint against God for the evil and suffering He permitted in His world. How lucky God was to live in heaven where there was no weeping, no fear, no hunger, no hatred! Indeed, what did God know about what man had been forced to endure in this world? "After all, God leads a pretty sheltered life," they said.

So each group sent out a leader, chosen because he had suffered the most. There was a Jew, a black, an untouchable from India, an illegitimate, a person from Hiroshima, and one from a Siberian slave camp. In the center of the plain they consulted with each other. At last they were ready to present their case. It was rather simple: before God would be qualified to be their judge, He must endure what they had endured. Their decision was that God should be sentenced to live on earth—as a man!

But because He was God, they set certain safeguards to be sure He could not use His divine powers to help Himself: Let Him be born a Jew. Let the legitimacy of His birth be doubted, so that none would know who is really His father. Let Him champion a cause so just, but so radical, that it brings down upon Him the hate, condemnation, and efforts of every major traditional and established religious authority to eliminate Him. Let Him try to describe what no man has ever seen, tasted, heard, or smelled—let Him try to communicate God to men. Let Him be betrayed by His dearest friends. Let Him be indicted on false charges, tried before a prejudiced jury, and convicted by a cowardly judge. Let Him see what it is to be terribly alone and completely abandoned by every living thing. Let Him be tortured and let Him die! Let Him die the most humiliating death—with common thieves.

As each leader announced his portion of the sentence, loud murmurs of approval went up from the great throngs of people. But when the last had finished pronouncing sentence, there was a long silence. No one uttered another word. No one moved. For suddenly all knew . . . God had already served His sentence.

6. OUT OF THE MOUTHS OF BABES

One Sunday on their way home from church, a little girl turned to her mother and said, "Mommy, the preacher's sermon this morning confused me." The mother said, "Oh? Why is that?" The little girl replied, "Well, he said that God is bigger than we are. Is that true?" The mother replied, "Yes, that's true, honey." "And he also said that God lives in us? Is that true Mommy?" Again the mother replied, "Yes." "Well," said the little girl, "if God is bigger than us and he lives in us, wouldn't He show through?"

7. GOD IN CHRIST—THE KING SEEKS A WIFE

The Danish philosopher Soren Kierkegaard once sought to describe the incarnation of God in Christ. He used this simple illustrative story:

A certain king was very rich. His power was known throughout the world. But he was most unhappy, for he desired a wife. Without a queen, the vast palace was empty.

One day, while riding through the streets of a small village, he saw a beautiful peasant girl. So lovely was she that the heart of the king was won. He wanted her more than anything he had ever desired. On succeeding days, he would ride by her house on the mere hope of seeing her for a moment in passing.

He wondered how he might win her love. He thought, *I will draw up a royal decree and require her to be brought before me to become the queen of my land.* But, as he considered, he realized that she was a subject and would be forced to obey. He could never be certain that he had won her love.

Then, he said to himself, "I shall call on her in person. I will dress in my finest royal garb, wear my diamond rings, my silver sword, my shiny black boots, and my most colorful tunic. I will overwhelm her and sweep her off her feet to become my bride." But, as he pondered the idea, he knew that he would always wonder whether she had married him for the riches and power he could give her.

Then, he decided to dress as a peasant, drive to the town, and have his carriage let him off. In disguise, he would approach her house. But, somehow the duplicity of this plan did not appeal to him.

At last, he knew what he must do. He would shed his royal robes. He would go to the village and become one of the peasants. He would work and suffer with them. He would actually become a peasant. This he did. And he won his wife.

So did God consider how He might win humankind. God in Christ became one of us. He took upon Him the form of human flesh to dwell among us. Paul says, "God was in Christ, reconciling the world to Himself."

8. GOD TAKING ON OUR WEAKNESS

It is the nature of God that he makes something out of nothing. Consequently, if someone is not nothing, God can make nothing out of him. Men make something into something else. But this is vain and useless work. Thus God accepts no one except the abandoned, makes no one healthy except the sick, gives no one sight except the blind, brings no one to life except the dead, makes no one pious except sinners, makes no one wise except the foolish, and in short, has mercy upon no one except the wretched, and gives no one grace except those who have not grace. Consequently, no proud person can become holy, wise or righteous, become the material with which God works, or have God's work in him, but he remains in his own works and makes a fabricated, false and simulated saint out of himself, that is a hypocrite. MARTIN LUTHER

9. A GIVING INCARNATION

Shortly after World War II came to a close, Europe began picking up the pieces. Much of the Old Country had been ravaged by war and was in ruins. Perhaps the saddest sight of all was that of little orphaned children starving in the streets of those war-torn cities. Early one chilly morning an American soldier was making his way back to the barracks in London. As he turned the corner in his jeep, he spotted a little lad with his nose pressed to the window of a pastry shop. Inside the cook was kneading dough for a fresh batch of doughnuts. The hungry boy stared in silence, watching every move. The soldier pulled his jeep to the curb, stopped, got out, and walked quietly over to where the little fellow was standing. Through the steamed-up window he could see the mouth-watering morsels as they were being pulled from the oven, piping hot. The boy salivated and released a slight groan as he watched the cook place them onto the glass-enclosed counter ever so carefully. The soldier's heart went out to the nameless orphan as he stood beside him. "Son . . . would you like some of those?" The boy was startled. "Oh, yeah . . . I would!" The American stepped inside and bought a dozen, put them in a bag, and walked back to where the lad was standing in the foggy cold of the London morning. He smiled, held out the bag, and said simply: "Here you are." As he turned to walk away, he felt a tug on his coat. He looked back and heard the child ask quietly: "Mister, . . . are you God?" We are never more like God than when we give.

10. MIRROR IMAGE OF GOD

There is a painting in a palace in Rome by Reni. It is painted into the ceiling of the dome, over 100 feet high. To stand at floor level and look upward, the painting seems to be surrounded by a fog which leaves its content unclear.

But in the center of the great dome room is a huge mirror, which in its reflection picks up the picture. By looking into the mirror you can see the picture with great clarity.

Jesus Christ, born in a manger at Bethlehem, is the mirror of God. In him we see a clear reflection of the Father. Jesus said, "If you have seen me, you have seen the Father." No power on earth has done more to tame the hostile forces of humankind, and cause us to beat our swords in tools of useful productivity and our spears into peaceful instruments of creativity than this Child of Bethlehem, who came in weakness to lead us in strength.

11. A PARABLE OF CHRISTMAS EVE

Once there lived a king who had power over all nations and peoples. His courts were of richest splendor; his tables were heavy with finest food. Music and laughter and gaiety floated from his castle. Clouds wrapped it in ethereal majesty. Peasants—in their valley of violence and hunger—stopped and looked at the castle for a long while, wishing they might know the king. But none were able to reach it.

In the cold of winter, the king's tailor entered the royal chambers with the latest additions to the king's wardrobe. He had selected the finest materials and woven them into the most beautiful garments that eyes had ever seen.

But the king was not pleased. He ordered his tailor out, vowing to make his own clothes. The door to the throne room was shut and locked. Weeks passed. The royal court waited with anticipation to see what the king would make for himself. They knew they were bound to be blinded by the glory of it. Finally the awaited day arrived. The door opened and the king appeared.

Everyone, especially the tailor, gasped in surprise. His Majesty was dressed in the simplest, cheapest, most unkingly garments imaginable. He had the choice of the world's finest materials, but he had chosen to wear the clothes of a beggar.

He spoke quietly to them all: "I am going into the valley!" MICHAEL DAVES

12. MUCH MORE

'Twas much, that man was made like God before.
But, that God should be made like man, much more. JOHN DONNE

13. THE KING AMONG US

King James V of Scotland would on occasion lay aside the royal robe of king and put on the simple robe of a peasant. In such a disguise, he was able to move freely about the land, making friends with ordinary folk, entering into their difficulties, appreciating their handicaps, sympathizing with them in their sorrow. And when as king he sat again upon the throne, he was better able to rule over them with fatherly compassion and mercy. God shares in human experience and thereby is better able to accept man.

14. PARABLE OF THE BIRDS
There once was a flock of birds who forgot to fly south for the winter. Now it was late in December and it was getting awfully cold. God loved those birds and didn't want them to freeze so He sent His only Son to become a bird and to show them the way to a warm barn where they would be saved from the cold. Most of the birds were leery of this cocky new bird who said he knew the way to safety. The leaders of the flock felt threatened by this bird so they killed him. Some of the flock believed this new bird and were saved from the cold by flying to the warm barn as the new bird had directed. Most of the flock however refused to believe this bird and they died from the cold.

EIGHTY
Individualism

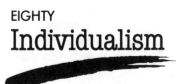

1. WHAT IS AN INDIVIDUALIST?
A man who lives in the city and commutes to the suburbs. MICHAEL MEANEY

2. DIFFERENT DRUM
Why should we be in such desperate haste to succeed, and in such desperate enterprises? If a man does not keep pace with his companions, perhaps it is because he hears a different drummer. Let him step to the music which he hears, however measured or far away. HENRY DAVID THOREAU

EIGHTY-ONE
Influence

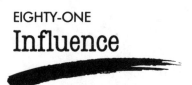

1. WHICH WAY DOES INFLUENCE FLOW?
A dignified old clergyman owned a parrot of which he was exceedingly fond, but the bird had picked up an appalling vocabulary of cuss words from a

previous owner and, after a series of particularly embarrassing episodes, the clergyman decided he would have to have his parrot put to sleep. But a lady in his congregation suggested a last-ditch remedy. She said, "I have a female parrot. She is an absolute saint. She sits quietly on her perch and prays constantly. Why don't you bring your parrot over and see if my own bird's good influence doesn't reform him?" The pastor said it was worth a try, and the next night he arrived with his pet. The bird took one look at the lady parrot and chirped, "Hi, Toots, how about a big kiss?" The lady parrot responded gleefully, "My prayers have been answered!"

2. RASPUTIN

A little bit of hell spilled over on the world because two people believed in a false prophet. In his brilliant book, *Nicholas and Alexandra,* Robert K. Massie tells how the czar and empress of Russia were misled by a miracle and thus brought their great empire down to dust.

After many years of anxious waiting for an heir to the Russian throne, Czar Nicholas II and his German wife, Alexandra, were blessed with a son. However, their hopes for the future were cruelly crushed six weeks later when doctors discovered the infant had hemophilia, an incurable blood disease that could kill at any moment. All of his short life was to be lived in the shadow of terror, with death stalking every footstep. This tragedy introduced into the royal family one of the most evil men who ever lived.

Several times the youngster slipped close to death. Seeing him writhe in excruciating pain, his tormented parents would beg doctors to do something, but they were helpless. In those moments they turned to Gregory Rasputin, a religious mystic of questionable credentials, later known as the mad monk of Russia. Invariably, he would pray for the boy and there would be a marked improvement. Even today doctors are at a loss to explain how these healings took place, but history testifies to them. Always, Rasputin would warn the parents the boy would only live as long as they listened to him.

Rasputin's power over the royal family became so great he could, with a word, obtain the appointment or dismissal of any government official. He had men appointed or dismissed on the basis of their attitudes toward him rather than their abilities. Consequently, the whole Russian government reeled under the unwise counsel of this evil man. Seeds of revolution were planted and watered with discontent. It erupted into the murder of the royal family, internal war, and the Communist takeover.

Alexander Kerensky, a key government figure during those trying times, later reflected, "Without Rasputin, there could have been no Lenin!"

EIGHTY-TWO
Integrity
*(See also Character,
Dignity, Nobility)*

1. MEN OF INTEGRITY
*God give us men. The time demands
Strong minds, great hearts,
True faith and willing hands;
Men whom the lust of office does not kill;
Men whom the spoils of office cannot buy;
Men who possess opinions and a will;
Men who have honor; men who will not lie;
Men who can stand before a demagogue
And damn his treacherous flatteries without winking;
Tall men, sun-crowned men, who live above the fog
In public duty and in private thinking.* JOHN G. HOLLAND

2. RIGHTEOUSNESS SUSPECTED
A traffic officer pulled a motorist over to the curb and demanded to see his driver's license. The driver produced a license, which the officer studied suspiciously for several minutes before waving him on. The officer explained, "You were driving so carefully, I thought for sure you had an invalid license."

3. PROGRAM PRESSURES
I'm sure you've heard the old story about the two men who met on the street. One said to the other, "Have you heard about Harry? He embezzled the company out of half a million dollars." The other man said, "That's terrible; I never did trust Harry." The first man said, "Not only that, he left town and took Tom's wife with him." The other man said, "That's awful; Harry has always been a ne'er-do-well." The first man said, "Not only that, he stole a car to make his getaway." The other man said, "That's scandalous; I always did think Harry had a bad streak in him." The first man said, "Not only that, they think he was drunk when he pulled out of town." The other man said, "Harry's no good. But what really bothers me is, who's going to teach his Sunday school class this week?"

4. WHEN THE FUN STOPS

Football great Bubba Smith has sworn off booze. Not drinking it, but selling it. Bubba never did drink, but he sold a ton of beer by making cute television ads. Not anymore. Bubba has kicked the habit.

As far as I know, Bubba Smith is the first athlete ever, maybe the first person ever, to give up a very lucrative, stupendously easy and really amusing job making beer commercials, just because he decided it was wrong.

Here's how it happened. "I went back to Michigan State for the homecoming parade last year," Bubba said. "I was the grand marshal and I was riding in the backseat of this car. The people were yelling, but they weren't saying, 'Go, State, go!' One side of the street was yelling, 'Tastes great!' and the other side was yelling 'Less filling.'

"Then we go to the stadium. The older folks are yelling 'Kill, Bubba, kill!' But the students are yelling 'Tastes great! Less filling!' Everyone in the stands is drunk. It was like I was contributing to alcohol, and I don't drink. It made me realize I was doing something I didn't want to do.

"I was with my brother, Tody, who is my agent. I told him, 'Tody, I'll never do another Lite beer commercial.'

"I loved doing the commercials, but I didn't like the effect it was having on a lot of little people. I'm talking about people in school. Kids would come up to me on the street and recite lines from my commercials, verbatim. They knew the lines better than I did. It was scary. Kids start to listen to things you say, you want to tell 'em something that is the truth.

"Doing those commercials, it's like me telling everyone in school, 'Hey, it's cool to have a Lite beer.' I'd go to places like Daytona Beach and Fort Lauderdale on spring breaks [as a spokesman for the brewery], and it was scary to see how drunk those kids were. It was fun talking to the fans, until you see people lying on the beach because they can't make it back to their rooms, or tearing up a city.

"As the years wear on, you stop compromising your principles."

EIGHTY-THREE
Justice

1. OBJECTIVITY OF A GENERAL
General Robert E. Lee was asked what he thought of a fellow officer in the Confederate army who had made some derogatory remarks about him. Lee rated him as being very satisfactory. The person who asked the question seemed perplexed. "General," he said, "I guess you don't know what he's been saying about you." "I know," answered Lee. "But I was asked my opinion of him, not his opinion of me!"

2. SEVERE JUDGMENT
A Christian lady wanted a parrot that could talk. She looked in several shops before finding one. The owner told her, however, that the parrot had been previously owned by a bartender and though he could say anything, he also on occasion used profanity. She told him she would buy him anyway and teach him to say good things. Everything went well for about a month. He learned to say "Praise the Lord" and a number of other Christian words and phrases. One day she forgot to feed him and when she came into the house she heard him cursing. She grabbed him up and said, "I told you not to talk that way. I'll teach you never to do it again." So she put him in the deep freeze and shut the door. A few minutes later she took him out and asked, "Have you learned your lesson?" The bird shivered and replied, "Yes, ma'am." She asked, "Are you going to talk that way anymore?" The parrot replied, "No, ma'am."

About seven months went by and not a bit of bad language. Apparently the bird was cured of his rascally habits. Then one day she forgot to feed him, water him, or change his cage. When she returned home that day he was carrying on worse than ever. She grabbed him and put him back in the freezer but forgot him for some time. He was almost frozen to death when she thought of him. She put him in his cage to thaw out. Finally he began to move and talk a little and she asked him again, "Did you learn your lesson?" "Yes, ma'am," he retorted. Then he sat there quietly for a few more minutes shivering and said, "Can I ask you a question?" She answered, "Yes." The parrot said, "I thought I knew all the bad words there were, but just what did that turkey in there say?"

3. RECIPROCITY

At a party, a doctor who was chatting with a lawyer was interrupted by a woman who insisted on telling the doctor about a pain in her leg and asking him what to do about it. The doctor advised her, then, after she went away, he asked the lawyer: "Do I have a right to send that woman a bill for my professional services?" The attorney replied, "Certainly." The next day the doctor sent the woman a bill. He also received a bill—from the lawyer.

4. JUDGED BY HIS OWN LAW

A new law on drunken driving in Louisiana is now one of the toughest in the nation. There is a mandatory prison sentence for anyone convicted of driving while intoxicated. Getting it passed was a major victory for various groups against drunk driving, and they could not have gotten it passed if it wasn't for the help of one particular state legislator who sponsored the bill. It wasn't long after the new law took effect that the first person to be arrested for driving under the influence was brought before the judge and found guilty and was sentenced to his prison term. Who was he? The same legislator who sponsored the bill! "For the way you judge, you will be judged, and by your standard of measure it shall be measured to you."

5. BESIDES BEING FORGIVEN

Many of us are like the little boy who had broken the glass of a streetlamp. Greatly disturbed, he asked his father, "What shall I do?" "Do?" exclaimed his father, "why we must report it and ask what you must pay, then go and settle it." This practical way of dealing with the matter was not what the boy was looking for, and he whimpered, "I—I—thought all I had to do was ask God to forgive me."

KINDNESS *(See Compassion)*

EIGHTY-FOUR
Leadership
(See also Authority)

1. A LEADER IS NOT THE CAUSE

A true leader is committed to the cause, and does not become the cause. Staying personally dedicated to the cause can become extremely difficult, particularly if the cause succeeds. A subtle change in thinking can overtake the leader of a successful ministry. He or she begins "needing" certain things to carry on the ministry—things that were not needed earlier. I admire Mother Teresa, who decided after winning the Nobel Prize that she would not go to accept any more recognition because it interfered with her work. She knew she was not in the business of accepting prizes; she was in the business of serving the poor of Calcutta. She maintained her dedication to the cause by refusing unrelated honors.

2. BOSSES AND LEADERS
A boss creates fear; a leader creates confidence. Bossism creates resentment; leadership breeds enthusiasm. A boss says, "I"; a leader says, "We." A boss fixes blame; a leader fixes mistakes. A boss knows how; a leader shows how. Bossism makes work drudgery; leadership makes work interesting. A boss relies on authority; a leader relies on cooperation. A boss drives; a leader leads.

3. ASSERTING LEADERSHIP
The lion was proud of his mastery of the animal kingdom. One day he decided to make sure all the other animals knew he was the king of the jungle. He was so confident that he bypassed the smaller animals and went straight to the bear. "Who is the king of the jungle?" the lion asked. The bear replied, "Why, you are, of course." The lion gave a mighty roar of approval.

Next he asked the tiger, "Who is the king of the jungle?" The tiger quickly responded, "Everyone knows that you are, O mighty lion."

Next on the list was the elephant. The lion faced the elephant and addressed his question: "Who is the king of the jungle?" The elephant immediately grabbed the lion with his trunk, whirled him around in the air five or six times, and slammed him into a tree. Then he pounded him onto the ground several times, dunked him under water in a nearby lake, and finally threw him up on the shore.

The lion—beaten, bruised, and battered—struggled to his feet. He looked at the elephant through sad and bloody eyes and said, "Look, just because you don't know the answer is no reason for you to get mean about it!"

4. THE HEADY TASTE OF POWER
A first grader was told to come directly home from school, but he arrived late almost every day. The difference in time amounted to as much as twenty minutes. His mother asked him, "You get out of school the same time every

day. Why can't you get home at the same time?" He said, "It depends on the cars."

"What do cars have to do with it?" The youngster explained, "The patrol boy who takes us across the street makes us wait until some cars come along so he can stop them."

5. FOLLOW ME
E. Stanley Jones tells of a missionary who got lost in an African jungle— nothing around him but bush and a few cleared places. He found a native hut and asked the native if he could lead him out. The native said he could. "All right," said the missionary, "show me the way." The native said, "Walk." So they walked and hacked their way through unmarked jungle for more than an hour. The missionary got worried. "Are you quite sure this is the way? Where is the path?" The native said, "Bwana, in this place there is no path. I am the path."

6. BAD ASSUMPTION
He who thinketh he leadeth and hath no one following him is only taking a walk. BENJAMIN HOOKS

7. HIDING THE TRUTH
Leadership is the ability to hide your panic from the others.

8. LEADERSHIP—TWO EXTREMES
The frogs wanted a leader. They bothered Jupiter so much with their requests that he finally tossed them a log into the pond, and, for awhile, the frogs were happy with their new leader. Soon, however, they found out they could jump up and down on their new leader and run all over him. He offered no resistance nor even a response. The log did not have any direction or purpose in his behavior, but just floated back and forth in the pond. This practice exasperated the frogs, who were really sincere about wanting "strong leadership."

They went back to Jupiter and complained about their log leader and appealed for much stronger administration and oversight. Because Jupiter was weary of the complaining frogs, he gave them a stork, who stood tall above the members of the group and certainly had the appearance of a leader. The frogs were quite happy with their new leader. Their leader stalked around the pond making great noises and attracting great attention. However, their joy turned to sorrow and ultimately to panic, for in a very short time the stork began to eat its subordinates.

This story, taken from Aesop, speaks of two kinds of leaders. The Lord does not want His leaders to be like logs who allow the people totally to run the church; neither does the Lord want His leaders to be like storks that eat up the people and only take advantage of them. May the Lord grant His leaders the divine balance that He so greatly desires.

EIGHTY-FIVE
Learning & Teaching

1. LIMITED VISION

Eight-year-old Frank had looked forward for weeks to this particular Saturday because his father had promised to take him fishing if the weather was suitable. There hadn't been any rain for weeks and as Saturday approached, Frank was confident of the fishing trip. But, wouldn't you know it, when Saturday morning dawned, it was raining heavily and it appeared that it would continue all day.

Frank wandered around the house, peering out the windows and grumbling more than a little. "Seems like the Lord would know that it would have been better to have the rain yesterday than today," he complained to his father who was sitting by the fireplace, enjoying a good book. His father tried to explain to Frank how badly the rain was needed, how it would make the flowers grow and bring much needed moisture to the farmers' crops. But Frank was adamant. "It just isn't right," he said over and over.

Then, about three o'clock, the rain stopped. Still time for some fishing, and quickly the gear was loaded and they were off to the lake. Whether it was the rain or some other reason, the fish were biting hungrily and father and son returned with a full string of fine, big fish.

At supper, when some of the fish were ready, Frank's mom asked him to say grace. Frank did—and concluded his prayer by saying, "And, Lord, if I sounded grumpy earlier today it was because I couldn't see far enough ahead."

No doubt much of our complaining is because we "can't see far enough ahead."

2. A GREAT INVENTION

If you could build a small package, something small enough to carry in your coat pocket, a machine which would instantly start and stop, in which you

could instantly reverse yourself or go forward, which would require no batteries or other energy sources, and which would provide you with full information on an entire civilization, what would you have? A book!
ISAAC ASIMOV

3. GOD'S NEEDS
John Wesley once received a note that said: "The Lord has told me to tell you that He doesn't need your book-learning, your Greek and your Hebrew."

Wesley answered, "Thank you, sir. Your letter was superfluous, however, as I already knew the Lord has no need for my 'book-learning,' as you put it. However, although the Lord has not directed me to say so, on my own responsibility I would like to say to you that the Lord does not need your ignorance either."

4. MAKING TRUTH RELEVANT
In trying to explain something to others it's wise to remember this fundamental rule of communications: "One specific is worth a hundred generalities." In 1847 the great naturalist Agassiz gave an address at a meeting of teachers. The subject was grasshoppers. "I passed round a jar of the insects and made every teacher hold one while I lectured," Agassiz recorded. And if a teacher dropped his grasshopper, Agassiz waited until he picked it up. He insisted that his abstract words be related to the real animal they held in their palms.

5. AN ACTIVE FLAME
The mind is a fire to be kindled, not a vessel to be filled. PLUTARCH

6. THE GREAT VALUE OF BOOKS
Commenting on 2 Timothy 4:13, where Paul asks Timothy to bring him a cloak, books, and the parchments, Charles Haddon Spurgeon wrote the following words:

"He is inspired, yet he wants books! He has been preaching at least for thirty years, yet he wants books! He has seen the Lord, yet he wants books. He has had a wider experience than most men, yet he wants books! He has been caught up into the third heaven, and has heard things which it is unlawful to utter, yet he wants books! He has written the major part of the New Testament, yet he wants books!"

7. SEND US BOOKS!
In 1814 the Methodists in Australia sent an urgent appeal to the Methodist Missionary Society in London:

"Send us a preacher. Send a faithful servant of the Lord to us. Disappoint us not! Deny us not! Leave us not forsaken in this benighted land. We call upon you on behalf of our children: let them not be left to perish.

"We call upon you on behalf of those who cannot speak for themselves: perishing, dying sinners, outcasts of society, leave them not in their blood. Send us one of yourselves, with a good supply of wearing apparel, house furniture, and, particularly, books."

8. FEEBLE REED
Man is a reed, the most feeble thing in nature, but he is a thinking reed. BLAISE PASCAL

9. CONFUSION BEGINS
The first real confusion in a child's life is when he decides girls are better than frogs but he isn't sure why.

10. TEACHER'S CREDENTIALS
Sometime ago there was a teacher who celebrated her eightieth birthday. It proved to be a marvelous occasion, highlighted by the presence of a great number of her former students. It seemed that she taught school in one of the worst sections of Baltimore. Before she came to that school to teach there had been repeated instances of juvenile crime and delinquency. When she began her work there came a change. The change in time became noticeable with so many of her students turning out to be good citizens, men and women of good character. Some became doctors, others lawyers, educators, ministers, honorable craftsmen, and skilled technicians. It was no accident, therefore, that on important anniversaries like her eightieth birthday she was remembered with gratitude and love from a great number of her students.

A newspaper got wind of this celebration and sent a reporter to interview her. He asked, among other things, what was her secret that made her teaching so rewarding? She said: "Oh, I don't know. When I look at the young teachers in our schools today, so well-equipped with training and learning, I realize that I was ill-prepared to teach. I had nothing to give but love." DON E. MCKENZIE, *Northway Christian Church, Dallas, Texas*

11. THE PROCESS OF LEARNING
It is remarkable how much you have to know before you realize how little you know.

12. DEPRIVATION
Man can live without air for a very few minutes, without water for a number of days, without food for about two months, without a new thought for years on end.

13. SO MUCH FOR TRAINING

Helene Hanff, author of *84 Charing Cross Road,* first went to New York City nearly forty years ago after winning a playwriting contest. She writes about the results of that contest:

"The Theatre Guild knocked its brains out training twelve of us to be playwrights because the year before we won our contest, two other contest winners had been given their fellowship money and went wandering off on their own. The Theatre Guild knew this was very bad because playwrights didn't need money as much as they needed training, so they held seminars for us and we went to all the plays on Broadway and we took lessons in how to produce, write, act, and direct. And when the year was up, everybody agreed it was a great success—except that not one of us ever became a Broadway playwright. The two writers who had been given the money and went wandering off on their own with no training were Tennessee Williams and Arthur Miller."

14. PRACTICE, PRACTICE

Hank, a landscape contractor, had his first full-fledged job. Of course he didn't want to appear to be the rank amateur he knew he was, so he feigned a casual kind of nonchalance and expertise. One of the first tasks he had to tackle was blasting out some stumps with dynamite for a farmer. Since the farmer was watching he went to some length to measure out the fuses and set the dynamite—just as if he really knew what he was doing. But his problem was he really didn't know how much dynamite would be just right to do the job.

When he was all set up he breathed a prayer that he had enough dynamite packed under each stump, and yet not too much to blow them all to kingdom come. The moment of truth came. Hank looked at the farmer with a knowing look of what he hoped came across as confidence and pushed down the plunger. A stump rose high in the air with a resounding boom and arched magnificently over towards his pickup truck and landed right on the roof of the cab, demolishing it.

The farmer turned to Hank and said, "Son, you didn't miss it by much—just a few feet. With a bit more practice you'll be able to land those suckers in the truck bed every time."

EIGHTY-SIX
Listening
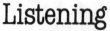

1. STRATEGY FOR PEOPLE
The only way to entertain some folks is to listen to them. KIN HUBBARD

2. THE NEED FOR BALANCE
Somewhere we know that without silence words lose their meaning, that without listening speaking no longer heals, that without distance closeness cannot cure. HENRI NOUWEN

3. BASIC REQUIREMENT FOR COMMUNICATION
Two men were talking one day. One of them said, "My wife talks to herself a lot." His friend answered, "Mine does, too, but she doesn't know it. She thinks I'm listening."

4. FAMILY PLOT
President Franklin D. Roosevelt got tired of smiling that big smile and saying the usual things at all those White House receptions. So, one evening he decided to find out whether anybody was paying attention to what he was saying. As each person came up to him with extended hand, he flashed that big smile and said, "I murdered my grandmother this morning." People would automatically respond with comments such as "How lovely!" or "Just continue with your great work!" Nobody listened to what he was saying, except one foreign diplomat. When the president said, "I murdered my grandmother this morning," the diplomat responded softly, "I'm sure she had it coming to her."

5. ATTENTION SPAN
The attention span of a typical human is ten praises, six promises, or one preachy statement. JOCCO GRAND

6. LISTEN WHILE SHUT
It's impossible for a worthwhile thought to enter your mind through an open mouth.

7. FRINGE BENEFIT
Good listeners are not only popular everywhere, but after a while they know something.

8. HEARING MAY NOT BE THE PROBLEM

Jed Harris, producer of *Our Town* and other plays, became convinced he was losing his hearing. He went to a specialist, who gave him a thorough checkup. The doctor pulled out a gold watch and asked, "Can you hear this ticking?" Harris said, "Of course." The specialist walked to the door and held up the watch again. "Now can you hear it?" Harris concentrated and said, "Yes, I can hear it clearly." The doctor walked out the door into the next room and said, "Can you hear it now?" Harris said, "Yes."

The doctor said, "Mr. Harris, there is nothing wrong with your hearing. You just don't listen."

9. LISTENING AT A PREMIUM

Patricia Goldman, the vice chairman of the National Transportation Safety Board, tells a story about a stewardess who, frustrated by passenger inattentiveness during her what-to-do-in-an-emergency talk at the beginning of each flight, changed the wording and said, "When the mask drops down in front of you, place it over your navel and continue to breathe normally." Not a single passenger noticed.

10. A GLORIOUS ATTRIBUTE

His thoughts were slow,
His words were few,
And never formed to glisten.
But he was a joy to all his friends—
You should have heard him listen.

EIGHTY-SEVEN

Loneliness

1. THE LONELY IN THE CROWD

A few years ago, the press carried a heartrending story of a young father who shot himself in a tavern telephone booth. James Lee had called a Chicago newspaper and told a reporter he had sent the paper a manila envelope outlining his story. The reporter frantically tried to trace the call, but was too late. When the police arrived the young man was slumped in the booth with a bullet through his head.

In his pockets they found a child's crayon drawing, much folded and worn. On it was written, "Please leave in my coat pocket. I want to have it buried with me." The drawing was signed in childish print by his daughter, Shirley Lee, who had perished in a fire just five months before. Lee was so grief-stricken he had asked total strangers to attend his daughter's funeral so she would have a nice service. He said there was no family to attend, since Shirley's mother had been dead since the child was two.

Speaking to the reporter before his death, the heartbroken father said that all he had in life was gone and he felt so alone. He gave his modest estate to the church Shirley had attended and said, "Maybe in ten or twenty years, someone will see one of the plaques and wonder who Shirley Ellen Lee was and say, 'Someone must have loved her very, very much.'" The grieving father could not stand loneliness or the loss so he took his own life. . . . He felt it better to be dead than live in an impersonal world.

How many James Lees are there in this world? They don't wear signs saying "I'm lonely . . . will you help me?" Let's discover these in His name.

EIGHTY-EIGHT
Love
(See also Compassion)

1. LIVING NOBLY
To act well in the world, one must die within oneself. Man is not on this earth only to be happy, he is not there to be simply honest, he is there to realize great things for humanity, to attain nobility and to surpass the vulgarity in which the existence of almost all individuals drags on.
ERNEST RENAN

2. INFILLING
The Scriptures often exhort us to be filled with various godly virtues—which means what? How do we know if we are "full of goodness" (Rom. 15:14), for example? Think a moment about a water-saturated sponge. If we push down with our finger even slightly, water runs out onto the table. We immediately know what fills the interior pockets of the sponge. The same is true of ourselves. We can tell what fills us on the inside by what comes out under pressure.

3. AFFIRMATION AND HUGGIN'

In a world where people are finding themselves being rejected in so many ways, it is vital that they find the affirmation that is in Christ through the ministry of the Church. Personally, I've always believed in the power of positive hugging as a form of affirmation. *Reader's Digest* mentioned Virginia Satir prescribing hugs for the blues. They quote her as saying: "Our pores are places for messages of love and physical contact. . . . Four hugs a day are necessary for survival, eight for maintenance and twelve for growth." According to the report I read, she delivered this happy prescription to those attending an orthopsychiatric convention, whatever that is.

4. FRUIT OF THE SPIRIT

Love is the key. Joy is love singing. Peace is love resting. Long-suffering is love enduring. Kindness is love's touch. Goodness is love's character. Faithfulness is love's habit. Gentleness is love's self-forgetfulness. Self-control is love holding the reins. DONALD GREY BARNHOUSE

5. CARE FOR MY SON

A wealthy man died, apparently without leaving a will. Consequently, according to law, the estate was to be divided among the several surviving cousins who were the next of kin. Also as prescribed by law, the deceased's household goods and other items of personal property were to be converted into cash in a public auction. During the sale, the auctioneer held up a framed photograph, but no one bid on it, including the cousins. Later, a woman approached the auctioneer and asked him if she might purchase the picture for a dollar, which was all she had. She said it was a photograph of the deceased man's only son. She went on to relate that she had been a servant in the deceased's household when the boy lost his life trying to rescue a drowning person, and that she had loved him very much. The auctioneer accepted the dollar and the woman went home and placed the photograph on a table beside her bed. It was then she noticed a bulge in the back of the frame. She undid the backing and there, to her amazement, was the rich man's will. The instructions in the will were simple: "I give and bequeath all my possessions to the person who cares enough for my son to cherish this photograph."

6. THE RAG DOLL

My daughter, like the typical American girl, has had her share of dolls and stuffed animals. Today, through modern technology, a little girl need not be content with dull, lifeless dolls, but can experience the thrill of owning a lifelike replica of a baby that can walk and talk, drink and wink, slurp and burp, cry, sigh and laugh—almost anything a real baby does, including wet itself and get diaper rash. After ten years of buying these mechanical marvels, I wondered which of these dolls was my daughter's favorite? To my surprise, I found her favorite was a small rag doll she had received on her third birthday. All the other performing dolls had gone, but this simple rag doll had allowed her to love it. The other dolls had caught her eye, but the rag doll had won her heart. To my daughter the rag doll was real and was loved just the way it was, and the scars of love showed as the hair was nearly gone, the eyes were missing, and the clothes were soiled and torn. But, missing all these parts, it was still what it had always been, just itself. We are, too often, like the high-tech dolls of my daughter. We try to impress others with skills, talent, education, speech, or mannerisms when what they want is someone just being themselves. Within every man lies the innate desire to be loved and accepted. Don't try to be something or someone that you are not. Just be yourself. Love is not won—a reward for performance or achievement. You don't have to sing, teach, preach, or pray well to be loved. People will not love us for what we do but rather for what we are. RANDY SPENCER

7. GIVING LOVE AWAY

One evening just before the great Broadway musical star, Mary Martin, was to go on stage in *South Pacific,* a note was handed to her. It was from Oscar Hammerstein, who at that moment was on his deathbed. The short note simply said:

"Dear Mary, A bell's not a bell till you ring it. A song's not a song till you sing it. Love in your heart is not put there to stay. Love isn't love till you give it away."

After her performance that night many people rushed backstage, crying, "Mary, what happened to you out there tonight? We never saw anything like that performance before." Blinking back the tears, Mary then read them the note from Hammerstein. Then she said, "Tonight, I gave my love away!"

8. LOVE OR INFATUATION?

Infatuation is instant desire. It is one set of glands calling to another. Love is friendship that has caught fire. It takes root and grows—one day at a time.

Infatuation is marked by a feeling of insecurity. You are excited and eager, but not genuinely happy. There are nagging doubts, unanswered question, little bits and pieces about your beloved that you would just as soon not examine too closely. It might spoil the dream.

Love is quiet understanding and the mature acceptance of imperfection. It is real. It gives you strength and grows beyond you—to bolster your beloved. You are warmed by his presence, even when he is away. Miles do not separate you. You want him nearer. But near or far, you know he is yours and you can wait.

Infatuation says, "We must get married right away. I can't risk losing him." Love says, "Be patient. Don't panic. Plan your future with confidence." Infatuation has an element of sexual excitement. If you are honest, you will admit it is difficult to be in one another's company unless you are sure it will end in intimacy. Love is the maturation of friendship. You must be friends before you can be lovers.

Infatuation lacks confidence. When he's away, you wonder if he's cheating. Sometimes you even check. Love means trust. You are calm, secure and unthreatened. He feels that trust, and it makes him even more trustworthy.

Infatuation might lead you to do things you'll regret later, but love never will. Love is an upper. It makes you look up. It makes you think up. It makes you a better person than you were before. ANN LANDERS

9. COMMUNICATING LOVE

Ole and Olga lived on a farm in Iowa. Olga was starved for affection. Ole never gave her any signs of love, and Olga's need to be appreciated went unfulfilled. At her wit's end, Olga blurted out, "Ole, why don't you ever tell me that you love me?" Ole stoically responded, "Olga, when we were married I told you that I loved you, and if I ever change my mind, I'll let you know."

That is not enough. Daily we need to express our love for one another just as God does for us daily in His Son, Jesus Christ. Love is new each day.

10. NO GRUDGING

You can give without loving, but you can't love without giving.

11. A CHILD'S VIEW OF LOVE

Some children were asked, "What is love?" One little girl answered, "Love is when your mommy reads you a bedtime story. True love is when she doesn't skip any pages."

12. UNASHAMED LOVE

We have some friends who have a little boy who was born with a severe handicap that would cause him to go into very violent seizures without any warning. The father would usually be the one holding their son during worship services, and I remember on one particular occasion when the little guy started into a seizure, the father got up and with a strong yet gentle love carried the boy to the back of the sanctuary where he held him close to his chest and rocked him, whispered to him, and did all he could to help his son through. One thing I noticed most of all was that there was no hint of embarrassment or frustration in that father's face—only love for his hurting son. I felt God speak to my own heart and in so many words say, "That's just the way I love you through your imperfections. I'm not embarrassed to have people know that you are my son." I have come to know that it's in my times of greatest frustration that my Father draws me close and weathers the storm with me. How good it is that with all of our faults we have a Savior who is "not ashamed to call us brothers." That's love!

13. LOVE THAT ABSORBS SUFFERING

This is supposed to be a true story from the time of Oliver Cromwell in England. A young soldier had been tried in military court and sentenced to death. He was to be shot at the "ringing of the curfew bell." His fiancée climbed up into the bell tower several hours before curfew time and tied herself to the bell's huge clapper. At curfew time, when only muted sounds came out of the bell tower, Cromwell demanded to know why the bell was not ringing. His soldiers went to investigate and found the young woman cut and bleeding from being knocked back and forth against the great bell. They brought her down and, the story goes, Cromwell was so impressed with her willingness to suffer in this way on behalf of someone she loved that he dismissed the soldier saying, "Curfew shall not ring tonight."

14. LOVE, WHATEVER

Once, while riding in the country, I saw on a farmer's barn a weather vane on the arrow of which was inscribed these words: "God is Love." I turned in at the gate and asked the farmer, "What do you mean by that? Do you think God's love is changeable; that it veers about as that arrow turns in the winds?" The farmer said, "Oh, no! I mean that whichever way the wind blows, God is still Love." CHARLES H. SPURGEON

15. AGAPE LOVE

Agape love is the love of T. E. McCully, father of Ed McCully, one of the missionaries slain by Auca Indians in Ecuador, who one night shortly after that experience prayed, "Lord, let me live long enough to see those fellows saved who killed our boys that I may throw my arms around them and tell them I love them because they love my Christ." That is love of the highest kind.

16. SAFE FROM LOVE

To love all is to be vulnerable. Love anything, and your heart will certainly be wrung and possibly broken. If you want to make sure of keeping it intact, you must give your heart to no one. . . . Wrap it carefully round with hobbies and little luxuries; avoid all entanglements; lock it safe in a casket or coffin of your selfishness. But in that casket—safe, dark, motionless, airless— it will change. It will not be broken; it will become unbreakable, impenetrable, irredeemable. . . . The only place outside heaven where you can be perfectly safe from all the dangers of love is—hell. DAVID WATSON, *I Believe in the Church*

17. LOVE OBSERVED
The world will not care what we know until they know we care.
GENE BARRON

18. THE RATIONALE OF GOD'S LOVE
He loved us not because we were lovable, but because He is love.
C. S. LEWIS

19. THE RISK OF LOVE
To love anyone is to hope in him always. From the moment at which we begin to judge anyone, to limit our confidence in him, from that moment at which we identify him, and so reduce him to that, we cease to love him, and he ceases to be able to become better. We must dare to love in a world that does not know how to love.

20. LOVE NEVER GIVES UP
A New England girl had just become engaged when the Civil War broke out. Her fiance was called into the army, so their wedding had to be postponed. The young soldier managed to get through most of the conflict without injury, but at the Battle of the Wilderness he was severely wounded. His bride-to-be, not knowing of his condition, read and reread his letters, counting the days until he would return. Suddenly the letters stopped coming. Finally she received one, but it was written in an unfamiliar handwriting. It read, "There has been another terrible battle. It is very difficult for me to tell you this, but I have lost both my arms. I cannot write myself. So a friend is writing this letter for me. While you are as dear to me as ever, I feel I should release you from the obligation of our engagement."

The letter was never answered. Instead, the young woman took the next train and went directly to the place her loved one was being cared for. On arrival she found a sympathetic captain who gave her directions to her soldier's cot. Tearfully, she searched for him. The moment she saw the young man, she threw her arms around his neck and kissed him. "I will never give you up!" she cried. "These hands of mine will help you. I will take care of you."

21. TESTING

A man and a woman who had been corresponding solely by mail fell in love with one another. They agreed to meet at the airport. Since they had never seen each other, they devised a plan that would help them recognize each other. She was to wear a green scarf and a green hat and have a green carnation pinned to her coat.

When the man got off his plane, he immediately began looking for her. Suddenly he saw a woman with a green scarf, green hat, and green carnation. His heart fell. She was one of the most homely women he had ever seen in his life. He was tempted to get back on the plane without approaching her. Nevertheless, he walked over to the woman, smiled, and introduced himself.

Immediately the woman said, "What is this all about, anyway? I don't know who you are. That woman over there gave me five dollars to wear these things." When the man looked over at the woman mentioned, he realized that she was one of the most beautiful women he had ever seen. The man approached the woman, who later explained, "All my life men have wanted to be with me, to be my friend, because of my beauty. They consider me beautiful. I want someone to love me, not just for my outward appearances, but for what I am *inside.*

22. LOVE DEFINED

Love does not consist in gazing at each other, but in looking outward together in the same direction. ANTOINE DE SAINT-EXUPERY

23. THE WHOLE DUTY

Some years ago there was a shipwreck off the coast of the Pacific Northwest. A crowd of fishermen in a nearby village gathered to watch the ship as it was smashed on the rocks. A lifeboat was sent to the rescue, and after a terrific struggle the rescuers came back with all of the shipwrecked sailors but one. "There was no room in the lifeboat for him, so we told him to stay by the ship and someone would come back for him," shouted a young man.

"Who will come with me?" shouted a young man.

Just then a little old lady cried out, "Don't go. Jim, my boy. Don't go. You are all I have left. Your father was drowned in the sea; your brother William sailed away and we've never heard from him; and now if you are lost, I'll be left alone. Oh, Jim, please don't go."

Jim listened patiently to his mother's pleading, then said, "Mother, I must go! It is my duty. I must go!"

The onlookers watched as the men in the lifeboat fought their way toward the wreck. Anxiously Jim's mother wept and prayed. They saw the boat start back, a frail little shell tossed about by the angry waves. At last it came close enough to hear, and they shouted, "Did you get him?"

And Jim shouted back, "Yes, and tell mother it's William!"

24. FATHER DAMIEN

In 1873, a Belgian Catholic priest named Joseph Damien De Veuster was sent to minister to lepers on the Hawaiian Island of Molokai. When he arrived he immediately began to meet each one of the lepers in the colony in hopes of building a friendship. But where ever he turned, people shunned him. It seemed as though every door was closed. He poured his life into his work, erecting a chapel, beginning worship services, and pouring out his heart to the lepers. But it was to no avail! No one responded to his ministry. After twelve years Father Damien made the decision to leave.

Dejectedly, he made his way to the docks to board a ship to take him back to Belgium. As he stood on the dock he wrung his hands nervously as he recounted his futile ministry among the lepers. As he did he looked down at his hands and noticed some mysterious white spots and felt some numbness. Almost immediately he knew what was happening to his body. He had contracted leprosy!

It was then that he knew what he had to do. He returned to the leper colony and to his work. Quickly the word about his disease spread through the colony. Within a matter of hours everyone knew. Hundreds of them gathered outside his hut, they understood his pain, fear, and uncertainty about the future.

But the biggest surprise was the following Sunday. As Father Damien arrived at the chapel, he found hundreds of worshipers there. By the time the service began, the chapel was crowded, and many were gathered outside. His ministry became enormously successful. The reason? He was one of them. He understood and empathized with them.

25. NEEDED—THE PERSONAL TOUCH

A man stopped at a flower shop to order some flowers to be wired to his mother who lived two hundred miles away. As he got out of his car he noticed a young girl sitting on the curb sobbing. He asked her what was wrong and she replied: "I wanted to buy a red rose for my mother. But I only have seventy-five cents and a rose costs two dollars." The man smiled and said, "Come on in with me. I'll buy you a rose." He bought the little girl her rose and ordered his own mother's flowers. As they were leaving he offered the girl a ride home. She said, "Yes, please! You can take me to my mother." She directed him to a cemetery, where she placed the rose on a freshly dug grave. The man returned to the flower shop, cancelled the wire order, picked up a bouquet and drove the two hundred miles to his mother's home.

26. THE GREAT DECISION

A little boy was told by his doctor that he could save his sister's life by giving her some blood. The six-year-old girl was near death, a victim of disease from which the boy had made a marvelous recovery two years earlier. Her only chance for restoration was a blood transfusion from someone who had previously conquered the illness. Since the two children had the same rare blood type, the boy was the ideal donor.

"Johnny, would you like to give your blood for Mary?" the doctor asked.

The boy hesitated. His lower lip started to tremble. Then he smiled, and said, "Sure, Doc. I'll give my blood for my sister."

Soon the two children were wheeled into the operating room—Mary, pale and thin; Johnny, robust and the picture of health. Neither spoke, but when their eyes met, Johnny grinned.

As his blood siphoned into Mary's veins, one could almost see new life come into her tired body. The ordeal was almost over when Johnny's brave little voice broke the silence, "Say Doc, when do I die?"

It was only then that the doctor realized what the moment of hesitation, the trembling of the lip, had meant earlier. Little Johnny actually thought that in giving his blood to his sister he was giving up his life! And in that brief moment, he had made his great decision!

27. OFFENDING THE LITTLE CHILDREN

One of the most arresting statements ever made by Jesus during his sojourn on earth was concerning the offending of children. He said it would be better for one to have a millstone tied around his neck and be cast into the sea.

An old woman was noticed to be picking up something in the street—a poor slum street. The policeman on the beat noticed the woman's action and watched her very suspiciously. Several times he saw her stoop, pick up something, and hide it in her apron. Finally, he went up to her and with a gruff voice and threatening manner demanded, "What are you carrying off in your apron?" The timid woman did not answer at first, whereupon the officer, thinking that she must have found something valuable, threatened her with arrest. The woman opened her apron and revealed a handful of broken glass. "I just thought I would like to take it out of the way of the children's feet," she said. Oh, how we need people like this timid little woman who cared about what hurts "children's feet."

28. GOING THE SECOND MILE

A salesman called his wife from a coin-operated phone in a distant city, finished the conversation, said good-bye, and replaced the receiver. As he was walking away, the phone rang. He went back and answered it, expecting to be informed of extra charges. But the operator said, "I thought you'd like to know. Just after you hung up, your wife said, 'I love you.'"

29. LOVE IS

Love is the filling from one's own,
Another's cup,
Love is the daily laying down
And taking up;
A choosing of the stony path
Through each new day,
That other feet may tread with ease
A smoother way.
Love is not blind, but looks abroad
Through other's eyes;
And asks not, "Must I give?"
But "May I sacrifice?"
Love hides its grief, that other hearts
And lips may sing;
And burdened walks, that other lives
May buoyant wing.
Hast thou a love like this?
Within thy soul?
'Twill crown thy life with bliss
When thou dost reach the goal.

30. LOVE THAT MUST EXPRESS ITSELF

A man was trying to read a serious book, but his little boy kept interrupting him. He would lean against his knees and say, "Daddy, I love you." The father would give him a pat and say rather absently, "Yes, Son, I love you too," and he would kind of give him a little push away so he could keep on reading. But this didn't satisfy the boy, and finally he ran to his father and said "I love you, Daddy," and he jumped up on his lap and threw his arms around him and gave him a big squeeze, explaining, "And I've just got to DO something about it!" That's it—as we grow in love, we aren't content with small-talk love, or pat-on-the-head love. We want to get involved and "do something about it."

31. THE CAPACITY FOR TENDERNESS

There is a tragic story about Lenin that persists to this day, revealing much about his inner soul. Vladimir Ulyanov was born in 1870 to a family that would suffer many tragedies in the years to come. Later, he used the pen name Lenin to promote his revolutionary ideas. He wrapped himself in his revolutionary work until he lost almost all capacity for human tenderness. Those about him said he was a most miserable man.

Although married, Lenin gave little love to his wife, Krupskaya. One night she rose, exhausted from her vigil beside her dying mother, and asked Lenin, who was writing at a table, to awaken her if her mother needed her. Lenin agreed and Krupskaya collapsed into bed. The next morning she awoke to find her mother dead and Lenin still at work. Distraught, she confronted Lenin, who replied, "You told me to wake you if your mother needed you. She died. She didn't need you."

EIGHTY-NINE

Marriage

1. NOTHING SACRED

Marriage used to be a contract. Now many regard it as a ninety-day option.

2. UNLUCKY MAN

He's been unlucky in both his marriages. His first wife left him and his second wife won't.

3. THE WAGES OF SIN IS STUPIDITY

Ann Landers received a letter from a woman who had broken off an affair with a married man and now ten years later wondered if she should have. She still had a nostalgic itch, and her mind was full of "what ifs" and "if onlys." She wondered if "you knew of a magic switch that could turn off that ever-present longing." After reading this, another reader sent in her story:

"I met the love of my life when I was twenty-two. He was forty-two and married. Today I am sixty-four. He is eighty-four. His poor sick wife is still with him. As recently as last night he repeated that familiar line: 'Please wait for me, darling, we will have a life together one of these days. Just be patient.'

"Just how much longer does he think he will live? The man is full of arthritis and has a devil of a time getting out of a chair. He repeats himself constantly and can never remember what he did with his eyeglasses. I must have been nuts to allow him to keep me on the string this long. Somehow the years just flew by and before I knew it he was an old man and I was no spring chicken. Several months ago when I told him what a fool I had been, he said, 'If you want to meet someone else go ahead, but you will never find anyone who loves you more than I do.' I'd give anything if I could turn the clock back to when I was twenty-two. I would have told him to call me up when his divorce was final."

4. THE ART
Marriage is the art of two incompatible people learning to live compatibly.

5. COMMUNICATION IN MARRIAGE
A happy couple had always raised cucumbers and made sweet pickles together. The husband just loved to watch things grow. Thus he spent his winters studying the seed catalogues to get the best possible cucumbers. The whole family enjoyed preparing the soil, planting and caring for the plants. He would often go out and just enjoy the way they grew. His wife loved to make sweet pickles. She studied the best recipes and the best methods of preparing and preserving them. They were such a happy family, and all their visitors went home with a jar of their famous pickles. The church always had a good supply of their pickles as well. People marveled at this family that had found a project to do together.

Finally, the man died. The next spring all the children returned home. They said to their mother, "We know how much you love making pickles, so we are going to prepare the garden and plant them for you." The mother smiled and said, "Thanks a lot children, but you don't have to do any planting for I really don't enjoy pickle making. I only did that because your father loved to grow the cucumbers so much." The children were all amazed, but the youngest son was upset, because the father had pulled him aside not too long before and shared with him that he really didn't like growing cucumbers, but only did it to please the mother!

Is this a happy or a sad story? I'm not sure. In many ways it is happy. They were happy doing for each other. People enjoyed being with them. But why is it also sad? Primarily, because they were not able to share their changing needs and joys with each other. Instead of growing, they stagnated in the performance of what they thought were their duties to each other.

6. THE SEVEN STAGES OF THE MARRIED COLD

A husband's reactions to his wife's colds during seven years of marriage:

Firt year: "Sugar dumpling, I'm really worried about my baby girl. You've got a bad sniffle and there's no telling about these things with all the strep going around. I'm putting you in the hospital this afternoon for a general checkup and a good rest. I know the food's lousy, but I'll be bringing your meals in from Rozzini's. I've already got it all arranged with the floor superintendent."

Second year: "Listen, darling, I don't like the sound of that cough and I've called Doc Miller to rush over here. Now you go to bed like a good girl, just for Poppa."

Third year: "Maybe you better lie down, honey. Nothing like a little rest when you feel lousy. I'll bring you something. Have we got any canned soup?"

Fourth year: "Now look, dear, be sensible. After you've fed the kids and got the dishes done and the floor finished, you better lie down."

Fifth year: "Why don't you take a couple of aspirin?"

Sixth year: "I wish you'd just gargle or something instead of sitting around barking like a seal all evening."

Seventh year: "For Pete's sake, stop sneezing! Are you trying to give me pneumonia?"

7. COMMUNICATION AFTER MANY YEARS

There is a story about a man and wife who were celebrating their golden wedding anniversary—fifty years of married life. Having spent most of the day with relatives and friends at a big party given in their honor, they were back home again. They decided, before retiring, to have a little snack of tea with bread and butter. They went into the kitchen, where the husband opened up a new loaf of bread and handed the end piece (the heel) to his wife. Whereupon she exploded! She said, "For fifty years you have been dumping the heel of the bread on me. I will not take it anymore; this lack of concern for me and what I like." On and on she went in the bitterest of terms, for offering her the heel of the bread. The husband was absolutely astonished at her tirade. When she had finished he said to her quietly, "But it's my favorite piece."

8. WISE STRATEGY

Keep your eyes open before marriage; half shut afterwards.
BENJAMIN FRANKLIN

9. THE ROLE OF A WIFE
Every man needs a wife, because many things go wrong that he can't blame on the government.

10. SPECIFICATIONS FOR A HUSBAND
When Ruth Bell was a teenage girl going off to Korea for schooling from her childhood home in China she fully intended to be a confirmed old maid missionary to Tibet. But she did give the thought of a husband some serious consideration. She wrote the following list of particulars:

"If I marry: He must be so tall that when he is on his knees, as one has said, he reaches all the way to heaven. His shoulders must be broad enough to bear the burden of a family. His lips must be strong enough to smile, firm enough to say no, and tender enough to kiss. Love must be so deep that it takes its stand in Christ and so wide that it takes the whole lost world in. He must be active enough to save souls. He must be big enough to be gentle and great enough to be thoughtful. His arms must be strong enough to carry a little child." RUTH BELL GRAHAM, *A Time for Remembering*

11. LUTHER ON MARRIAGE
Along comes the clever harlot, namely natural reason, looks at married life, turns up her nose and says: "Why, must I rock the baby, wash its diapers, change its bed, smell its odor, heal its rash, take care of this and take care of that, do this and do that? It is better to remain single and live a quiet and carefree life. I will become a priest or a nun and tell my children to do the same." But what does the Christian faith say? The father opens his eyes, looks at these lowly, distasteful, and despised things and knows that they are adorned with divine approval as with the most precious gold and silver. God, with his angels and creatures, will smile—not because diapers are washed, but because it is done in faith. MARTIN LUTHER

12. COMMUNICATION AFTER MANY YEARS (II)
A golden anniversary party was thrown for an elderly couple. The husband was moved by the occasion and wanted to tell his wife just how he felt about her. She was very hard of hearing, however, and often misunderstood what he said. With many family members and friends gathered around, he toasted her: "My dear wife, after fifty years I've found you tried and true!" Everyone smiled approval, but his wife said, "Eh?" He repeated louder, "AFTER FIFTY YEARS I'VE FOUND YOU TRIED AND TRUE!" His wife harumped and shot back, "Well, let me tell you something—after fifty years I'm tired of you, too!"

13. PREVIEW
If you wish to know how she will talk to you after marriage, listen while she talks to her younger brothers.

14. TENDER SYMBOLISM
I was escorted to a wedding by my twenty-four-year-old bachelor son. He appeared unaffected by the ceremony until the bride and groom lighted a single candle with their candles and then blew out their own. With that he brightened and whispered, "I've never seen that done before." I whispered back, "You know what it means, don't you?" His response: "No more old flames?"

15. WATCH OUT FOR THE LITTLE BUGS
A mighty tree stood high upon the mountain. It survived the hail, the heavy snows, the storms, the bitter cold of many years. Then finally it was felled by an attack of little beetles. And so it is with marriage.

16. HEAVY METAL
A teenage girl was examining her grandmother's wedding ring. The girl said, "Wow, what heavy and cumbersome rings those were fifty years ago." The grandmother replied, "That's true, but don't forget that in my day they were made to last a lifetime."

17. THE POLICY
Love is not an emotion. It is a *policy*. HUGH BISHOP

18. NO SUBSTITUTES
A woman was suffering from depression, so her concerned husband took her to a psychiatrist. The doctor listened to the couple talk about their relationships, and then said, "The treatment I prescribe is really quite simple." With that he went over to the man's wife, gathered her up in his arms, and gave her a big kiss. He then stepped back and looked at the woman's glowing face and broad smile. Turning to the woman's husband, he said, "See! That's all she needs to put new life back into her." Expressionless, the husband said, "OK, Doc, I can bring her in on Tuesdays and Thursdays."

19. BECAUSE SHE WAS LOVED
I once knew a very old married couple who radiated a tremendous happiness. The wife especially, who was almost unable to move because of old age and illness and in whose kind old face the joys and sufferings of many years had etched a hundred lines, was filled with such a gratitude for life that I was touched to the quick. Involuntarily, I asked myself what could possibly be the

source of this kindly person's radiance. In every other respect they were common people, and their room indicated only the most modest comfort. But suddenly I knew where it all came from, for I saw those two speaking to each other, and their eyes hanging upon each other. All at once it became clear to me that this woman was dearly loved.

It was not because she was a cheerful and pleasant person that she was loved by her husband all those years. It was the other way around. Because she was so loved she became the person I saw before me. HELMUT THIELICKE, *How the World Began*

20. CHARLES DICKENS ON MARRIAGE
Sam Weller addressing his son: "When you're a married man, Samivel, you'll understand a good many things as you don't understand now; but vether it's worth while goin' through so much to learn so little, as the charity boy said ven he got to the end of the alphabet, is a matter of taste." CHARLES DICKENS, *Pickwick Papers*

21. IDEAL MARRIAGE
A deaf husband and a blind wife are always a happy couple. *Danish proverb*

22. GAMBLE
Marriage is a lottery in which a man stakes his liberty and a woman her happiness. MME. DE RIEUX

23. FOR AN ANNIVERSARY
Companioned years have made them comprehend
The comradeship that lies beyond a kiss.
The young ask much of life—they ask but this,
To fare the road together to its end. ROSELLE MERCIER MONTGOMERY

24. DON'T MARRY TOO QUICKLY
Thus grief still treads upon the heels of pleasure,
Marry'd in haste, we may repent at leisure.
WILLIAM CONGREVE, *The Old Bachelor*

25. PROMO AND REALITY
The difference between courtship and marriage is the difference between the pictures in the seed catalog and what comes up. JAMES WHARTON

26. APPEARANCE OF EASE
Marriage is like twirling a baton, turning handsprings, or eating with chopsticks. It looks easy until you try it. HELEN ROLAND

27. GROWING MORE VALUABLE

An archaeologist is the best husband any woman can have—the older she gets, the more interested he is in her. AGATHA CHRISTIE

28. MUTUALITY

Another important emphasis in speaking on the gifts and/or fruits of the Spirit is mutuality. By our differences we complement one another in the body of Christ. I think it was in the *Reader's Digest* I saw the story about the woman who was away for a few days at a teachers' convention. Suddenly she remembered it was Monday, trash day, and she expressed her concern to her friend. But her friend tried to calm her fears, reminding her that her husband was still at home and he could certainly put out the trash by himself. But she said, "It takes both of us to take out the trash. I can't carry it and he can't remember it."

29. THE OBLIVIOUS DRUNK

A fellow frequently came home drunk and he was so far gone that he would fall into bed fully clothed, pass out, and then snore loudly all night long. Finally, his wife was losing so much sleep because of his snoring that she went to her doctor and said, "Doc, I can't take it any longer. If you'll only tell me how to keep him from snoring, I'll pay you anything." The doctor said there was no problem at all. He could give her the answer and he wouldn't even charge her. He told her that whenever her husband passed out, and started to snore she was to take a ribbon and tie it around his nose, and his snoring would stop. Well, that night her husband came in as usual, fell across the bed, fully dressed, passed out and started snoring. The wife got up, pulled a blue ribbon from her dresser, and tied it around his nose. Sure enough, the snoring stopped. Next morning, the wife, fully refreshed, was preparing breakfast and asked her husband, as he was awakening, "Honey, where were you last night?" The husband, still fully clothed, looked in the mirror and seeing the blue ribbon around his nose, replied, "I don't know, but wherever I was, I won first prize!"

30. WHO'S THE BOSS?

A farmer's boy decided to get married. His father said to him, "John, when you get married, your liberty is gone."

The boy said he did not believe it. The father said, "I'll prove it to you. Catch a dozen chickens, tie their legs together and put them in the wagon. Hitch up the two horses to the wagon and drive into town. Stop at every house you come to, and wherever you find the man is boss, give him a horse.

Wherever you find the woman is boss, give her a chicken. You'll give away all your chickens and come back with two horses."

The boy accepted the proposition and drove to town. He had stopped at every house and had given away ten chickens when he came to a nice little house and saw an old man and his wife standing out on the front lawn. He called to them and asked, "Who is boss here?"

The man said, "I am." Turning to the woman, the boy said, "Is he boss?" The woman replied, "Yes, he's boss." The boy asked them to come down to the street. He then explained his reason for asking and told the man to pick out one of the horses. He said he would bring the horse back to him that afternoon. The old man and the old lady looked over the horses carefully, and the husband said, "I think the black horse is the better of the two."

The wife then said, "I think that bay horse is in every way the better horse. I would choose him."

The old man took a careful look at the bay horse and said, "I guess I'll take the bay horse."

The boy smiled and said, "No, you won't; you'll take a chicken."

31. HOW TO GET ALONG
A lawyer and a psychologist were making small talk at a party. "You and your wife get along very well," said the lawyer. "Do you ever have differences of opinion?" "Definitely," said the psychologist, "very often—but we get over them quickly." "How do you do that?" asked the lawyer. "Simple," said the psychologist, "I never tell her about them."

32. REAL SATISFACTION, OF SORTS
Lucy: What happened when you showed your new engagement ring to the women in the office. Did they admire it?
Lois: Admire it? Four of them recognized it!

33. TWO BECOME ONE
Newly added to our wedding service is the ceremony of lighting the wedding candle by the bride and groom. Explaining the procedure ahead of time, I tell the couple they each take a small burning candle, representing their solitary life thus far, and together they light the large, middle, wedding candle. When they put their small candles back into holders, they can either extinguish them, or leave them burning to represent their unique personalities. During the wedding it is interesting to see whether they leave the individual candles aglow or put them out. At a recent wedding, the bride and groom put the individual candles back into their holders with the flames burning. Then the bride, an impish gleam in her eye, bent over and blew out her husband's

candle. The congregation burst into laughter. When I told of the incident at a ministerial meeting, Father Tom Glen commented wryly, "During the marriage ceremony two become one—on the honeymoon they discover which one."

34. THE COLOR OF YOUR MARRIAGE
When I walk on the beach to watch the sunset I do not call out, "A little more orange over to the right, please," or "Would you mind giving us less purple in the back?" No, I enjoy the always-different sunsets as they are. We do well to do the same with people we love." CARL ROGERS

35. I MARRIED YOU BECAUSE YOU PROMISED
In Thornton Wilder's play *The Skin of Our Teeth* the character Mrs. Antrobus says to her husband, "I didn't marry you because you were perfect. . . . I married you because you gave me a promise." She takes off her ring and looks at it. "That promise made up for your faults and the promise I gave you made up for mine. Two imperfect people got married, and it was the promise that made the marriage."

36. ONE LAST CHANCE
A man never opened the car door for his wife or any other woman. He felt it was a sissy Emily Post kind of thing to do and "Besides," he was fond of saying, "she doesn't have two broken arms." His table manners left much to be desired, and manners in general were looked upon by him as quite unnecessary.

After many years of marriage, the wife died and her husband was heartbroken because he truly loved her. Somehow, as the pallbearers brought her casket out of the funeral service, the husband and his family reached the hearse ahead of them. The mortician was back a few feet and, since he knew the husband quite well, he called him by name and said, "Open the door for her, will you?" The man reached for the door handle and then, for one second, just froze. He realized he had never opened a car door for her in life; now in her death it would be the first, last, and only time. It was a moment for him when years of regrets came crashing down around him.

37. DOUBLE MESSAGE
A young woman quickly signed for a library book, the title page of which read:

HOW—
To Reach Men
To Hold Men

To Win Men

It Has Been Done

When she got home and examined the fine print at the bottom of the page, she read: A Manual of Useful Information on How to Build a Men's Bible Class.

NINETY

Materialism

(See also Money, Stewardship)

1. PRUDENT ROMANCE

No woman marries for money; they are all clever enough, before marrying a millionaire, to fall in love with him first. CESARE PAVESE

2. SENDING IT ON AHEAD

Sigmund Freud's favorite story was about the sailor shipwrecked on one of the South Sea islands. He was seized by the natives, hoisted to their shoulders, carried to the village, and set on a rude throne. Little by little, he learned that it was their custom once each year to make some man a king, king for a year. He liked it until he began to wonder what happened to all the former kings. Soon he discovered that every year when his kingship was ended, the king was banished to an island, where he starved to death. The sailor did not like that, but he was smart and he was king, king for a year. So he put his carpenters to work making boats, his farmers to work transplanting fruit trees to the island, farmers growing crops, masons building houses. So when his kingship was over, he was banished, not to a barren island, but to an island of abundance. It is a good parable of life: We're all kings here, kings for a little while, able to choose what we shall do with the stuff of life.

"Lay not up for yourselves treasures upon earth, where moth and rust doth corrupt, and where thieves break through and steal. But lay up for yourselves treasures in heaven, where neither moth nor rust doth corrupt, and where thieves do not break through nor steal" (Matt. 6:19-20).

3. WHO TOOK WHAT WITH HER?

The story is told of Rose Greenhow, a Confederate spy during the Civil War, who tried to evade capture and the loss of her fortune by sewing the gold she had gained into the seams of her dress. But the ship she boarded sank, and the weight of the gold made it impossible for the life preserver to support her. She sank to the bottom with all her wealth. Dr. Pierce Harris, who told the story, pointed out that death did to her what it does to all of us, because we "cannot take it with us" when we die. But sometimes, we might add, it takes us with it!

4. MONEY MAGNATES
In 1923 at the Edgewater Beach Hotel in Chicago, Illinois, eight of the most powerful money-magnates in the world gathered for a meeting. These eight, if they combined their resources and their assets, controlled more money than the U.S. Treasury. In that group were such men as Charles Schwab. He was the president of a steel company. Richard Whitney was the president of the New York Stock Exchange, and Arthur Cutton was a wheat speculator. Albert Fall was a presidential cabinet member, personally a very wealthy man. Jesse Livermore was the greatest bear on Wall Street in his generation. Leon Fraser was the president of the International Bank of Settlements. Ivan Krueger headed the largest monopoly. Quite an impressive group of people!

Let's look at the same group later in life. Charles Schwab died penniless. Richard Whitney spent the rest of his life serving a sentence in Sing Sing Prison. Arthur Cutton, that great wheat speculator, became insolvent. Albert Fall was pardoned from a federal prison so he might die at home. Leon Fraser, the president of that big international bank? He committed suicide. Jesse Livermore? He committed suicide. Ivan Krueger? He committed suicide. Seven of those eight great big money magnates had lives that were disasters before they left planet Earth.

What mistake did they make? Thinking that what they had and what they controlled belonged to them.

5. COPING WITH WEALTH
Most people can't stand prosperity . . . but then again, most people don't have to.

6. KISSING POWER
Husbands who kiss their wives every morning before leaving for work usually live five years longer than those who do not. A kissing husband has fewer automobile accidents, loses up to 50 percent less time from work because of illness, and earns 20–30 percent more than a nonkissing husband. No statistics were available for benefits to kissing wives. Perhaps along with special rates for nonsmokers and nondrinkers, there'll soon be a special policy for kissers.

7. HOW MUCH?

Russian author Leo Tolstoy tells the story of a rich man who was never satisfied. He always wanted more and more. He heard of a wonderful chance to get more land. For a thousand rubles he could have all that he could walk around in a day. But he had to make it back to the starting point by sundown or he would lose it all.

He arose early and set out. He walked on and on, thinking that he could get just a little more land if he kept going on. But he went so far that he realized he must walk very fast if he was to get back in time to claim the land. As the sun got lower in the sky, he quickened his pace. He began to run. As he came within sight of the starting place, he exerted his last energies, plunged over the finish line, fell to the ground, and collapsed. A stream of blood poured out of his mouth and he lay dead. His servant took a spade and dug a grave. He made it just long enough and just wide enough and buried him.

The title of Tolstoy's story is "How Much Land Does a Man Need?" He concludes by saying, "Six feet from his head to his heels was all he needed."

8. THE TRUTH COMES OUT

A man entered a sporting goods store and told the proprietor he was taking up tennis and needed some equipment. He was sold a designer warm-up suit for $250, a pair of shoes for $100, three cans of balls for $30, a book of tennis tips for $15, and a membership in a local tennis club for over a $1,000. As he was leaving the store the sportsman realized that he had forgotten the most important thing. He asked, "Could you also supply me with a racket?" The owner beamed with joy and replied, "Of course, how about a half interest in this shop?"

9. LOYALTY TO THE END

The wealthy old man was very enthusiastic about his lovely young bride but sometimes wondered whether she might have just married him for his money, so he asked: "If I lost all my money, would you still love me?" She retorted, "Of course I would still love you. Don't be silly. But I would miss you!"

10. THE POWER OF ASSUMPTION

A man was inviting a friend to his wedding anniversary celebration and was explaining how to get to his place. He said: "We're on the seventh floor, apartment D. Just touch the elevator button with your elbow." "With my elbow? Why should I use my elbow?" And he responded, "For goodness' sake, man. You're not coming empty-handed, I hope!"

11. LET ME PUT IT ANOTHER WAY

Once a young man proposed to his girl as they sat looking over the beautiful lake. "Darling, I want you to know that I love you more than anything else in the world. I want you to marry me. I'm not wealthy. I don't have a yacht or a Rolls-Royce like Johnny Green, but I do love you with all my heart."

She thought for a minute and then replied, "I love you with all my heart, too, but tell me more about Johnny Green."

12. QUESTIONABLE HONESTY

A teacher was trying to impress her students with the importance of honesty. She asked her class, "Suppose you found a briefcase with a half a million dollars in it. What would you do?" Johnny raised his hand immediately and replied, "If it belonged to a poor family I'd return it."

13. ACID TEST

Beware of all enterprises that require new clothes. HENRY DAVID THOREAU

14. THE KILLJOY

I can't think of anything that's as much fun to own as it is to look forward to owning. JIM VORSAS

15. SUPERIOR AND INFERIOR

The superior man understands what is right; the inferior man understands what will sell. CONFUCIUS

16. THE COMMERCIAL CHRISTMAS

It was the first day back to school after Christmas vacation, and the teacher used a good bit of the morning by going around the room and asking each child to tell how they spent Christmas. The first boy said, "Well, we are Catholics and we went to midnight mass and came home and went right to bed. The next morning we had a big breakfast and sat around the Christmas tree and opened all our presents." The second child then told her experience. "We are United Methodists but we did about the same thing. We went to the Christmas Eve candlelight service and came home and went to bed. We had a big Christmas breakfast and then opened all our presents." The third child then said, "Well we aren't Christians. But we did have a big breakfast and opened presents around the tree. Then we all got into the car and went downtown to my dad's department store. He showed us all the empty shelves. He showed us all the money. Then we made a circle around the cash register, joined hands, and sang, 'What a Friend We Have in Jesus.'"

17. LET'S GET PRACTICAL

And then there was the wife who said to her husband, "This year let's give each other more practical gifts like socks and fur coats."

18. CHANGING VALUES, UNCHANGING VALUES
Conversation overheard between two young women: "I hear you broke your engagement to Joe. What happened?" "Oh, it's just that my feelings toward him aren't the same." "Are you returning his ring?" "Oh, no! My feelings toward the ring haven't changed a bit!"

19. THE SECRET OF PROGRESS
All progress is based upon a universal innate desire on the part of every organism to live beyond its income. SAMUEL BUTLER

20. REAL NEEDS?
Every girl has certain needs. From birth to age eighteen she needs her parents. From age eighteen to thirty-five she needs good looks. From age thirty-five to age fifty-five she needs a good personality. After fifty-five, she needs CASH! SOPHIE TUCKER

21. OLD AND GREEDY
A reporter asked a man on his ninety-fifth birthday, "To what do you credit your long life?" The old timer responded, "Well, I'm not sure yet. My lawyer's negotiating with two breakfast cereal companies."

NINETY-ONE
Maturity

1. THE OPPOSITE OF STEWARD IS VICTIM
In his book, *The Search for Power,* Harvard Professor David C. McClelland contends that there are four stages in the development of the individual to maturity:

Stage 1: Power is perceived as coming from others, but is directed toward oneself.

Stage 2: Power is perceived as residing within oneself, and is used for the needs of the self.

Stage 3: Power is perceived as residing within oneself, but is used for the sake of others.

Stage 4: Power is perceived as residing outside, coming through the self, but used for the sake of others.

This stage is what religion is all about. And faith. And theology. And Jesus.

It is the task of career development to help remove the last vestiges of Stage 1 (where we feel like "victims") from our lives, by teaching that even in the world of work, power resides within us, and can be used for the sake of others. So as long as men and women do not know or believe this, theology may well beckon them in vain, to Stage 4. We must first learn that we are not victims, before we learn that we are stewards.

2. MATURITY AND CHANGE
To exist is to change; to change is to mature; to mature is to create oneself endlessly. HENRI BERGSON

3. YOUR HIDDEN POTENTIAL
An American Indian tells about a brave who found an eagle's egg and put it into the nest of a prairie chicken. The eaglet hatched with the brood of chicks and grew up with them. All his life, the changeling eagle, thinking he was a prairie chicken, did what the prairie chickens did. He scratched in the dirt for seeds and insects to eat. He clucked and cackled. And he flew in a brief thrashing of wings and flurry of feathers no more than a few feet off the ground. After all, that's how prairie chickens were supposed to fly. Years passed. And the changeling eagle grew very old. One day, he saw a magnificent bird far above him in the cloudless sky. Hanging with graceful majesty on the powerful wind currents, it soared with scarcely a beat of its strong golden wings. "What a beautiful bird!" said the changeling eagle to his neighbor. "What is it?" "That's an eagle—the chief of the birds," the neighbor clucked. "But don't give it a second thought. You could never be like him." So the changeling eagle never gave it another thought. And it died thinking it was a prairie chicken. TED ENGSTROM, *The Pursuit of Excellence*

4. GROWING UP FOR SURE
Maturity is the ability to do a job whether or not you are supervised, to carry money without spending it, and to bear an injustice without wanting to get even. ANN LANDERS

5. CHILDISH FEAR
When I was ten, I read fairy tales in secret and would have been ashamed if I had been found doing so. Now that I am fifty, I read them openly. When I became a man, I put away childish things—including the fear of childishness and the desire to be grown-up. C. S. LEWIS

NINETY-TWO

Mercy

(See also Forgiveness)

1. THE FULL RANGE OF GOD'S MUSIC

I used to go out in the morning to get the paper when we lived in El Paso. Our house was a good four miles from the main parade ground at Fort Bliss. On most mornings I could hear the *whump, whump, whump* of the thirteen-gun salute which was sounded every morning at seven o'clock. But on some mornings I could hear the sound of the drum corps as they rolled their cadences.

However, if the morning was clear and still, as in the winter time when the air was crisp and cold, I could also hear the sound of the music of the army band, the blast of the trumpets, the wail of the clarinets, and the mellow tone of the horns.

But on the mornings I could only hear the cannon, I knew the drum and the horns were there, whether I could hear them or not.

Our fathers, in their theology, heard the cannon and the drum, the stirring of the wrath of God. Modern ears have heard the soft music of the flute and the horn, but have not listened for the cannon and the drum.

But the music of God's message demands the whole gamut of sound. He is just, but He is also loving. He is strong, but He is also merciful. Kindness without justice is mushiness. Justice without mercy has no power to move or change the stubborn heart. The cross is the only place where the picture is in focus. God's justice and mercy come together in His love for us sinners.

2. GETTING RID OF AN ENEMY

In the days of the Revolutionary War there lived at Ephrata, Pennsylvania, a Baptist pastor by the name of Peter Miller who enjoyed the friendship of General Washington. There also dwelt in that town one Michael Wittman, an evil-minded man who did all in his power to abuse and oppose this pastor. One day Michael Wittman was involved in treason and was arrested and sentenced to death. The old preacher started out on foot and walked the whole seventy miles to Philadelphia to plead for this man's life. He was admitted into Washington's presence and at once begged for the life of the traitor. Washington said, "No, Peter, I cannot grant you the life of your friend." The preacher exclaimed, "He is not my friend—he is the bitterest enemy I have." Washington cried, "What? You've walked seventy miles to save the life of an enemy? That puts the matter in a different light. I will grant the pardon." And he did. And Peter Miller took Michael Wittman from the very shadow of death back to his own home in Ephrata—no longer as an enemy, but as a friend.

3. WORDS ON AN EPITAPH
As Copernicus, the great astronomer, was dying, a copy of his great book, *The Revolution of the Heavenly Bodies,* was placed in his hands. But it was not his brilliant work that was on his mind. Instead he directed that the following epitaph be placed on his grave at Frauenburg: "O Lord, the faith thou didst give to St. Paul, I cannot ask; the mercy thou didst show to St. Peter, I dare not ask; but, Lord, the grace thou didst show unto the dying robber, that, Lord, show to me." There is no one who cannot come to God under those terms.

4. THE HIGHEST ATTRIBUTE
Among the attributes of God, although they are all equal, mercy shines with even more brilliancy than justice. MIGUEL DE CERVANTES

5. THWARTING SATAN
Mercy imitates God and disappoints Satan. ST. JOHN CHRYSOSTOM

6. THE QUALITY OF MERCY
The classic quote on mercy is that of Portia in Shakespeare's *The Merchant of Venice,* Act IV, Scene I, lines 186–197.
The quality of mercy is not strain'd
It droppeth as the gentle rain from heaven
Upon the place beneath: It is twice blest;
It blesseth him that gives and him that takes:
'Tis mightiest in the mightiest: it becomes
The throned monarch better than its crown;
His sceptre shows the force of temporal power,
The attribute to awe and majesty,
Wherein doth sit the dread and fear of kings;
But mercy is above this sceptred sway;
It is enthroned in the hearts of kings;
It is an attribute to God himself;
And earthly power doth then show likest God's
When mercy seasons justice.

7. FORGIVEN AND PARDONED

A young employee secretly misappropriated several hundred dollars of his business firm's money. When this action was discovered the young man was told to report to the office of the senior partner of the firm. As he walked up the stairs toward the administrative office the young employee was heavy-hearted. He knew without a doubt he would lose his position with the firm. He also feared the possibility of legal action taken against him. Seemingly his whole world had collapsed.

Upon his arrival in the office of the senior executive the young man was questioned about the whole affair. He was asked if the allegations were true and he answered in the affirmative. Then the executive surprisingly asked this question: "If I keep you in your present capacity, can I trust you in the future?" The young worker brightened up and said, "Yes, sir, you surely can. I've learned my lesson."

The executive responded, "I'm not going to press charges, and you can continue in your present responsibility." The employer concluded the conversation with his younger employee by saying, "I think you ought to know, however, that you are the second man in this firm who succumbed to temptation and was shown leniency. I was the first. What you have done, I did. The mercy you are receiving, I received. It is only the grace of God that can keep us both." Don Mallough, *Crowded Detours*

NINETY-THREE

Middle Age

(See also Aging)

1. COUPLES APART

Middle age is that time of life when a man will let his wife go anywhere as long as she doesn't insist on his coming along.

2. REALLY FAST . . .

Forget about jets, racing cars, and speed boats. Nothing goes as fast as middle age.

3. SINNING IN MIDDLE AGE

Middle age is when you have two temptations—and you choose the one that will get you home by nine. Ronald Reagan

4. THE IMPOSSIBLE YEARS

Middle age is that difficult period between adolescence and retirement when you have to take care of yourself.

5. FINDING THE ACTION

Middle age is when you try to find out where the action is so you can go someplace else. PATRICIA LEIMBACH

NINETY-FOUR

Ministry

(See also Church Life)

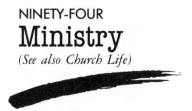

1. WHAT IS A PARABLE?

Let me offer a few thoughts on illustrations. Illustration is an art with three purposes. First, its purpose is to find the listener, and second, to help the listener find the speaker. It is like a bridge. Third, an illustration establishes contact between the listener and the text, so that a participation and a communication occurs in a new way between the listener and the text.

This means that an illustration often transforms the idea content present in a text with a concrete form that is then perceived at a different level than before. Where does the preacher find the right illustration to make use of as a window upon a text or as a bridge between the listener and the speaker?

Palmer suggests there are four basic places to look for illustrations: within the biblical text itself, in life experiences of oneself and friends, within the vast resource of literature, and in the image-building creativity of the preacher's own imagination.

He says: "An illustration needs the same attention to accuracy that the text deserves, because each illustration from life is close to some listener's area of familiarity."

2. HE DOESN'T COST ME A DOLLAR

The trouble is, you are always asking for money. You are probably right. But let me tell you a personal story. I had a little boy—my firstborn. He was a delight to our hearts, but he was always costing me something. He needed clothing, shoes, food, and had special needs that I gladly provided, for he was my son. Then one day he died. It was an experience that I hope you will never have. He does not cost me a dollar now.

Every need is an unfailing sign of life and growth. Body, mind, and soul have their needs and they must be met continually. A ministry that is constantly in need of funds is alive and growing and going somewhere. A dead ministry has no need, and will not bother you. PRESIDENT PEARSON, *Miami Christian College*

3. EVEN THE WORST OF SERMONS

An English vicar was most unhappy to learn, after preaching a powerful sermon against betting, that one of his own wardens was a heavy gambler. Immediately, the vicar hurried over to explain that he had not meant for the sermon to come across as a personal attack on him. The warden said, "Don't worry about it. It's a pretty poor sermon that doesn't hit me somewhere."

4. IN CASE OF SWELLING HEAD

The young preacher had just announced to his congregation that he was requesting the dissolution of the pastoral relationship in order to accept another call. He was standing at the door after the service and greeting people, as preachers are wont to do, when one of the elderly saints approached him, her eyes swimming with tears. She sobbed, "Oh, pastor, I'm so sorry you've decided to leave. Things will never be the same again." The young man was flattered, but was equal to the situation and took her hands in his and most benevolently replied, "Bless you, dear lady, but I'm sure that God will send you a new pastor even better than I." She choked back a sob and was heard to say, "That's what they all say, but they keep getting worse and worse."

5. NO URGENCY

Sign on the desk of church administrator: "Lack of planning on your part does not justify an emergency on my part."

6. A VERSE FOR ALL OCCASIONS

A young pastor had rung the doorbell at the home of one of his parishioners and was waiting to be received but no one came to the door. He sensed that someone was at home, but repeated ringing of the bell brought no response. As a final departing act he wrote Revelation 3:20 on the back of one of his calling cards and stuck it under the door: "Behold, I stand at the door and knock; if any one hears my voice and opens the door, I will come in."

Two days later the pastor received his calling card back in an envelope with a brief note attached that simply contained the text from Genesis 3:10: "I heard the sound of thee in the garden, and I was afraid, because I was naked; and I hid myself."

7. DESIGNATED GIVING

The congregation was taking up a special collection to add to the salaries of pastors who received very inadequate salaries because they worked in very small churches that simply couldn't pay more. On the face of one check was written, "For some inadequate pastor." Pastor, does your paycheck seem to send you this kind of message? Or are you being paid with the coin of another realm?

8. RANK IN THE CLERGY

In case you don't think rank still exists about various members of the clergy—consider this true story that came from the mother-in-law of a former staff member of the large Lexington Chapel in Lexington, Massachusetts.

It was summer and the pastor was on vacation. On this particular day the associate pastor also happened to be away. The Christian education director was the only pastor on duty. A phone call came into the office from a nonmember asking to speak to the pastor. The secretary informed the lady that the pastor was not available. She then asked for the associate pastor. The secretary explained that he wasn't there either, and trying to be helpful, she asked, "Would the director of Christian education do?" The caller paused very briefly and replied, "No, I don't want to go that low," and hung up.

9. HOW ABOUT YOUR LASTING IMPACT?

Several years ago a reader of the *British Weekly* wrote a letter to the editor as follows: "Dear Sir! I notice that ministers seem to set a great deal of importance on their sermons and spend a great deal of time in preparing them. I have been attending services quite regularly for the past thirty years and during that time, if I estimate correctly, I have listened to no less than three thousand sermons. But, to my consternation, I discover I cannot remember a single one of them. I wonder if a minister's time might be more profitably spent on something else? Sincerely . . ."

The letter kicked up quite an editorial storm of angry responses for weeks. The pros and cons of sermons were tossed back and forth until, finally, one letter ended the debate. This letter said: "My Dear Sir: I have been married for thirty years. During that time I have eaten 32,850 meals—mostly of my wife's cooking. Suddenly I have discovered that I cannot remember the menu of a single meal. And yet, I received nourishment from every one of them. I have the distinct impression that without them I would have starved to death long ago. Sincerely . . ."

10. THE DISTAFF VIEW

When the pastor of a conservative small-town congregation received the gift of a white suit from a friend, he was a bit reluctant to wear it. But since it was so attractive and a perfect fit, he decided to put in on one warm Sunday. As he was leaving for church, he asked his wife what she thought of his attire. After giving him the once-over, she replied, "It depends. Are you going to preach or sell chicken?" *Partnership*

11. DEALING WITH DEATH—THEORY AND PRACTICE

Philip Anderson of Chicago Theological Seminary tells a favorite story to illustrate that long, long distance between pedagogical theories of pastoral care and the actual practice of parish ministries.

Shortly after graduation one year Phil received a frantic phone call from a former student newly established in his first parish. "Phil," panted his young caller, "what do you do at a funeral?"

"We covered funeral practices in my spring course on pastoral care," answered Phil.

"I know we did," said the caller, "but this guy is really dead!"

12. FACT AND FAITH

A pastor was speaking to his people on the relationship between fact and faith. He said, "That you are sitting before me in this church—is fact. That I am standing here, speaking from this pulpit—is fact. That I believe anyone is listening to me—is faith!"

13. STAY ALERT

The easiest way to stay awake during a sermon is to deliver it.

14. REACHING TO HEAVEN

A farmer asked the district superintendent to assign a pastor to his community. "How big a man do you want?" asked the superintendent. "Well," the man replied, "we're not overly particular, but when he's on his knees we'd like to have him reach heaven."

15. THE SOUND OF MY VOICE

I overheard two laymen discussing the direction that my sermons for several weeks had been taking.

Apparently, one of the men felt quite satisfied with himself and where he was in his walk with the Lord. "I suppose the pastor will give another altar call next week, calling for further commitment of our lives. I'll sure be glad when he finds something else to talk about."

The other's reply sent me on my way with a song.

"Well, I hope our pastor keeps preaching the deeper walk with the Lord. I want more and more of Him. When I get to heaven, I don't want to have to pull out my wallet and show the Lord my driver's license to prove who I am. I want Him to know me by the sound of my voice."

16. MINISTERIAL MALADY
Never trust someone who has to change his tone to ask something of the Lord. ROBERT EVERETT

17. BODY LANGUAGE
Charles Haddon Spurgeon was sharing with a class of ministerial students about the importance of making the facial expression harmonize with the sermon. "When you speak of heaven," he said, "let your face light up, let it be irradiated with a heavenly gleam, let your eyes shine with reflected glory. But when you speak of hell ... well, then your ordinary face will do!"

18. DON'T GET TOO HUMBLE
After a worship service an old lady stopped and spoke to the pastor who had only been with them a few months. She said, "I'm deaf, and I can't hear a word you say, but I still come to get my plate full." Hoping to console her, the pastor said, "Well, maybe you haven't missed much." She replied, "Yes, that's what they all tell me."

19. ONE PASTOR'S ANSWER TO WHAT HE DOES
The pastor proclaims eternal truths to people who would rather hear the latest baseball score. He teaches, though he must solicit his own classes. He heals, though without pills or knife. He prays for people and hopes they pray for him. He leads worship and tries to make God real to those present. He sows God's Word and cultivates God's vineyard so that we may have deep roots in Christ and bear abundant fruits of the Spirit. He is a manager, administrator, correspondent, keeper of official records. He is sometimes a lawyer, often a social worker, frequently a one-man emergency squad. He is the favorite target of panhandlers and a decorative piece at public functions. He is a writer, speech maker, something of an editor, a bit of a scholar, philosopher, entertainer, salesman, and arbitrator. He is the theologian in residence and interpreter of the church at large. He seeks the lost, visits the sick, counsels the troubled. He comforts the afflicted and afflicts the comfortable. He tries to get people ready for baptism, confirmation, ministry, marriage, parenthood, old age, and finally death. He tries to keep people focused on eternity as they rush through time. He also tries to stay sweet when chided for either doing or not doing his duty, and often discovers that doing his duty can be just as offensive as not doing it. He plans programs

and recruits and trains workers when he can get them. He is determined to multiply ministry and not monopolize it. He wants people to experience the joy of being givers of Christian service as well as being recipients. Then he spends considerable time in keeping people out of each other's hair. Between all this he prepares a sermon and preaches it on Sunday to those who don't happen to have any other engagement. Then on Monday he smiles when some jovial chap roars,

"What a job—one day a week!"

20. SUMMER PERILS

In a small church during the summer, a pastor was preaching with gusto. Due to the warmth of the evening, the windows were open and bugs of all sizes were attracted to the sanctuary lights. As the pastor was making an energetic point, a large moth flew into his open mouth. The congregation was silent, awaiting some reply after the ingestion of the fluttering creature. After some coughing and throat clearing he responded, "Ladies and gentlemen, with some difficulty, a moth has entered the ministry."

21. DESCENT INTO MEDIOCRITY

The church is filled with fifty-year-old men who started brilliantly, who worked in places of real prominence and in the process have lost the very ways of doing their work that give them some insight as to what to do with their power. They are just holding on and frantically trying to survive.
JOHN CLAYPOOL, *The Wittenburg Door*

22. GETTING DOWN TO CASES

There once was a young preacher who had just landed his first congregation. Now this church was rather a small one and was composed entirely of the population of a small logging town. Everyone in town worked for the town's lumber mill, which was its only business and was involved in fierce competition with the mill just upstream. The preacher wasn't in town long before he had an experience that shook him up a bit. He was taking a walk through the woods and chanced to see the workers at the town mill pulling logs branded for the other mill out of the stream, cutting off the branded ends, and running them through their own mill. The preacher was very distressed with this and so worked the rest of the week on a powerful sermon. That Sunday he got up and preached his sermon entitled "Thou Shalt Not Covet Thy Neighbor's Property." The sermon seemed to go over well. Everyone told him, as they went out the door, just how much they loved his preaching. "You really moved me preacher" and "Best sermon I ever heard." were some of the remarks they made. But that next Monday morning it was business as usual at the mill. They were still stealing logs. So the next Sunday the preacher delivered a real "pulpit pounder" called "Thou Shalt Not Steal." "Fantastic!" the people told him. "Wonderful!" they cried. But on Monday morning the other company's logs were still being swiped by the town mill. Enough was enough! There's only so much a man can take and then he's got to act—this time he wasn't going to hold anything back. The following Sunday he got up and preached on the topic: "Thou Shalt Not Cut the Branded Ends Off Someone Else's Logs!" They ran him out of town!

23. APPLICATION IS ALMOST EVERYTHING

A soap manufacturer and a pastor were walking together down a street in a large city. The soap manufacturer casually said, "The gospel you preach hasn't done much good, has it? Just observe. There is still a lot of wickedness in the world, and a lot of wicked people, too!" The pastor made no reply until they passed a dirty little child making mud pies in the gutter. Seizing the opportunity, the pastor said, "I see that soap hasn't done much good in the world; for there is much dirt, and many dirty people around." The soap manufacturer replied, "Oh, well, soap is only useful when it is applied." And the pastor said, "Exactly, so it is with the gospel."

24. WAITING FOR GUIDANCE

Do you ever step up to the pulpit on Sunday morning knowing you are not as well prepared as you should be? My friend Ken Johnson shared a story with me that he heard Ian Pitt-Watson tell at Arcadia Presbyterian Church. Pitt-Watson said: "Because I'm leaving on Tuesday for Korea, I am not as well prepared as I ought to be. And I am reminded of the pastor who thought, when he had difficulty preparing a particular sermon, 'Perhaps the Holy Spirit will tell me what to say on Sunday morning.' This thought returned to him several times during the week, and when at last he stood silently before his congregation, he turned to the Holy Spirit for guidance, and a celestial voice said to him, 'Tell the people you are unprepared!'"

25. PUTTING FORTH EFFORT

A sermon is something a pastor would drive five hundred miles to deliver but wouldn't walk across the street to hear.

26. WE MAY NOT UNDERSTAND

In an age in which time is more and more limited and valuable, why do millions return to our sanctuaries week after week to listen to sermons? Though there are multiplied reasons, for many it is the desire to hear an authentic word from God. In lives that are torn by stress, puzzled by ethical questions, filled with anxiety about the future, they come to you as God's messenger to be reminded that their lives matter, that God cares, that there is hope. They come, as the Greeks came to Philip, saying, "Sir, we would see Jesus."

One young preacher expressed feelings of frustration about his place in the pulpit. He wrote: "I wish I did not hate preaching so much, but the degradation of being a Brighton preacher is almost intolerable . . . the pulpit has lost its place."

The writer was F. W. Robertson, who—within a few years of his premature death in 1853—was being called one of England's greatest preachers. Perhaps more important than the accolades of historians are the words of one of his church members:

"I cannot describe . . . the strange sensation, during his sermon of union with him and communion with one another which filled us as he spoke. . . . Nor can I describe the sense we had of a higher Presence with us as he spoke—the sacred awe which filled our hearts—the hushed stillness in which the smallest sound was startling—the calm eagerness of men who listened as if waiting for a word of revelation to resolve the doubt or to heal the sorrow of a life."

27. PEOPLE OF A CAUSE
Some pastors are crusaders. They have a cause that is larger than life. And occasionally they touch home base and do some nitty-gritty pastoral work. I'm sure we've seen them on all sides of the ecclesiastical spectrum—the public figures like William Sloane Coffin popping up in Iran, Jerry Falwell crusading for morality. Don't get me wrong—there are many good causes. History tells us of the Henry Ward Beechers who stumped against slavery and Martin Luther Kings crusading for civil rights. I don't mean to be critical, but there is a potential trap as well as an appeal in this kind of ministry. It is possible to get a Richard the Lion Heart fixation. You know, he was king of England for ten years but only spent six months of that time at home. He was busy off crusading to rescue the Holy Land. It is possible to see yourself as some sort of heroic and legendary figure—sort of a theological "Bear" Bryant.

28. CHURCH STAFF JOB DESCRIPTIONS
Pastor: Able to leap tall buildings in a single bound. More powerful than a locomotive. Faster than a speeding bullet. Walks on water. Gives counsel to God. *Associate Pastor:* Able to leap short buildings in a single bound. As powerful as a switch engine. Just as fast as a speeding bullet. Walks on water when the sea is calm. Talks with God. *Minister of Music:* Leaps short buildings with a running start. Almost as powerful as a switch engine. Faster

than a speeding BB. Is occasionally addressed by God. Walks on water if she knows where the stumps are. *Minister of Youth:* Runs into small buildings. Recognizes locomotive two out of three times. Uses a squirt gun. Knows how to use the water fountain. Mumbles to himself. *Church Secretary:* Lifts building to walk under them. Kicks locomotives off the track. Catches speeding bullets in her teeth. Freezes water with a single glance. When God speaks, she says, "May I ask who is calling?"

29. COMMUNICATIONS FEEDBACK

William Barclay, world-famed Scottish Bible scholar who died in February of 1978, claimed that his unique ability to communicate the gospel was due to an old Scot lady who lived alone in an humble house when he was a minister of Trinity Church, Renfrew. During her illness one winter, Barclay visited her regularly until she recovered. On his last visit, she remonstrated, "When you've been here, talking to me, and sometimes putting up a wee prayer, it's been grand, and I've understood every word you said. But man, when you're in yon pulpit on the Sabbath, you're awa' o'er ma head!"

30. WHAT MAKES THE DIFFERENCE

Two pastors' wives sat mending their husbands' pants. One of them said to the other, "My poor John, he is so discouraged in his church work. He said just the other day he was considering resigning. It seems nothing goes right for him."

The other replied, "Why, my husband was saying just the opposite. He is so enthused, it seems like the Lord is closer to him than ever before."

A hushed silence fell as they continued to mend the trousers; one patching the seat and the other the knees.

31. BACK TO BASICS

It's about time we gave up all the theological grand opera and went back to practicing the scales. VANCE HAVNER

32. THE REAL THING

A man had to fill in at the last minute for Billy Graham who was scheduled to preach in a big old church. He was a bit overwhelmed by the enormity of such a substitution. As he was sitting and thinking about playing this role he thought of a way to tie into the situation. So, as he got up to speak he alluded to his problem of having to substitute for such a celebrated preacher. He pointed out, "As I was sitting here I looked up at your large stained glass window and I noticed that one of the small sections of glass is broken out and a piece of cardboard has been substituted. I'm like that bit of cardboard.

Not the real thing, but better than nothing." Then he launched into his sermon.

At the close of the service he was greeting people at the door. One little old lady came up to him and said, "Preacher, I just wanted you to know that you mustn't see yourself as a cardboard substitute. You're a real pane!"

33. THE PREVIOUS PASTOR

The previous pastor had been a paragon of virtue. He lived up to all the people's expectations and was willing to live on a very low salary to boot. He loved to work around the manse and keep both house and grounds in repair. But the new pastor wasn't that type. He hired someone to do a lot of these chores, including the mowing of the manse and church lawns. Naturally this cost more money. This change of pattern was of concern to some of the elders of the church. One day one of them approached the new pastor and tried to bring this up tactfully. He said to the new pastor, "You know, our previous pastor mowed the lawn himself. Have you considered this approach?" The new pastor came back, "Yes, I'm aware of this. And I asked him, but he doesn't want to do it anymore!"

34. FAITHFUL PREACHING

There is an incredible hunger for the things of God in our day. Only a clear proclamation of biblical truth can assuage that need. Many a preacher has discovered that when he taught the Word with exegetical accuracy and expository excellence he was applauded for his creativity and originality. The reason is obvious—most moderns do not know the Scriptures. What a privilege to be "Servants of the Word" and "Heralds of God." Good preaching must not only be biblical, but also must be present tense. In 1928 Fosdick said that people are not interested in coming to church to hear about the Jebusites. Of course! They want a Word from God that has a distinct point of contact with the here-and-now. A sermon exists at the intersection of the Eternal Word and the life in the spirit today. Every sermon worthy of the name addresses us in the midst of the throbbing nowness of life. It also must be interesting. It is a sin to be boring. The gospel is never dull, only teachers and preachers are. This is where the preacher must stretch—he needs to develop the art of storytelling, to frame his thoughts with poignancy, to be creative in structure, and to maximize the preaching event through appropriate, enthused delivery. When a sermon is biblical, present tense and interesting, it passes the essential tests. Most other homiletical norms are superfluous. J. DANIEL BAUMAN, *Theology, News and Notes*

35. VALUED PET

The minister preached a very short sermon. He explained, "My dog got into my office and chewed up some of my notes." At the close of the service a visitor asked, "If your dog ever has pups, please let my pastor have one of them."

36. STERN INTERVIEWING

A young minister was being interviewed by a church board for the position of pastor. One old hard-working Irishman who was on the board looked at the young man sternly and asked, "Young man, did God send you here?"

He replied, "Well, I don't know if God sent me here. I am here trying to find the will of God and find out if you would like me for your next pastor."

The board member replied, "Young man, did God send you here?"

The young minister was somewhat at a loss for words and came back again, "Well, I just stopped by to talk with the board . . ."

The board member interrupted again and said, "Young man, did God send you here?"

Finally he screwed up his courage and said, "Well, I guess God didn't send me here. I just stopped by to see about whether we could get together."

The old board member leaned back in his seat and said, "That's good. The last four said that God had sent them, and we have had nothing but trouble with all four of them!"

NINETY-FIVE
Missions
(See also Evangelism, Witnessing)

1. DOING ONE THING RIGHT

Charles Malik, Lebanese ambassador to the United Nations, asked in a speech: "What has been the greatest American contribution to the rest of the world? Has it been money? Has it been food? Has it been medical skill? Has it been military might? Has it been industrial know-how?" Then he answered: "The greatest thing to come out of America has been the American missionary effort: the quiet, selfless men and women who have left the comfort and security of their homeland to bring the gospel of Christianity to less favored nations."

2. WHO IS A MISSIONARY?

For a helpful look at what or who a missionary is or should be, I recommend *A Hitchhiker's Guide to Missions* by Ada Lum (InterVarsity Press, 1984). Lum gives some helpful definitions and analysis of just what the missionary enterprise is all about. "A missionary is a prepared disciple whom God sends into the world with His resources to make disciples for His kingdom." She suggests six biblical images:

1. A Witness—Acts 1:8; Isaiah 43:10-12
2. An Evangelist—Luke 2:10-11; Acts 11:19-21
3. A Pioneer—Hebrews 12:2; Acts 20:22-24
4. A Herald—1 Timothy 2:7; 2 Timothy 1:11, 4:2
5. An Ambassador—2 Corinthians 5:20; Ephesians 6:19-20
6. A Servant—1 Corinthians 4:1; 2 Timothy 2:24

Lum points out similarities between Jesus and Paul in Preparation and in Ministry.

Similar Preparation: They had a deep sense of commission, they were well trained by life, they were full of the Spirit and they each had the heart of a servant.

Similar Ministry: Their message was reconciliation to God, they had a worldwide vision, they had a strategy, they focused on basic ministries, they trained disciple makers to carry on the work, they were men of perseverance, they were part of a team, they were men of compassion, and they were men of passion.

3. LOSING AND FINDING ONESELF

Here is the losing and finding of life in a person. Marian Preminger was born in Hungary in 1913, raised in a castle with her aristocratic family, surrounded with maids, tutors, governesses, butlers, and chauffeurs. Her grandmother, who lived with them, insisted that whenever they traveled, they take their own linen, for she believed it was beneath their dignity to sleep between sheets used by common people.

While attending school in Vienna, Marian met a handsome young Viennese doctor. They fell in love, eloped, and married when she was only eighteen. The marriage lasted only a year, and she returned to Vienna to begin her life as an actress.

While auditioning for a play, she met the brilliant young German director, Otto Preminger. They fell in love and soon married. They went to America soon thereafter, where he began his career as a movie director. Unfortunately and tragically, Hollywood is a place of dramatic illustrations of people "biting, devouring, and consuming" one another. Marian was caught up in the glamor, lights, and superficial excitement and soon began to live a sordid life. When Preminger discovered it, he divorced her.

Marian returned to Europe to live the life of a socialite in Paris. In 1948 she learned through the newspaper that Albert Schweitzer, the man she had read about as a little girl, was making one of his periodic visits to Europe and was staying at Gunsbach. She phoned his secretary and was given an appointment to see Dr. Schweitzer the next day. When Marian arrived in Gunsbach she discovered he was in the village church playing the organ. She listened and turned pages of music for him. After a visit he invited her to have dinner at his house. By the end of the day she knew she had discovered what she had been looking for all her life. She was with him every day thereafter during his visit, and when he returned to Africa he invited her to come to Lambarene and work in the hospital.

Marian did—and found herself. There in Lambarene, the girl who was born in a castle and raised like a princess, who was accustomed to being waited on with all the luxuries of a spoiled life, became a servant. She changed bandages, bathed babies, fed lepers . . . and became free. Marian wrote her autobiography and called it *All I Ever Wanted Was Everything*. She could not get the "everything" that would satisfy and give meaning until she could give everything. When she died in 1979, the New York Times carried her obituary, which included this statement from her: "Albert Schweitzer said there are two classes of people in this world—the helpers, and the nonhelpers. I'm a helper."

4. SEND MORE!

Alexander Mackay of Scotland was sent to Africa by the Church Missionary Society (Anglican) in 1876. He was an engineer by profession and a jack of all trades who was conversant in linguistics and theology. Mackay's heart was set on Africa and at last the call came. On November 15, 1875, a letter appeared in the columns of the *Daily Telegraph*. It was from H. M. Stanley, the famous explorer who had found Livingstone, and it told of the needs of the ancient kingdom of Uganda.

"Here, gentlemen, is your opportunity," it concluded. "Embrace it! The people on the shores of the Nyanza call upon you."

At age twenty-six Alexander Mackay headed for Africa. But before he left he and the seven other missionaries who were bound together for service in Africa met for a farewell meeting with the committee of the Church Missionary Society.

Each of the missionaries said a few words, the last speaker being the youngest of the party, Alexander Mackay. There was a stillness in the room as the erect young Scot spoke:

"There is one thing," he said, "which my brethren have not said, and which I want to say. I want to remind the committee that within six months they will probably hear that one of us is dead."

All eyes were fastened on him as he went on: "Yes, is it at all likely that eight English men should start for Central Africa and all be alive six months after? One of us at least—it may be I—will surely fall before that. But when the news comes, do not be cast down, but send someone else immediately to take the vacant place."

Mackay's words were still ringing in the directors' ears when the news came that one of the eight had died. A ghastly total of five of them succumbed to the African graveyard in the first year, and by the end of the second, Mackay was the only one left.

5. JONATHAN GOFORTH—THE SPIRIT OF CALEB

Some years back there was a missionary with the same kind of persevering passion as we find in Caleb in the Book of Joshua. His name was Jonathan Goforth—of China. At an advanced age his mission was turned over to the United Church of Canada. He was now separated from his life's labor in China. His wife was weak with illness, and he was accompanied by two lady missionaries who were now semi-invalids and a young man who did not know the languages. Closed doors and nothing but difficulties surrounded him. But at seventy years of age when most are retired or dead, Goforth set out for a new field to preach the name of Christ where it had not been named. Goforth tried to enter five different fields in Manchuria—and every door closed. But his faith was steadfast. Then came a call to northwest Manchuria, and another miracle of modern missions took place. In a few short years almost two thousand people came to Christ through his ministry—when all doors seemed shut.

6. THE POWER OF BEING

Legend has it that a missionary, lost at sea, was by chance washed up out of the sea on the edge of a remote native village. Half-dead from starvation, exposure, and sea water, he was found by the people of the village and was nursed back to full health. Subsequently, he lived among these people for twenty years. During the whole of that time he confessed no faith. He uttered no songs. He preached no sermons. He neither read nor recited any Scripture. He made no personal faith claim. But when people were sick, he attended them, sitting long into the night. When people were hungry, he gave them food. When people were lonely, he was a source of company. He taught the ignorant. He was a source of enlightenment to those who were more knowledgeable. He always took the side of those who had been wronged. There was not a single human condition with which he did not identify.

After twenty years had passed, missionaries came from the sea to the village and began talking to the people about a man called Jesus, and after hearing of Jesus, the natives insisted that he had lived among them for the past twenty years. "Come, we will introduce you to the man about whom you have been speaking." The missionaries were led to a hut, and there they found their long-lost fellow missionary whom they had thought dead.

NINETY-SIX
The Modern World

1. I KNOW HOW HE FEELS
Our family had gathered around the television to witness the arrival of Pope John Paul II in America. As we watched the Pontiff step from the plane and symbolically kiss the ground, my eighty-year-old aunt turned to me and confided, "I know just how he feels. I hate to fly, too." VIRGINIA SPRING

2. STEPPING BACKWARD
We are on the move from false certainty to true uncertainty.
Attributed to HENRI NOUWEN

3. PUT IT OUT
A three-watt bulb has been burning in a northern California fire station continually for eighty-five years. General Electric would like to examine it—to make sure they never make that mistake again.

4. ABSENCE OF MUSIC
The trouble with a lot of songs you hear nowadays is that somebody forgot to put them to music.

5. SIGN OF THE TIMES
The big thing today is computer dating. If you don't know how to run a computer, it really dates you.

6. COMMERCIAL COMMUNICATION

In the first twenty years of an American kid's life, he or she will see something approaching one million television commercials at the rate of about a thousand a week. This makes the TV commercial the most voluminous information source in the education of your child. These commercials are about products only in the sense that the story of Jonah is about the anatomy of whales. A commercial teaches a child three interesting things. The first is that all problems are resolvable. The second is that all problems are resolvable quickly. And the third is that all problems are resolvable quickly through the agency of some technology. It may be a drug. It may be a detergent. It may be an airplane or some piece of machine, like an automobile or computer. The essential message is that the problems that beset people—whether it is lack of self-confidence or boredom or even money problems—are entirely solvable if only we will allow ourselves to be ministered to by a technology. . . . Commercials teach these important themes through parables. In eight to ten seconds, the middle part comes, which is Hawaii or a new car. Then there's a moral. The moral is nailed down at the end, where we are shown what happens if a person follows this advice. And the actor, of course, is usually ecstatic. One has simply got to wonder what the effects are on a young adult who has seen a million of these little vignettes. One has to ask, "What is being taught?" NEILL POSTMAN

7. THE GRASS MAY NOT BE GREENER

I have had few difficulties, many friends, great successes; I have gone from wife to wife, and from house to house, visited great countries of the world, but I am fed up with inventing devices to fill up twenty-four hours of the day. SUICIDE NOTE LEFT BY RALPH BARTON, CARTOONIST

8. NAMES

I went to a restaurant one day recently wearing a shirt with the designer's signature on the right sleeve. As I stood in line to wait for a table, an elderly gentleman tapped me on the shoulder. Pointing to the label, he said, "Nice name." Then, in a curious tone, he asked, "What do you call your other arm?"

9. GETTING EVERYTHING TO COME OUT EVEN

I'm working as hard as I can to get my life and my cash to run out at the same time. If I can just die after lunch Tuesday, everything will be perfect. DOUG SANDERS, *former professional golfer*

10. ELECTRONIC PROGRESS
A computer expert reveals that it would take a hundred clerks working for a hundred years to make a mistake as monumental as a single computer can make in 1/1000th of a second.

11. YOU'D BE MISSED
If you think nobody cares if you're alive, try missing a couple of car payments. EARL WILSON

12. LET'S TALK LOUD
The loudest sound known to man is the first rattle in a brand new car. EARL WILSON

13. CANDOR ABOUT ADVERTISING
Advertising deals in open sores. . . . Fear. Greed. Anger. Hostility. You name the dwarfs and we play on every one. We play on all the emotions and on all the problems, from not getting ahead . . . to the desire to be one of the crowd. Everyone has a button. If enough people have the same button, you have a successful ad and a successful product. *Ad executive* JERRY DELLA FEMINA

14. THE SIMPLIFIED LIFE
A magazine cartoon shows a middle-aged lady talking to her boss at work. She says: "I've decided to simplify my life. Just send my paycheck to Visa."

15. LOOK FOR THE MUSIC
Herbert Feis relates how George Gershwin was talking to a friend on the crowded beach of a resort near New York City. The sounds and shrieks of voices pierced their conversation. Clanking tunes ground out from a nearby merry-go-round, while barkers and hucksters shouted themselves hoarse. From underground came the deep roar of the subway; beside them crashed the relentless tumble of the sea. Gershwin listened and then remarked to his friend, "All of this could form such a beautiful pattern of sound. It could turn into a magnificent musical piece expressive of every human activity and feeling with pauses, counterpoints, blends and climaxes of sound that would be beautiful. . . . But it is not that. . . . It is all discordant, terrible and exhausting—as we hear it now. The pattern is always being shattered." It is a parable of our time. So many confusing sounds and noises, so much unrest, so much rapid change. But somewhere, in the midst of it, there could be a pattern emerging, a meaning coming out of it, and our job is to look for the music in the noise.

16. IS THAT PROGRESS?

It only took the movies fifty years to go from silent to unspeakable.

17. OUR MOBILE GENERATION

I read recently of a man who lived in the same town in the Midwest all of his life—in fact, until recently he even had lived in the same house all of that time. He was satisfied that the town had all the things that he needed, so why move? Then one day he up and sold his house and moved into a new one—right next door! His friends were surprised that he had done this and asked him for the reason. He simply answered, "Oh, I guess it's just the gypsy in me."

18. SECURITY IN FLIGHT

Whenever I am flying and I engage people in conversation a confession is almost always forthcoming when they find out I am a psychiatrist. A few years ago, before all of the modern security measures were installed at the nation's airports, a man I was sitting next to on a coast-to-coast flight told me, "You know, I used to be deathly afraid of flying. It all started after that man brought a bomb on board a flight to Denver to kill his mother-in-law. I could never get it out of my mind that someone on board one of my flights might also be carrying a bomb."

I asked, "Well, what did you do about it?"

He replied, "Well, I went to one of those special schools for people who are afraid of flying and they told me there was only one chance in ten thousand that someone would be on board my flight with a bomb. That didn't make me feel much better. The odds were still too close. But then I reasoned that if there was only one chance in ten thousand that one bomb would be on the plane, there was only one chance in 100 million that two bombs would be on board. And I could live with those odds."

So I asked, "But what good would that do you?"

He quickly replied, "Ever since then, I carry one bomb on board myself—just to improve the odds." DR. JEROME FRANK, *professor of psychiatry at Johns Hopkins University*

19. BUREAUCRACY

An office worker in a San Francisco company applied through channels for a job with a government agency in Washington. While he was waiting for a reply, the head of the agency heard about him from a mutual friend in California and hired him for the job. Several months later, while the man was working in Washington, a letter was forwarded to him from his old address in San Francisco. It contained his original application for the job he now held, together with a letter from the agency regretfully turning him down because he was not qualified for the position. Looking more closely at the letter, the man found that he had signed it himself.

20. MEDIA INFLUENCE

A market research interviewer was stopping people in the grocery store after they picked up their bread. One fellow picked up a loaf of Wonder Bread and the man asked him, "Sir, would you be willing to answer a couple of questions about your choice of bread?" The man responded, "Yes, I'd be happy to."

"Fine," the man said. "The question I'd like to ask you is this: Do you feel that your choice of Wonder Bread has been at all influenced by their advertising program?" The fellow looked shocked and said, "Of course not. I'm not influenced by that sort of thing at all!"

"Well then," he said, "could you tell me just why you did choose Wonder Bread?" And he replied, "Of course I can! Because it builds strong bodies eight ways!"

21. FRIVOLOUS DIMENSIONS OF MODERN LIFE

Bathrooms collect fads. Hundreds of things end up on shelves or in cabinets. They fill the corners and line the tub. Some of them make for interesting reading, when one has time to browse. Recently I was visiting in a home on a trip, and was in the bathroom. My eyes roamed to a plain plastic bottle which drew no attention to itself. The white label with simple black print read: "Strawberry Bubbling Milk Bath." On the bottom of the same label in bold face black was NO FRILLS. How I cackled to myself at the utter, total incongruity. No way strawberry bubbling milk bath could be "no frill." It seemed at that moment pure frill. Nothing more than catchpenny. Another way to snag an unsuspecting dollar. What a commentary—on life, on aspirations, on self-deception!

22. THE FAST LANE RELIGIOUS LEADERS

An ethics professor at Princeton Seminary asked for volunteers for an extra assignment. At two o'clock, fifteen students gathered at Speer Library. There he divided the group of fifteen into three groups of five each. He gave the first group of five envelopes telling them to proceed immediately across campus to Stewart Hall and that they had fifteen minutes to get there. If they didn't arrive on time it would affect their grade. This he called the "High Hurry" group. A minute or two later he handed out envelopes to five others. Their instructions were to also go over to Stewart Hall, but they were given forty-five minutes. After they departed he gave the last of the envelopes with instructions to the third group, the "Low Hurry" group. They were given three hours to arrive at Stewart Hall. Now, unknown to any of these students, the teacher had arranged with three students from the Princeton University Drama Department to meet them along the way, acting as people in great need. In front of Alexander Hall one of the drama students was going around covering his head with his hands and moaning out loud in great pain. As they passed by Miller Chapel on their way to Stewart Hall they found a fellow who was on the steps lying face down as if unconscious. And finally on the very steps of Stewart Hall the third drama student was acting out an epileptic seizure. It's interesting that of the first group no one stopped, of the second, two of the five stopped, and of the third group all five stopped.

Maybe one of the reasons that the Good Samaritan was able to stop and help was because he had a more leisurely agenda, while the religious "pros" of Jesus' day were living in the fast lane and simply had no time for interruptions. Their calendars may well have been filled with commitments that left them no leeway.

23. AT THE CROSSROADS
Civilization stands at the crossroads. Down one road is despondency and despair, and down the other is total annihilation. Let us pray that we choose the right road. WOODY ALLEN

24. UNDERSTANDING LOUDNESS
The amount of noise which anyone can bear undisturbed stands in inverse proportion to his mental capacity. ARTHUR SCHOPENHAUER

25. WHEN THINGS DON'T SEEM TO WORK
A young mother examined a toy rather dubiously, then asked the salesman, "Isn't this rather complicated for a small child?" The clerk replied, "It's an educational toy. It's designed to adjust a child to live in the world today. Any way he puts it together, it's wrong."

26. THE HUMAN SCENE
Perhaps you picked up your newspaper one morning and read an editorial that went something like this:

"The world is too big for us. Too much going on, too many crimes, too much violence and excitement. Try as you will, you get behind in the race, in spite of yourself. It's an incessant strain to keep pace ... and still, you lose ground. Science empties its discoveries on you so fast that you stagger beneath them in hopeless bewilderment. The political world is news seen so rapidly you're out of breath trying to keep pace with who's in and who's out. Everything is high pressure. Human nature can't endure much more!"

Was that editorial written last week or last month or last year? Believe it or not, it appeared in a newspaper called *The Atlantic Journal* on June 16, 1833—more than 150 years ago.

27. HUMAN DILEMMA
This sign was seen at the desk of a country inn in Stow on the Wold, England: Please introduce yourself to your fellow guests since we are one big happy family. Do not leave valuables in your room.

28. ROCK AND CLASSICAL
Concert pianist Wladimir Jan Kochanski was asked if he liked any of the rock groups. He said, "One, Mount Rushmore."

29. LOGIC OF FLIGHT
If God had meant for us to fly, he'd have put the airports closer to town.

30. VALS
According to William Meyers in *The Image Makers,* Madison Avenue's most widely used categorization of people in our society is that suggested by SRI International's VALS (Values and Life-Styles). This divides people into five basic groups, as follows:

Belongers: The typical traditionalist, the cautious and conforming conservative. Archie Bunker is a Belonger; he believes in God, country and family. These are those who are the staunch defenders of the status quo (33 percent of the population).

Emulators: Not so set in their ways, a small but impressionable group of young people in desperate search of an identity and a place in the adult working world. They will do almost anything to fit in. They lack self-confidence and are discouraged about their prospects. They are into hedonism and finding solutions to their postadolescent dilemmas (about 15 percent of the population).

Emulator-Achievers: America's materialists, have it made already—own a Mercedes, drink Dom Perignon, shop at Tiffany's or Gucci's. They are a bit frustrated, just below the top rung on the ladder. Though affluent, they are somewhat dissatisfied (20 percent of the population).

Societally Conscious Achievers: These are the flower children of America's consumer culture. Baby-boomers, they care more about inner peace and environmental safety than about financial success and elegant surroundings. They are looking for personal, not necessarily professional fulfillment. They will try things from Zen to acupuncture. These are the gradually graying hippies. They shop for their clothes by mail from L. L. Bean, and have dropped out of the commercial rat-race to run antique stores. They have organic gardens and they hike in the woods. They are Madison Avenue's toughest challenge (20 percent of the population).

Need-Directed: These are the survivors, those who barely subsist on low incomes. They are on welfare and/or earn minimum wages. Ad Alley ignores them because they don't have much in the way of disposable income (15 percent of the population).

Meyers says that if you are going to communicate in the twentieth century—you need to know what kind of group you are trying to get through to.

31. AN UPTIGHT PEOPLE
There is a harrassed, knife-edge quality to daily life. Nerves are ragged and, as the scuffles and shootings in subways or on gas queues suggest, tempers are barely under hair-trigger control. Millions of people are terminally fed up. ALVIN TOFFLER, *The Third Wave*

NINETY-SEVEN
Money
(See also Materialism, Stewardship)

1. MONEY AND EXPERIENCE
When a person with experience meets a person with money, the person with experience will get the money, and the person with the money will get some experience. LEONARD LAUDER, *CEO of Estee Lauder*

2. IRS POLICY
When you consider the taxes the average person has to pay, the IRS seems to have a policy of "handicap the hired."

3. CONSOLATION
Money can't buy you friends, but your enemies treat you a little better.

4. WOULD IT WORK FOR ME?
Money can't buy happiness, we're told. But a lot of people would like the chance to prove it for themselves.

5. SMALL WONDER

Two Irishmen who were traveling in the Holy Land came to the Sea of Galilee. They discovered that it would cost them fifty dollars each to cross the lake by boat. They cried out in protest. "The Lakes of Killarney are the most beautiful lakes in the world and one can cross them for a few shillings."

The guide explained: "Oh, but this is the lake Jesus walked on!"

The Irishman quickly retorted: "Small wonder, at the prices you charge for taking a boat."

6. GOD'S DESIGN

God divided the hands into fingers so that money could slip through. MARTIN LUTHER

7. OUT OF DATE

Among the things that money can't buy is what it used to.

8. THE MISER

A miser isn't any fun to live with—but he makes a wonderful ancestor.

9. MONEY BUYS WHAT?

Many people have finally realized that money can't buy happiness. Now they're trying credit cards.

10. BOILING IT DOWN TO THE ESSENCE

A visiting American textile buyer told a long but amusing anecdote at a luncheon in Seoul, Korea. The translator repeated it to the group in just a few words and the audience laughed and applauded. Later, the textile buyer commented to the translator, "I think it was wonderful the way they appreciated my joke. It's amazing how you were able to shorten it in Korean." The interpreter replied, "Not at all. I merely said, 'Man with big checkbook has told funny story. Do what you think is appropriate.'"

11. LEADING INTO SIN

The income tax has made more liars out of the American people than golf has. WILL ROGERS

12. INCOME MANAGEMENT

People try to live within their income so that they can afford to pay taxes to a government that can't live within its income. ROBERT HALF

13. FAMILY MONEY

The average family's ambition is to make as much money as they're spending.

14. NOT A STATE OF MIND

Rich isn't just a state of mind. It's not having to arrange your vacation so that you arrive home on pay day.

15. CLOUT—WHO HAS IT?

An ad appeared in the classified section of the newspaper that read: "I would like to announce that the ad I put in this newspaper last Saturday was in error. I will be responsible for any debts incurred by my wife. And I will start paying as soon as I get out of the hospital."

16. PSEUDO-CONCERN

A knock at the door brought the lady of the house face to face with a man of sad countenance. He said, "I am sorry to disturb you, but I am collecting money for an unfortunate family in your neighborhood." He went on with great sympathy. "The husband is out of work, the kids are hungry, the utilities are soon to be cut off, and worst of all, they are going to be kicked out of their home if they cannot get the rent money by this afternoon." The woman replied with great concern, "I will be happy to help, but who are you?" He replied, "I am the landlord."

17. REAL POWER

Billy Graham was speaking in the San Jose area, and on the closing day told this story. It seems there was a strong man who traveled with a circus. One of his most impressive stunts was to take an orange and squeeze every last drop of juice out of it. Then he would offer one thousand dollars to anyone who could manage to squeeze as much as one additional drop from it. He went from town to town making his offer, but no one was able to win the one thousand dollars from him. Then one day he came to a small town in California and made his demonstration of juice-squeezing prowess and his challenge. A small, wizened, ninety-eight pound weakling type man came forward and said he'd like to take a try at the challenge. He took the crushed orange and proceeded to squeeze six more drops of juice from it. The strong man was amazed. He could hardly believe his eyes. He asked how he was possibly able to do this. The man shrugged and said, "Oh, I'm the treasurer down at the Baptist church and we do this all the time."

18. POVERTY PERSPECTIVE

In Hollywood there is an exclusive school attended by children of movie stars, producers, and directors. Asked to write a composition on the subject of poverty, one little girl started her literary piece: "Once there was a poor little girl. Her father was poor, her mother was poor, her governess was poor, her chauffeur was poor, her butler was poor. In fact, everybody in the house was very, very poor."

19. NOW I SEE!

Rev. Don Holesapple, a Baptist preacher, tells the story on himself about the time he received a call from a woman who was quite upset over the death of her pet cat, Homer. She wanted the preacher to conduct the funeral service for Homer! Holesapple explained that this was a little out of his line and referred her to a friend, a Presbyterian pastor at a church down the street.

Later, Holesapple learned that the Presbyterian preacher had referred her to a Methodist minister, who had referred her to someone else. About an hour later, she called Holesapple back, still upset. The woman said she was at her wit's end, couldn't find a preacher to conduct Homer's services, and didn't know what to do. She said she planned to give one thousand dollars to the church of the minister who performed this service for Homer. Holesapple said it took him only a moment to mull this over, and then he said to her, "Well, why didn't you tell me Homer was a Baptist cat in the first place?!"

20. JESUS AND FINANCE

Jesus talked a great deal about money. Sixteen of the thirty-eight parables were concerned with how to handle money and possessions. In the Gospels, an amazing one out of 10 verses (288 in all) deal directly with the subject of money. The Bible offers 500 verses on prayer, less than 500 verses on faith, but more than 2,000 verses on money and possessions.
HOWARD DAYTON, JR.

21. SIMPLE RULES FOR INVESTING

Don't gamble. Take all your savings and buy some good stock and hold it until it goes up, then sell it. If it don't go up, don't buy it. WILL ROGERS

22. MAKING MONEY

If you make money at poker, that's gambling. If you make it playing bridge, it's a social activity. If you make it outguessing the commodities, that's a miracle.

23. THE OGRE IN THE PIT

Once upon a time there was a White Knight looking for adventure. He came to a village where legend told of a terrible ogre in a pit. Bravely the White Knight took up the challenge. He would do battle with the terrible ogre in the pit. The people remembered several courageous men had climbed down into the pit, but no one could remember even one of those champions returning.

The White Knight stood looking at the deep, dark hole. The opening was so narrow he stripped himself of armor and unnecessary clothing. He took only a long dagger, which he tied around his neck with a leather strap. After securing a rope at the opening and testing its strength, he gripped it firmly and began lowering himself, hand under hand, letting the rope slip between his feet. Soon he felt the cool, smooth floor of the chamber. It took several minutes for his eyes to adjust to the darkness, but soon he focused on a large mound. Then he realized it was the bones of his predecessors, along with their assorted weapons. A little way off he spotted another mound, but he wasn't sure what it was.

Suddenly he was surprised by the inhabitant of the pit—surprised because he didn't anticipate that the ogre would be only as tall as a rabbit. The ogre waved his arms and screeched with its squeaky voice, trying to appear as fierce as possible. The White Knight picked up a sword from the floor and prepared to do battle, but quick as a rat, the ogre ran into a hole near the second mound.

The White Knight followed, and as the second mound became clearer and again he was surprised. Before his eyes there glittered balls of gold as big as grapefruits and diamonds as big as plums. With only a small part of that treasure, any commoner would be a prince for life. The little ogre lost its importance in view of this great treasure.

But the White Knight had a problem. How would he carry it out of the hole? He had no pockets. Who would believe him if he didn't bring back at least one piece?

He suddenly had an idea. He would take one of the diamonds in his mouth and carry it that way until he had climbed out of the hole. He could always come back later for the rest. Hurriedly he chose one of the larger diamonds. It fit comfortably into his mouth, and he began the arduous climb out of the pit, hand over hand, gripping the rope with his feet. His tongue held the diamond tightly against the roof of his mouth. Higher and higher he climbed until the heavy exertion began to render him breathless. He would have to breathe through his mouth in order to get enough air. As he took in a large gulp of air the diamond slipped and stuck in his throat. The White Knight choked on his treasure, lost consciousness, and fell to his death on the mound of bones below.

You see, the terrible ogre in the pit was not the little troll. The ogre in the pit was greed—greed in the hearts of men who saw easy treasure and the hope of unearned gain. The glitter of this world had choked him to death.

24. A WORKABLE BUDGET

Husband to wife as they plan a budget in the current inflationary times: "Let's start with the basic necessities—food, clothing, and shelter. We have a choice of any two." RALPH DUNAGAN

25. WIN A LITTLE, LOSE A BUNCH

Several centuries ago one of the popes, an avid patron of the arts, is said to have surveyed the vast artistic riches he had amassed and to have gloated: "No longer can the church of Jesus Christ say, 'Silver and gold have I none.'" And a subordinate replied, "But then neither can she now say, 'Rise up and walk.'" DAVID BARRETT

26. MODERN REVOLUTION

If Patrick Henry thought taxation without representation was bad, he should see it *with* representation.

27. TAKING IT WITH HIM

The story is told by the chief accountant for one of the wealthiest men who ever lived—John D. Rockefeller, Sr. Someone asked the accountant one day, "How much did John D. leave? We know he was an immensely wealthy man." Without a moment's hesitation, the accountant answered, "Everything!"

28. MONEY AS AN INDEX OF CHARACTER

Money is one of the acid tests of character and a surprising amount of space is given to it in Scripture. . . . Whether a man is rich or poor, observe his reaction to his possessions and you have a revealing index to his character. OSWALD SANDERS, *A Spiritual Clinic*

29. MAKING VAST SUMS OF MONEY

Jenny Lind, the great Swedish soprano, disappointed many of her friends because she turned down so many big contracts that would have made her world-famous. One day a friend surprised her sitting on a sunny seashore reading the New Testament. The friend rebuked the singer for not seizing her chances. Quickly, Jenny Lind put her hand over her Testament and said, "I found that making vast sums of money was spoiling my taste for this."

30. THE SOLUTION TO THE PROBLEM OF MONEY

I fear, wherever riches have increased (exceeding few are the exceptions), the essence of religion, the mind that was in Christ has decreased in the same proportion. Therefore I do not see how it is possible, in the nature of things, for any revival of true religion to continue long. For religion must necessarily produce both industry and frugality; and these cannot but produce riches.

But as riches increase, so will pride, anger, and love of the world in all its branches.

What way then can we take that our money may not sink us to the nethermost hell? There is one way, and there is no other under heaven. If those who "gain all they can," and "save all they can," will likewise "give all they can," then the more they gain, the more they will grow in grace, and the more treasure they will lay up in heaven. JOHN WESLEY

31. THEOLOGICAL ACCOUNT
A budget is a theological document. It indicates who or what we worship.

32. BETTER YOU THAN US
One Alaska storekeeper's philosophy regarding credit: "You ask for credit, we don't give you—you get mad. We give you credit, you don't pay—we get mad. Better you get mad."

NINETY-EIGHT
Mothers

1. GIVING
Years ago, a young mother was making her way across the hills of South Wales, carrying her tiny baby in her arms, when she was overtaken by a blinding blizzard. She never reached her destination and when the blizzard had subsided her body was found by searchers beneath a mound of snow. But they discovered that before her death, she had taken off all her outer clothing and wrapped it about her baby. When they unwrapped the child, to their great surprise and joy, they found he was alive and well. She had mounded her body over his and given her life for her child, proving the depths of her mother love. Years later that child, David Lloyd George, grown to manhood, became prime minister of Great Britain, and, without a doubt, one of England's greatest statesmen.

2. THE SELF-GIVING MOTHER
About 6:00 A.M. on a Wednesday morning James Lawson of Running Springs, California (in the San Bernardino mountains) left home to apply for a job. About an hour later his thirty-six-year-old wife Patsy left for her fifth

grade teaching job down the mountain in Riverside—accompanied by her two children, five-year-old Susan and two-year-old Gerald—to be dropped off at the baby-sitter's. Unfortunately, they never got that far. Eight and a half hours later the man found his wife and daughter dead in their wrecked car, upside down in a cold mountain stream. His two-year-old son was just barely alive in the forty-eight-degree water. But in that death the character of a mother was revealed in a most dramatic and heart-rending way. For when the father scrambled down the cliff to what he was sure were the cries of his dying wife, he found her locked in death, holding her little boy's head just above water in the submerged car. For eight and a half hours Patsy Lawson had held her beloved toddler afloat and had finally died, her body almost frozen in death in that position of self-giving love, holding her baby up to breathe. She died that another might live. That's the essence of a mother's love.

3. THE PLACE IS EMPTY

A cartoon in the *Saturday Evening Post* showed a young boy about five or six years old talking on the telephone, saying, "Mom is in the hospital, the twins and Roxie and Billie and Sally and the dog and me and Dad are all home alone."

4. THE STRATEGIC ROLE OF THE SUCCESSFUL MOTHER

When all is said, it is the mother, and the mother only, who is a better citizen than the soldier who fights for his country. The successful mother, the mother who does her part in rearing and training aright the boys and girls who are to be the men and women of the next generation, is of greater use to the community, and occupies, if she would only realize it, a more honorable as well as a more important position than any man in it. The mother is the one supreme asset of the national life. She is more important, by far, than the successful statesman, or businessman, or artist, or scientist.
THEODORE ROOSEVELT

God could not be everywhere and therefore He made mothers. *Ancient Jewish proverb*

Mother is the name of God in the lips and hearts of little children.
WILLIAM MAKEPEACE THACKERAY

5. MAMA'S BOY

A mother was concerned about her only son going off to college. She wrote the following letter to the college president:

"Dear Sir: My son has been accepted for admission to your college and soon he will be leaving me. I am writing to ask that you give your personal attention to the selection of his roommate. I want to be sure that his roommate is not the kind of person who uses foul language, or tells off-color jokes, smokes, drinks, or chases after girls. I hope you will understand why I am appealing to you directly. You see, this is the first time my son will be away from home, except for his three years in the Marine Corps."

6. TELL ME ABOUT YOUR MOTHER

A small boy went to the lingerie department of a store to purchase a gift for his mother. He bashfully told the clerk that he wanted to buy a slip for his mom but he didn't know her size. The lady explained that it would be helpful if he could describe her—was she fat, thin, short, tall? The youngster replied, "Well, she's just about perfect." So the clerk sent him home with a size 34. A few days later, the mother came to exchange the gift, as it was too small. She needed a size 52! Just about perfect!

7. A MOTHER IS WAITING

John Todd was born in Rutledge, Vermont, into a family of several children. They later moved to the village of Killingsworth back in the early 1800s. And there, at a very young age, both John's parents died. The relatives wondered what they would do with so many children, how they could parcel them out to other friends and relatives. One dear and loving aunt said she would take little John. The aunt sent a horse and a slave to get John, who was only six at the time. The slave, Caesar, came and put the little boy on the back of the horse. On the way back an endearing conversation took place:

John: Will she be there?

Caesar: Oh, yes, she'll be there waiting up for you.

John: Will I like living with her?

Caesar: My son, you fall into good hands.

John: Will she love me?

Caesar: Ah, she has a big heart.

John: Will I have my own room? Will she let me have a puppy?

Caesar: She's got everything all set, son. I think she has some surprises, too.

John: Do you think she'll go to bed before we get there?

Caesar: Oh, no! She'll be sure to wait up for you. You'll see when we get out of these woods. You'll see her candle shining in the window.

When they got to the clearing, sure enough, there was a candle in the window and she was standing in the doorway. She reached down, kissed him, and said "Welcome home!" She fed him supper, took him to his room, and waited until he fell asleep. John Todd grew up to be a great minister of the gospel. But it was there at his aunt's, his new mother, that he grew up. It was always a place of enchantment because of his aunt. It awed him that she had given him a second home. She had become a second mother to him. Years later, long after he had moved away, his aunt wrote to tell him of her impending death. Her health was failing and she wondered what was to become of her. This is what John Todd wrote her:

"My Dear Aunt,

Years ago I left a house of death not knowing where I was to go, whether anyone cared, whether it was the end of me. The ride was long but the slave encouraged me. Finally, he pointed out your candle to me, and there we were in the yard and you embraced me and took me by the hand into my own room that you had made up. After all these years I still can't believe it—how you did all that for me! I was expected; I felt safe in that room—so welcomed. It was my room.

Now it's your turn to go, and as one who has tried it out, I'm writing to let you know that Someone is waiting up. Your room is all ready, the light is on, the door is open, and as you ride into the yard—don't worry, Auntie. You're expected! I know. I once saw God standing in your doorway—long ago!"

8. LUTHER ON MOTHER

In commenting on the nature of women, Martin Luther is reported to have said: "When Eve was brought unto Adam, he became filled with the Holy Spirit, and gave her the most sanctified, the most glorious of appellations. He called her Eve, that is to say, the Mother of All. He did not style her wife, but simply mother, mother of all living creatures. In this consists the glory and the most precious ornament of woman."

9. IS THIS COMPASSION?

A fifteen-year-old boy came bounding into the house and found his mom in bed. He asked if she were sick or something. He was truly concerned. Mom replied that, as a matter of fact, she didn't feel too well. The son replied, "Well, don't worry a bit about dinner. I'll be happy to carry you down to the stove."

10. TYPE CASTING

After years of hauling children, pets, groceries and camping gear, the family station wagon sputtered to a stop. My wife told me she was ready for a change, but I didn't realize how big a change until we got to the car dealer and she fell in love with a foreign sports car. I pointed out, "But honey, this eight-passenger wagon over here has power steering, luggage rack, and fold-down seats, all for the same price as the sports car." She glared resentfully at the big car. She snapped, "I don't like it." "But why not?" "It has 'Mother' written all over it!"

11. THE MOTHERING EXPERIENCE

My thirteen-year-old daughter is perhaps having more trouble than some teens "discovering who she is" because she is adopted from South Korea and we have no idea who her birth mother might be.

Recently Amy received braces on her teeth and she was more and more uncomfortable as the day wore on. By bedtime she was miserable. I gave her some medication and invited her to snuggle up with me for awhile. Soon she became more comfortable and drowsy. In a small voice that gradually tapered off to sleep she said, "Mom, I know who my real mom is, it is the one who takes away the hurting." MARGARET H. COBB

12. FAMOUS MOTHERS, CAUGHT UNAWARES

Alexander the Great's mother: "How many times do I have to tell you—you can't have everything you want in this world."

Franz Schubert's mother: "Take my advice, Son. Never start anything you can't finish."

Achilles's mother: "Stop imagining things. There's nothing wrong with your heel."

Sigmund Freud's mother: "Stop pestering me! I've told you a hundred times the stork brought you!"

13. MATERNAL CONVERSIONS

An ounce of mother is worth a pound of clergy. *Spanish Proverb*

14. BEAUTY OF MOTHER

It was mid-October, and the trees along the Blue Ridge Parkway were ablaze with color. At an overlook, we stood next to a woman who was showing the view to her elderly mother. "Isn't it wonderful of God to take something just before it dies and make it so beautiful?" the daughter commented as she gazed at some falling leaves. "Wouldn't it be nice if he did that with people?" the mother mused. The younger woman looked at the stooped, white-haired figure beside her. "Sometimes he does," she answered so softly that she thought no one heard. B. G. WHITE

15. MOTHER'S HARD TASK TO LOVE

Kahlil Gibran, in *The Prophet,* expresses well the hard task of a mother to love completely and deeply and yet always with the task of letting go. "You may give them your love but not your thoughts, for they have their own thoughts.

You may house their bodies but not their souls, for their souls dwell in the house of tomorrow, which you cannot visit. You may strive to be like them, but seek not to make them like you, for life goes not backward nor tarries with yesterday. You are the books from which your children as living arrows are sent forth."

16. FAVORITE CHILD

Every mother has a favorite child. She cannot help it. She is only human. I have mine—the child for whom I feel a special closeness, with whom I share a love that no one else could possibly understand. My favorite child is the one who was too sick to eat ice cream at his birthday party . . . who had measles at Christmas . . . who wore leg braces to bed because he toed in . . . who had a fever in the middle of the night, the asthma attack, the child in my arms at the emergency ward.

My favorite child spent Christmas alone away from the family, was stranded after the game with a gas tank on E, lost the money for his class ring.

My favorite child is the one who messed up the piano recital, misspelled *committee* in a spelling bee, ran the wrong way with the football, and had his bike stolen because he was careless.

My favorite child is the one I punished for lying, grounded for insensitivity to other people's feelings, and informed he was a royal pain to the entire family.

My favorite child slammed doors in frustration, cried when she didn't think I saw her, withdrew and said she could not talk to me.

My favorite child always needed a haircut, had hair that wouldn't curl, had no date for Saturday night, and a car that cost $600 to fix. My favorite child was selfish, immature, bad-tempered and self-centered. He was vulnerable, lonely, unsure of what he was doing in this world—and quite wonderful.

All mothers have their favorite child. It is always the same one: the one who needs you at the moment. Who needs you for whatever reason—to cling to, to shout at, to hurt, to hug, to flatter, to reverse charges to, to unload on—but mostly just to be there. ERMA BOMBECK

17. ONLY A HOUSEWIFE?

Too many times women are made to feel that they should apologize for being mothers and housewives. In reality, such roles can be noble callings. When I was on the faculty of the University of Pennsylvania, there were gatherings from time to time to which faculty members brought their spouses. Inevitably, some woman lawyer or sociologist would confront my wife with the question, "And what is it that you do, my dear?" My wife, who is one of the most brilliantly articulate individuals I know, had a great response: "I am socializing two homo sapiens in the dominant values of the Judeo-Christian tradition in order that they might be instruments for the transformation of the social order into the teleologically prescribed utopia inherent in the eschaton." When she followed that with, "And what is it that you do?" the other person's "A lawyer" just wasn't that overpowering.

ANTHONY CAMPOLO, *The Power Delusion*

18. NOT TOO FAR FROM WRONG

It was a Rally Day program at the church and a little girl was to recite the Scripture she had memorized for the occasion. When she got in front of the crowd, the sight of hundreds of eyes peering at her caused her to forget her memory work.

Every line that she had so carefully rehearsed faded from her mind and she stood there unable to utter a single word. In the front row, her mother was almost as frantic as the little girl. The mother gestured, moved her lips, trying to form the words for the girl, but it did no good.

Finally, the mother, in desperation, whispered the opening phrase of the memorized Scripture: "I am the light of the world."

Immediately the child's face lit up and a smile appeared on it as she said with supreme confidence: "My mother is the light of the world!"

Of course, everybody smiled and some laughed out loud. Then they soberly reflected that the girl, in some ways, was not far from wrong. For the mother is the light of the child's world.

19. POWERFUL EVIDENCE UNREFUTED

When Robert Ingersoll, the notorious skeptic, was in his heyday, two college students went to hear him lecture. As they walked down the street after the lecture, one said to the other, "Well, I guess he knocked the props out from under Christianity, didn't he?" The other said, "No, I don't think he did. Ingersoll did not explain my mother's life, and until he can explain my mother's life I will stand by my mother's God."

20. MATERNAL LEGACY

When the will of Henry J. Heinz, wealthy distributor of the famous "57 Varieties" line, was read, it was found to contain the following confession:

"Looking forward to the time when my earthly career will end, I desire to set forth at the very beginning of this will, as the most important item in it, a confession of my faith in Jesus Christ as my Savior. I also desire to bear witness to the fact that throughout my life, in which there were unusual joys and sorrows, I have been wonderfully sustained by my faith in God through

Jesus Christ. This legacy was left me by my consecrated mother, a woman of strong faith, and to it I attribute any success I have attained."

21. SUMMING IT UP

On Mother's Day a minister gave this perfect tribute: "My mother practices what I preach."

22. ALL GROWN UP

I finally found a Mother's Day card that expressed my feelings for my mother in real terms. It said, "Now that we have a mature, adult relationship, there's something I'd like to tell you. You're still the first person I think of when I fall down and go boom!"

23. A CHILD'S PERSPECTIVE

A little boy was talking to the girl next door. "I wonder what my mother would like for Mother's Day." The girl answered, "Well, you could promise to keep your room clean and orderly. You could go to bed as soon as she calls you. You could brush your teeth after eating. You could quit fighting with your brothers and sisters, especially at the dinner table." The boy looked at her and said, "No, I mean something practical."

24. APPRECIATING MOTHER

Not until I became a mother did I understand how much my mother had sacrificed for me. Not until I became a mother did I feel how hurt my mother was when I disobeyed. Not until I became a mother did I know how proud my mother was when I achieved. Not until I became a mother did I realize how much my mother loves me. VICTORIA FARNSWORTH

25. THE BEST PREACHER

The preacher G. Campbell Morgan had four sons, all of whom were preachers. The youngest son, Howard, considered a fine preacher, once took his father's place on this side of the Atlantic while Dr. Morgan preached in London. Someone came into the drawing room when the family was there and, thinking to find out what Howard was made of, asked this question: "Howard, who is the greatest preacher in your family?" Without a moment's hesitation he answered, "My mother." Sometimes men and women who never stand at a pulpit preach the greatest sermons through living out the Word in their daily lives.

26. MY NAME IS . . .

A teacher had just given her second-grade class a lesson on magnets. Now came the question session, and she asked a little boy, "My name starts with an *M* and I pick up things. What am I?" The boy replied instantly, "A mother."

27. NOT ON MOTHER'S DAY
After dinner on Mother's Day a mother was washing the dishes when her teenage daughter wandered into the kitchen. Horrified to see her mother at the sink, she exclaimed, "Oh, Mama, you shouldn't have to do dishes on Mother's Day." The mother was touched by this seeming thoughtfulness and was about to take off her apron and give it to her daughter when the daughter added, "They'll keep till tomorrow."

28. EDISON'S TRIBUTE
I did not have my mother long, but she cast over me an influence which has lasted all my life. The good effects of her early training I can never lose. If it had not been for her appreciation and her faith in me at a critical time in my experience, I should never likely have become an inventor. I was always a careless boy, and with a mother of different mental caliber, I should have turned out badly. But her firmness, her sweetness, her goodness were potent powers to keep me in the right path. My mother was the making of me.

29. FAMILY HARDWARE
A child without a mother is like a door without a knob. *Jewish proverb*

30. FAMILY MATH
A teacher was giving a lesson in fractions. "Johnny, suppose there were seven in your family—five children and mother and father—a total of seven. Suppose there was pie for dessert. What fraction of the pie would you get?" Johnny answered, "One-sixth." "What do you mean?" asked the teacher. "Don't you know about fractions?" Johnny replied, "I know about fractions and I know about my mother, too. Mother would say she didn't want any." LESLIE FLYNN

31. RETROSPECTIVE
A little girl was shown pictures of her mom and dad on their wedding day. She asked her father, "Daddy, is that the day you got Mom to come and work for us?"

32. LOOKING OUT FOR MOM
A penny-pinching miser defended himself against criticism aimed at his parsimonious ways. He said, in his own defense, "Why, I couldn't stand for my mother to go on year after year working every night scrubbing and cleaning office floors, so I just bought the office building." The listener

asked, "Well, what did you do for your dear mother then?" The miser smiled proudly and said, "Well, she was immediately moved to the day shift."
MARVIN CROW

NINETY-NINE

Motivation

1. UNSPOILED MOTIVATION

My wife, Avis, taught a second-grade Sunday school class that was emphasizing the memorization of Scripture. One little seven-year-year old, Christian, was beginning to get into the program and was working on his memory work at home. His dad was inquiring into the whole procedure and asked Christian, "Well, what do you get if you learn these verses? What's the prize or reward?" Christian eyed him with that simple childlike look and said, "We get to learn more!"

2. CLEAR MOTIVATION

People go to college for a variety of reasons, but Bob Kuechenberg, formerly of the Miami Dolphins, may have given the best reason yet in an interview with *Newsweek*:

"My father and uncle were human cannonballs in carnivals. My father told me, 'Go to college or be a cannonball.' Then one day my uncle came out of the cannon, missed the net and hit the ferris wheel. I decided to go to college."

3. MOTIVATION THAT WORKS

The loaded station wagon pulled into the only remaining campsite. Four youngsters leaped from the vehicle and began feverishly unloading gear and setting up a tent. The boys then rushed off to gather firewood, while the girls and their mother set up the camp stove and cooking utensils. A nearby camper marveled to the youngsters' father: "That, sir, is some display of teamwork." The father replied, "I have a system. No one goes to the bathroom until the camp is set up."

4. MORE POWERFUL COMMUNICATION

A citizen received a "Second Notice" from the IRS stating that his tax payment was overdue, and that unless it was immediately forthcoming, the

IRS would be forced to take legal action. The very next day the citizen appeared at the IRS office with the overdue payment in hand, saying: "I would have paid sooner, but I never received your 'First Notice.'" The clerk replied, "We ran out of 'First Notices.' Besides, we discovered that the 'Second Notices' are much more effective."

5. THE GIFT OF MOTIVATION

Richard Halvorson tells the story in *Leadership* about the frog who fell in the pothole and couldn't get out. Even his friends couldn't get him to muster enough strength to jump out of the deep pothole. They gave up and left him to his fate. But the next day they saw him bounding around just fine. Somehow he had made it out and so they asked him how he did it. They said to him, "We thought you couldn't get out." The frog replied, "I couldn't, but a truck came along and I had to."

6. GRAVE MATTERS

There was a young man who took a short cut home late one night through the cemetery. And he fell in an open grave. He called, he tried to climb out. To no avail. There was no one around to hear his cries or lend a hand. So he settled down for the night in a corner of the darkened grave to await morning. A little while later another person came the same route through the cemetery, taking the same short cut home and fell in the same grave. He started clawing and shouting and trying to get out just as the first had done. Suddenly, the second fellow heard a voice out of the dark corner of the grave saying, "You can't get out of here." But he did!

7. DANGEROUS WATERS

A wealthy businessman hosted a spectacular party in which he had filled his swimming pool with sharks, barracuda, and other assorted dangerous fish. He announced to his guests that he would like to challenge any of them to try swimming across the pool, and he would offer a first prize of either a new home in the mountains, a trip around the world for two, or a piece of his business. No sooner had he made the announcement than there was a splash and a man swam rapidly across the infested waters and bounded up out on the other side. The millionaire said to the dripping man, "That was a stunning performance. What prize do you want?" He answered tersely, "Right now I really don't care about the prize. I just want to get the name of the turkey who pushed me in."

8. GETTING CREDIT FOR STEWARDSHIP

There's the story of the careless Scot who tossed a crown into the collection plate thinking it was a penny. When he saw his mistake he asked to have it back. The deacon refused, and then the Scot grunted, "Aweel, aweel, I'll get credit for it in heaven." The deacon responded "Na, na, ye'll get credit for the penny."

9. RIGHT TRACK
Even if you are on the right track, you'll get run over if you just sit there.

10. MOTIVATED TO DO HER BEST
The opera star Mary Garden, considered one of the greats of her profession, said there was one thing she always told herself before going on stage: "There's one person in that vast audience who has made a sacrifice to come and hear me, and for that person I'm going to give my very best."

11. FAITH OR HUNGER?
My husband is a minister who conducts an expanded altar call at the end of his sermon. He asks those who wish to accept Jesus Christ as their personal Lord and Savior, as well as those with prayers or other requests, to come forward.

To the surprise and delight of the congregation our three-year-old daughter, without a word to me, got up and made her way forward. She waited patiently while the others ahead of her made a request.

When her turn came, my husband leaned down to ask for her request. She whispered, "Can we go to the restaurant after church?"
ELLEN HAMMONDS

12. ONE HUNDRED PERCENT
Everybody but Sam had signed up for a new company pension plan that called for a small employee contribution. The company was paying the rest.

Unfortunately, 100 percent employee participation was needed; otherwise the plan was off.

Sam's boss and his fellow workers pleaded and cajoled, but to no avail. Sam said the plan would never pay off.

Finally the company president called Sam into his office. "Sam," he said, "here's a copy of the new pension plan and here's a pen. I want you to sign the papers. I'm sorry, but if you don't sign, you're fired. As of right now."

Sam signed the papers immediately.

"Now," said the president, "would you mind telling me why you couldn't have signed earlier?"

"Well, sir," replied Sam, "nobody explained it to me quite so clearly before."

ONE HUNDRED
Nature

1. SPRING DEFINED
Spring is God thinking in gold, laughing in blue, and speaking in green.

2. AUTUMN
I like autumn best of all, because its leaves are a little yellow, its tone mellower, its colors richer, and it is tinged a little with sorrow. Its golden richness speaks not of the innocence of spring, nor of the power of summer, but of the mellowness and kindly wisdom of approaching age. It knows the limitations of life and is content. LIN YUTANG

3. HIGH FLIGHT
In December 1941, Pilot Officer John Gillespie Magee, Jr., a nineteen-year-old American serving with the Royal Canadian Air Force in England, was killed when his Spitfire collided with another airplane inside a cloud. Discovered among his personal effects was this sonnet, written on the back of a letter at the time he was in flying school at Farnborough, England.

Oh, I have slipped the surly bonds of earth,
And danced the skies on laughter-silvered wings;
Sunward I've climbed and joined the tumbling mirth
Of sunsplit clouds—and done a hundred things
You have not dreamed of—wheeled and soared and swung—
High in the sunlit silence. Hov'ring there,
I've chased the shouting winds along, and flung
My eager craft through footless halls of air.
Up, up the long, delirious, burning blue,
I've topped the windswept heights with easy grace,
Where never lark or even eagle flew.
And, while with silent, lifting mind I've trod
The high untrespassed sanctity of space,
Put out my hand, and touched the face of God.

4. AN APPOINTMENT
Harvard philosophy professor George Santayana was giving a lecture one day when he paused to look at the brilliant yellow forsythia blooming outside the window. Many long seconds passed. Then he said: "Gentlemen, I very much

fear that that last sentence will never be completed. You see, I have an appointment with April." He left the room and never gave regular lectures again.

ONE HUNDRED ONE

Nobility

(See also Character, Dignity, Integrity)

1. VARIATIONS ON A THEME

To laugh often amid much; to win the respect of intelligent people and the affection of children; to earn the appreciation of honest critics and endure the betrayal of false friends; to appreciate beauty, to find the best in others, whether by a healthy child, a garden patch, or a redeemed social condition; to know that even one life has breathed easier because you lived.

This is to have succeeded. RALPH WALDO EMERSON

2. SYMPHONY

To live content with small means;
To seek elegance rather than luxury,
and refinement rather than fashion;
To be worthy, not respectable,
and wealthy, not rich;
To study hard, think quietly, talk gently,
act frankly;
To listen to stars and birds,
to babes and sages, with open heart;
To bear all cheerfully, do all bravely,
await occasion, hurry never;
In a word, to let the spiritual, unbidden and
unconscious, grow up through the common:
This is to be my symphony. WILLIAM ELLERY CHANNING

ONE HUNDRED TWO

Opportunity

1. THE LONG RIDE
A fellow comes up to a cab driver in New York and says, "Take me to London." The cab driver tells him there is no possible way for him to drive the cab across the Atlantic. The customer insists there is. "You'll drive me down to the pier and we'll put the taxi on a freighter and when we get off at Liverpool, you'll drive me to London and I'll pay you whatever is on the meter." The driver agrees and when they arrive in London, good to his word, the passenger pays the total on the meter and gives him a thousand dollar tip. Now the driver is roaming around London and doesn't know what to do. A Britisher hails him and says, "I want you to drive me to New York." The cab driver can't believe his good luck. How often can you pick up a fare in London who wants to go to New York? The passenger says, "First, we take a boat. . . ." The driver says, "That I know. But where to in New York?" The passenger says, "Riverside Drive and 104th Street." And the driver responds, "Sorry, I don't go to the west side." How about your church? Do you refuse to go the west side and thereby miss great opportunity?

2. WASTEFUL
As if you could kill time without injuring eternity. HENRY DAVID THOREAU

3. GOOD IMPRESSION
You never get a second chance to make a good first impression.

4. LIFE STILL HAPPENS
Life is what happens to you while you're busy planning more important things.

5. OUR VARIED ROLES
We are all manufacturers in a way—making good, making trouble, or making excuses. H. V. ADOLF

6. MISSED OPPORTUNITIES
The other day I ran across the story of a man who had a great opportunity that he missed. His friend took him for a ride one day way out in the country. They drove off the main road and drove through groves of trees to a large uninhabited expanse of land. A few horses were grazing, and a couple

of old shacks remained. The friend, Walter, stopped the car, got out, and started to describe with great vividness the wonderful things he was going to build. He wanted his friend Arthur to buy some of the land surrounding his project to get in on the ground floor.

But Arthur thought to himself, *Who in the world is going to drive twenty-five miles for this crazy project? The logistics of the venture are staggering.*

And so Walter explained to his friend Arthur, "I can handle the main project myself. But it will take all my money. But the land bordering it, where we're standing now, will in just a couple of years be jammed with hotels and restaurants and convention halls to accommodate the people who will come to spend their entire vacation here at my park." He continued, "I want you to have the first chance at this surrounding acreage, because in the next five years it will increase in value several hundred times."

"What could I say? I knew he was wrong," Arthur tells the story today. "I knew that he had let this dream get the best of his common sense, so I mumbled something about a tight-money situation and promised that I would look into the whole thing a little later on."

"Later on will be too late," Walter cautioned Arthur as they walked back to the car. "You'd better move on it right now."

And so Art Linkletter turned down the opportunity to buy up all the land that surrounded what was to become Disneyland. His friend Walt Disney tried to talk him into it. But Art thought he was crazy.

7. LABOR FOR THE CHANCE
The reason some people don't recognize opportunity is because it often comes disguised as hard work.

8. THE CHANCE FOR EVANGELISM
One of the great disasters of history took place in 1271. In 1271 Niccolo and Matteo Polo (the father and uncle of Marco) were visiting the Kubla Khan. Kubla Khan at that time was a world ruler, for he ruled all China, all India, and all of the East. He was attracted to the story of Christianity as Niccolo and Matteo told it to him. And he said to them: "You shall go to your high priest and tell him on my behalf to send me a hundred men skilled in your religion and I shall be baptized, and when I am baptized all my barons and great men will be baptized and their subjects will receive baptism, too, and so there will be more Christians here than there are in your parts." Nothing was done. Nothing was done for about thirty years, and then two or three missionaries were sent. Too few and too late. It baffles the imagination to think what a difference to the world it would have made if in the thirteenth century China had become fully Christian, if in the thirteenth century India

had become fully Christian, if in the thirteenth century the East had been given to Christ. In that, we have seen man frustrating God's purpose in history. WILLIAM BARCLAY

9. THE LAST MINUTE
If it weren't for the last minute, a lot of things would never get done.

10. OPPORTUNITY ETYMOLOGY
Our English word *opportunity* comes from the Latin and means "toward the port." It suggests a ship taking advantage of the wind and tide to arrive safely in the harbor. The brevity of life is a strong argument for making the best use of the opportunities God gives us.

11. REALLY LAZY
Mere longing for a better world can be a lazy person's way to face life. There is an old story of a farmer who said lightning struck an old shed and thus saved him the trouble of tearing it down, and rain washed off his car and saved him that chore too. When asked what he was doing now, he replied, "Waiting for an earthquake to shake the potatoes out of the ground."
W. A. POOVEY, *The Prayer He Taught*

12. FORMULA FOR SUCCESS
An ambitious young man asked an experienced salesman for the secret of his success in selling. The salesman said, "There's no great secret, you just have to jump at every opportunity that comes along." The young man replied, "But how can I tell when an opportunity is coming?" The salesman responded, "You can't. You have to keep jumping."

13. DANGEROUS OPPORTUNITY
In the language of China there is hardly a more suggestive or challenging word that *crisis*. It is made up of two characters, *way gee*. Each of these is half a word, the first being *danger* and the second *opportunity*. Hence a "crisis" is literally a "dangerous opportunity." EARLE H. BALLOU

14. TIMELY OPPORTUNITIES TO DO GOOD
A young man was busy at his job of taking out the groceries for the local supermarket. He had been in and out of the store on his helpful errands a number of times that morning. Something drew his attention to a woman in the parking lot who was struggling with her groceries. Her cart was abundantly filled, as were her arms.

His path back to the store took him in her direction. Like many people, she put one of her packages on the roof of the car while she hunted for her keys and opened the door. Then she began to load her packages from the cart to the automobile. But as she got in, started up her car and began to drive away, the young man saw that she had forgotten to retrieve the package she'd placed on the roof. Now he was closer to the car and he began to run after her. When she made a turn to exit the parking lot the package on the roof rolled off.

Fortunately, the young man caught the package—a baby—just before it hit the pavement!

15. CONFRONTATION
We are confronted with insurmountable opportunities. POGO

16. HOME RULE
All you need to grow fine, vigorous grass is a crack in your sidewalk.

17. THE GOSPEL OF THE SECOND CHANCE
On New Year's Day, 1929, Georgia Tech played University of California in the Rose Bowl. In that game a man named Roy Riegels recovered a fumble for California. Somehow, he became confused and started running in the wrong direction. One of his teammates, Benny Lom, overtook and downed him sixty-five yards away, just before he scored for the opposing team. When California attempted to punt, Tech blocked the kick and scored a safety, which was the ultimate margin of victory.

That strange play came in the first half, and everyone who was watching the game was asking the same question: "What will Coach Nibbs Price do with Roy Riegels in the second half?" The men filed off the field and went into the dressing room. They sat down on the benches and on the floor, all but Riegels. He put his blanket around his shoulders, sat down in a corner, put his face in his hands, and cried like a baby.

If you have played football, you know that a coach usually has a great deal to say to his team during halftime. That day Coach Price was quiet. No doubt he was trying to decide what to do with Riegels. Then the timekeeper came in and announced that there were three minutes before playing time. Coach Price looked at the team and said simply, "Men, the same team that played the first half will start the second."

The players got up and started out, all but Riegels. He did not budge. The coach looked back and called to him. Still he didn't move. Coach Price went over to where Riegels sat and said, "Roy, didn't you hear me? The same team that played the first half will start the second."

Then Roy Riegels looked up and his cheeks were wet with a strong man's tears. "Coach," he said, "I can't do it to save my life. I've ruined you. I've ruined the University of California. I've ruined myself. I couldn't face that crowd in the stadium to save my life."

Then Coach Price reached out and put his hand on Riegels' shoulder and said to him: "Roy, get up and go on back; the game is only half over." And Roy Riegels went back. Those Tech men will tell you they have never seen a man play football as Roy Riegels played that second half.

We take the ball and run in the wrong direction. We stumble and fall and are so ashamed of ourselves that we never want to try again. And God comes to us and bends over us in the person of His Son and says, "Get up and go on back; the game is only half over." That is the gospel of the grace of God. It is the gospel of a second chance, of a third chance, of the hundredth chance.

18. PERSPECTIVES—A PUZZLER

During World War II, a general and his aide, a lieutenant, were traveling from one base to another. They were forced to travel with civilians aboard a passenger train. They found their compartment where two other folks were already seated—an attractive young lady and her grandmother. For most of the trip, they conversed freely. The train entered a long and rather dark tunnel. Once inside the tunnel, the passengers in this particular car heard two distinct sounds—the first was the smack of a kiss; the second was the loud sound of a slap.

Now, although these four people were in the same compartment aboard the passenger train, they came to four differing perspectives. The young lady thought how glad she was that the young lieutenant got up the courage to kiss her, but she was somewhat disappointed at her grandmother for slapping him for doing it; the general thought to himself how proud he was of his young lieutenant for being enterprising enough to find this opportunity to kiss the attractive young lady but was flabbergasted that she slapped him instead of the lieutenant; the grandmother was flabbergasted to think that the young lieutenant would have the gall to kiss her granddaughter, but was proud of her granddaughter for slapping him for doing it; and the young lieutenant was trying to hold back the laughter, for he found the perfect opportunity to kiss an attractive young girl and slap his superior officer all at the same time!

ONE HUNDRED THREE
Optimism
(See also Hope)

1. WHEN IN DOUBT, STALL

The sorcerer had fallen out of favor of the court, and the king sentenced him to death. On the day of the planned execution, the sorcerer told the king that if he would allow him to live for one year, the king could become famous around the world—because the sorcerer would make the king's horse talk. If the sorcerer failed, the king could kill him—and the sorcerer wouldn't object. The king agreed, and the sorcerer was spared for one year and dispatched to a dungeon. A duke, who was friendly to the sorcerer, sneaked up to the dungeon and said: "You are indeed a fool. I know and you know that you do not have the power to make animals speak. Now you will surely die." The sorcerer answered: "I have a year. Many things can happen in a year. The king might die. Or I might die. And who knows? In a year perhaps the horse might talk."

2. THE RECESSION

A mayor who was very proud of his city was asked how the recession had affected it. He answered, "We don't have a recession here, but I will admit we are having the worst boom in many years."

3. HANG IN THERE WITH OPTIMISM

Two frogs fell into a deep cream bowl,
One was an optimistic soul;
But the other took the gloomy view,
"I shall drown," he cried, "and so will you."
So with a last despairing cry,
He closed his eyes and said, "Good-bye."
But the other frog, with a merry grin,
Said, "I can't get out, but I won't give in!
I'll swim around till my strength is spent.
For having tried, I'll die content."
Bravely he swam until it would seem
His struggles began to churn the cream.
On the top of the butter at last he stopped
And out of the bowl he happily hopped.

What is the moral? It's easily found.
If you can't get out—keep swimming around!

4. CHEERFULNESS
Cheerfulness keeps up a kind of daylight in the mind, filling it with a steady and perpetual serenity. An inward cheerfulness is an implicit praise and thanksgiving to Providence under all dispensations. It is a kind of acquiescence in the state wherein we are placed, and a secret approbation of the Divine Will in His conduct towards man. JOSEPH ADDISON

5. VIEW OF INSECTS
The optimist is the kind of person who believes a housefly is looking for a way out. GEORGE JEAN NATHAN

6. BIG FISHERMAN
I'm such an optimist I'd go after Moby Dick in a rowboat and take the tartar sauce with me. ZIG ZIGLAR

ONE HUNDRED FOUR
Parents
(See also Family)

1. TEN GOOD THINGS
Parenting—Ten Things for Which You as a Parent Will Never Be Sorry
1. For doing your level best even when discouraged.
2. For hearing before judging in family quarrels.
3. For thinking before speaking when emotionally upset.
4. For not harboring unkind thoughts of a talebearer.
5. For being generous to an enemy, perhaps the next door neighbor.
6. For stopping your ears to gossip over the fence.
7. For standing by your principles in dealing with your teenagers.
8. For asking pardon, when in error, even of your child.
9. For being square in business dealings with the newsboy.
10. For accepting the stewardship of "another" child. *Encounter, published monthly by the National Research Bureau, Inc.*

2. TURTLE PARENTING
Good parents are like turtles—hard on the outside and soft on the inside.

ONE HUNDRED FIVE
Patience

1. COPING WITH IRRITATION
A pearl is a garment of patience that enclosed an annoyance.

2. LET'S HELP EACH OTHER
A man's car stalled in the heavy traffic as the light turned green. All his efforts to start the engine failed, and a chorus of honking behind him made matters worse. He finally got out of his car and walked back to the first driver and said, "I'm sorry, but I can't seem to get my car started. If you'll go up there and give it a try, I'll stay here and blow your horn for you."

3. RAPID TRANSIT
The antiquated train on a branch line was creeping slowly through the countryside when suddenly it came to a dead stop. The only passenger in the car, a salesman riding the line for the first time, asked the conductor why they had stopped. The conductor said, "Nothing to worry about, sir. There's a cow on the tracks." In about ten minutes the train got under way again, but after chugging along for a mile or two, it again ground to a halt. "Just a temporary delay," the conductor said. "We'll be on our way shortly." The exasperated salesman asked, "What is it now? Did we catch up to the cow again?"

4. MARKING TIME
The secret of patience is doing something else in the meanwhile.

5. THE UNEXPECTED ANSWER
Then there was the woman who prayed for patience and God sent her a poor cook. HENRY WARD BEECHER

ONE HUNDRED SIX

Patriotism

1. LONG AND STEADY
I venture to say that patriotism is not a short and frenzied outburst of emotion but the tranquil and steady dedication of a lifetime.
ADLAI STEVENSON

2. A ONE-SIDED VIEW
In the annals of sheep the wolves are always defeated and disgraced.
PAUL ELDRIDGE

3. DEDICATION TO COUNTRY
Our country, right or wrong. When right, to be kept right; when wrong, to be put right. CARL SCHURZ

4. EVERYDAY PATRIOTS
I don't think the United States needs superpatriots. We need patriotism, honestly practiced by all of us, and we don't need these people that are more patriotic than you or anybody else. DWIGHT D. EISENHOWER

5. THE FLAG AND THE CROSS
Several times during my ministry I shared in military funerals. Finally a very significant lesson dawned. I've seen military funerals on the news, and have participated in six or seven across the years. And not once have I seen the American flag go down with the deceased. At every instance the flag was removed at the end of the service, and neatly folded and handed to the survivors. It's true. A nation cannot die for someone; it is powerless to do so; indeed it must not die. A nation survives, and the removal of the flag from the casket symbolizes that, though all it's citizens die, the nation continues. I am impressed that the symbol of our faith is the cross of Jesus, who died for men and women of all nations so that they may have life. A nation will finally say its farewell to us all, but the Savior will not.

6. ALEXANDER GRAHAM BELL, PATRIOT
We can demonstrate our love of country in many ways. When Bell prepared his gravestone's epitaph, he had it read:
Alexander Graham Bell
Inventor-Teacher

Born Edinburgh, March 3, 1847
Died a Citizen of the U.S.A., 1922

He could have listed his numerous inventions and honors. But that he was a citizen of the U.S.A. was his most cherished accomplishment.

7. CATCHING UP

President Reagan tells how we could match Russia's record after its more than half a century of socialism: "We'd have to cut our paychecks by more than 80 percent; move 33 million workers back to the farm; destroy 59 million television sets; tear up fourteen of every fifteen miles of highway; junk nineteen of every twenty cars; tear up two-thirds of our railroad track; knock down 70 percent of our houses; and rip out nine of every ten telephones. Then all we have to do is find a capitalist country to sell us wheat on credit to keep us from starving."

8. THE PRICE THEY PAID

Have you ever wondered what happened to those fifty-six men who signed the Declaration of Independence?

Five signers were captured by the British as traitors and tortured before they died. Twelve had their homes ransacked and burned. Two lost their sons in the Revolutionary Army, another had two sons captured. Nine fought and died from wounds or the hardships of the Revolutionary War.

What kind of men were they? Twenty-four were lawyers and jurists. Eleven were merchants, nine were farmers and large plantation owners, men of means, well educated. But they signed the Declaration of Independence knowing full well that the penalty would be death if they were captured.

They signed and they pledged their lives, their fortunes and their sacred honor.

Carter Braxton of Virginia, a wealthy planter and trader, saw his ships swept from the seas by the British navy. He sold his home and properties to pay his debts and died in rags.

Thomas McKeam was so hounded by the British that he was forced to move his family almost constantly. He served in the Congress without pay, and his family was kept in hiding. His possessions were taken from him, and poverty was his reward.

Vandals or soldiers or both looted the properties of Ellery, Clymer, Hall, Walton, Gwinnett, Heyward, Ruttledge, and Middleton.

At the Battle of Yorktown, Thomas Nelson, Jr., noted that the British General Cornwallis, had taken over the Nelson home for his headquarters. The owner quietly urged General George Washington to open fire, which was done. The home was destroyed, and Nelson died bankrupt.

Francis Lewis had his home and properties destroyed. The enemy jailed his wife and she died within a few months.

John Hart was driven from his wife's bedside as she was dying. Their thirteen children fled for their lives. His fields and gristmill were laid waste. For more than a year he lived in forests and caves, returning home after the war to find his wife dead, his children vanished. A few weeks later he died from exhaustion and a broken heart.

Norris and Livingston suffered similar fates.

Such were the stories and sacrifices of the American Revolution. These were not wild-eyed, rabble-rousing ruffians. These were soft-spoken men of means and education. They had security, but they valued liberty more. Standing tall, straight and unwavering, they pledged: "For the support of this declaration, with a firm reliance on the protection of the Divine Providence, we mutually pledge to each other, our lives, our fortunes, and our sacred honor."

They gave us an independent America. Can we keep it?

9. A CYNICAL VIEW
History is largely the glorification of the iniquities of the triumphant.
PAUL ELDRIDGE

10. DOLLEY'S COURAGEOUS RESCUE
President Madison's declaration of war against Great Britain in 1812 was not popular with many Americans, especially when the first year of conflict brought a series of shattering American defeats. New England was in a virtual state of secession; the governor of Vermont ordered the state militia to resign from national service; and in Massachusetts there was talk of negotiating a separate peace with the enemy.

After threatening for a year, the British actually attacked the capital in August 1814. While President Madison rode out to the battlefield in an attempt to instill confidence in the untrained troops, the citizens of Washington streamed out of the city into Virginia. Even the militia assigned to protect the White House deserted their posts. But First Lady Dolley Madison refused to budge.

Before the White House was burned, Dolley saved her husband's papers, a framed copy of the Declaration of Independence, and a valuable portrait of George Washington. She would leave only at the last minute—and returned as soon as Madison sent word that the British had left Washington.

Dolley's dramatic rescue of George Washington's portrait silenced her husband's critics and infused the once-divided nation with a new spirit. When news of the British burning of the White House spread, people who had been denouncing the war and talking surrender abruptly changed their minds. Confronted by a united, determined people, the British were more than willing to sign a peace treaty six months later.

11. GODLY MEN IN GOVERNMENT

A traveling man came into a hotel to secure a room for the night. Upon being informed that every room in the building had been taken, he was naturally quite perturbed, until a portly gentleman standing nearby kindly offered to share his room with him. The offer was thankfully accepted.

Upon retiring, the portly man knelt and prayed, tenderly mentioning his guest for the night in his petition. In the morning his host informed him that it was his custom to read a portion of the Word of God and pray before taking up the responsibilities of the day. The effect upon the man was moving; a strange feeling came over him; something had been working in his heart all the night. When gently pressed by this stranger to accept the Lord Jesus as his personal Savior, his resistance went down in a heap. A soul had been won for Christ!

But who is this humble ambassador of Christ, who so strikingly resembles a member of President Wilson's cabinet? When business cards were exchanged before parting, to the guest's amazement he read, "William Jennings Bryan, Secretary of State."

12. CHRISTIANITY AND PATRIOTISM

Christianity and patriotism have much in common. It is significant to note that:

Our patriotic hymn, "My Country, 'Tis of Thee," was written by a Baptist clergyman, Samuel Francis Smith.

The Pledge of Allegiance to the flag was written in 1892 by a Baptist minister, Francis Bellamy.

The words, "In God We Trust," carried on all of our coins, are traced to the efforts of the Rev. W. R. Watkinson of Ridleyville, Pennsylvania. His letter of concern, addressed to the Hon. S. P. Chase, was dated November 13, 1861. Seven days later Mr. Chase wrote to James Pollock, Director of the U.S. Mint as follows:

"No nation can be strong except in the strength of God, or safe except in His defense. The trust of our people in God should be declared on our national coins. Will you cause a device to be prepared without delay with a motto expressing in the finest and tersest words possible, this national recognition."

The president of the College of New Jersey, the Reverend John

Witherspoon (Presbyterian), was the only clergyman to sign the Declaration of Independence.

He is too much forgotten in our history books: John Witherspoon had a far-reaching influence on democracy. He had personally taught several of the signers of the document, and nine of them were graduates of the little college over which he presided at Princeton.

When he took up his pen to put his name to the document, Witherspoon declared: "There is a tide in the affairs of men, a spark. We perceive it now before us. To hesitate is to consent to our own slavery. That noble instrument upon the table, that insures immortality to its author, should be subscribed this very morning by every pen in this house. He that will not respond to its accents, and strain every nerve to carry into effect its provisions, is unworthy of the name of free man. For my own part, of property I have some; of reputation, more. That reputation is staked, that property is pledged on the issue of this contest; and although these gray hairs must soon descend into the sepulcher, I would infinitely rather that they descend thither by the hand of the executioner than desert at this crisis the sacred cause of my country."

13. LINCOLN'S FATHER'S FAITH
We have forgotten the gracious Hand which has preserved us in peace and multiplied and enriched and strengthened us, and have vainly imagined in the deceitfulness of our hearts that all these blessings were produced by some superior wisdom and virtue of our own. ABRAHAM LINCOLN

14. EMPHASIZE THE PEOPLE
The late Bishop G. Bromley Oxnam tells of giving the annual Memorial Day address at the National Monument at Gettysburg. Like most other speakers, he felt the need to conclude his speech by reciting Lincoln's famous address. After he finished he felt all had gone well. That is, until an old, old man made his way forward and remarked: "Son, you made an awful mess of Lincoln's speech." Oxnam asked: "What do you mean? I didn't miss a word of it. Here, look at my notes." The old man replied: "Oh, I don't need your notes. I know it by heart. You see, I heard it the first time 'round." By now Bishop Oxnam realized that this man had been present when Lincoln originally delivered his words. He was curious about how his recitation had differed from that of the president. The old-timer explained it this way: "Abe put his hands out over the people like a benediction, and said, 'That the government of the people, by the people, and for the people, should not perish from the earth.' You got the words right, son, but you missed the message. You emphasized *government;* Lincoln talked about *people.*"

15. THE DOLLAR CARRIES THE MESSAGE

Like so many other everyday things, even our money bears witness to the fact that ours is a God-founded nation, and it emphasizes the additional fact that as a nation we rely upon Divine Providence.

On the dollar bill is a pyramid, which represents the building of our country. The fact that it is broken emphasizes that our nation is not yet completed. Directly above the pyramid is an eye symbolizing the eye of God. This stresses the importance of putting spiritual welfare above material prosperity. Our Founding Fathers firmly believed that our strength was rooted in God and that our progress must always be under the watchful eye of Providence.

Another important symbol is contained in the words *Annuit Coeptis* in a semicircle at the top of the seal. Referring to the Almighty, they mean "He has smiled on our undertakings."

And, finally, three Latin words appear directly under the pyramid, meaning "A new order of the ages." That statement suggests that our nation, under God, is introducing a new age in the life and freedom of mankind.
NORMAN VINCENT PEALE, *One Nation Under God*

16. THE NEED FOR DEMOCRACY

Man's capacity for justice makes democracy possible, but man's inclination to injustice makes democracy necessary. REINHOLD NIEBUHR

ONE HUNDRED SEVEN
Peace

1. PEACE, PEACE

A true story: A retired couple was alarmed by the threat of nuclear war so they undertook a serious study of all the inhabited places on the globe. Their goal was to determine where in the world would be the place to be least likely affected by a nuclear war. A place of ultimate security. They studied and traveled, traveled and studied. Finally they found *the place*. And on Christmas they sent their pastor a card from their new home—in the Falkland Islands. However, their "paradise" was soon turned into a war zone by Great Britain and Argentina. Jesus said, "Peace I leave with you; my peace

I give to you. Not as the world gives do I give to you. Let not your hearts be troubled, neither let them be afraid."

2. SPONTANEOUS BROTHERHOOD
Amid the horrors of World War I, there occurred a unique truce when, for a few hours, enemies behaved like brothers.

Christmas Eve in 1914 was all quiet on France's Western Front, from the English Channel to the Swiss Alps. Trenches came within fifty miles of Paris. The war was only five months old, and approximately eight hundred thousand men had been wounded or killed. Every soldier wondered whether Christmas Day would bring another round of fighting and killing, but something happened:

British soldiers raised Merry Christmas signs, and soon carols were heard from German and British trenches alike.

Christmas dawned with unarmed soldiers leaving their trenches as officers of both sides tried unsuccessfully to stop their troops from meeting the enemy in the middle of no-man's-land for songs and conversation. Exchanging small gifts—mostly sweets and cigars—they passed Christmas Day peacefully along miles of the front. At one spot, the British played soccer with the Germans, who won three to two.

In some places, the spontaneous truce contained the next day, neither side willing to fire the first shot. Finally the war resumed when fresh troops arrived, and the high command of both armies ordered that further "informal understandings" with the enemy would be punishable as treason.

3. ENEMIES' SECRETS
If we could read the secret history of our enemies, we should find in each man's life sorrow and suffering enough to disarm all hostility.
HENRY WADSWORTH LONGFELLOW

4. THE DESIRE FOR PEACE
Ramsey MacDonald, one-time prime minister of England, was discussing with another government official the possibility of lasting peace. The latter, an expert on foreign affairs, was unimpressed by the prime minister's idealistic viewpoint. He remarked cynically, "The desire for peace does not necessarily ensure it." This MacDonald admitted, saying, "Quite true. But neither does the desire for food satisfy your hunger, but at least it gets you started toward a restaurant."

5. OUT OF TOUCH WITH THE WORLD
One of the strangest tales to come out of World War II concerns the story of two young men who were captured by the Americans in Germany near the end of the war.

The two were shipped to a POW camp in this country, but attempts to integrate them were to no avail. They would not or could not speak to American authorities. They kept to themselves and refused to talk to anyone, even their fellow German prisoners. In fact, the other German prisoners insisted that they knew nothing of the pair.

The American officers were puzzled. The two men seemed frightened and bewildered but not sullen or rebellious. After a few weeks in their new quarters they even seemed willing to cooperate, but when they finally did speak no one could understand a word they said. There was something else too. They did not look like Germans. Since their features were more Asiatic in appearance, an expert in Asiatic languages was called in. He soon solved the mystery. The two were Tibetans, and they were overjoyed that at last someone was able to understand them and to listen to their incredible, almost unbelievable, story.

It seems that in the summer of 1941 the two friends, lured by a desire to see something of the world outside their tiny village, crossed the northern frontier of Tibet and for weeks wandered happily in Soviet Russian territory. Abruptly they were picked up by Russian authorities, put on a train with hundreds of other young men, and shipped west.

Outside a large city, at an army camp, they were issued uniforms and rifles and given some rudimentary military training. After a few days they were loaded onto trucks with the other soldiers and shipped to the Russian front.

They were horrified at what they saw. Men were killing each other with artillery, rifles—even hand-to-hand fighting. Because they were good Buddhists, killing was against their moral principles. They started to flee to the rear, but in their flight they were overtaken by the Germans and made prisoners. Once again they were loaded onto a train and shipped, this time to Germany. After the Normandy invasion, as the American forces neared Germany, they were put into an auxiliary service in the German army. As the Americans continued to advance the two were given guns and told to fight with the Germans. Once again they tried to flee, but this time were captured by the Americans. When they had finished their story, the interpreter asked them if they had any questions. They had only one: "Why were all those people trying to kill each other?"

6. A FABLE ON PEACE

When Christ was born, the angel declared to the frightened shepherds, "Glory to God in the highest, and on earth peace to people of good will."

But the world has seen very few years of peace since Christ our Prince of Peace came. I discovered this fable on peace which challenges me.

"Tell me the weight of a snowflake," a sparrow asked a wild dove.

"Nothing more than nothing," was the answer.

"In that case, I must tell you a marvelous story," the sparrow said. "I sat on the branch of a fir, close to its trunk, when it began to snow—not heavily, not in a raging blizzard—no, just like in a dream, without a sound, and without any violence. Since I did not have anything better to do, I counted the snowflakes settling on the twigs and needles of my branch. Their number was exactly 3,741,952. When the 3,741,953rd dropped onto the branch, nothing more than nothing, as you say, the branch broke off."

Having said that, the sparrow flew away.

The dove, since Noah's time an authority on the matter, thought about the story for awhile, and finally said to herself, "Perhaps only one person's voice is lacking for peace to come to the world."

ONE HUNDRED EIGHT

Perfection

1. A PERFECTIONIST

A perfectionist is someone who takes infinite pains—and gives them to others.

2. PUNCTUAL PEOPLE

People who are too punctual lead lonely lives. GERALD ROTHSTEIN

3. THE PERFECT HUSBAND

While vacationing recently in Palm Desert, California, I heard Pastor Dean Miller share this story about perfection: It seems the pastor was saying to the people that none of us is perfect, and not only that, none of us today even has the opportunity of knowing a perfect person. In fact, he went so far as to challenge the people, asking them if any of them had even heard of a perfect person among their contemporaries. One fellow stood up and allowed as he knew of such a person. The pastor pressed him for details: Did he really know him? Had he met him? The man admitted that he didn't know the man personally, but he had certainly heard a great deal about him. In fact, this storied man of many perfections was his wife's first husband.

4. SO CLOSE

The closest to perfection a person ever comes is when he fills out a job application form.

ONE HUNDRED NINE
Persuasion

1. NEGOTIATION SKILLS

The art of negotiation is something you learn at an early age. You'd be amazed how many teenagers get their first car by asking for a motorcycle.

2. STRATEGY FOR INTERPERSONAL CONVINCING

Never try to prove to the other person that you are right. It is human nature to object to anyone who insists he is right. Rather, always present your arguments in such a manner as to do your best to prove that you are wrong. If you follow this approach, especially when you are sure you are right, the person you are trying to convince will bring up strong evidence in behalf of your cause and prove to himself and to the world that your stand is correct. LOUIS PASTEUR

3. MANIPULATION VERSUS PERSUASION

The line between manipulative and persuasive motivators is very difficult to draw sometimes. The manipulative person is persuasive and deceptive. You may get manipulated into doing something because of trickery. For example, a woman who is pretending to be hurt and doesn't really feel that way is being a manipulator. Her emotions are delivered in counterfeit form. A persuasive person, on the other hand, seeks to convince people because he believes that following his course will be best, most successful. F. LEE BAILEY

4. POWERFUL SALESMANSHIP

Elizabeth Brinton, thirteen-year-old Girl Scout, explaining how she sold 11,200 boxes of cookies: "You have to look people in the eye and make them feel guilty."

ONE HUNDRED TEN
Pessimism
(See also Cynics)

1. OUT OF THE WAY
Man who say it cannot be done should not interrupt man doing it.
Chinese proverb

2. PHILOSOPHY OF DREAD
Charlie Brown: "I have a new philosophy. I'm only going to dread one day at a time." CHARLES SCHULZ

3. NATURE, THE FAULT FINDER
Murphy's Third Law: Nature always sides with the hidden flaw.

4. SUSPICIOUS ALTRUISM
Nothing is more generally suspected than an altruistic gesture and those who throw bread upon waters are accused of pollution. PAUL ELDRIDGE

5. IT COULDN'T BE DONE
Listen to these examples of inventions and ideas that some people said "couldn't be done" so they resisted the new.
1. The first successful cast-iron plow, invented in the United States in 1797, was rejected by New Jersey farmers under the theory that cast iron poisoned the land and stimulated the growth of weeds.
2. An eloquent authority in the United States declared that the introduction of the railroad would require the building of many insane asylums, since people would be driven mad with terror at the sight of locomotives rushing across the country.
3. In Germany it was proved by "experts" that if trains went at the frightful speed of 15 miles an hour, blood would spurt from the travelers' noses and passengers would suffocate when going through tunnels.
4. Commodore Vanderbilt dismissed Westinghouse and his new air brakes for trains, stating, "I have no time to waste on fools."
5. Those who loaned Robert Fulton money for his steamboat project stipulated that their names be withheld for fear of ridicule were it known they supported anything so "foolhardy."
6. In 1881, when the New York YWCA announced typing lessons for women, vigorous protests were made on the grounds that the female constitution would break down under the strain.

7. Men insisted that iron ships would not float, that they would damage more easily than wooden ships when grounding, that it would be difficult to preserve the iron bottom from rust, and that iron would deflect the compass.

8. Joshua Coppersmith was arrested in Boston for trying to sell stock in the telephone. "All well-informed people know that it is impossible to transmit the human voice over a wire."

9. The editor of the *Springfield Republican* refused an invitation to ride in an early automobile, claiming that it was incompatible with the dignity of his position.

6. HAVE A NICE DAY

Most of us in our more cynical moments have questioned the sincerity of people who tell everybody to "have a nice day." One lady was overheard saying to someone who told her to have a nice day, "I have other plans."

7. REGULAR KILLJOYS

An optimist may see a light where there is none, but why must the pessimist always run to blow it out? MICHEL DE SAINT-PIERRE

8. THE EXPERTS HAVE SPOKEN

Everything that can be invented has been invented. CHARLES H. DUELL, *U.S. Patent Office director, 1899*

Who the h—— wants to hear actors talk? H. M. WARNER, *Warner Bros. Pictures, c. 1927*

Sensible and responsible women do not want to vote.
GROVER CLEVELAND, *1905*

There is no likelihood man can ever tap the power of the atom.
ROBERT MILLIKAN, *Nobel prize winner in physics, 1923*

Heavier than air flying machines are impossible. LORD KELVIN, *president, Royal Society, c. 1895*

Ruth [Babe Ruth] made a big mistake when he gave up pitching.
TRIS SPEAKER, *1927*

The horse is here to stay, but the automobile is only a novelty. *The Michigan banker who advised Henry Ford's lawyer not to invest in the new motor car company*
Gone with the Wind *is going to be the biggest flop in Hollywood history. I'm just glad it'll be Clark Gable who's falling flat on his face and not me.*
GARY COOPER

ONE HUNDRED ELEVEN
Point of View
(See also Attitude)

1. SEEING WITH A DIFFERENT PERSPECTIVE

Sculptress Louise Nevelson says that she collects things "for my eye." And she has an exceptional eye. She believes that any of us can live in great beauty anywhere, as long as we're alive to our environment. She lives near the Bowery in New York City. Even from there, she can "see the world." Sitting in her dining room and looking out at the huge building that stands across the street, she can find varying patterns in the way the sun and the moon reflect on its windows. She can look at a chair and say, "The chair isn't so hot, but look at its shadow."

2. FINDING WHAT WE LOOK FOR

Jim Smith went to church on Sunday morning. He heard the organist miss a note during the prelude, and he winced. He saw a teenager talking when everybody was supposed to be bowed in silent prayer. He felt like the usher was watching to see what he put in the offering plate and it made him boil. He caught the preacher making a slip of the tongue five times in the sermon by actual count. As he slipped out through the side door during the closing hymn, he muttered to himself, "Never again, what a bunch of clods and hypocrites!"

Ron Jones went to church one Sunday morning. He heard the organist play an arrangement of "A Mighty Fortress" and he thrilled at the majesty of it. He heard a young girl take a moment in the service to speak her simple moving message of the difference her faith makes in her life. He was glad to see that this church was sharing in a special offering for the hungry children of Nigeria. He especially appreciated the sermon that Sunday—it answered a question that had bothered him for a long time. He thought as he walked out the doors of the church, "How can a man come here and not feel the presence of God?"

Both men went to the same church, on the same Sunday morning. Each found what he was looking for. What do we look for on Sunday morning?

3. NAIVE OR WHAT?

There was a women's tournament at the golf club, and the turnout was so great the women had to use the men's locker room as well as their own.

Naturally, on that day the room was off-limits to men. But eight-year-old Tommy didn't realize that. When he walked nonchalantly into the men's locker room, he was greeted with shrieks as the women grabbed for cover. Tommy asked, "What's the matter, haven't you ever seen a little boy before?"

4. WAS LINCOLN HANDSOME?

A mother came to President Lincoln seeking the pardon of her son, under sentence of death. The result of her pleading was that Lincoln issued a pardon. After leaving him, as she passed through a corridor, she exclaimed to Thaddeus Steven, who accompanied her, "I knew it was a lie!" Stevens asked, "What do you refer to?" She replied with vehemence, "Why, they told me he was an ugly-looking man, but he is the handsomest man I ever saw in my life."

5. MY TIME IS YOUR TIME

A man asked God how long a million years was to Him. God replied, "It's just like a single second of your time, my child." So the man asked, "And what about a million dollars?" The Lord replied, "To me, it's just like a single penny." So the man gathered himself up and said, "Well, Lord, could I have one of your pennies?" And God said, "Certainly, my child, just a second."

6. YOU AND YOUR NEIGHBOR

Have you ever noticed: When the other fellow acts that way, he is ugly; when you do, it's nerves. When others are set in their ways, they're obstinate; when you are, it is firmness. When your neighbor doesn't like your friend, he's prejudiced; when you don't like his, you are a good judge of human nature. When he tries to treat someone especially well, he's toadying; when you try it, you are being thoughtful.

When he takes time to do things well, he's a slowpoke or lazy; when you do, you are deliberate and careful. When he spends a lot, he is a spendthrift; when you do, you're generous. When someone picks flaws in things, he's cranky and critical; when you do, you are creative. When he is mild-mannered, you call him weak; when you are, it is graciousness. When someone dresses especially well, that person is extravagant; when you do, it is tastefulness. When he says what he thinks, he's spiteful; when you do, you are being frank. When he takes great risks in business, he's foolhardy; when you do, you are a wise financier.

7. NOVA SCOTIA PERSPECTIVE

Former Undersecretary of the Interior John C. Whitaker was reminded of how easy it is to get an out-of-perspective feeling about one's importance in government whenever he thinks of an eighty-five-year-old woman who has lived her life in one spot in Nova Scotia. The population there swells to nine in summer and stays steady at two during the winter.

Whitaker, who has been fishing there every year since he was twelve, flew in one day. Miss Mildred welcomed him into her kitchen and said, "Johnny, I hate to admit I don't know, but where is Washington?" When Whitaker realized that she wasn't kidding, he explained: "That's where the president is. That's like where you have the prime minister in Ottawa."

Then she asked how many people lived there, and Whitaker said there were about 2 million. She said, "Think of that, 2 million people living so far away from everything."

8. CHANGING TASTE
Novelist and editor William Dean Howells was talking with an author who was known for having a very high regard for himself. The author said, "You know, my books are selling very well. I'm getting rich, but I think my work is falling off. I don't think my recent writing is as good as my earlier works." Howells retorted, "Nonsense, you write as well as you ever did. Your taste is improving, that's all."

9. BOTH TOP AND BOTTOM
Corrie ten Boom often showed a piece of embroidery to her audiences. She would hold up the piece of cloth, first showing the beauty of the embroidered side, with all the threads forming a beautiful picture, which she described as the plan God has for our lives. Then she would flip it over to show the tangled, confused underside, illustrating how we view our lives from a human standpoint.

10. GRAND CANYON PERSPECTIVE
Three people were visiting and viewing the Grand Canyon—an artist, a pastor, and a cowboy. As they stood on the edge of that massive abyss, each one responded with a cry of exclamation. The artist said, "Ah, what a beautiful scene to paint!" The minister cried, "What a wonderful example of the handiwork of God!" The cowboy mused, "What a terrible place to lose a cow!"

11. THE BEAM IN THE EYE
Father Murphy stopped in the local barber shop for a shave and haircut to find the barber hung over from a heavy weekend. He endured the shaking hand but when the shave was over decided a brief sermon was in order. "Look at this cut on my throat!" he exclaimed. "And this one by the ear, and

this other one on my upper lip, it might have cost me my nose. And all due to whiskey!" The barber replied, "You're right, Father, drinking does make the skin very tender."

12. DIFFERING STANDARDS

Everyone looks at life with their own perspective, bringing their own standards, their own ways of assessing a situation. A. H. Livingstone is a man who sells etchings to hotel managers. He is always trying to get his potential customer to raise his sights in the matter of standards of art. His product costs more, but he feels it is one that makes the room look better than the usual sporting prints or flower pictures that are more typically found in hotel rooms. When he tried to sell his product to a Los Angeles hotel the manager was unimpressed, and reminded him that the typical pictures he bought were only half as much as his prints. Finally Livingstone said, "Don't you care about the quality of art you give your guests? Don't you have any standards?" The manager replied, "Standards, sure, I have one standard, and that's all I need. Any picture that goes into one of my bedrooms has to be too large to fit into a suitcase."

13. SUNDAY JOB

If you can smile when everything is going wrong, the chances are you're a plumber working on a Sunday.

14. YOU HAVE TO START FROM SOMEWHERE

One morning an elementary school teacher asked her class how many points a compass has. She was surprised when one little boy stuck up his hand and said, "Five." She asked him, "Five? What are they?" He counted them off: "North, south, east, west, and where I am." JAMES HARNISH, *Jesus Makes the Difference*

15. OUR OWN AGENDA

In the recreation room of a California retirement home, four ladies were playing bridge and chatting. An elderly gentleman wandered into the room. They recognized him as a newcomer, and they all perked up. One of the ladies said, "Hello, there. You're new here, aren't you?" He smiled and replied that he was, indeed, new. He had just moved in that morning. Another lady said, "Where did you live before you moved in?" He replied, "I was just released from San Quentin, where I spent the last twenty years." A third lady said, "Oh, really? What were you in for?" He replied, "I murdered my wife." The fourth lady sat up, smiled brightly, and said, "Oh, then you're single?"

412

16. NOT MUCH VALUE ANYMORE

A book collector ran into an unbookish acquaintance who soon revealed that old books didn't mean anything to him. In fact, he observed he had just thrown away a big old Bible which had been packed away in the attic of his ancestral home for generations. He was describing it and said, "Somebody named Guten-some-thing had printed it." The bibliophile gasped. "Not Gutenberg! You idiot! You've just thrown away one of the first books ever printed. A copy sold recently at an auction for over a million dollars!" But the other man was unmoved. He responded, "No, not my copy. It wouldn't have brought a dime. Some fellow named Martin Luther had scribbled notes all through it!"

17. OVERSIZED TARGET

Saul's soldiers thought Goliath was too big to kill. David thought he was too big to miss!

18. DIFFERENT MENTALITIES

The Stanford Research Institute was making a study of how different people think, how they perceive things differently. They devised a short but succinct test to use in their interviews and proceeded to call in several people from different walks of life.

The first to come in was an engineer. The researchers asked him: "Tell us, what does two plus two make?" The engineer didn't hesitate a moment— but simply said, "Well, if you mean in absolute terms—two and two make four." The researchers made their notes, thanked the engineer and dismissed him.

Next, they called in an architect. They asked him the same question and he said, "Well, there are several possibilities: two and two make four, but so do three and one—or two and one-half and one and one-half—they also make four. So, it is all a matter of choosing the right option." The researchers thanked him and made their notes.

The last of the three to come in was an attorney. They said to him, "What does two and two make?" The attorney looked around furtively, asked if he could close the door for privacy, and then came over close, leaned toward them and said, "Well, tell me, what would you like it to be?"

19. CAN YOU TOP THIS?

The story is told about an old minister who survived the great Johnstown flood. He loved to tell the story over and over in great detail. Everywhere he went he would spend all his time talking about this great historic event in his life. One day he died and went to heaven and there in a meeting all the saints had gathered together to share their life experiences. The old minister got all excited and ran to Peter (who, naturally, was in charge) and asked if he might tell the exciting story of his survival from the Johnstown flood. Peter hesitated for a moment and then said, "Yes, you may share, but just remember that Noah will be in the audience tonight."

20. PERSONAL CONTEXT
The easiest things to decide are what you'd do if you were in someone else's shoes.

21. A FLEXIBLE BIAS
A woman who was called to jury duty told the presiding judge that she was not qualified to serve because she did not believe in capital punishment. The judge said, "You don't understand, madam. This is a civil case involving a man who spent five thousand dollars of his wife's money on gambling and other women." To which the woman replied eagerly, "I'll be happy to serve, your honor, and I've changed my mind about capital punishment."

22. JUMPING TO CONCLUSIONS
Two men came to Miami from the Arctic regions, where they had lived all their life. On the bus to the hotel they passed one of the bays where some people were water-skiing. Having only seen their kayaks and other hand-propelled boats throughout their lifetime, one man asked the other, "What makes that boat go so fast?" The other man watched for a few seconds, then replied, "Man on string push it."

23. NOT EVERYONE WAS FESTIVE
After the Sunday school teacher told the story of the Prodigal Son to the class, she asked, "Was anyone sorry when the Prodigal Son returned?" One boy answered, "The fatted calf."

24. HALF THE TRUTH
The difference between ourselves and others is that we don't tell half of what we know, while they don't know half of what they tell.

25. HOME IMPROVEMENT STRATEGY
A good architect can improve the looks of an old house merely by discussing the cost of a new one.

26. THRUST OUT INTO THE SKY
There is an awkward moment at the top of a ferris wheel when, having come up the inside curvature, where we are facing into a firm structure of confident girders, suddenly that structure disappears, and we are thrust out

into the sky for the outward curve down. Such perhaps is the present
moment. JULIAN JAYNES

27. PERVASIVE ODOR
If a man has limburger cheese on his upper lip, he thinks the whole world
smells.

28. DISINTERESTED PARTY
There are two sides to every question—as long as it doesn't concern us
personally.

29. BASIC VISION
If I think of you as a friend and collaborator, my emotions on meeting you
will be warm and positive. If I see you as an enemy and competitor, my
emotions will be just the opposite. You will remember the little verse:
Two men looked out from prison bars.
One saw mud, one saw stars.

In the pursuit of the fullness of human life, everything depends on this
frame of reference, this habitual outlook, this basic vision that I have of
myself, others, life, the world, and God. What we see is what we get.

Consequently, if you or I are to change, to grow into persons who are more
fully human and more fully alive, we shall certainly have to become aware of
our vision and patiently work at redressing its imbalances and eliminating its
distortions. All real and permanent growth must begin here. A shy person
can be coaxed into assuming an air of confidence, but it will only be a
mask—one mask replacing another. There can be no real change, no real
growth in any of us until and unless our basic perception of reality, or vision,
is changed. JOHN POWELL

30. LAZY PERSPECTIVE
The city man bought a farm and was visited by his new neighbor. He asked
him, "Can you tell me where the property line runs between our farms?" The
farmer looked him over and asked, "Are you talking owning or mowing?"

31. SELF-FULFILLING
We lost because we told ourselves we lost. LEO TOLSTOY, *War and Peace*

ONE HUNDRED TWELVE

Prayer

1. PRAYER OR SWEAR
There is more religion in some men's curses than in some men's prayers, especially if the former is sincere and the latter perfunctory.
J. W. MacGorman

2. DOMINIE AT THE BEDSIDE
Leslie Weatherhead tells the story of an old Scot who was quite ill, and the family called for their dominie, or minister. As he entered the sick room and sat down, he noticed another chair on the opposite side of the bed, a chair which had also been drawn close. The pastor said, "Well, Donald, I see I'm not your first visitor for the day."

The old man looked up, was puzzled for a moment, then recognized from the nod of the head that the pastor had noticed the empty chair. "Well, Pastor, I'll tell you about that chair. Many years ago I found it quite difficult to pray, so one day I shared this problem with my pastor. He told me not to worry about kneeling or about placing myself in some pious posture. Instead, he said, 'Just sit down, put a chair opposite you, and imagine Jesus sitting in it, then talk with Him as you would a friend.'" The aged Scot then added, "I've been doing that ever since."

A short time later the daughter of the Scot called the pastor. When he answered, she informed him that her father had died very suddenly and she was quite shaken for she had no idea death was so near. Then she continued, "I had just gone to lie down for an hour or two, for he seemed to be sleeping so comfortably. When I went back he was dead." Then she added thoughtfully, "Except now his hand was on the empty chair at the side of the bed. Isn't that strange?"

The minister said, "No, it's not so strange. I understand."

3. A SAINT'S PRAYER
Give me, O Lord, a steadfast heart, which no unworthy affection may drag downwards; give me an unconquered heart, which no tribulation can wear out; give me an upright heart, which no unworthy purpose may tempt aside.
Thomas Aquinas

4. PRAYER IS VITAL

It seems to me that it is of more than just passing interest that virtually every month the lectionary readings include some important passages on prayer. You'd almost get the idea that prayer was vital to the Christian's life.

I was never deeply interested in any object, I never prayed sincerely and earnestly for anything, but it came at some time. No matter how distant the day, somehow, in some shape, probably the last I should have advised, it came. ADONIRAM JUDSON.

I have lived to thank God that all my prayers have not been answered. JEAN INGELOW

5. GOD'S TIME

God answers prayer; sometimes, when hearts are weak,
He gives the very gifts believers seek.
But often faith must learn a deeper rest,
And trust God's silence, when He does not speak;
For he whose name is Love will send the best.
Stars may burn out nor mountain walls endure,
But God is true; His promises are sure
To those who speak. M. G. PLANTZ

6. THE SOUL'S SINCERE DESIRE

Prayer is the soul's sincere desire,
Uttered or unexpressed—
The motion of a hidden fire,
That trembles in the breast.
Prayer is the burden of a sigh,
The falling of a tear,
The upward glancing of an eye,
When none but God is near. JAMES MONTGOMERY

7. PRIORITIES

I'd rather be able to pray than be a great preacher; Jesus Christ never taught his disciples how to preach, but only how to pray. D. L. MOODY

8. PRAYER REMINDER

George Reindrop, in his book *No Common Task,* tells how a nurse once taught a man to pray and in doing so changed his whole life from being a dull, disgruntled, and dispirited person into a man of joy. Much of the nurse's work was done with her hands, and she used her hands as a scheme of prayer. Each finger stood for someone. Her thumb was the nearest to her, and it reminded her to pray for those who were closest to her. The second finger was used for pointing and it stood for all her teachers in school and in the hospital. The third finger was the tallest and it stood for the leaders in every sphere of life. The fourth finger was the weakest, as every pianist knows, and it stood for those who were in trouble and pain. The little finger was the smallest and the least important and to the nurse it stood for herself.

9. A METHOD OF PRAYING

Be simple and direct in your secret prayer. The grace of simplicity is not to be despised in public prayer; but when we call on God in secret, any formality or elaborateness in our petitions is an offense.

Pray audibly. You need not lift your voice to be heard in the street, but it is vastly better to pray not merely in your thoughts but also with words. The utterance of our wants helps to define them.

Be honest in your secret prayer. Do not express any want that you do not feel. Do not confess any fault that you do not mean to forsake. Do not keep anything back. Remember that it is He that searcheth the heart to whom you are speaking.

Pray earnestly. The words need not be loud, but the desire should be intense. "The fervent, energetic prayer of a righteous man availeth much." "The kingdom of heaven suffereth violence, and the violent take it by force." No listless, drowsy petitioning will serve.

Do not mock God in your prayers. Do not beg him to come to you. You know that he is never far from any soul that seeks him. That prayer is answered before you utter it. Do not ask God to do for you that which he has expressly bidden you to do.

Pray always with special reference to the needs of the day and the hour— the warfare to be waged, the temptations to be resisted, the work to be done, the sorrow to be borne; put your life into your prayer; and let it be the most real and the most immediate business of your life. WALTER RAUSCHENBUSCH

10. HIGHER GROUND

Prayer is the contemplation of the facts of life from the highest point of view. RALPH WALDO EMERSON

11. POWERFUL POSITIONS FOR PRAYER

Three ministers were talking about prayer in general and the appropriate and effective positions for prayer. As they were talking, a telephone repairman was working on the phone system in the background. One minister shared that he felt the key was in the hands. He always held his hands together and pointed them upward as a form of symbolic worship. The second suggested that real prayer was conducted on your knees. The third suggested that they both had it wrong—the only position worth its salt was to pray while stretched out flat on your face.

By this time the phone man couldn't stay out of the conversation any longer. He interjected: "I found that the most powerful prayer I ever made was while I was dangling upside down by my heels from a power pole, suspended forty feet above the ground."

12. ANSWERED PRAYER—WITH CATTLE

Shortly after Dallas Theological Seminary was founded in 1924, it almost came to the point of bankruptcy. All the creditors were going to foreclose at noon on a particular day. That morning they met in the president's office with Dr. Chafer for prayer that God would provide. In that prayer meeting was a man by the name of Harry Ironside. When it was his turn to pray, he prayed in his characteristic manner: "Lord, we know that the cattle on a thousand hills are Thine. Please sell some of them and send us the money."

While they were praying, a tall Texan with boots on and an open collar stepped up to the business office and said, "I just sold two carloads of cattle in Ft. Worth. I've been trying to make a business deal but it fell through, and I feel compelled to give the money to the seminary. I don't know if you need it or not, but here's the check!"

A little secretary took the check and, knowing how critical things were financially, went to the door of the prayer meeting and timidly tapped. When she finally got a response, Dr. Chafer took the check out of her hand. It was exactly the amount of the debt! When he looked at the name, he recognized the cattleman in Ft. Worth, and turning to Dr. Ironside said, "Harry, God sold the cattle!"

13. PRAYER IN CONGRESS

When Edward Everett Hale was chaplain of the U.S. Senate, someone asked him, "Do you pray for the senators, Dr. Hale?" He replied, "No, I look at the senators and pray for the country."

14. ASSUME THE SAFEST POSITION

George Adam Smith tells us that he was once climbing the Weisshorn above the Zermatt Valley in Switzerland with two guides on a stormy day. They had made the ascent on the sheltered side. Reaching the top, and exhilarated by the thought of the view before him, Smith sprang to the top of a peak—and was almost blown away by the gale. The guide caught hold of him and pulled him down saying, "On your knees, sir! You are safe here only on your knees."
J. W. ROBERTS

15. PREPARATION FOR PRAYER

I have a friend who took his little six-year-old boy fishing with him one day. They put out the line and then went up to the cabin. After an hour, they went back down to the river to see if they had caught anything.

Sure enough, there were several fish on the line. The boy said, "I knew there would be, Daddy."

The father asked, "How did you know?"

He replied, "Because I prayed about it."

So they baited the hooks again and put out the line and went back to the cabin for supper.

Afterward, they went back to the river; again, there were fish on the line. The boy said, "I knew it."

The father said, "How?"

"I prayed again."

So they put the line back into the river and went to the cabin. Before bedtime, they went down again. This time there were no fish.

The child said, "I knew there wouldn't be," and the father asked, "How did you know?"

The boy said, "Because I didn't pray this time."

The father asked, "And why didn't you pray?"

And the boy said, "Because I remembered that we forgot to bait the hooks." ROBERT GOODRICH, *What's It All About*

16. EVEN THE ANIMALS

Once upon a time there was a man who went hunting. He was hunting bears. As he trudged through the forest looking for bears, he came upon a large and steep hill. He climbed the hill and, just as he was pulling himself up over the last outcropping of rocks, a huge bear met him nose to nose. The bear roared fiercely. The man was so scared that he lost his balance and fell down the hill with the bear not far behind. On the trip down the hill the man lost his gun. When he finally stopped tumbling, he found that he had a broken leg. Escape was impossible and so the man, who had never been particularly religious (in fact he was hunting on Sunday morning), prayed: "God if you will make this bear a Christian I will be happy with whatever lot you give me for the rest of my life." The bear was no more than three feet away from the man when it stopped dead in its tracks, looked up to the heavens quizzically, and then fell to its knees and prayed in a loud voice: "Lord bless this food of which I am about to partake. Amen."

420

17. PRAYER TOO AVAILABLE?

Our failure to think of prayer as a privilege may be partly due to the fact that we can pray any time. The door to prayer is open so continuously that we fail to avail ourselves of an opportunity which is always there.

HARRY EMERSON FOSDICK, *The Meaning of Prayer*

18. UNCEASING PRAYER

You've heard someone say, "I don't know what to pray about." Or, people will get a prayer list and pray for missionaries because they don't know what else to do. A lady said to me not too long ago, "I can't pray for more than two minutes at a time. What can I do?" When people say that to me, I reply, "What have you been thinking or worrying about this last week? Pray about that." Convert your thoughts into prayer. Prayer is not only thinking about new things, but prayer is thinking in dialogue. It is a move from self-centered monologue to a conversation with God.

19. YOUR BEST PRAYER

Listen, my friend! Your helplessness is your best prayer. It calls from your heart to the heart of God with greater effect than all your uttered pleas. He hears it from the very moment that you are seized with helplessness, and He becomes actively engaged at once in hearing and answering the prayer of your helplessness. He hears today as He heard the helpless and wordless prayer of the man sick with the palsy. O. HALLESBY, *Prayer*

20. THE PROPER FOCUS OF PRAYER

There is a shrine in the French Pyrenees where people come to pray for healing. A war veteran who had lost a leg appeared at the shrine sometime after World War II. As he hobbled his way along the street to the shrine someone said, "Look at that silly man! Does he think God is going to give him back his leg?" The young man overheard the remark and turned toward the speakers and said: "Of course I do not expect God to give me back my leg. I am going to pray to God to help me live without it!"

21. THE POSITION FOR TROUBLES

If all your troubles are deep-seated and longstanding, try kneeling.

22. GLADSTONE AND PRAYER

Prayer is one of those topics that gathers so many marvelous stories to illustrate its many facets. In particular I like the story that William Gladstone told that illustrates prayer coupled with a sort of persistent (if also perverse) action. It seems Gladstone knew of a little girl in his neighborhood who believed strongly in the efficacy of prayer. Her current concern was a trap that her brother had made to catch birds. Being a bird lover herself, she prayed that God would frustrate her brother's designs and he would be unsuccessful in his plan. She had shared this resolution with Gladstone and told him how hard she was praying.

One day, upon encountering her, Gladstone observed a particular radiance to her countenance. He said to her, "Julia, you look so pleased. Are you still confident your prayers will be answered?" Julia smiled a knowing smile and retorted, "I know for sure that my prayers will be answered. Yesterday I kicked my brother's trap to pieces."

23. ESSENCE OF PRAYER
It is no use to ask God with factitious earnestness for A when our whole mind is in reality filled with B. We must lay before him what is in us, not what ought to be in us. C. S. LEWIS, *Letters to Malcolm, Chiefly on Prayer*

24. HANGING ON TO GOD
Prayer is not overcoming God's reluctance; it is laying hold of his highest willingness. ARCHBISHOP TRENCH

25. TO PRAY IS HUMAN
More things are wrought by prayer
Than this world dreams of. Wherefore, let thy voice
Rise like a fountain for me night and day.
For what are men better than sheep or goats
That nourish a blind life within the brain,
If, knowing God, they lift not hands of prayer
Both for themselves and those who call them friends? ALFRED LORD TENNYSON

26. THE STRUGGLE OF PRAYER
One day a boy was watching a holy man praying on the banks of a river in India. When the holy man completed his prayer the boy went over and asked him, "Will you teach me to pray?" The holy man studied the boy's face carefully. Then he gripped the boy's head in his hands and plunged it forcefully into the water! The boy struggled frantically, trying to free himself in order to breathe. Finally, the holy man released his hold. When the boy was able to get his breath, he gasped, "What did you do that for?" The holy man said: "I just gave you your first lesson." "What do you mean?" asked the astonished boy. "Well," said the holy man, "when you long to pray as much as you longed to breathe when your head was underwater—only then will I be able to teach you to pray." MARK LINK, *Breakaway*

27. TO PRAY IS HUMAN

A farmer was paid a visit by one of his city relatives. Before dinner the farmer bowed his head and said grace. His sophisticated relative jeered: "This is old-fashioned; nobody with an education prays at the table anymore."

The farmer admitted that the practice was old and even allowed that there were some on his farm who did not pray before their meals. Justified, the relative remarked: "So enlightenment is finally reaching the farm. Who are these wise ones?"

The farmer replied: "My pigs."

28. TURNING TO HEAVEN

A prayer, in its simplest definition, is merely a wish turned heavenward.
PHILLIPS BROOKS

29. SINCERE PRAYER

O God, if in the day of battle I forget Thee, do not Thou forget me.
WILLIAM KING

30. WHAT ARE WE LOOKING FOR?

There was a five-year-old attending a formal wedding some years ago. The girl was sitting with her grandmother. She had been in Sunday school but had never attended a formal church service. During the wedding, the minister said: "Let us pray." Each person bowed his head in prayer. The little girl looked around and saw all the heads bowed and eyes turned toward the floor and she cried: "Grandmother, what are they all looking for?"

What are we all looking for when we pray?

31. OUR DUTY BEYOND PRAYER

We cannot merely pray to You, O God, to end war;
For we know that You have made the world in a way
That man must find his own path to peace
Within himself and with his neighbor.
We cannot merely pray to You, O God, to end starvation;
For you have given us the resources
With which to feed the entire world
If we would only use them wisely.
We cannot merely pray to You, O God,
To root out prejudice,
For You have already given us eyes
With which to see the good in all men
If we would only use them rightly.

We cannot merely pray to You, O God, to end despair,
For You have already given us the power
To clear away slums and to give hope
If we would only use our power justly.
We cannot merely pray to You, O God, to end disease,
For you have already given us great minds with which
To search out cures and healing,
If we would only use them constructively.
Therefore we pray to You instead, O God,
For strength, determination, and willpower,
To do, instead of just to pray,
To become, instead of merely to wish.

32. USES AND MISUSES

The great baseball catcher Yogi Berra was involved in a ball game in which the score was tied, with two outs in the bottom of the ninth inning. The batter from the opposing team stepped up to the batting box and made the sign of the cross on home plate with his bat. Berra was a Catholic, too, but he wiped off the plate with his glove and said to the pious batter, "Why don't we let God just watch this game?" That is good theology when applied to the outcome of a baseball game. It's terrible when applied to the way we live our lives and carry out the work of God. Worse than that, it is fatal. God is merely in attendance at the game, our prayers are merely ceremonial functions: tips of the hats, verbal recognition over the loudspeaker between innings, or requests to throw out the game ball. Prayer is always getting nudged aside, neglected or perfunctorily performed. Many of us feel we just have too much to do to have time to pray.

33. DIVINE INTERCESSION

An elderly gentleman passed his granddaughter's room one night and overheard her repeating the alphabet in an oddly reverent way. He asked her, "What on earth are you up to?" She explained, "I'm saying my prayers, but I can't think of exactly the right words tonight, so I'm just saying all the letters. God will put them together for me, because he knows what I'm thinking."

34. MIGHTY PRAYER

One might estimate the weight of the world, tell the size of the celestial city, count the stars of heaven, measure the speed of lightning, and tell the time of the rising and the setting of the sun—but you cannot estimate prayer-power.

Prayer is as vast as God because He is behind it. Prayer is as mighty as God because He has committed Himself to answer it. LEONARD RAVENHILL

35. THE GREAT KEY
Prayer is the key that unlocks all the storehouses of God's infinite grace and power. All that God is, and all that God has, is at the disposal of prayer. R. A. TORREY

36. TOO MUCH TO DO
We are too busy to pray, and so we are too busy to have power. We have a great deal of activity but we accomplish little; many services but few conversions; much machinery but few results. R. A. TORREY

37. LUTHER AND MYCONIUS
It was a sense of being in the center of God's will that gave Luther his great boldness in prayer. In 1540 Luther's great friend and assistant, Frederick Myconius, became sick and was expected to die within a short time. On his bed he wrote a loving farewell note to Luther with a trembling hand. Luther received the letter and instantly sent back a reply: "I command thee in the name of God to live because I still have need of thee in the work of reforming the church. . . . The Lord will never let me hear that thou art dead, but will permit thee to survive me. For this I am praying, this is my will, and may my will be done, because I seek only to glorify the name of God." The words are almost shocking to us, as we live in a more sensitive and cautious day, but they were certainly from God. For although Myconius had already lost the ability to speak when Luther's letter came, in a short time he revived. He recovered completely, and he lived six more years to survive Luther himself by two months. JAMES MONTGOMERY BOICE

38. THE WHITE BIRDS
There was once a man who had a waking dream. He dreamed he was in a spacious church. He had wandered in to pray, and after his prayers were finished, he knelt on, his eyes open, gazing around at the beauty of the ancient building, and resting in the silence. Here and there in the great building were quiet kneeling figures across the dim darkness of the nave and aisles. Shafts of sunlight streamed into the church from upper windows. In the distance a side door was open, letting in scents of summer air, fragrant with the smell of hay and flowers, and the sight of trees waving in the breeze, and beyond, a line of blue hills, dim and distant as an enchanted land.

Presently the man withdrew his eyes from the pleasant outdoor world and looked again at the church. Suddenly, close to the spot where he was kneeling, there was a gentle whir of wings and he saw a little white bird fluttering about in the dim nave; it flew uncertainly hither and thither, and once or twice he thought it would fall to the ground. But gradually it gathered strength, rose toward the roof, and finally, with a purposeful sweep of its wings, sped upward, and out through one of the open windows into the sunshine.

The stranger looked down again at the kneeling men and women, scattered singly throughout the building; and now he saw, what he had not noticed before, that by the side of each worshiper there hovered, close to the stone floor, a little white bird. Just then he saw another bird rise from the floor and try to reach the roof. But it, too, was in difficulties; it flew round and round in circles, occasionally beating its wings in a futile way against the great lower windows, rich with stained glass. Finally it sank down exhausted, and lay still. A little later another bird rose from the ground, with a swift and easy flight; for a moment it seemed that it would reach the open window and the open air beyond; but suddenly, it whirled round, fell helplessly over and over, and came to the ground with a thud, as if it had been shot. The man rose from his knees and went over to see what had happened; the little bird was dead.

He went back to his place and sat down on one of the chairs; then he noticed an ugly bird, its white feathers dirty and bedraggled, rise from the ground. At first this bird labored heavily, but it soon gathered speed, for it was strong, and it soared up and out into the sunlit world beyond the walls of the great church. More and more the man wondered what all this might mean. He looked again at the persons at prayer near him, and he noticed one, kneeling very reverently, by whose side lay a very beautiful bird, snowy white and perfectly formed. But when he looked at it more closely he saw that its eyes were glazed, its wings stiff; it was a lifeless shell. "What a pity!" he murmured under his breath. At that moment, a gentle whir of wings a few feet away attracted his attention; another bird was rising from the ground, steadily and quietly, at first with some appearance of effort, but more and more easily and lightly as it gathered strength; this bird flew straight up, past the carved angels which seemed to be crying "Hallelujah!" to one another across the dim spaces of the church, and out through the open window into the blue sky, where it was soon lost to sight.

Pondering on what he had seen, the man looked round again, and this time he saw standing close to him, an angel, tall and strong, with a face of great kindness, wisdom and compassion. It all seemed perfectly natural (as things do in dreams), and the man whispered to him: "Can you explain to me about these white birds?"

"Yes," said the angel, in a low voice, as he seated himself beside him, "for

I am the guardian of this place of prayer. These white birds are the outward sign of the prayers of the people who come here to pray. The first bird, which found it difficult to rise, but then succeeded, is the prayer of a woman who has come here straight from a very busy life; she has very little time to herself; in fact she usually comes here in the midst of her shopping. She has a great many duties and claims, and her mind was full of distractions when she first knelt down and tried to pray. But she persevered, for her heart is right with God, and He helped her; her prayer was real and her will good, so her prayer reached God."

"And what about the bird that flew around in circles?" asked the man.

The angel smiled slightly, with a tinge of faint amusement. "That," he said slowly, "is the prayer of a man who thinks of no one but himself; even in his prayers he only asks for 'things'—success in his business and things like that; he tries to use God for his own ends . . . people think he is a very religious man . . . but his prayer does not reach God at all."

"But why did that other bird fall to the ground as if it had been shot?"

The angel looked sad as he replied: "That man began his prayer well enough; but suddenly he remembered a grudge against someone he knew; he forgot his prayer and brooded in bitter resentment, and his bitterness killed his prayer. . . . And the ugly bird," he went on after a moment's silence, "is the prayer of a man who hasn't much idea of reverence; his prayer is bold, almost presumptuous, some people might call it; but God knows his heart, and He sees that his faith is real; he does really believe God, so his prayer reaches Him."

"And the beautiful lifeless bird that never stirred from the ground at all?" said the man.

"That," said the angel, "is a beautifully composed prayer; the language is perfect, the thought is doctrinally correct; the man offered it with the greatest solemnity and outward reverence. But he never meant a word of it; even as he said the words his thoughts were on his own affairs, so his prayer could not reach God."

"And what about the last bird that flew upstairs so easily?"

The angel smiled. "I think you know," he said gently. "That is the prayer of a woman whose whole heart and will is set upon God. . . . Her prayer went straight to God." OLIVE WYON, *The School of Prayer*

39. LIKE A FORT

Deep in the Arabian desert is a small fortress. It stands silently on the vast expanse of the ageless desert. Thomas Edward Lawrence, known as "Lawrence of Arabia," often used it. Though unpretentious, it was most sufficient. Its primary commendation was its security. When under attack, often by superior forces, Lawrence could retreat there. Then the resources of the fortress became his. The food and water stored there were life supporting. The strength of the fortification became the strength of its occupants. When Lawrence defended it, it defended him. As one relying on the garrison, he was the object of its protection. Its strength was his. Old desert dwellers living around there have told me that Sir Lawrence felt confident and secure within its walls. He had on occasion to depend on the fort; it provided his need. He learned to trust it; his experience proved its worth. Like that fort, "The Lord is good, a strong hold in the day of trouble; and he knoweth them that trust in him." Through prayer we enter God's fortress.

40. THE LORD'S WILL

An overweight business associate of mine decided it was time to shed some excess pounds. He took his new diet seriously, even changing his driving route to avoid his favorite bakery. One morning, however, he arrived at work carrying a gigantic coffee cake. We all scolded him, but his smile remained cherubic. "This is a very special coffee cake," he explained. "I accidentally drove by the bakery this morning and there in the window were a host of goodies. I felt this was no accident, so I prayed, 'Lord, if you want me to have one of these delicious coffee cakes, let me have a parking place directly in front of the bakery.' And sure enough," he continued, "the eighth time around the block, there it was!"

41. CHILDREN'S CANDID RESPONSES

Our kindergarten class went to the fire station for a tour and some instruction in fire safety. The fireman was explaining what to do in case of a fire. He said, "First, go to the door and feel the door to see if it's hot." Then he said, "Fall to your knees. Does anyone know why you ought to fall to your knees?" One of the little tykes said, "Sure, to start praying to ask God to get us out of this mess!"

42. THE POWER THAT TAKES US UP

One day in Lucerne, Switzerland, a man went up to the summit of Mount Pilatus in a cable car operated by hydraulic power. As he ascended, he marveled at the miracles of modern engineering. More than halfway up, his attention was caught by a waterfall. The water poured down the mountainside. If the railway symbolized modern science, then that waterfall was the symbol of primitive nature. *What a contrast!* he thought. Then it suddenly occurred to him that the waterfall was not a contrast but a complement. It was the source of that hydraulic power. It was the force of that water that was driving him up.

So it is with prayer. The power that takes us up to God is the same power that comes from God. KENNETH D. HARVEY

43. GETTING WHAT YOU WANT

"Be careful," runs the old saying, "or you may get what you want."

One who would agree is a man who lived in a squalid tenement on a side street in East Boston. He was a tailor and worked long hours each day to eke out a meager existence. He allowed himself but one luxury: a ticket each year to the Irish Sweepstakes. And each year he would pray fervently that this would be the winning ticket that would bring him his fortune.

For fourteen years his life continued in the same impoverished vein, until one day there came a loud knocking on his door. Two well-dressed gentlemen entered his shop and informed him that he had just won the sweepstakes. The grand prize was $1,000,000!

The little tailor could hardly believe his ears. He was rich! No longer would he have to slave away making pant cuffs, hemming dresses. Now he could really live!

He locked his shop and threw the key into the Charles River. He bought himself a wardrobe fit for a king, a new Rolls Royce, a suite of rooms at the Ritz, and soon was supporting a string of attractive women.

Night after night he partied until dawn, spending his money as if each day was his last. Of course the inevitable happened. One day the money was gone. Furthermore, he had nearly wrecked his health.

Disillusioned, ridden with fever and exhausted, he returned to his little shop and set up business once more. And from force of habit, once again each year set aside from his meager savings the price of a sweepstakes ticket.

Two years later there came a second knock at his door. The same two gentlemen stood there once again. "This is the most incredible thing in the history of the sweepstakes," exclaimed one. "You have won again!"

The little tailor staggered to his feet with a groan that could be heard for miles. "Oh, no," he protested, "do you mean I have to go through all that again?"

44. LUTHER ON THE PRIORITY OF PRAYER

It is well to let prayer be the first employment in the early morning and the last in the evening. Avoid diligently those false and deceptive thoughts which say, "I will pray an hour hence; I must first perform this or that." For with such thoughts a man quits prayer for business, which lays hold of and

entangles him so that he comes not to pray the whole day long.
MARTIN LUTHER

45. CHILDREN, TEACH US TO PRAY

I was sitting in with my wife one Wednesday evening as she was teaching a five-year-old's Bible class. It came time to have some animal crackers, and she asked one of the little boys, Joey, to lead the prayer for the crackers. Of course it is always so precious to see children pray, and as Joey bowed his head along with the other children he began a most thorough sweet prayer: "Dear God, thank you for my mommy, my daddy, my brother, my sister . . . great-grandfather . . . and thank you for my teacher. And God, thank you for the animal crackers . . ." Joey stopped right there in the middle of the prayer. Everyone began to squirm and get restless. We waited and waited and finally my wife quietly asked Joey if there was anything wrong. Joey slowly raised his head and in a very low whisper asked, "Are we going to have anything to drink?" My wife said no, and immediately he bowed his head and said, "Amen."

What a lesson in prayer this is for those adults who ritualistically roll through leading prayers, not really conscious of the need of those they are praying for.

46. PRAYER AND WORK

Men do not really pray until they are willing to work. Former Governor William E. Russell, of Massachusetts, had his boat overturn about a mile from shore. He was not a good swimmer, and those on shore despaired of his life. When he reached safety, they exclaimed, "Mr. Russell, how on earth did you ever make it?" He replied, "I don't know. All I know is that I prayed to God, and kept my arms and legs in stroke." Prayer changes people to change things. HERSHELL HOBBS

47. NONTAXABLE

I don't know of a single foreign product that enters this country untaxed except the answer to prayer. MARK TWAIN

48. GOD'S VIEW OF PRAYER

God warms his hands at man's heart when he prays. JOHN MASEFIELD

49. WRESTLING WITH GOD

Whoever wrestles with God in prayer puts his whole life at stake.
JACQUES ELLUL, *Prayer and Modern Man*

50. IMPROVEMENT OF THE PRAYING MAN
Whoever riseth from prayer a better man, his prayer is answered.
GEORGE MEREDITH

51. PRAYER OF A DILIGENT SAINT
Teach us, good Lord, to serve Thee as Thou deservest: to give and not to count the cost; to fight and not to heed the wounds; to toil and not to seek for rest; to labor and not to ask for any reward save that of knowing that we do thy will. IGNATIUS OF LOYOLA

PREACHING *(See Ministry)*

ONE HUNDRED THIRTEEN
Prejudice

1. AN UNDERSTANDABLE BIAS
The judge glared down from his bench at the prospective juror. "And just why is it," he asked, "that you don't want to serve on this jury?" The man replied, "Well, judge, I'm biased. One look at that man convinced me that he is guilty." The judge scowled and replied, "That man is not the defendant, he's the district attorney."

2. PASSION AND PREJUDICE IN CHARGE
Passion and prejudice govern the world, but only under the name of reason. JOHN WESLEY

3. UNDERGIRDING
Prejudices are the props of civilization. ANDRE GIDE

4. MATURING IN BIAS
The older the prejudice, the hardier. Some are perennials. PAUL ELDRIDGE

5. THE TENACIOUS NATURE OF PREJUDICE
A Chinese man and a Jewish man were eating lunch together. Suddenly, without warning the Jew gets up, walks over to the Chinese fellow and smashes him in the mouth, sending him sprawling. The Chinese man picks himself up, rubs his jaw and asks, "What in the world did you do that for?"

And the answer comes back: "For Pearl Harbor!" His response is total astonishment—"Pearl Harbor? I didn't have anything to with Pearl Harbor. It was the Japanese that bombed Pearl Harbor!" The Jew responds, "Chinese, Japanese, Taiwanese—they're all the same to me." With that they both sit down again, and before too long the Chinese man gets up, walks over to the Jew and sends him flying with a hard slap to the jaw. The Jew yells out, "What did you do that for?" And the answer comes back: "The Titanic." "The Titanic? Why, I didn't have anything to do with the Titanic!" Whereupon the Chinese man replies, "Goldberg, Feinberg, Iceberg . . . they're all the same to me!"

6. THE LAST WORD

The following is a bit of homely psychological insight by that delightful commentator on life, Momma, by Mel Lazarus.

Momma's youngest son, Francis, drops by her house and says, "Momma, I'm bringing my new girlfriend in to meet you. Now, will you keep an open mind?" Momma replies, "Yes, dear." "Remember, Momma, an open mind!" "Open mind, open mind." She waits, smiling to herself, and in the last frame, she turns to the reader and remarks, "You'd be surprised how much prejudice can be crammed into an open mind."

7. ANTIPREJUDICE

A first grader went on her first day to a newly integrated school at the height of the segregation storm. An anxious mother met her at the door to inquire, "How did everything go, honey?" "Oh, Mother! You know what? A little black girl sat next to me!" In fear and trepidation, the mother expected trauma, but tried to ask calmly: "And what happened?" "We were both so scared that we held hands all day."

8. A WORD FOR PREJUDICE

Without the aid of prejudice and custom, I should not be able to find my way across the room. WILLIAM HAZLITT

Pretense and Hypocrisy
(See also Appearances)

1. THE AMBIGUITY OF SAINTS
There is the story of the man who came down from the North Carolina mountains. He was all dressed up and carrying his Bible. A friend saw him and asked, "Elias, what's happening? Where are you going all dressed up like that?" Elias said, "I've been hearing about New Orleans. I hear that there is a lot of free-runnin' liquor and a lot of gamblin' and a lot of real good naughty shows." The friend looked him over and said, "But Elias, why are you carrying your Bible under your arm?" And Elias replied, "Well, if it's as good as they say it is, I might stay over until Sunday."

2. DOUBLE MESSAGE NOTED
A man sat down to supper with his family and said grace, thanking God for the food, for the hands which prepared it, and for the source of all life. But during the meal he complained about the freshness of the bread, the bitterness of the coffee, and the sharpness of the cheese. His young daughter questioned him, "Dad, do you think God heard the grace today?"

He answered confidently, "Of course."

Then she asked, "And do you think God heard what you said about the coffee, the cheese, and the bread?" Not so confidently, he answered, "Why, yes, I believe so."

The little girl concluded, "Then which do you think God believed, Dad?"

The man was suddenly aware that his mealtime prayer had become a rote, thoughtless habit rather than an attentive and honest conversation with God. By not concentrating on that important conversation, he had left the door open to let hypocrisy sneak in.

3. THE BETTER WAY
Hypocrisy is the homage which vice renders to virtue. LA ROCHEFOUCAULD

4. ONE MUST OBSERVE
A certain Irish priest, newly arrived in New York City, decided to visit the section known as the Bowery, haven of homeless alcoholics and other derelicts. As he walked along one of the Bowery blocks at night he suddenly

felt a gun against his ribs. Then he heard a raspy voice: "All right mister, gimme all your money!" Quickly, he reached for his wallet and, as he did, the holdup man noticed his clerical garb. The thief was overcome with shame. He said, "Forgive me, Father. I didn't know you were a priest." To which the victim replied, "That's all right, Son. Just repent of your sin. Here, have a cigar." The thief replied, "Oh, no, thank you, Father, I don't smoke during Lent."

5. LEVELS OF LOVE

A little girl stayed for dinner at the home of her first-grade friend. The vegetable was buttered broccoli, and the mother asked if she liked it. The child replied very politely, "Oh, yes, I love it." But when the bowl of broccoli was passed she declined to take any. The hostess said, "I thought you said you loved broccoli." The girl replied sweetly, "Oh, yes, ma'am, I do, but not enough to eat it!"

6. SELF-DECEPTION

Before God can deliver us from ourselves we must undeceive ourselves.
AUGUSTINE

7. OUR FEELINGS OF HYPOCRISY

In the "guilt versus grace" discussion it seems that most people have a deep sensitivity about their own guilt, flaws, and inadequacies. Most of us don't need to be told we are hypocrites; we already know this about ourselves. We can identify with the feelings expressed by Jules Feiffer in his poem first published in *The Village Voice.*

I felt like a fraud,
So I learned to fly an airplane.
At 50,000 feet I thought,
"A fraud is flying an airplane."
So I crossed the Atlantic in a rowboat.
I docked at Cherbourg.
And I thought,
"A fraud has crossed the Atlantic in a rowboat."
So I took a space shot to the moon.
On the way home I thought,
"A fraud has circled the moon."
So I took a full page ad in the newspaper,
And confessed to the world that I was a fraud.
I read the ad and thought—
"A fraud is pretending to be honest."

8. POTENCY

We cannot make a tiger eat grass by removing his teeth or turn a lamb into a bull by tying horns onto his head. PAUL ELDRIDGE

9. THE OBVIOUS TRUTH

If I were two-faced, would I be wearing this one? ABRAHAM LINCOLN

10. APPEARANCE OF GOODNESS

To win over certain people to something, it is only necessary to give it a gloss of love of humanity, nobility, gentleness, self-sacrifice—and there is nothing you cannot get them to swallow. FRIEDRICH NIETZSCHE

11. MOVING UP

Members of the Methodist Women's Church Circle in one Wisconsin town some years ago were disturbed because a widowed church member and her three small daughters were staying away from services. Finding the reason to be a lack of suitable clothes, the ladies' group corrected the situation in a generous manner. When the little girls still failed to appear at Sunday school, some of the ladies called to inquire about their absence. The mother thanked them sweetly for the clothing and explained: "The girls looked so nice, I sent them to the Presbyterian church."

12. WAR OF PRETENSE

In a small college town a tavern frequented by students ran the following ad in the campus paper during the days before Parents Weekend: "Bring Your Parents for Lunch Saturday. We'll Pretend We Don't Know You!"

The ad was soon challenged by the college chaplain, who posted a revised version on the campus bulletin board. It read: "Bring Your Parents to Chapel Sunday. We'll Pretend We Know You!"

13. LOVELY LIES

The Devil can cite Scripture for his purpose.
An evil soul, producing holy witness,
Is like a villain with a smiling cheek;
A goodly apple rotten at the heart.
Oh, what a goodly outside falsehood hath.
SHAKESPEARE, *The Merchant of Venice, Act III*

14. A DECEIVABLE WORLD

The world is still deceiv'd with ornament.
In law, what plea so tainted and corrupt
But, being season'd with a gracious voice,
Obscures the show of evil? In religion,

What damned error, but some sober brow
Will bless it and approve it with a text,
Hiding the grossness with fair ornament?
There is no vice so simple but assumes
Some mark of virtue in its outward parts.
SHAKESPEARE, *The Merchant of Venice, Act III*

15. FLOWER AND SERPENT
To beguile the time,
Look like the time; bear welcome in your eye,
Your hand, your tongue; look like the innocent flower,
But be the serpent under 't. SHAKESPEARE, *Macbeth, Act I*

16. THE TRUTH IN OTHERS' EYES
However much we guard ourselves against it, we tend to shape ourselves in the image others have of us. It is not so much the example of theirs we imitate, as the reflection of ourselves in their eyes and the echo of ourselves in their words. ERIC HOFFER

17. CAUGHT
A brand new lawyer in his brand new office on his first day in practice sees a prospective client walk in the door. He decides he should look busy, so he picks up the phone and starts talking: "Look, Harry, about that amalgamation deal. I think I better run down to the factory and handle it personally. Yes. No. I don't think 3 million will swing it. We better have Rogers from Seattle meet us there. OK. Call you back later." He looks up at the visitor and says, "Good morning, how may I help you?" And the prospective client says, "You can't help me at all. I'm just here to hook up your phone."

18. THE POWER OF HYPOCRISY
Years ago in Germany there was a young Jewish boy who had a profound sense of admiration for his father. The life of the family centered around the acts of piety and devotion prescribed by their religion. The father was zealous in attending worship and instruction and demanded the same from his children. While the boy was a teenager the family was forced to move to another town in Germany. In the new location there was no synagogue, and the pillars of the community all belonged to the Lutheran church. Suddenly the father announced to the family that they were all going to abandon their Jewish traditions and join the Lutheran church. When the stunned family asked why, the father explained that it was necessary to help his business. The youngster was bewildered and confused. His deep disappointment soon

gave way to anger and a kind of intense bitterness that plagued him throughout his life.

He left Germany and went to England to study. He sat daily at the British Museum formulating his ideas and composing a book. In that book he introduced a whole life and worldview and conceived of a movement that was designed to change the world. In the book he described religion as an "opiate for the masses" that could be explained totally in terms of economics. Today there are billions of people in the world who live under the system invented by this embittered man. His name, of course, is Karl Marx. The influence of this father's hypocrisy is still being keenly felt around the world. R. C. SPROUL, *Objections Answered*

19. SCULPTING THE FACE
We mold our faces to fit our masks. PAUL ELDRIDGE

20. HATING HYPOCRISY
We hate the hypocrite more keenly than the mere liar because the hypocrite adds to his lie the lacquer of flattery, which we are gullible enough to accept as tribute to our merit. PAUL ELDRIDGE

21. PEACEFUL?
Washington is full of peace monuments. We build one after every war.

22. FORM AND SUBSTANCE
A devout Christian who had a cat used to spend several minutes each day at prayer and meditation in his bedroom. He read a portion of Scripture and a devotional book, followed by a period of silent meditation and prayer. As time went on his prayers became longer and more intense.

He came to cherish this quiet time in his bedroom, but his cat came to like it, too. She would cozy up to him, purr loudly, and rub her furry body against him. This interrupted the man's prayer time, so he put a collar around the cat's neck and tied her to the bedpost whenever he wanted to be undisturbed while at prayer. This didn't seem to upset the cat, and it meant that the man could meditate without interruption.

Over the years, the daughter of this devout Christian had noted how much his devotional time had meant to him. When she began to establish some routines and patterns with her own family, she decided she should do as her father had done. Dutifully she, too, tied her cat to the bedpost and then proceeded to her devotions. But time moved faster in her generation and she couldn't spend as much time at prayer as did her father.

The day came when her son grew up and wanted to make sure that he preserved some of the family traditions which had meant so much to his

437

mother and his grandfather. But the pace of life had quickened all the more and there simply was no time for such elaborate devotional proceedings. So he eliminated the time for meditation, Bible reading, and prayer. But in order to carry on the religious tradition, each day while he was dressing he tied the family cat to the bedpost.

Thus forms become more important than the faith they are meant to convey.

ONE HUNDRED FIFTEEN
Pride
(See also Self-centeredness)

1. FILLING IN
The bigger a man's head gets, the easier it is to fill his shoes.

2. SILLY GOOSE
Every goose is certain she could lay golden eggs if only properly fed.
PAUL ELDRIDGE

3. KEEPING UP WITH THE JONESES
Two wellborn and blueblooded dogs were walking daintily along the street with their noses held high in the air. Along came a big alley dog of the Heinz 57 Varieties type. Embarrassed at being in the company of such a no-account dog, one of the lady dogs said, "We must go. My name is Miji, spelled M-I-J-I." The other blueblood said, "My name is Miki, spelled M-I-K-I." The low-class alley dog put his nose up in the air also and said, "My name is Fido— spelled P-H-Y-D-E-A-U-X."

4. TOUGH INITIATION
Two Texans were trying to impress each other with the size of their ranches. One asked the other, "What's the name of your ranch?" He replied, "The Rocking R, ABC, Flying W, Circle C, Bar U, Staple Four, Box D, Rolling M, Rainbow's End, Silver Spur Ranch." The questioner was much impressed and exclaimed, "Whew! That's sure some name! How many head of cattle do you run?" The rancher answered, "Not many. Very few survive the branding."

5. COMPLIMENTS UNFINISHED

The only things wrong about getting an unexpected compliment is the nagging suspicion that they have not said quite enough.

6. HEAD SWELLING

I once heard a missionary tell how he was trying to do translation work in a particular tribe and found it hard to translate the word *pride* or at least the concept. He finally came to the idea to use their word or words for the ears being too far apart. In other words, he conveyed the idea of an "inflated head" which is probably hard to improve on when we talk of the problem of pride.

7. SHELLEY ON PRIDE

I met a traveler from an antique land
Who said: Two vast and trunkless legs of stone
Stand in the desert. Near them, on the sand,
Half sunk, a shattered visage lies, whose frown
And wrinkled lip, and sneer of cold command,
Tell that its sculptor well those passions read
Which yet survive, stamped on these lifeless things,
The hand that mocked them and the heart that fed;
And on the pedestal these words appear:
"My name is Ozymandias, king of kings;
Look on my works, ye Mighty, and despair!"
Nothing beside remains. Round the decay
Of that colossal wreck, boundless and bare
The lone and level sands stretch far away. PERCY BYSSHE SHELLEY

8. SELF AND EGOCENTRICITY

A newly elected politician was visiting Washington, D.C., to get acquainted. He was visiting in the home of one of the ranking senators who was trying to interpret the bizarre wonder of the capitol. As they stood looking out over the Potomac River, an old deteriorating log floated by in view on the river. The old-timer said, "This city is like that log out there." The fledgling politician asked: "How's that?" The senator came back, "Well, there are probably more than one hundred thousand grubs, ants, bugs and critters on that old log as it floats down the river. And I imagine every one of them thinks that he's steering it."

9. FATHER AND PRAYER

Father expected a good deal of God. He didn't actually accuse God of inefficiency, but when he prayed his tone was lucid and angry, like that of a dissatisfied guest in a carelessly managed hotel. CLARENCE DAY, *Life with Father*

ONE HUNDRED SIXTEEN
Repentance and Confession
(See also Change and Conversion)

1. A HEARTY SORROW
Repentance is a hearty sorrow for our past misdeeds, and a sincere resolution and an endeavor to the utmost of our power, to conform all our actions to the law of God. It does not consist in one single act of sorrow, but in doing works meet for repentance; in a sincere obedience to the law of Christ for the remainder of our lives. JOHN LOCKE

2. DOUBLE-SIDED
Repentance has a double aspect; it looks upon things past with a weeping eye, and upon the future with a watchful eye. ROBERT SOUTH

3. THE SIN OR THE PENALTY
True repentance hates the sin, and not merely the penalty; and it hates the sin most of all because it has discovered and felt God's love. W. M. TAYLOR

4. CEASING
True repentance is to cease from sin. AMBROSE OF MILAN

5. REPENTANCE AT THE LAST MOMENT
There is one case of deathbed repentance recorded—that of the penitent thief, that none should despair; and only one that none should presume. AUGUSTINE

6. THE JOY OF THE REPENTANT HEART
When the soul has laid down its faults at the feet of God, it feels as though it had wings. EUGENIE DE GUERIN

7. VERBALIZING
From listening comes wisdom and from speaking comes repentance.

8. TRUE REPENTANCE—THE CYNICAL VIEW
Repentance is not so much remorse for what we have done as the fear of consequences. LA ROCHEFOUCAULD

ONE HUNDRED SEVENTEEN
Responsibility

1. BLAME
Wives feel resentment when it is assumed that they are responsible for everything that goes wrong around the house. This is epitomized in the television ad in which the husband is upset because there's a "ring around the collar." The wife breaks into tears because her detergent has not removed the dirt from her husband's shirt. The ring around the collar is seen as telltale evidence of her failure. The ad never asks the obvious question— Why didn't he wash his neck? TONY CAMPOLO

2. ROLE OF THE INDIVIDUAL
No snowflake in an avalanche ever feels responsible.

3. ULCERS REQUIRED
If you haven't got an ulcer, you're not carrying your share of the load.

4. THE REAL EDUCATION
The man who blames others for his problems hasn't begun his education. The man who blames himself has begun his education. And the man who blames no one has finished his education.

RESURRECTION
(See Easter, Eternity)

REVENGE *(See Vengeance)*

ONE HUNDRED EIGHTEEN
Role Models

1. IRRITATING BUT GOOD
Few things are harder to put up with than the annoyance of a good example.
MARK TWAIN

2. PASSING IT ON
Small boys learn to be large men in the presence of large men who care about small boys. PHYLLIS THEROUS

3. AMAZING BUT TRUE
Professor Lowell of Harvard University was speaking many years ago to a gathering on Columbus Day. He said that there were three profound things about Christopher Columbus' discovery of America: First, when he left Spain he didn't know where he was going. Second, when he arrived in the New World he didn't know where he was. Third, when he returned to Ferdinand in his court he didn't know where he had been. Later wags have also added, "And he did it all on borrowed money!"

4. INSPIRED BY THE BEST
Leonardo da Vinci had started work on a large canvas in his studio. For awhile he worked at it—choosing the subject, planning the perspective, sketching the outline, applying the colors, with his own inimitable genius. Then suddenly he ceased, the painting still unfinished, and, summoning one of his students, invited him to complete the work. The student protested that he was both unworthy and unable to complete the great painting which his master had begun. But da Vinci silenced him. "Will not what I have done inspire you to do your best?"

Our Master began two thousand years ago—by what he said, by what he did, and supremely by what he suffered. He illustrated his message and he has left us to finish the picture.

ONE HUNDRED NINETEEN
Sacrifice

1. THE SURRENDERED SELF

E. Stanley Jones, well-known Christian missionary to India, tells of a situation where the fellow members of his ashram helped him in a problem regarding his spiritual reputation. It seems that for a number of years Jones had supported a prominent man financially. And when the time came that he could no longer support him, the man turned on Jones and attacked him in the public press. So E. Stanley Jones sat down and wrote a letter of reply of a few sentences, the kind of reply in which you don't give your opponent a leg to stand on. As he put it, "the kind of reply you are proud of the first five minutes, the second five minutes you're not so certain, and the third five minutes you know you're wrong." But before he mailed this letter he sent this reply to the people of the ashram to get their opinion of it. They sent it back with three words written on the margin: "Not sufficiently redemptive." As Jones read those words he was devastated. He knew that he was winning the argument, but losing his man. He knew immediately that the "Christian is not in the business of winning arguments, but of winning people." So he tore up the letter and said, "Lord, you'll have to take care of my reputation." A few weeks later he received a letter of apology from the man who had turned on him.

When the self is unsurrendered, it tends to be touchy, easily provoked, unable to bear insults. When the self is surrendered to Christ and the love of Jesus fills and cleanses the self, then we can bear all things, endure all things, and men and women are impacted by our lives.

2. SURRENDER TO CHRIST

Why do people resist surrendering themselves to Christ? For many, the reason they give is that they don't really trust God to handle their lives to their suiting. A young lady stood talking to an evangelist on the subject of consecration, of giving herself wholly to God. She said, "I dare not give myself wholly to the Lord, for fear He will send me out to China as a missionary." The evangelist said, "If some cold, snowy morning a little bird should come, half-frozen, pecking at your window, and you would let you take it in and feed it, thereby putting itself entirely in your power, what would you do? Would you grip it in your hand and crush it? Or would you give it shelter, warmth, food, and care?" A new light came into the girl's eyes. She said, "Oh, now I see, I see. I can trust God!" Two years later she again met the evangelist and recalled to him the incident. She told of how she had finally abandoned herself to God—and then her face lit up with a smile and said, "And do you know where God is going to let me serve Him?" And there was now a twinkle in her eye—"In China!"

3. THE SACRIFICIAL LIFE

When Dawson Trotman passed away he probably left a legacy of discipleship on this earth that will never be matched except perhaps in the life of Jesus Christ Himself. I've become a real student of Dawson Trotman and believe wholeheartedly in the methods of discipleship that he taught and emulated throughout his days. He died in Schroon Lake, New York. He died of all things in the midst of an area that he was expert in—he drowned. He was an expert swimmer. The last few moments he had in the water he lifted one girl out of the water. He went down and got the other girl and lifted her out of the water and then submerged and was not found again until the dragnet found him a few hours later. A man named Larsen was on that boat when Trotman died, and he said, "The entire United States Navy couldn't have saved Trotman that day—it was God's time." *Time* ran an article on Trotman's life the next week, and they put a caption beneath his name, and it read, "Always Holding Somebody Up." In one sentence, that was Trotman's life—investment in people, in honesty and humility, holding them up. Are you doing that? Who are you holding up? CHARLES SWINDOLL

4. THE HIGH COST OF MAKING PEACE

At the International Youth Triennium in Bloomington, Indiana, in July 1980 Professor Bruce Riggins of McCormick Theological Seminary was sharing with thirty-eight hundred attendees that he had met a very dedicated Christian working in an amazing way with the underprivileged people in London, England. He wanted to know what inspired her Christian faith and action. She shared her story of how seeing another Christian's faith converted her: She was a Jew fleeing the German Gestapo in France during World War II. She knew she was close to being caught and she wanted to give up. She came to the home of a French Huguenot. A widow lady came to that home to say that it was time to flee to a new place. This Jewish lady said, "It's no use, they will find me anyway. They are so close behind." The Christian widow said, "Yes, they will find someone here, but it's time for you to leave. Go with these people to safety—I will take your identification and wait here."

The Jewish lady then understood the plan; the Gestapo would come and find this Christian widow and think she was the fleeing Jew.

As Professor Riggins listened to this story, the Christian lady of Jewish descent looked him in the eye and said, "I asked her why she was doing that and the widow responded, 'It's the least I can do; Christ has already done that and more for me.'" The widow was caught and imprisoned in the Jewish lady's place, allowing time for her to escape. Within six months the Christian widow was dead in the concentration camp.

This Jewish lady never forgot that. She too became a follower of Jesus Christ and lived her life serving others. She met God through the greatest love a person can give—personal self-sacrifice. In faith, an authentic Christian lives his life serving others, saying, "That's the least I can do considering what great sacrifices Christ has already made for me."

5. UNAMBIGUOUS SELF-DENIAL
One single act performed with true self-denial, in renunciation of the world, is infinitely more of a revival and more of Christianity than 1,000 or 10,000 or 100,000 or 1,000,000 persons, so long as they keep it ambiguous.
SØREN KIERKEGAARD

6. HE WHO LOSES HIS LIFE FINDS IT
On one occasion Sadhu Sundar Singh and a companion were traveling through a pass high in the Himalayan Mountains. At one point they came across a body lying in the snow. Sundar Singh wished to stop and help the unfortunate man, but his companion refused, saying, "We shall lose our lives if we burden ourselves with him."

But Sundar Singh would not think of leaving the man to die in the ice and snow. As his companion bade him farewell, Sundar Singh lifted the poor traveler onto his back. With great exertion on his part, he bore the man onward, but gradually the heat from Sundar Singh's body began to warm up the poor frozen fellow, and he revived. Soon both were walking together side by side. Catching up with his former companion, they found him dead— frozen by the cold.

In the case of Sundar Singh, he was willing to lose his life on behalf of another, and in the process found it; in the case of his callous companion, he sought to save his life but lost it.

ONE HUNDRED TWENTY
The Secular World and the Christian

1. CHRISTIANS *CONTRA MUNDUM*

Thus it was from the beginning and so it is today. Yet the early Christians had one great advantage over us; then it was clear that the surrounding culture was groping in the darkness of paganism, and thus it was clear that the culture should have no hand in defining the role of God's people in the world. But today we have grown accustomed to thinking of ourselves as a part of the "Christian West," living in a "Christian nation." That habit is hard to kick, for it has the narcotic effect of easing the painful reality of the stark contrast between twentieth-century American culture and the calling of Christ to His Church.

Yet we must kick that habit if by serving heaven we are to be any earthly good. Our challenge is clear: We must reject the illusions, seductions, and false alternatives of the current political scene and reassert the ageless truth that Christ is Lord of lords, King of kings. With Athanasius, the great fourth-century champion of the faith, we must stand for Christ against the world. In the very moment of our clearest opposition to the world, we will find that as witnesses to the Truth and Life we will have the inestimable privilege of helping to make His invisible kingdom visible in the world. For with Christ we will "preach good news to the poor ... proclaim freedom for the prisoners, and recovery of sight for the blind, ... release the oppressed, [and] proclaim the year of the Lord's favor" (Luke 4:18-19, NIV).

2. THE HUMANIST'S PRAYER

Lyman Abbot once paraphrased the Lord's Prayer to reflect the philosophy of those without God. We might call it the Humanist's Prayer:

Our brethren who art on earth,
hallowed be our name.
Our kingdom come,
our will be done on earth,
for there is no heaven.
We must get this day our daily bread;
we neither forgive nor are forgiven.

We fear not temptation,
for we deliver ourselves from evil.
For ours is the kingdom and the power,
and there is no glory and no forever.

3. EPITAPH FOR A GODLESS PEOPLE
A cry from the North, from the West, from the South
Whence thousands travel daily to the timekept City;
Where My Word is unspoken,
In the land of lobelias and tennis flannels
The rabbit shall burrow and the thorn revisit,
The nettle shall flourish on the gravel court,
And the wind shall say: "Here were decent, godless people;
Their only monument the asphalt road
And a thousand lost golf balls." T. S. ELIOT, *Choruses from "The Rock"*

4. WE PLAY THE GAME UNFAIRLY
A Hasidic story tells of a little boy playing hide-and-seek with his friends. For some unknown reason they stopped playing while he was hiding. He began to cry. His old grandfather came out of the house to see what was troubling him. After learning what had happened, the grandfather said, "Do not weep, my child, because the boys did not come to find you. Perhaps you can learn a lesson from this disappointment. All of life is like a game between God and us. Only it is God who is weeping, for we are not playing the game fairly. God is waiting to be found, but many have gone in search of other things."

5. PLAIN CROSS
A Denver woman told her pastor of a recent experience that she felt was indicative of the times in which we live. She was in a jewelry store looking for a necklace and said to the clerk, "I'd like a gold cross." The man behind the counter looked over the stock in the display case and said, "Do you want a plain one, or one with a little man on it?"

6. COOLING LOTHARIO'S ARDOR
An attractive young woman whose career necessitated a good deal of traveling was asked if she was ever bothered by uninvited male attention. She answered, "Never, I just say five words and immediately I am left alone." "What are the five words?" She said, "I simply ask, 'Are you a born-again Christian?'"

7. NO STRENGTH TO RISE
Like the eagle that sat down on the frozen ground to feed upon its prey, and when it would have arisen, found its great wings so frozen to the ice that it

could never rise again but perished beside its costly pleasure; like the ship that sailed so close to the current that it was not possible to stem the awful tide that drove it over the abyss—so Christian men and women are trifling with forbidden things until they have neither heart nor strength to rise to their heavenly calling.

8. IS THE CHURCH IMPORTANT?

The Christian Communications Laboratory relates the story of a small Midwestern weekly paper which ran a story saying, "We are pleased to announce that the cyclone which blew away the Methodist church last Friday did no real damage to the town." Kind of scary! Perhaps our failure today is not that we kill the King's Son or practice violence and bloodshed so much as being irrelevant and without impact.

9. CYPRIAN'S TESTIMONY

This is a cheerful world as I see it from my garden under the shadows of my vines. But if I were to ascend some high mountain and look out over the wide lands, you know very well what I should see: brigands on the highways, pirates on the sea, armies fighting, cities burning; in the amphitheaters men murdered to please applauding crowds; selfishness and cruelty and misery and despair under all roofs. It is a bad world, Donatus, an incredibly bad world. But I have discovered in the midst of it a quiet and holy people who have learned a great secret. They are despised and persecuted, but they care not. They are masters of their souls. They have overcome the world. These people, Donatus, are the Christians—and I am one of them.

CYPRIAN, *third-century martyr*

ONE HUNDRED
TWENTY-ONE
Self-
Centeredness
(*See also Pride*)

1. EGO PERSPECTIVE

Conversation between a six-year-old and a five-year-old:

"Are you in Linda's room at school?"

"No, I'm not. But she's in my room!"

2. REAL CONSOLATION

A woman was heartbroken when her dog disappeared. She put an ad in the paper offering a reward for its return. The next morning the phone rang. It was the voice of a woman: "I'm calling about your dog." Then she began to cough. She explained she wasn't feeling too well. In fact, she hadn't felt well for three years since her husband had died. She went on to say that after her mother and father had passed away, that recently her sister had contracted cancer and was undergoing painful treatments. Her friends weren't doing well, either. She gave details of their various illnesses and went on to describe the funerals of several of them. After thirty minutes of this, the woman who had lost the dog tried to get the caller back on the subject. She asked, "But what about my dog?" The other woman replied, "Oh, I don't have him, but I thought you might be feeling badly about losing it, so I thought I'd just call to cheer you up!" CHARLES KRIEG

3. ARROWS OFF COURSE

Søren Kierkegaard, in an essay on humility, suggests that we conceive of an arrow racing on its course when suddenly it halts in its flight, perhaps in order to see how far it has come or how high it has soared above the earth or how its speed compares to that of another arrow (or to see and admire the gracefulness with which it flies); at that very moment it falls to the ground. So, the philosopher insists, self-preoccupation is always dangerous and self-destructive.

4. STRONG SELF-IMAGE

"What is your opinion of my painting?" "It isn't worth anything." "I know—but I'd like to hear it anyway."

5. NO RIVALS

He that falls in love with himself will have no rivals. BENJAMIN FRANKLIN

6. HARSH REALITY

A man said to the Universe: "Sir, I exist." "However," replied the Universe, "that fact has not created in me a sense of obligation." STEPHEN CRANE

7. FORGETTING OTHERS

Selfishness is not living as one wishes to live. It is asking others to live as one wishes to live. OSCAR WILDE

8. GOOD MANNERS

Even folks with bad manners know how to be polite to those who can do something for them.

449

9. STRATEGIC SPOT
An admirer once asked Leonard Bernstein, celebrated orchestra conductor, what was the hardest instrument to play. He replied without hesitation: "Second fiddle. I can always get plenty of first violinists, but to find one who plays second violin with as much enthusiasm or second French horn or second flute, now that's a problem. And yet if no one plays second, we have no harmony."

10. STAR OF THE SHOW
One of Teddy Roosevelt's children said of him: "Father always wanted to be the bride at every wedding and the corpse at every funeral."

11. IRKSOME OTHERS
All discourses but my own afflict me; they seem harsh, impertinent, and irksome. BEN JONSON

12. COPING WITH OTHERS
Coping with difficult people is always a problem, particularly if the difficult person happens to be oneself. ASHLEIGH BRILLIANT

13. NEIGHBORHOOD RENEWAL
A woman lived in a big city neighborhood that was going downhill very fast. The area was becoming increasingly overcrowded, noisy, and dirty. It was a bad situation. The woman decided something would have to be done about it. She knew that money would be required to change the situation. Consequently, she started a fund-raising drive. She called people. She sent letters. She got some financial support from a private foundation. She finally raised eighty-five thousand dollars and then she used the money to move to another neighborhood.

14. TURNABOUT
A cold wind was howling and a chilling rain was beating down when the telephone rang in the home of a doctor. The caller said that his wife needed urgent medical attention. The doctor was understanding. "I'll be glad to come, but my car is being repaired," he said. "Could you come and get me?" There was indignation at the other end of the phone as an angry voice sputtered, "What, in this weather?"

15. PEOPLE OF THE LIE
Utterly dedicated to preserving their self-image of perfection, they are unceasingly engaged in the effort to maintain the appearance of moral purity. They worry about this a great deal. They are acutely sensitive to social norms and what others might think of them. . . . They dress well, go to work on

time, pay their taxes, and outwardly seem to live lives that are above reproach.

The words "image," "appearance," and "outwardly" are crucial to understanding the morality of the evil. While they seem to lack any motivation to be good, they intensely desire to appear good. Their "goodness" is all on a level of pretense. It is, in effect, a lie. That is why they are the "people of the lie."

Actually, the lie is designed not so much to deceive others as to deceive themselves. They cannot or will not tolerate the pain of self-reproach.
M. SCOTT PECK, *People of the Lie*

16. AFFIRMATION
Everyone needs recognition for his accomplishments, but it is possible to carry the need too far. Such people are like the little boy who says to his father: "Let's play darts. I'll throw and you say 'Wonderful!'"

17. IMPORTANCE IS RELATIVE
George had a friend with an inflated opinion of himself. As a friend should, George decided to help his friend lose this quirk. Subtly, George mentioned that he knew Johnny Carson. The friend said, "Oh, yeah, prove it." In a few minutes they were in front of a large house near the beach. After knocking, out came Johnny Carson saying, "Come on in, George, and bring your friend." On the way home the friend grudgingly said, "OK, so you know Johnny Carson."

Obviously, this was not enough, so George said offhandedly, "Yes, he and I and the president are well-acquainted." The friend looked in the air, at nothing, and cried out, "That's too much, I'll pay the costs—let's go to D.C. and see." At the White House, they just arrived, and out came the president to greet them, saying, "Come on in, George, and bring your friend." Later George's friend looked around sheepishly and admitted, "Well, yeah, you do know the president."

George sensed his friend needed further deflation. So casually he remarked, "Yeah, but you know the pope has a nicer office." "What!" yelled his wide-eyed friend. "You know the pope! I'll bet you ten thousand dollars you can't even get in to see the pope." In a few days they were in Rome, with George knocking on a door to the Vatican. A cardinal came out extending his hand to George, but saying, "Your friend will have to stay outside!" About an hour went by, when out came the pope onto the balcony, waving at the crowd, with one arm around George. Later, outside, George looked around for his friend and found him out cold in the courtyard. George rushed over and helped his friend up and apologized for shocking him so. But his friend simply shook his head and mumbled, "It's not that you knew the pope. It was the crowd! They kept asking each other, 'Who's the guy with George?'"

18. WITH FRIENDS LIKE THAT . . .

Two friends went camping out in the woods. They woke up the first morning and were standing by their tent having their first cup of coffee for the day when they suddenly spotted a grizzly bear heading for them at full speed. Quickly, the one man reached down and grabbed his tennies and started putting them on. The other man looked at him and said, "What are you doing? Do you think you can outrun that grizzly bear?" And the first man said, "No, and I don't need to. All I need to do is to outrun you!"

ONE HUNDRED
TWENTY-TWO

Servanthood

1. THE SERVANT HEART

Arnold Billie is a rural mail carrier in southern New Jersey. For the last quarter century his daily route has taken him sixty-three miles through two counties and five municipalities. Mr. Billie not only delivers mail, he brings personal service. Anything you can get at the post office you can get from Mr. Billie—stamps, money orders, and pickup service. All the customer has to do is leave the flag up on the mailbox. One elderly woman has trouble starting her lawn mower, so when she wants to use it, she leaves it by her mailbox and Mr. Billie starts it when he arrives. Who says personal service is no more?

2. SAVED FOR A PURPOSE

God did not save you to be a sensation; He saved you to be a servant.

3. GOD'S SERVANTS

Archbishop Secker used to say, "God has three sorts of servants in the world: some are slaves, and serve Him from fear; others are hirelings, and serve for wages; and the last are sons, who serve because they love."

4. THE SERVANT CHURCH

The life of the one holy Universal Church is determined by the fact that it is the fulfillment of the service as ambassador enjoined upon it.

Where the life of the Church is exhausted in self-serving, it smacks of death; the decisive thing has been forgotten, that this whole life is lived only in the exercise of what we called the Church's service as ambassador, proclamation, kerygma. A Church that recognizes its commission will neither desire nor be able to petrify in any of its functions, to be the Church for its own sake. There is the "Christ-believing group"; but this group is sent out: "Go and preach the gospel!" It does not say, "Go and celebrate services!" "Go and edify yourselves with the sermon!" "Go and celebrate the Sacraments!" "Go and present yourselves in a liturgy, which perhaps repeats the heavenly liturgy!" "Go and devise a theology which may gloriously unfold like the Summa of St. Thomas!" Of course, there is nothing to forbid all this; there may exist very good cause to do it all; but nothing, nothing at all for its own sake! In it all the one thing must prevail: "Proclaim the gospel to every creature!" The Church runs like a herald to deliver the message. It is not a snail that carries its little house on its back and is so well off in it that only now and then it sticks out its feelers and then thinks that the "claim of publicity" has been satisfied. No, the Church lives by its commission as herald, it is *la compagnie de Dieu.*

Where the Church is living, it must ask itself whether it is serving this commission or whether it is a purpose in itself. If the second is the case, then as a rule it begins to smack of the "sacred," to affect piety, to play the priest and to mumble. Anyone with a keen nose will smell it and find it dreadful! Christianity is not "sacred"; rather there breathes in it the fresh air of the Spirit. Otherwise it is not Christianity. For it is an out-and-out "worldly" thing open to all humanity: "Go into all the world and proclaim the gospel to every creature." KARL BARTH, *Dogmatics in Outline*

ONE HUNDRED
TWENTY-THREE
Sin

1. THE RAVAGED LIFE

When Leonardo da Vinci was painting his masterpiece, *The Last Supper,* he selected as the person to sit for the character of the Christ a young man, Pietri Bandinelli by name, connected with the Milan Cathedral as chorister. Years passed before the great picture was completed, and when one character only—that of Judas Iscariot—was wanting, the great painter noticed a man in the streets of Rome whom he selected as his model. With shoulders far bent toward the ground, having an expression of cold, hardened, evil, saturnine, the man seemed to afford the opportunities of a model terribly true to the artist's conception of Judas.

When in the studio, the profligate began to look around, as if recalling incidents of years gone by. Finally, he turned and with a look half-sad, yet one which told how hard it was to realize the change which had taken place, he said, "Maestro, I was in this studio twenty-five years ago. I, then, sat for Christ."

2. MIGHT IT BE SIN?

Why is it if we are all so well-educated and brilliant and gifted and artistic and idealistic and distinguished in scholarship, that we are so selfish and scheming and dishonest and begrudging and impatient and arrogant and disrespectful of others? M. C. Richards

3. REVEALING SLIP

At the close of a sermon one Sunday morning one of the members of the church came forward at the invitation. He was noticeably disturbed and moved by his conviction of sin in his life. With tears flowing and a halt in his voice he took my hand and meant to tell me that his life was full of sin. But what came out was, "My sin is full of life." As soon as he had spoken he realized his mistake and changed it, but in reality his first statement was the real reason for the second. His sin was full of life and that is why his life was full of sin. Praise God that the blood of Jesus Christ is the remedy and he found it that day.

4. THE PASSION OF ENVY

What we have not poisons what we have. . . . Our urge to acquire things is due less to the passion to possess them than to the vanity of feeling superior to those who envy our possession of them. . . . Envy transmutes other people's base metals into gold. . . . Our envy is the yeast that swells the fortune of others. . . . No form of hatred is as keen as envy. It magnifies the importance of our enemy—and belittles our own. PAUL ELDRIDGE

5. PROFESSIONAL DEMEANOR REQUIRED

There was this young priest who was going to confessional for the first time. He went with another priest, his senior. After a day of hearing confessions he was approached by the older pastor who said, "You know, I think that when a person finishes with a confession, you should say something on the order of, 'I agree it is terrible what you have done, and I would encourage you to stay away from that kind of behavior from now on,' instead of saying, 'WOW!'"

6. CLOCKS IN HEAVEN

During a dream I had last night, I died and promptly met with St. Peter at the famous "Pearly Gate." Upon being taken into heaven, Peter began to show me around. One immediate observation I made was that on the walls of an enormous warehouse I saw thousands of clocks. All of these clocks were ticking away but at different rates. I then noticed that under each clock was a name plate with a name engraved on it. Naturally, I asked the significance of all this. Peter informed me that each clock was designed to keep track of an individual still on earth. Each time the person, represented by the clock, committed a sin, the hands on the clock made a complete revolution. Upon closer examination I began to recognize a few names. After searching for [insert the name of the person you're trying to rib] name, and not finding it, I inquired as to the location of his clock. St. Peter replied, "Oh, his clock! Well, we moved his into the office and are using it for a fan."

7. VARIETIES OF SIN

In a sermon on sin, a preacher announced that there were 789 different sins. A few days later the mailman delivered 94 requests from members of his congregation for a list of the 789 sins.

8. HIDDEN SIN

Working in my garden, I was admiring the large, green, healthy-looking squash plant. The stems appeared to be strong, and the leaves were large. A few days later I noticed that the plant was terribly wilted, and within a couple of days the squash plant was completely dead. Pulling up the plant and examining its roots, I discovered that a bore worm, which could not be seen from the outside, had eaten the heart out of the stem of the plant. Hidden sin, like the bore worm, can eat away the heart of one's Christian experience and leave him spiritually dead.

9. SIN OF DISHONESTY

The "credibility gap" that once alienated the public from people in high places now seems to separate us from one another in all walks of life. Americans lie on their income tax returns to the tune of millions of dollars a year. Doctors fake reports in order to profit from Medicare patients. Prize athletes at great universities are kept eligible for competition through bogus credits and forged transcripts of academic records. Children soon acquire the cynical assumption that lying is the normal tack for TV advertisers. In the words of a *Time* magazine essay, ours is "a huckstering, show-bizzy world, jangling with hype, hullabaloo, and hooey, bull, baloney, and bamboozlement." After a while, people tend to expect not to hear the truth anymore; in 1976, a national poll showed that 69 percent of Americans believed that the country's leaders had, over the last decade, consistently lied to the people. LEWIS SMEDES, *Mere Morality*

10. PRIORITY LEVELS

One Sunday morning a preacher in Virginia began his sermon: "There are three points I want to make today: First: Because we're not really hearing the Word of God, the whole world is in danger of annihilation. Second: Most people don't give a damn about that! Third: You are more worried about the fact that I just used the word *damn* than you are about the world being in danger of annihilation."

11. OVERMUCH GUILT

Martin Luther was one who struggled with his sins. Before his break with the Catholic church he went to confession every day and was so guilt-ridden by his sins he would almost have gone every hour.

On most nights Luther slept well, but he even felt guilty about that, thinking, *Here am I, sinful as I am, having a good night's sleep.* So he would confess that. One day the older priest to whom Luther went for confession said to him, "Martin, either find a new sin and commit it, or quit coming to see me!"

12. MORALS AND LOOPHOLES

Everybody looks for different things in the Ten Commandments. Some look for Divine guidance, some look for a code to live by, but most of us are looking for loopholes.

13. JUVENILE INSIGHT

The Sunday school teacher asked her class: "What are sins of omission? After some thought one little fellow said: "They're the sins we should have committed but didn't get around to."

14. DECALOGUE BARGAINING

A cartoon in the Hong Kong *Tattler* showed Moses just come down from the top of the mountain with the tablets in his hand. He's reporting to the children of Israel and says, "It was hard bargaining—we get the milk and honey, but the anti-adultery clause stays in."

15. GETTING THE PICTURE

Each week a New York youngster would bring home from Sunday school an illustrated card that dramatized one of the Ten Commandments. The first week showed people worshiping at church. Another week, to illustrate "Thou shalt not kill," the picture showed Cain in the act of slaying Abel. The child's father reports: "I was waiting with considerable alarm for the seventh week. But fortunately, tact and delicacy prevailed. Under the caption, "Thou shalt not commit adultery" was a picture of a dairyman, leering villainously, as he poured a huge pail of water into a can of milk.

SLANDER *(See Gossip)*

ONE HUNDRED TWENTY-FOUR
Small Towns

1. YOU KNOW YOU'RE IN A SMALL TOWN WHEN . . .

The airport runway is terraced. . . . Third Street is on the edge of town. . . . Every sport is played on dirt. . . . You don't use your turn signal because everyone knows where you're going. . . . You dial a wrong number and talk for fifteen minutes anyway. . . . You drive into the ditch five miles out of town and the word gets back into town before you do. . . . You write a check on the wrong bank and it covers it for you. . . . The pickup trucks on main street outnumber the cars three to one. . . . You miss a Sunday at church and receive a get-well card. . . . Someone asks you how you feel then listens to what you say.

SORROW *(See Adversity, Grief)*

ONE HUNDRED
TWENTY-FIVE
Stewardship
(See also Giving, Money)

1. RADICAL GIVING

At a church meeting a very wealthy man rose to tell the rest of those present about his Christian faith. "I'm a millionaire," he said, "and I attribute it all to the rich blessings of God in my life. I remember that turning point in my faith. I had just earned my first dollar and I went to a church meeting that night. The speaker was a missionary who told about his work. I knew that I only had a dollar bill and had to either give it all to God's work or nothing at all. So at that moment I decided to give my whole dollar to God. I believe that God blessed that decision, and that is why I am a rich man today."

He finished and there was an awed silence at his testimony as he moved toward his seat. As he sat down a little old lady sitting in the same pew leaned over and said to him: "I dare you to do it again."

2. BUMPER STICKER WISDOM

Tithe if you love Jesus; any idiot can honk!

3. FIRST FRUITS TITHING

There was a knock on the door of the hut occupied by a missionary in Africa. Answering, the missionary found one of the native boys holding a large fish in his hands. The boy said, "Reverend, you taught us what tithing is, so here—I've brought you my tithe." As the missionary gratefully took the fish, he questioned the young lad. "If this is your tithe, where are the other nine fish?" At this, the boy beamed and said, "Oh, they're still back in the river. I'm going back to catch them now."

4. MOTIVATING STEWARDSHIP

One year the pastor took drastic action to get a more generous response from the congregation at stewardship time. He called in an electrician and wired the pews. Next day, when the collection time came, the pastor announced to the congregation, "Hereafter all pledges will be made publicly in the worship service." Then he added, "All those who will pledge ten dollars per week, stand." At that moment the switch was thrown that sent the juice through the wires in the pews. The response was immediate—about one half of the congregation jumped to their feet. Then the pastor said, "All those who will pledge twenty dollars please stand." The electrician raised the voltage and a second, stronger shock wave caused more persons to rise. The whole process was repeated several more times. Each time the amount was raised and so was the voltage. The ushers had to work frantically to get all the names and pledges written down. Later, in the counting room, the pastor and his staff were busy adding up the totals and congratulating themselves on the great success of the campaign—until the sexton appeared at the door and announced that four parishioners had stubbornly remained glued to their seats and were electrocuted.

5. STEWARDSHIP OF YOUR LIFE

Life is a leaf of paper white
Whereon each one of us may write
His word or two
And then comes night.
Greatly begin, though thou have time
But for a line. Be that sublime.
Not failure, but low aim, is crime. JAMES RUSSELL LOWELL

6. LET THE CHURCH CRAWL

One Sunday morning the pastor encouraged his congregation to consider the potential of the church. He told them, "With God's help we can see the day when this church will go from crawling to walking."

The people responded, "Let the church walk, Pastor, let the church walk."

He continued, "And when the church begins to walk, next the church can begin to run."

And the people shouted, "Let the church run, Pastor, let the church run!"

The pastor continued, "And finally the church can move from running to flying. Oh, the church can fly! But of course, that's going to take lots of money for that to happen!"

The congregation grew quiet, and from the back, someone mumbled, "Let the church crawl, Pastor, let the church crawl."

7. HIGH TECH STEWARDSHIP

I read of one pastor who perceived the whole concept of encouragement from a financial point of view. He announced one Sunday that he had made a new offering box for the weekly collection of the tithes and offerings. He claimed that it was designed to encourage people to become better stewards of their money.

"This new box," he explained, "has some interesting features. When you drop in a check or paper money in large amounts, the box makes no sound at all. Put a quarter in and it tinkles like a bell. A dime blows a whistle, and a penny fires a shot. When you put in nothing, the box takes your picture."

8. DID YOU NOTICE THE DIFFERENCE?

A priest once asked one of his parishioners to serve as financial chairman of his parish. The man, manager of a grain elevator, agreed on two conditions: No report would be due for a year, and no one would ask any questions during the year.

At the end of the year he made his report. He had paid off the church debt of $200,000. He had redecorated the church. He had sent $1,000 to missions. He had $5,000 in the bank.

"How did you do all this?" asked the priest and the shocked congregation.

Quietly he answered, "You people bring your grain to my elevator. As you did business with me, I simply withheld 10 percent and gave it to the church. You never missed it."

9. HOW MUCH TO GIVE?

"Go give to the needy sweet charity's bread.
For giving is living," the angel said.
"And must I be giving again and again?"
My peevish, petulant answer ran.
"Oh, no," said the angel, piercing me through,
"Just give till the Master stops giving to you."

10. ONLY ONE *T* IN *DIRTY*

He was not too well-educated and his manner was somewhat crude and rough, but he became a Christian and was on fire for the Lord. He constantly pestered his pastor to help him be of some genuine service to his church. In desperation, the pastor gave him a list of ten people, saying, "These are members who seldom attend services; some are prominent men of the city. Contact them any way you can and try to get them to be more faithful. Use the church stationery to write letters if you want, but get them back in church." He accepted the challenge with enthusiasm. About three weeks later, a letter arrived from a prominent physician, whose name was on the list. In the envelope was a one thousand dollar check and a note: "Dear Pastor: Enclosed is my check to make up for my missed offerings. I'm sorry for missing worship so much, but be assured I am going to be present every Sunday from now on and will not by choice miss services again. Sincerely, M. B. Jones, M.D. P.S. Would you kindly tell your secretary that there is only one *t* in *dirty* and no *c* in *skunk.*"

11. THE LOCUS CLASSICUS
The pastor got up at the beginning of the huge stewardship rally, held his hands up for silence, and said, "Friends, I have a marvelous announcement to make about our building fund and our stewardship program for the coming year." He paused for the import of his opening remark to sink in. He then added with dramatic phrasing, "Friends, we have the money!" A buzz of excitement went through the congregation. He held up his hands for quiet once again. He finished, "Yes, we have all the money we need. Now all we have to do is give it!"

12. THE CHURCH OF ALL TITHERS
Dr. Hugh McKean of Chiengmai, Thailand, tells of a church of four hundred members where every member tithes. They receive a weekly wage of forty stangs [less than twenty cents] and their rice. Of this meager existence, each gives a tenth every week. Because of this, they have done more for Christ in Thailand than any other church. They pay their own preacher and have sent two missionary families to spread the gospel in a community cut off from the outside world. They are intensely interested in all forms of Christian work, especially work for unfortunates of every kind; and their gifts for this kind of work are large. They have not only accepted Christ, but, having found Him good, they are making Him known to others. Oh, by the way, this church of all tithers is also a church of all lepers—every person has leprosy.

13. TITHING AND TRUSTING
A church member was having trouble with the concept of tithing. One day he revealed his doubts to his minister: "Pastor, I just don't see how I can give 10 percent of my income to the church when I can't even keep on top of our bills."

The pastor replied, "John, if I promise to make up the difference in your bills if you should fall short, do you think you could try tithing for just one month?"

After a moment's pause, John responded, "Sure, if you promise to make up any shortage, I guess I could try tithing for one month."

"Now, what do you think of that," mused the pastor. "You say you'd be willing to put your trust in a mere man like myself, who possesses so little materially, but you couldn't trust your Heavenly Father who owns the whole universe!" The next Sunday, John gave his tithe, and has been doing so faithfully ever since.

14. ONLY FIFTY-SEVEN PENNIES

Fifty-seven pennies that were found under a little girl's pillow when she died left their mark on Philadelphia. The girl wanted to enter a little Sunday school in Philadelphia years ago, and was told that there was not enough room. She began saving her pennies to "help the Sunday school have more room."

Two years later she became ill and died, and they found a small pocket book under her pillow with fifty-seven pennies and a piece of paper that had the following note written very neatly: "To help build the Little Temple bigger, so more children can go to Sunday school."

The pastor told the story to his congregation, and the newspaper took the story across the country. Soon the pennies grew, and the outcome can be seen in Philadelphia today. There is a church which will seat 3,300 persons, a Temple University which accommodates thousands of students, a Temple Hospital, and a large Temple Sunday school. And it all began with a beautiful, dedicated spirit—and fifty-seven pennies.

It takes concern and commitment and dedication and love to give one's self. In the words of Jesus at the conclusion of the parable of the Good Samaritan: "Go thou and do likewise."

15. DOES YOUR GIFT REPRESENT YOU?

It happened one time after a pastor had made an appeal in church for a great and worthy cause, that a certain woman, a member of the church, came to him and handed him a check for $50, asking at the same time if her gift was satisfactory. The pastor immediately replied, "If it represents you."

There was a moment of soul-searching thought and she asked to have the check returned to her. She left with it and a day or two later she returned handing the pastor a check for $5,000 and again asked the same question, "Is my gift satisfactory?" The pastor gave the same answer as before, "If it represents you." As before, a truth seemed to be driving deeply. After a few moments of hesitation she took back the check and left.

Later in the week she came again with a check. That time it was for $50,000. As she placed it in the pastor's hand, she said, "After earnest, prayerful thought, I have come to the conclusion that this gift does represent me and I am happy to give it."

Perhaps in this light the words from 1 Corinthians 16:2, "as God hath prospered him," may take on new meaning. JOHN ALLAN LAVENDER

16. DON'T BE CHEAP WITH THE SEED

While in Canada, I visited one believer who operated a large grain farm. His spread included some twenty-five hundred acres. I asked him how he planted the seed. He reached in a bin and pulled out an ear of corn. Then he proceeded to pop out the kernels one by one as he walked along, demonstrating the planting process. Do you believe that?

No, sir! That's not what he said nor is it what he did. He showed me a distributor that was some thirty feet wide. "We take that double tandem truck, fill it with certified seed, back it up to the distributor, open the slots, and pour in the seed." He went on to say, "If you're ever going to be cheap, *don't be cheap with the seed.*"

One bushel of seed invested yields thirty bushels of grain harvested in a good year. Thirty to one—not a bad return, if you are ready to believe and willing to invest. God says, "Believe Me, trust Me, try My plan, prove My ways, and see the kind of harvest I will give." So Paul guarantees this principle of truth in the Scripture with the promise, "And God is able to make all grace abound toward you; that ye, always having all sufficiency in all things, may abound to every good work" (2 Corinthians 9:8).

All grace, all ways, all sufficiency, all things! There are four promises in one breath. Knowing it is one thing, believing it is quite another. JACK EXUM

17. THE PASTOR'S INVOLVEMENT WITH STEWARDSHIP

A man called at the church and asked if he could speak to the Head Hog at the Trough. The secretary said, "Who?"

The man replied, "I want to speak to the Head Hog at the Trough!"

Sure now that she had heard correctly, the secretary said, "Sir, if you mean our pastor, you will have to treat him with more respect—and ask for 'The Reverend' or 'The Pastor.' But certainly you cannot refer to him as the Head Hog at the Trough!"

At this, the man came back, "Oh, I see. Well, I have ten thousand dollars I was thinking about donating to the Building Fund."

Secretary: "Hold the line—I think the Big Pig just walked in the door."

18. DEBT COLLECTORS

The pastor responded to a member: "You say you can't give to the church because you owe everyone. Don't you feel that you owe the Lord something?" The member responded: "Yes, of course I do. But He isn't pushing me like the others."

19. TALK ABOUT MONEY
I have never felt any hesitation in speaking to my congregation about money. . . . I thrill to it. I revel in it. I love to see the liberal enjoy it. I love to watch the stingy suffer. CLOVIS G. CHAPPELL

20. WESLEY ON STEWARDSHIP
When the Possessor of heaven and earth brought you into being and placed you in this world, He placed you here not as an owner but as a steward—as such He entrusted you for a season with goods of various kinds—but the sole property of these still rests in Him, nor can ever be alienated from Him. As you are not your own but His, such is likewise all you enjoy. JOHN WESLEY

ONE HUNDRED
TWENTY-SIX
Stubbornness

1. TOO LATE
Sign on the desk of an airline executive in Chicago: "Don't bother to agree with me, I've already changed my mind."

2. YOU CAN'T GET HERE FROM THERE
A summer visitor was asking a local farmer how to get off Southport Island in Maine and find his way back to Boothbay Harbor. The farmer began to explain how to find the road back to the bridge. The visitor insisted, "But I didn't cross any bridge to get here." The farmer looked at him skeptically and replied, "Well, now, if you didn't cross any bridge, then you ain't here in the first place, so you got nothing to worry about."

3. DEFINITELY GRAPE JUICE
There was this teetotaling mother who was very vocal from time to time about her theory that only grape juice—not wine—was served at the Last Supper. During one of these discussions her daughter said: "But mother, don't you remember at Cana Jesus turned the water into wine?" The mother, eyes blazing, said, "Yes! And He *never* should have done it either!"

4. UNENDING LOGIC

After a lecture on the solar system, philosopher William James was approached by a determined elderly lady with a theory. "We don't live on a ball rotating around the sun," she said. "We live on a crust of earth on the back of a giant turtle." James decided to be gentle. "If your theory is correct, madam, what does this turtle stand on?" "The first turtle stands on the back of a second, far larger, turtle, of course." "But what does this turtle stand on?" The old lady crowed triumphantly. "It's no use, Mr. James—it's turtles all the way down!"

5. SMALL CHANGE

One of the early novels of William Thackeray first appeared as a serial in a magazine. After a few chapters had been published, the novelist was summoned to the editor's office.

The editor said, "Our readers are becoming impatient for the hero to marry the heroine."

Thackeray answered, "I have no plans for them to marry. It would weaken the plot."

But the editor came back strongly, "Nevertheless, I think they should marry."

It was obviously more a command than a suggestion and Thackeray, who was financially trapped, was in no position to debate the subject.

He said, "If you insist, I'll marry them in the next episode. But," he added, "I cannot guarantee that it will be a happy marriage."

6. HEARING PROBLEM OR HARDHEADEDNESS?

One of the most frustrating conversations in theatrical history is recorded by *Theatre Arts* magazine: A subscriber dialed "Information" for the magazine's number. "Sorry," drawled the lady, "but there is nobody listed by the name of 'Theodore Arts.'" The subscriber insisted: "It's not a person; it's a publication. I want Theatre Arts." The operator's voice rose a few decibels. She repeated, "I told you, we have no listing for Theodore Arts." By now the subscriber was hollering, "Confound it, the word is Theatre: T-H-E-A-T-R-E!" The operator came back with crushing finality: "That—is not the way to spell Theodore."

ONE HUNDRED
TWENTY-SEVEN

Success

(*See also Failure*)

1. GLYME'S FORMULA

The secret of success is sincerity. Once you can fake that you've got it made.
MICHAEL MEANEY

2. THE BIG SECRET

J. Paul Getty's formula: "Rise early, work late, and strike oil!"

3. THE MAN WE WANT

When Mike Kollin was a linebacker for the Dolphins and a graduate of
Auburn University, his former college coach, Shug Jordan, asked him if he
would do some recruiting for him. Mike said, "Sure, coach. What kind of
player are you looking for?"

The coach said, "Well, Mike, you know there's that fellow, you knock him
down, he just stays down?" Mike said, "We don't want him, do we, coach?"

"No, that's right. Then there's that fellow, you knock him down and he
gets up, but you knock him down again and he stays down."

Mike answered, "We don't want him either, do we, coach?"

Coach said, "No, but Mike, there's a fellow, you knock him down, he gets
up. Knock him down, he gets up. Knock him down, he gets up. Knock him
down, he gets up."

Mike said, "That's the guy we want, isn't it, coach?"

The coach answered, "No, we don't want him either. I want you to find
that guy who's knocking everybody down. That's the guy we want!"

4. GREENER GRASS

Two disillusioned college presidents were discussing what they'd do if they
had their lives to live over. One said, "I'd like to run an orphanage—no
parents to contend with." The other said, "I'd rather run a penitentiary, no
alumni pressure groups."

5. GREATNESS, REAL GREATNESS

We who sit in history's bleachers are inclined to confuse fame with greatness.
We seem willing to let the press, television, and radio determine whom we
shall call great. Prominence, however, is a poor yardstick with which to
measure greatness.

If one would know the truth, he must pull the pedestal out from under the man and see what is left. Many of the men we place on pedestals would stand tall without the pedestal. And many whom we never think of in terms of pedestals deserve the accolade of greatness.

It has been said that that nation is proudest and noblest and most exalted which has the greatest number of really great men and women—not just those whom it honors, but also the "anonymous" great, the citizens who, in their little bailiwicks, live exemplary lives—the kind it would be wonderful if all of us lived. These are the persons James Russell Lowell had in mind when he wrote:

The wisest man could ask no more of Fate
Than to be simple, modest, manly, true,
Safe from the Many, honored by the Few:
To count as naught in World, or Church, or State:
But inwardly in secret to be great.

6. A LITTLE FAILURE
If you're not failing now and again, it's a sign you're playing it safe.
WOODY ALLEN

7. FIGURING THE PROFIT
A small businessman from the old country kept his accounts payable in a cigar box, his accounts receivable on a spindle, and his cash in the cash register. His son said, "I don't see how you can run your business this way. How do you know what your profits are?" The businessman replied, "Son, when I got off the boat, I had only the pants I was wearing. Today your sister is an art teacher, your brother is a doctor, and you're an accountant. I have a car, a home, and a good business. Everything is paid for. So you add it all up, subtract the pants, and there's your profit.

8. SMELL OF SUCCESS
Like perfume, success is to be sniffed, not taken internally.
RUSS REID, *Eternity*

9. IT MAKES SENSE, SORT OF
An old storekeeper, who was also the community's postmaster, was a real go-getter. He had no helper, and when he had to leave his store to meet the mail train, he was tormented by thoughts of tourists stopping for gas and soft drinks, and finding him gone and his store closed. Finally he hit upon a shrewd solution. He printed a sign in bold letters which explained everything during his enforced absences: Back in 15 minutes—Already been gone 10.

10. LOOK THE PART
The greatest help to a man struggling to succeed is to look as if he has already succeeded.

11. HELPING OUT
You can't help a man uphill without getting closer to the top yourself.

12. SUCCESS AND FAILURE
If you really want to succeed, form the habit of doing the things that people who are failures don't like to do.

13. SPORTS AND POLITICS
In 1930 Babe Ruth earned eighty thousand dollars—a huge sum in those days. When asked if he thought it was fair that he receive more than President Hoover, he said, "Well, I had a better year."

14. THE SECRET OF SUCCESS
Sam Findley decided it was time to retire from the garment business. So he called in his son Mervyn and gave him the news and a bit of advice: "Son, it's all yours. I've made a success of this business because of two principles: reliability and wisdom. First, take reliability. If you promise goods by the tenth of the month, no matter what happens, you must deliver by the tenth. Even if it costs you overtime, double time, golden time. You deliver what you promise."

Mervyn thought about this for a few moments and then asked. "But what about wisdom?" His father shot back: "Wisdom is never making such a stupid promise."

15. THE GREAT CONTRAST
Success breeds a thousand parents, failure is an orphan.
Film producer STEPHEN SPIELBERG

16. DRIFTING
Following the path of least resistance is what makes people and rivers crooked. People seldom drift to success.

17. THE MATH THAT COUNTS
On the occasion of the twentieth anniversary of their graduation some college alumni were gathered for a class reunion. They were scattered about in little groups, reminiscing about college days. In one group the conversation turned to a classmate they all remembered named Harvey. The thing they remembered most about Harvey was that whenever he was asked what he was going to do after graduation he always replied, "I'm going to be a millionaire." Harvey always expected he would make his millions. But another

thing they remembered about Harvey was that he was one of the slowest students in their class intellectually. And he was especially poor in mathematics. Here was a man who expected to make millions, but he could hardly add up a column of figures.

As the members of the group were exchanging Harvey stories, up pulled a brand new, chauffeur-driven Rolls Royce and out stepped Harvey wearing an expensive, tailor-made, three-piece suit and everything that went with it. His classmates quickly gathered around him and began throwing questions at him. "Hey, Harvey, where did you get that car? Harvey! Wow! What happened? How did you do it?"

Harvey said, "Well, you see, I came upon an invention that costs me only five dollars to manufacture and I sell it for one hundred dollars. And you'd be surprised how fast that 10 percent profit adds up!"

18. THE IMPORTANCE OF LITTLE EXTRAS

We had just moved into a new apartment and were besieged by salesmen for everything from laundry service to life insurance. One busy day a dairyman came to the door. "No," I said firmly, "my husband and I don't drink milk."

"Be glad to deliver a quart every morning for cooking."

"That's more than I need," I replied, starting to close the door.

"Well, ma'am, how about some cream? Berries comin' in now, and ..."

"No," I said curtly, "we never use cream."

The dairyman retired slowly, and I congratulated myself on my sales resistance. The truth was that I had already ordered from a dairy, and this seemed to be the easiest way out. The following morning, however, the same dairyman appeared at the door, a bowl of dewy strawberries held carefully in one hand and a half-pint bottle of cream in the other.

"Lady," he said, as he poured the cream over the berries and handed them to me, "I got to thinkin'—you sure have missed a lot!" Needless to say, we changed dairies.

19. THE LION'S SHARE

Eighty percent of success is showing up. WOODY ALLEN

20. LOSING LESS

The scene was the campus of the University of Florida in the early 1960s. The football team was in practice session. They were running wind sprints for conditioning. One of the large linemen, Jack Katz, who played tackle, had proven himself to be the fastest lineman on the team. Katz walked up to coach Ray Graves and asked if he might run sprints with the faster backs. Permission was granted.

For the next several days Katz managed to finish last in every race with the backfield runners. Nobody was surprised. The coach asked if he wouldn't rather be a winner with the linemen than a loser in the competition with the backs.

Katz responded, "I'm not out here to outrun the linemen. I already know I can do that. I'm here to learn how to run faster; and if you've noticed, I'm losing by a little less every day."

21. SUCCESS VERSUS FAILURE

The difference between success and failure is that successful people make themselves do what they hate to do and failures wait for their managers to make them do it, or to do it for them. CHARLIE "TREMENDOUS" JONES

22. HISTORY OF REJECTION

British novelist John Creasey has published 564 books. But he didn't make his first sale until after he'd received 774 rejection slips.

23. MOTHER TERESA

Mother Teresa of Calcutta once was asked, "How do you measure the success of your work?" She looked puzzled for a moment and then replied, "I don't remember that the Lord ever spoke of success. He spoke only of faithfulness in love. This is the only success that really counts."

24. LOOKING AHEAD

When architect Frank Lloyd Wright was asked at age eighty-three which of his works he would select as his masterpiece, he replied, "My next one!"

25. THE SECRET

Paul Harvey said, "Someday, I hope to enjoy enough of what the world calls success so that if somebody asks me, 'What's the secret of it?' I shall say this: 'I get up when I fall down.'"

26. SELF-ENCOURAGEMENT

A young boy walked into a drugstore and asked to use the telephone. He asked the operator to give him a certain number: "Hello, Dr. Anderson . . . do you want to hire a boy to cut the grass and run errands for you? Oh, you already have a boy? Are you completely satisfied with the boy you have? OK then, good-bye, Doctor."

As the boy thanked the druggist, the druggist said: "Just a minute, Son. . . . If you are looking for work, I could use a boy like you."

"Thank you, sir, but I have a job," the boy replied.

"But didn't I just hear you trying to get a job from Dr. Anderson?"

"No, sir," said the boy, "you see, I'm the boy who is working for Dr. Anderson. I was just checking up on myself."

27. MAKING THE PORT
To reach the port of success we must sail, sometimes with the wind and sometimes against it—but we must sail, not drift or lie at anchor.
OLIVER WENDELL HOLMES

28. NOT BY CHANCE
Success doesn't happen. It is organized, preempted, captured by concentrated common sense. FRANCES E. WILLARD

29. THE MARK OF SUCCESS
You are not really successful until someone claims he sat beside you in school.

30. 57 RULES FOR SUCCESS
First, deliver the goods. Second, the other fifty-six do not matter.

31. THE BEST MOTIVATION
Try not to become a man of success but rather try to become a man of value.
ALBERT EINSTEIN

32. TECHNIQUES FOR DAILY SUCCESS
We all need to be reminded from time to time about the basics of getting through the work that is before us. Debra Smith presented these seven classic techniques for daily success at a Time Management seminar sponsored by the Dible Management Development Seminar people (yes, that's Dible, not Bible). They are:
1. Complete daily priorities—central concerns and essentials first.
2. Group together related activities in order to save time as well as create more time.
3. Divide big tasks into workable steps which also helps to maintain confidence.
4. Always construct a timetable.
5. For maximum results, concentrate on and complete one step at a time.
6. To maintain a high energy level, finish each task fully.
7. To prevent procrastination—"do it now."

33. INCLINED TO SUCCEED
You can tell when you're on the right track—it's usually uphill.

SUFFERING *(See Adversity)*

ONE HUNDRED
TWENTY-EIGHT
Tact and Diplomacy

1. A THIN LINE
Tact is the art of making a point without making an enemy.

2. THE DIFFICULTY OF BEING RIGHT
A passenger on a dining car looked over the luncheon menu. The list included both a chicken salad sandwich and a chicken sandwich. He decided on the chicken salad sandwich, but absentmindedly wrote chicken sandwich on the order slip. When the waiter brought the chicken sandwich the customer angrily protested. Most waiters would have immediately picked up the order slip and shown the customer that the mistake was his. This waiter didn't. Instead, expressing regret at the error, he picked up the chicken sandwich, returned to the kitchen, and a moment later placed the chicken salad sandwich in front of the customer. While eating his sandwich the customer picked up the order slip and saw that the mistake was his. When it came time to pay the check the man apologized to the waiter and offered to pay for both sandwiches. The waiter's response was, "No, sir. That's perfectly all right. I'm just happy you've forgiven me for being right."

3. THE ART OF APOLOGIZING
It takes real talent to be able to apologize in a manner that makes the offended person feel guilty.

4. SAYING IT NICELY
Firing an employee is one of the toughest jobs a supervisor ever faces. An insurance sales manager was known for his tact and diplomacy. One of his young salesmen was performing so poorly that he had to be terminated. The manager called him in and said, "Son, I don't know how we're ever going to get along without you, but starting Monday we're going to try."

5. DIPLOMACY FROM THE GROUND UP
A young man was applying for a job as clerk in a shoe store. The store owner asked him, "Suppose that a lady customer asked you, 'Don't you think one of my feet is bigger than the other?' What would you say?" The young man

responded promptly, "I'd say, 'Oh, no ma'am! If anything, one is a little smaller than the other.'"

Talk

(See also Communication, Gossip)

1. RARE RESTRAINT
Albert Einstein had a wholesome disregard for the tyranny of custom. Once as a guest of honor at a dinner given for him by the president of Swarthmore College he was called on for a speech. He said, "Ladies and gentlemen, I am very sorry but I have nothing to say" and sat down. A few seconds later he stood back up and said, "In case I do have something to say, I'll come back." Six months later he wired the president of the college with the message: "Now I have something to say." Another dinner was held and Einstein made a speech.

2. FEELING IMPORTANT
The secret of making another person feel important is to tell him a secret. He will feel important when he shares it with someone else.

3. BENEFIT OF APOLOGY
An apology is a good way to have the last word.

4. A WISE RULE
If your mind should go blank, don't forget to turn off the sound.

5. SO MUCH JARGON
Teachers never seem to put down kids anymore. A young lad had a notation on his report card that he was very adept in the creative use of visual aids for learning. His father called up his teacher and said, "What does that mean— 'the creative use of visual aids'?" Teacher: "That means he copies from the kid in the next seat."

6. THE RIGHT NOT TO
As precious as the right to speak is the right not to listen.

7. ROLE OF THE MOUTH
Maybe the eyes are the windows of the soul—but that still doesn't make the mouth the door to the brain.

8. TALKING CEASED
If nobody ever said anything unless he knew what he was talking about, a ghastly hush would descend upon the earth. SIR ALAN HERBERT

9. SILENCE IS GOLDEN
The unspoken word never defeats one. What one does not say does not have to be explained. SAM RAYBURN

10. A TIP ON STYLE
No one is exempt from talking nonsense; the misfortune is to do it solemnly. MONTAIGNE

11. QUIET COMMUNICATION
Silence need not be awkward or embarrassing, for to be with one you love, without the need for words, is a beautiful and satisfying form of communication.

I remember times when our children used to come running to me, all of them chattering at once about the events of their day—and it was wonderful to have them share their feelings with me. But there were also the times when they came to me wanting only to be held, to have me stroke their heads and caress them into sleep. And so it is, sometimes, with us and with God our Father. COLLEEN TOWNSEND EVANS

12. TRUE CONVERSATION
No man would listen to you talk if he didn't know it was his turn next. ED HOWE

13. DISCUSSION AS CONFIRMATION
Discussion is a method of confirming others in their errors. AMBROSE BIERCE

14. BURIED TALENT
A hotheaded woman told John Wesley, "My talent is to speak my mind." Replied Mr. Wesley, "Woman, God wouldn't care a bit if you would bury that talent."

15. VANITY
We often say things because we can say them well, rather than because they are sound and reasonable. WALTER SAVAGE LANDOR

474

16. PENN'S RULES OF CONVERSATION

Avoid company where it is not profitable or necessary, and in those occasions, speak little, and last. Silence is wisdom where speaking is folly, and always safe. Some are so foolish as to interrupt and anticipate those that speak instead of hearing and thinking before they answer, which is uncivil, as well as silly. If thou thinkest twice before thou speakest once, thou wilt speak twice the better for it. Better to say nothing than not to the purpose. And to speak pertinently, consider both what is fit, and when it is fit, to speak. In all debates, let truth be thy aim, not victory or an unjust interest; and endeavor to gain, rather than to expose, thy antagonist. WILLIAM PENN

17. REAL POWER

Empty barrels make the loudest noises, but the full ones silently crush one's toes. PAUL ELDRIDGE

18. THE TONGUE

"The boneless tongue, so small and weak,
Can crush and kill," declares the Greek.
"The tongue destroys a greater horde,"
The Turk asserts, "than does the sword."
The Persian proverb wisely saith,
"A lengthy tongue—an early death!"
Or sometimes takes this form instead,
"Don't let your tongue cut off your head."
"The tongue can speak a word whose speed,"
Say the Chinese, "outstrips the steed."
The Arab sages said in part,
"The tongue's great storehouse is the heart."
From Hebrew was the maxim sprung,
"Thy feet should slip, but ne'er the tongue."
The sacred writer crowns the whole,
"Who keeps the tongue doth keep his soul."

19. PRESENTING THE EVIDENCE

Blessed is the man who, having nothing to say, abstains from giving wordy evidence of the fact. GEORGE ELIOT

20. SILENCE IN VARIOUS MODES

A tribute was once paid to a great linguist, that he not only had learned seven languages well—but he had also learned when to be silent in all seven.

21. HOW TO SAVE FACE
Saving face is often accomplished by keeping the lower part of it shut.

22. CONVERSATIONAL GRACE
An attractive woman was taken to dinner one night by William E. Gladstone, the distinguished British statesman. The next evening she attended a dinner where she sat next to Benjamin Disraeli, his equally distinguished opponent. Asked her opinion of the two men, she replied thoughtfully: "When I left the dining room after sitting with Mr. Gladstone, I thought he was the cleverest man in England. But after sitting next to Mr. Disraeli, I thought I was the cleverest woman in England."

23. TOO GOOD TO KEEP
Some secrets are worth keeping. Others are too good to keep.

24. THE REAL SPARKLER
A gossip is one who talks to you about other people. A bore is one who talks to you about himself. And a brilliant conversationalist is one who talks to you about yourself. WILLIAM KING

25. TAKING A STAND
Learn to say no; it will be of more use to you than to be able to read Latin. CHARLES H. SPURGEON

26. VIRTUE OF SILENCE
A closed mouth gathers no feet.

27. NOTHING TO SAY
There is nothing wrong with having nothing to say—unless you insist on saying it.

TEENAGERS *(See Youth)*

ONE HUNDRED THIRTY
Temptation

1. DEALING WITH TEMPTATION
There are several good protections against temptation, but the surest is a cowardly response to the fact that you might get caught.

2. PERSISTENT KNOCKING
Why is it that opportunity knocks only once, yet temptation bangs on the door constantly?

3. EVER NOTICE?
Ever notice that the whisper of temptation can be heard farther than the loudest call to duty? EARL WILSON

4. THE READY MEANS
Have you noticed that when we decide to do something wrong the means are so readily available?

5. THE MASTER IS ALWAYS IN
The father of a small boy would occasionally sneak into a neighbor's orchard and pluck some of the choicest fruit. He always made sure, however, that "the coast was clear." One day with his son tagging along, after carefully looking in every direction and seeing no one, he crept through the fence. He was just about ready to help himself when the youngster startled him by crying out, "Dad! Dad! You didn't look UP! You forgot to see if God is watching." When temptation besets you and you're inclined to yield because no one else seems to be around, remember, if you're a Christian, your "Master is always in!"

ONE HUNDRED
THIRTY-ONE
Time

1. SURE-FIRE TIMEPIECE
Victor Borge told a friend that he could tell time by his piano. His friend was incredulous, so Borge volunteered to demonstrate. He pounded out a crashing march. Immediately there came a banging on the wall and a shrill voice screamed, "Stop that noise. Don't you know it's 1:30 in the morning?"

2. NEWS TOO LATE
A man had a checkup and then went in to see his doctor to get the results. The doctor said he had bad news and worse news for him, which did he want to hear first? The man was a bit nonplussed and said he'd rather hear

the bad news first. The doctor said, "The bad news is that you only have twenty-four hours to live."

At this the man jumped up, totally flabbergasted and distraught. He paced the doctor's office and complained, "Twenty-four hours to live? I can't possibly get my affairs in order that quickly. I can't believe this, it is incredible! What could be worse news than this?"

The doctor said, "The worse news is that I was supposed to tell you this yesterday but I forgot."

3. CYNICAL VIEW OF HISTORY
History is an account, mostly false, of events, mostly unimportant, which are brought about by rulers, mostly knaves, and soldiers, mostly fools.
AMBROSE BIERCE

4. FILL THE SPACES
Select a large box, and place in it as many cannon balls as it will hold, and it is, after a fashion, full; but it will hold more if smaller matters be found. Bring a quantity of marbles; very many of these may be packed in the spaces between the larger globes; the box is now full, but still only in a sense; it will contain more yet. There are spaces in abundance, into which you may shake a considerable quantity of small shot, and now the chest is filled beyond all question; but yet there is room. You cannot put in another shot or marble, much less another ball; but you will find that several pounds of sand will slide down between the larger materials, and even then between the granules of sand; if you empty yonder jug, there will be space for all the water and for the same quantity several times repeated. Where there is no space for the great, there may be room for the little; where the little cannot enter, the less can make its way; and where the less is shut out, the least of all may find ample room. So where time is, as we say, fully occupied, there must be stray moments, occasional intervals, and bits of time which might hold a vast amount of little usefulness in the course of months and years.
CHARLES H. SPURGEON

5. WAITING FOR FAME
Millions long for immortality who do not know what to do with themselves on a rainy Sunday afternoon. SUSAN ERTZ

6. TIMING IS EVERYTHING
It isn't what you know that counts; it's what you can think of in time.

7. HURRY!
An insurance agent received a phone call from an excited woman. "I want to insure my house," she said. "Can I do it by phone?" "I'm sorry," answered

the man, "but I'd have to see it first." "Then you'd better get here right away," exclaimed the woman, "because the place is on fire!"

8. SLOW DOWN

A woman who had been living a very high-pressured life moved with her family from the city to the country. The family had resolved to reduce the stresses and tensions that they had been under by entering into a gentler, easier life-style. A neighbor called on the mother one day and noticed something that had been pinned on the family bulletin board. She asked about it and the mother said, "Oh, that's a poem that represents what our moving here was all about. The poem starts out, 'Lord, slow me down . . .' But I haven't had time to read the rest of it."

ONE HUNDRED
THIRTY-TWO

Trust

1. LIFT UP YOUR HEAD

When my son was a toddler, washing his hair was always a problem. He would sit in the bathtub while I put shampoo on his hair. Then, when I poured on the water to make a lather, he would tip his head down so that the shampoo ran into his eyes, causing pain and tears. I explained that if he just looked straight up at me, he could avoid getting the shampoo in his face. He would agree; then, as soon as I started to rinse his hair, his fear would overcome his trust, and he would look down again. Naturally the shampoo would run into his face again, and there would be more tears.

During one of our sessions, while I was trying to convince him to lift up his head and trust me, I suddenly realized how this situation was like my relationship to God. I know God is my Father, and I'm sure He loves me. I believe that I trust Him, but sometimes, in a difficult situation, I panic and turn my eyes away from Him. This never solves the problem; I just become more afraid, as the "shampoo" blinds me.

Even though my son knew I loved him, he had a hard time trusting me in a panicky situation. I knew I could protect him, but convincing him of that wasn't easy, especially when all he could see was water coming down. His lack of trust hurt me, but it hurt him more. He was the one who had to suffer the pain. I'm sure my lack of trust hurts God very much, but how much more does it hurt me?

Often in the Bible, we are told to lift up our head to God when problems come. He knows how to protect us if we remember to listen to Him. Now, when I find myself in a situation where it would be easy to panic, I picture my son sitting in the bathtub, looking up at me, learning to trust me. Then I ask God what I should do. Sometimes the answer may seem scary, but, one thing I'm sure of—He'll never pour shampoo in my face! JEANETTE STRONG

2. IN A LONELY PLACE
What is more lonely than distrust?

3. SECOND OPINION
A tourist came to close to the edge of the Grand Canyon, lost his footing and plunged over the side, clawing and scratching to save himself. After he went out of sight and just before he fell into space, he encountered a scrubby bush which he desperately grabbed with both hands. Filled with terror, he called out toward heaven, "Is there anyone up there?" A calm, powerful voice came out of the sky, "Yes, there is." The tourist pleaded, "Can you help me? Can you help me?" The calm voice replied, "Yes, I probably can. What is your problem?" "I fell over the cliff and am dangling in space holding to a bush that is about to let go. Please help me." "The voice from above said, "I'll try. Do you believe?" "Yes, yes, I believe!" "Do you have faith?" "Yes, yes. I have strong faith." The calm voice said, "Well, in that case, simply let loose of the bush and everything will turn out fine." There was a tense pause, then the tourist yelled, "Is there anyone else up there?"

4. SAFE IN HIS HANDS
There is an old ploughman in the country I sometimes talk with, and he often says, though in uncouth words, some precious things. He said to me one day, "The other day, sir, the Devil was tempting me and I tried to answer him; but I found he was an old lawyer and understood the law a great deal better than I did, so I gave over and would not argue with him any more; so I said to him, 'What do you trouble me for?' 'Why,' said he, 'about your soul.' 'Oh!' said I, 'that is no business of mine; I have given my soul over into the hand of Christ; I have transferred everything to him; if you want an answer to your doubts and queries, you must apply to my Advocate.'" CHARLES H. SPURGEON

5. TRUST, QUALIFIED
Trust everybody, but cut the cards.

ONE HUNDRED
THIRTY-THREE
Truth
(See also Honesty)

1. DISTORTION
Get your facts first, and then you can distort them as much as you please.
MARK TWAIN

2. HEAD AND HEART
We arrive at the truth not by reason alone, but also by the heart.
BLAISE PASCAL

3. SOUND REASONS
The soundest reasoning leads to the wrongest conclusions when the premises
are false. VILHJALMUR STEFANSSON

4. COMMUNICATING IDEAS
You may treat ideas as bullets . . . or seeds! You may shoot ideas . . . or you
may sow them! You may hit people in the head with them, or you may plant
them in their hearts. Use them as bullets, they kill inspiration and neutralize
motivation. Use them as seeds, they take root, grow, and become a reality in
the life in which they are planted. The only risk taken when seeds are planted
is that they become a part of the one in whom they grow. The originator will
probably get no credit for the idea. If one is willing not to get credit for an
idea, a rich harvest will be reaped. "It is more blessed to give than to
receive." RICHARD C. HALVERSON

5. TRUTH AND THE BETTER LIFE
Honesty of thought and speech and written word is a jewel, and they who
curb prejudice and seek honorably to know and speak the truth are the only
builders of a better life. JOHN GALSWORTHY

6. PRECIOUS TRUTH
Most writers regard the truth as their most valuable possession, and therefore
are most economical in its use. MARK TWAIN

7. COMMUNICATING TRUTH
It takes two to speak the truth—one to speak and another to hear.
HENRY DAVID THOREAU

8. THE BEAUTY OF IT

Truth is beautiful, without doubt; but so are lies. RALPH WALDO EMERSON

9. TRUTH AS THE IRREDUCIBLE MINIMUM

Ian Pitt-Watson, professor at Fuller Theological Seminary, said: "I heard a silly story about an elderly Scottish couple who had never flown before, but who decided they going to visit their children in New York and see their grandchildren for the first time. They were on a charter flight in a Lockheed TriStar. They were about halfway out over the Atlantic when their pilot's voice came over the intercom: 'This is your captain speaking. Ladies and gentlemen, I feel I ought to let you know that one of our three engines has failed. There is, of course, no need for alarm. This plane is entirely airworthy flying on two engines, but I regret to say we will be one hour late in arriving in New York.'

"Half an hour later, inevitably, with that desperate calm that is reserved by air pilots and astronauts for conditions of extreme emergency, the pilot of the TriStar spoke again: 'This is your captain speaking. I regret that we have lost the second of our engines. But I would like to reassure you that we have every expectation of making a normal and safe landing at JFK Airport. We shall, however, be three hours late in arriving.'

"At this, Grandma turned to Grandpa with a hint of irritation in her voice and said, 'My dear, if that third engine goes—we shall be up here all night.'"

10. FRAGILE

Truth is like fine china: It can be broken. It can be mended. But it can never be the same again.

11. FACE THE TRUTH, WARTS AND ALL

Are we disposed to be of the number of those who, having eyes, see not, and having ears, hear not the things which so nearly concern their temporal salvation? For my part, whatever anguish of spirit it might cost, I am willing to know the whole truth, to know the worst, and to provide for it.
PATRICK HENRY

12. TRUTH AND ERROR

There has long been debate as to which is the speedier, truth or error; which spreads faster, false report or denial. Some have maintained that truth has sturdier and surer wings. Others contend that fiction and careless rumor find more willing tongues to speed them on their way. Long ago, Tacitus, the Roman historian, gave his judgment in these words: "Truth is confirmed by inspection and delay: falsehood by haste and uncertainty."

13. FACING THE HARSH TRUTH

A popular comic strip is "Momma" by Mel Lazarus. One of his strips shows
Momma entertaining her perpetual suitor, Mr. K. Frankly, he's not much of a
catch, but he is persistent. As the two sit on the couch, Mr. K. says, "Mrs.
Hobbs, I am at a low ebb, psychologically. My ego is flattened." Mrs. Hobbs
responds in an affirming way, "Mr. K., let me hasten to state that you're a
fine, interesting and attractive man."

Mr. K. perks up at this and asks, "Oh, Mrs. Hobbs, is that the truth?"

Mrs. Hobbs says, "No. There'll be plenty of time for the truth when
you're emotionally stronger."

14. UNCHANGING REALITY

Lincoln was trying to make a point. His hearer was unconvinced and
stubborn. So Lincoln tried another tack. He said to the disputer, "Well, let's
see now. How many legs does a cow have?" The disgusted reply came back
"Four, of course." Lincoln agreed, "That's right. Now, suppose you call the
cow's tail a leg; how many legs would the cow have?" The opponent replied
confidently, "Why, five, of course." Lincoln came back, "Now that's where
you're wrong. Calling a cow's tail a leg doesn't make it a leg!"

15. APPROPRIATE TO SPEAK

The commandment tells us to speak truthfully whenever it is appropriate for
us to speak at all. Respect for truthfulness does not compel us to reveal our
minds to everyone or on every occasion. The Ninth Commandment assumes,
no doubt, a situation that calls on us to speak. It does not ask us to tell the
people at the next table in a restaurant that their manners are repulsive. It
does not obligate a nurse to contradict a physician at a sick person's bedside.
Nor does it require me to divulge all of my feelings to a stranger on the bus.
We are called to speak the truth in any situation in which we have a
responsibility to communicate.

Further, the command requires only a revelation that is pertinent to the
situation. A politician ought to speak the truth about public matters as he
sees them; he does not need to tell us how he feels about his wife. A doctor
ought to tell me the truth, as he understands it, about my health; he does not
need to tell me his views on universal health insurance. A minister ought to
preach the truth, as he sees it, about the gospel; he does not need to tell the
congregation what he feels about the choir director. The commandment does
not call us to be garrulous blabbermouths. Truthfulness is demanded from us
about the things that we ought to speak about at all. LEWIS SMEDES, *Mere
Morality*

16. YOUR ATTITUDE TO THE NARROW WAY

Truth is narrow. If we were hiking and came to a wide river, and we learned that there was one bridge, down the river a mile or two, we wouldn't stomp in disgust and moan about how that was such a narrow way to think and that the bridge should be right there, where we were. Instead, thankful that there was a bridge, we would go to it and cross over.

Or consider the following. When we go to the doctor, we want a prescription for exactly what we will need to get well. We would be quite startled if the doctor said, "These pills ought to cure you if you're sincere. After all, we believe in health, don't we?" Or would you trust yourself to a surgeon who had received no specialized training but was simply a really good person who meant well? Of course not! You know that truth is narrow. And you will trust your life only to someone who knows exactly what he or she is doing.

ONE HUNDRED
THIRTY-FOUR

Uniqueness

1. CONSIDERING MYSELF

If I try to be like him, who will be like me? *Russian proverb*

2. THERE'S ALWAYS ONE

We need to treasure our uniqueness. Even those aspects of uniqueness that don't always fit in. I saw this illustrated in a cartoon that showed the foreman of a jury at the door of the jury room giving the lunch order to the bailiff. You know the jury is in for a long time when you hear the order: "Eleven cheeseburgers and one hot dog. Eleven coffees and one hot chocolate. Eleven fruit pies and one prune Danish."

3. SHE THINKS I'M REAL

A waitress was taking orders from a couple and their young son; she was one of the class of veteran waitresses who never show outright disrespect to their customers, but who frequently make it quietly evident by their unhurried pace and their level stare that they fear no mortal, not even parents. She jotted on her order pad deliberately and silently as the father and mother gave their luncheon selection and gratuitous instructions as to what was to be substituted for what, and which dressing changed to what sauce. When she finally turned to the boy, he began his order with a kind of fearful desperation. "I want a hot dog—," he started. And both parents barked at once, "No hot dog!" The mother went on. "Bring him the lyonnaise potatoes and the beef, both vegetables, and a hard roll and—"

The waitress wasn't even listening. She said evenly to the youngster, "What do you want on your hot dog?" He flashed an amazed smile. "Ketchup, lots of ketchup, and—and bring a glass of milk."

"Coming up," she said as she turned from the table, leaving behind her the stunned silence of utter parental dismay. The boy watched her go before he turned to his father and mother with astonished elation to say, "You know what? She thinks I'm real! She thinks I'm real!" FREDERICK B. SPEAKMAN

4. ADMIRE THEIR UNIQUENESS

Once a wise teacher was speaking to a group of eager young students. He gave them the assignment to go out and find a small, unnoticed flower somewhere. He asked them to study the flower for a long time. "Get a magnifying glass and study the delicate veins in the leaves, and notice the nuances and shades of color. Turn the leaves slowly and observe their symmetry. And remember that this flower might have gone unnoticed and unappreciated if you had not found and admired it." After the class returned, the teacher observed, "People are like that. Each one is different, carefully crafted, uniquely endowed. But you have to spend time with them to know this. So many people go unnoticed and unappreciated because no one has ever taken time with them and admired their uniqueness." JOHN POWELL

ONE HUNDRED
THIRTY-FIVE

Vengeance

1. DON'T GET MAD, JUST GET EVEN

Jack's mother ran into the bedroom when she heard him scream and found his two-year-old sister pulling his hair. She gently released the little girl's grip and said comfortingly to Jack, "There, there. She didn't mean it. She doesn't know that hurts." Mom was barely out of the room when the little girl

485

screamed. Rushing back in, she said, "What happened?" "She knows now," little Jack explained.

2. SWEET REVENGE
Abe Lemmons was asked if he was bitter at Texas Athletic Director Deloss Dodds who fired him as the Longhorn's basketball coach. He replied, "Not at all, but I plan to buy a glass-bottomed car so I can watch the look on his face when I run over him."

3. TRUE CLOUT
Three burly fellows on huge motorcycles pulled up to a highway cafe where a truck driver, just a little guy, was perched on a stool quietly eating his lunch. As the three fellows came in, they spotted him, grabbed his food away from him and laughed in his face. The truck driver said nothing. He got up, paid for his food, and walked out. One of the three cyclists, unhappy that they hadn't succeeded in provoking the little man into a fight, commented to the waitress: "Boy, he sure wasn't much of a man, was he?" The waitress replied, "Well, I guess not." Then, looking out the window, she added, "I guess he's not much of a truck driver, either. He just ran over three motorcycles."

4. TOYS FOR REVENGE
If thine enemy wrong thee, buy each of his children a drum.
Old Chinese proverb

WEALTH *(See Materialism)*

ONE HUNDRED
THIRTY-SIX
Wisdom

1. PRUDENT SLEEPERS
It's better to sleep on what you plan to do than to be kept awake by what you've done.

2. SENSIBLE CROSSING
Never insult an alligator until you've crossed the river. CORDELL HULL

3. LOOKING AND ACTING
See everything, overlook a lot, correct a little. POPE JOHN XXIII

4. HIGHER FACULTY
Imagination is more important than knowledge. ALBERT EINSTEIN

5. PROBLEMS AND SOLUTIONS
There is always an easy solution to every human problem—neat, plausible, and wrong. H. L. MENCKEN

6. DANCING BEARS
If you dance with a grizzly bear, you'd better let him lead.

7. PLANNING WELL
He who rides a tiger must make plans for dismounting. WILLIAM R. INGE

8. REPAIR WORK
If it ain't broke, don't fix it. BILLY CARTER

9. PROXIMITY OF DRAGONS
It does not do to leave a live dragon out of your calculations, if you live near him. J. R. R. TOLKIEN

10. RODENT WISDOM
Consider the little mouse, how sagacious an animal it is . . . which never entrusts its life to one hole only.

11. PEACE IN THE STORM
An appeaser is one who feeds a crocodile hoping it will eat him last. WINSTON CHURCHILL

12. FIRST PRIORITY
A young ensign, after nearly completing his first overseas cruise, was given an opportunity to display his capabilities at getting the ship under way. With a stream of commands, he had the decks buzzing with men, and soon the ship was steaming out the channel en route to the states.

His efficiency established a new record for getting a destroyer under way, and he was not surprised when a seaman approached him with a message from the captain. He was a bit surprised, though, to find it a radio message and even more surprised to read: "My personal congratulations upon completing your underway preparation exercise according to the book and with amazing speed. In your haste, however, you have overlooked one of the unwritten rules—make sure the captain is aboard before getting under way."

13. WHO ARE THE WISE MEN?
Who were the Wise Men in the long ago?
Not Herod, fearful lest he lose his throne;
Not Pharisees, too proud to claim their own;

Not priests and scribes whose province was to know;
Not money changers running too and fro;
But three who traveled, weary and alone,
With dauntless faith, because before them shone
The star that led them to a manger low.
Who are the Wise Men now, when all is told?
Not men of science; not the great and strong;
Not those who wear a kingly diadem;
Not those whose eager hands pile high the gold;
But those amid the tumult and the throng
Who follow still the star of Bethlehem.

14. UNFAIR ADVANTAGE
Never wrestle with a pig. You will both get all dirty . . . and the pig likes it.

15. ESOTERIC CHEATING
In Woody Allen's movie *Annie Hall,* Woody has his protagonist say: "I was thrown out of New York University for cheating on a Metaphysics test. The professor caught me looking deeply into the soul of the student seated next to me."

16. SHOPPING FOR A CAR
No one ever got rid of an old car because it ran too well.

17. BALANCE
The archer strikes the target, partly by pulling, partly by letting go.

18. LIMITATIONS
Genius has limits; stupidity does not.

19. NARROW VISION
In the year 1870 the Methodists in Indiana were having their annual conference. At one point, the president of the college where they were meeting said, "I think we live in a very exciting age." The presiding bishop said, "What do you see?" The college president responded, "I believe we are coming into a time of great inventions. I believe, for example, that men will fly through the air like birds." The Bishop said, "This is heresy! The Bible says that flight is reserved for the angels. We will have no such talk here." After the conference, the bishop, whose name was Wright, went home to his two small sons, Wilbur and Orville. And you know what they did to their father's vision.

20. KIND OF A TRUST
Trust in God, but tie your camel. *Persian proverb*

21. THE WISDOM THAT COMES IN CRISIS

There's a true story that comes from the sinking of the *Titanic*. A frightened woman found her place in a lifeboat that was about to be lowered into the raging North Atlantic. She suddenly thought of something she needed, so she asked permission to return to her stateroom before they cast off. She was granted three minutes or they would have to leave without her.

She ran across the deck that was already slanted at a dangerous angle. She raced through the gambling room with all the money that had rolled to one side, ankle deep. She came to her stateroom and quickly pushed aside her diamond rings and expensive bracelets and necklaces as she reached to the shelf above her bed and grabbed three small oranges. She quickly found her way back to the lifeboat and got in.

Now that seems incredible because thirty minutes earlier she would not have chosen a crate of oranges over even the smallest diamond. But death had boarded the *Titanic*. One blast of its awful breath had transformed all values. Instantaneously, priceless things had become worthless. Worthless things had become priceless. And in that moment she preferred three small oranges to a crate of diamonds. CHARLES SWINDOLL

22. MORE IMPORTANT KNOWLEDGE

A young man was being interviewed to be a pilot for a steamboat on the Mississippi River. The interviewer, doubtful that the young man could know the dangers of the river, asked if he knew where all the rocks were. To this he replied, "No, sir, I do not know where all the rocks are, but I know where they aren't." He got the job.

23. PRACTICAL CONSIDERATION

As the fame of Auguste Renoir spread, so did the number of Renoir forgeries. The painter was understandably upset by the proliferation of these bogus pictures, but after a time, he came to accept their presence.

On occasion, as a favor to collectors who had been stuck with one of these fakes, he would even touch up the canvas and sign it, so that the collector could pass it off as an original. Angry friends urged him to get tough with the forgers and to take legal action against them, but Renoir could see no benefit in litigation. He pointed out, "It takes less time to touch up a painting than to go to court about it."

ONE HUNDRED
THIRTY-SEVEN

Witnessing

(See also Evangelism, Missions)

1. A BIAS THAT SHOWS

Did you read about the little boy who returned home after his first Sunday school class? His mother asked, "Who was your teacher?' and the little boy answered, "I don't remember her name, but she must have been Jesus' grandmother because she didn't talk about anyone else."

Does our conversation reflect our love of Jesus? Would our words give away our relationship with him?

2. C. S. LEWIS—COST OF A PUBLIC FAITH

C. S. Lewis fell into grace. But instead of simply entering a monastery, he did worse. He ended up publicly explaining and openly defending his personal God to millions of listeners and readers. Such undignified behavior embarrassed the hierarchy at his college at Oxford and cost Lewis his chance of ever advancing to a higher position on the faculty there. Lewis learned that if you speak about beauty, truth or goodness, and about God as a great spiritual force of some kind, people will remain friendly. But he found that the temperature drops when you discuss a God who gives definite commands, who does definite acts, who has definite ideas and character.
KATHRYN LINDSKOOG

3. GOOD NEWS IS FOR SHARING

I recall one night very late in the evening when I was called to the hospital. As I was walking down the semidark hall, with no people around, a man suddenly ran out of one of the patient rooms. He ran up to me—I had never seen him before—and he said to me with joy in his face, "She's going to make it. She's better. She is going to make it," and then he made his way on down the hall. I have not seen the man since. I do not know who he was talking about. I assume it was someone very near and dear to him, and he had just received good news. He could not wait to share it. He did not even have to know the person with whom he shared it; it just flowed from him because he had received good news, and good news is to be shared.
DON MCKENZIE

4. THE POWER OF A SMILE

One day as a woman was crossing a street at London station, an old man stopped her. He said to her, "Excuse me, ma'am, but I want to thank you."

She looked up and exclaimed, "Thank me?"

He replied, "Yes'm, I used to be a ticket collector, and whenever you went by you always gave me a cheerful smile and a good morning. I knew that smile must come from inside somewhere. Then one morning I saw a little Bible in your hand. So I bought one, too, and I found Jesus.

5. THE LITTLE SECRETS OF SNOWFLAKES

The complex shapes and uniqueness of snowflakes have confounded scientists for hundreds of years. In the past, it was generally recognized that the formation of a snowflake is a two-step process: making a single crystal and then having it grow.

This process begins as a microscopic speck of dust is trapped in a molecule of water vapor inside the winds of a winter storm. As the particle is frosted with droplets of supercooled water, it becomes heavier and begins its plunge to earth. The falling ice crystal is sculpted by the varying temperature and humidity—lengthening here, a spiky branch pushing out there—until it grows into a shape as unique as a person's fingerprint.

But in the past few years, as our ability to study these beautiful flakes has improved with the development of new technology, a great mystery has emerged. Scientists have discovered that very few snowflakes contain a speck of dust or any other particle which has long been believed to be necessary for a snowflake to form! How are these unique flakes formed?

Dr. John Hallett, a physicist at the University of Nevada, has discovered the answer. As snowflakes are being formed, extremely dry or cold air cause snowflakes to break up into smaller parts. The small fragments then act as seeds for new flakes to develop. In other words, it takes snow to make snow!

Sometimes we forget that it is necessary for Christians to give a personal witness of their faith in order for others to discover the love and life Christ has for them. In other words, Christ uses Christians to make Christians!

Whenever we experience pressures and difficult burdens, when we see a part of our lives broken or shattered, these are often the circumstances God uses to let our faith touch someone close to us and be the seed for a new and beautiful life in Christ. To many, the reason we face difficulties in life is a great mystery. But to us, we live expecting to bear burdens for our Savior and anticipating that the pressures we endure will be used by God to produce new life in others!

Remember, Christ uses Christians to make Christians. Look for Him to use you! CHAD MILLER, *St. Paul's Lutheran Church, West Frankfort, Illinois*

6. PRESENTING THE GLORY OF GOD

Speakers and writers must present the glory of God as clearly and compellingly as human language will permit. Otherwise both preacher and people will be reduced to dreaming little dreams and attempting for God only little things, when they could be doing so much more. Otherwise they will succumb to what Annie Dillard terms "the enormous temptation in all of life to diddle around making itsy-bitsy friends and meals and journeys for itsy-bitsy years on end." The trouble with that, says Dillard, is that God and "the world is wider than that in all directions, more dangerous and more bitter, more extravagant and bright. We are making hay when we should be making whoopee; we are raising tomatoes when we should be raising Cain, or Lazarus."

7. SILENT VIOLINS

Luigi Tarisio was found dead one morning with scarce a comfort in his home, but with 246 exquisite violins, which he had been collecting all his life, crammed into an attic, the best in the bottom drawer of an old rickety bureau. In his very devotion to the violin, he had robbed the world of all that music all the time he treasured them; others before him had done the same, so that when the greatest of his collection, a Stradivarius, was first played it had had 147 speechless years. Yet, how many of Christ's people are like old Tarisio? In our very love of the church we fail to give the glad tidings to the world; in our zeal for the truth we forget to publish it. When shall we all learn that the Good News needs not just to be cherished, but needs to be told? All people need to hear it.

ONE HUNDRED
THIRTY-EIGHT

Words

1. A THOUGHTLESS WORD

In a country church of a small village an altar boy serving the priest at Sunday mass accidentally dropped the cruet of wine. The village priest struck the altar boy sharply on the cheek and in a gruff voice shouted: "Leave the altar and don't come back!" That boy became Tito, the Communist leader. In the cathedral of a large city an altar boy serving the bishop at Sunday Mass accidentally dropped the cruet of wine. With a warm twinkle in his eyes the bishop gently whispered: "Someday you will be a priest." That boy grew up to become Archbishop Fulton Sheen. Oh, the power of words, be they written or spoken!

2. POWER OF THE WRITTEN WORD

A few years ago we visited the castle of Elsinore of Denmark. The guide reminded us that around A.D. 1200, the king of Pomerania built Elsinore Castle and also another fortified castle across the Skagerrak Channel in what is now Sweden. He thought that with these two bastions, one on each side of the channel, he could control entrance to the heart of Europe. The castle at Elsinore is in decay, the one in Sweden is gone, the Pomeranian king's name is forgotten—at least by me. But on the day of my visit, tourist buses were lined up for blocks as they are every day, bringing visitors to that spot. Why? Because one William Shakespeare chose Elsinore as the locale of his drama, *Hamlet.* The power of the pen outlasts the power of the sword. Sparta had the strongest army in ancient Greece, but its site is rubble. Athens with its Parthenon and its Mars Hill still draws millions of awe-inspired visitors. RALPH W. SOCKMAN

3. WORDS, WORDS, WORDS

Dr. Wilfred Funk, the well-known dictionary publisher, was asked to select the ten most expressive words in the English language. Here is the list:

- the most bitter word—alone
- the most tragic—death
- the most reverend—mother
- the most beautiful—love
- the most cruel—revenge
- the most peaceful—tranquil
- the saddest—forgotten
- he warmest—friendship
- the coldest—no
- the most comforting—faith

4. SAMUEL GOLDWYN AS COMMUNICATOR

Stephen Birmingham's book *The Rest of Us* chronicles the story of the Eastern European Jews, particularly the Russian Jews, who came to America through New York between 1882 and 1915 in flight from the pogroms of Czarist

493

Russia. One of the characters he tells about is film producer Sam Goldwyn, famous for his fractured English sayings that were widely quoted in his day. Here are a few of them:

"Let me sum it up for you in two words—im possible!"

"Let me pinpoint for you the approximate date."

"Include me out."

"A verbal contract isn't worth the paper it's written on."

"Every Tom, Dick, and Harry is named John."

Edna Ferber told him she was writing her autobiography. He asked her, "What's it about?"

When filming *Romeo and Juliet* was proposed to him, Goldwyn liked the story but wondered if it couldn't have a happy ending. Jokingly, an associate said, "I don't think Bill Shakespeare would like that, Sam." Goldwyn replied, "Pay him off!"

ONE HUNDRED
THIRTY-NINE

Work

1. MODEL MOTIVATION
On employee bulletin board: "In case of fire, flee the building with the same reckless abandon that occurs each day at quitting time."

2. DOCTRINE OF FAITH
If you don't believe in the resurrection of the dead, you ought to be here five minutes before quitting time! *Sign in a San Francisco wholesale florist shop*

3. TARDINESS EXPLAINED
Albert I. Furth, former editor of *Fortune,* used to explain his lateness in answering his correspondence by remarking, "Every six months my secretary comes in and turns the compost on my desk."

4. ANY OPPORTUNITY
You know business is bad when you start treating wrong numbers like solid sales prospects.

5. HOW TO KNOW WHEN IT'S TIME TO MOVE
You know it's time to move to another job when some mornings you'd rather go to the dentist and have a root canal than go to work.

6. REAL FATIGUE
He is most fatigued who knows not what to do. NICOLAS BOILEAU

7. CULTURAL EXCHANGE
When we were borrowing customs from other cultures, who passed up the siesta?

8. THE BRAIN
The brain is an organ that starts working the moment you get up in the morning and does not stop until you get into the office.

9. ENTHUSIASTIC TYPE
Did you ever notice that when you run into a man with real enthusiasm for hard work, he turns out to be your boss?

10. THE ACTIVE AND THE PASSIVE
There are those who grab hold of life and those who are out to lunch. A man was driving on a lonely road one summer day. He saw a car with a flat tire pulled over on the shoulder of the road. A woman was standing next to the car and looking down in dismay at the flat tire. The man decided to pull over and play the Good Samaritan. He grew hot and sweaty and dirty in the hot sun as he changed the tire. The woman was watching him and when he was finished she said, "Be sure and let the jack down easily now, because my husband is sleeping in the back seat of the car!"

11. PRIORITIES FOR SOCIETY
An excellent plumber is infinitely more valuable than an incompetent philosopher. The society which scorns excellence in plumbing because it is a humble activity and tolerates shoddiness in philosophy because it is an exalted activity will have neither good plumbing nor good philosophy; neither its pipes nor its theories will hold water. JOHN GARNER, *former U.S. Secretary of Health, Education and Welfare*

12. STRANGE INTERLUDE
A vacation is that brief period of time between trying to get ahead so you can leave and trying to catch up when you get back. JIM VORSAS, SARATOGA

13. THE FRUIT OF HARD WORK
A management consultant makes the following observation: "Be the first in the office every morning, be the last to leave every night, never take a day

off, slave through the lunch hour, and the inevitable day will come when the boss will summon you to his office and say, 'I've been watching your work very carefully, Jackson. Just what the devil are you up to, anyhow?'"

ONE HUNDRED FORTY
Worry

1. COSTLY ANXIETY
Worry is the interest we pay on tomorrow's troubles. E. STANLEY JONES

2. THE CHANNEL
Worry is a thin stream of fear trickling through the mind. If encouraged, it cuts a channel into which all other thoughts are drained.
ARTHUR SOMERS ROCHE

3. GETTING RID OF THE RODENT
Years ago, in the pioneer days of aviation, a pilot was making a flight around the world. After he had been gone for some two hours from his last landing field, he heard a noise in his plane, which he recognized as the gnawing of a rat. He realized that while his plane had been on the ground a rat had gotten in. For all he knew the rat could be gnawing through a vital cable or control of the plane. It was a very serious situation. He was both concerned and anxious. At first he did not know what to do. It was two hours back to the landing field from which he had taken off and more than two hours to the next field ahead. Then he remembered that the rat is a rodent. It is not made for the heights; it is made to live on the ground and under the ground. Therefore the pilot began to climb. He went up a thousand feet, then another thousand and another until he was more than twenty thousand feet up. The gnawing ceased. The rat was dead. He could not survive in the atmosphere of those heights. More than two hours later the pilot brought the plane safely to the next landing field and found the dead rat.

Brothers and sisters in Christ, worry is a rodent. It cannot live in the secret place of the Most High. It cannot breathe in the atmosphere made vital by prayer and familiarity with the Scripture. Worry dies when we ascend to the Lord through prayer and His Word. CLOVIS CHAPPELL, *Questions Jesus Asked*

ONE HUNDRED
FORTY-ONE
Youth

1. CLARIFYING THE MESSAGE
From a father's letter to a son in college: "Am enclosing $10 as you requested in your letter. Incidentally, $10 is spelled with one zero, not two."

2. FATHER'S ADVICE
Maybe you should start shifting for yourself now while you still know everything.

3. THE HIGH COST OF WISDOM
When I have ceased to break my wings
Against the faultiness of things
And learned that compromises wait
Behind each hardly opened gate.
When I can look life in the eyes,
Grown calm and very coldly wise,
Life will have given me the Truth
And taken in exchange—my youth. SARA TEASDALE

4. TEEN INDEPENDENCE
A mother was overheard talking about her teenage daughter: "She's very independent—she lives alone at our house."

5. WISE YOUTH
The best substitute for experience is being sixteen.

6. GRIM WARNING
Sign seen in an orthopedic physician's office: Give your son a motorcycle for his last birthday.

7. TIMING
Why can't life's big problems come when we are twenty and know everything?

8. THOSE ROTTEN KIDS
Our youths love luxury. They have bad manners, contempt for authority— they show disrespect for their elders and love to chatter in place of exercise. Children are now tyrants, not the servants of their households. They no

longer rise when their elders enter the room. They contradict their parents, chatter before company, gobble up food, and tyrannize teachers.
SOCRATES, C. 400 B.C.

9. POSTER WISDOM
Attention Teenagers—If you are tired of being hassled by unreasonable parents, now is the time for action! Leave home and pay your own way while you still know everything!

10. LEARNING FROM DEPRIVATION
Sending a youngster to college these days is very educational. It teaches parents how to do without a lot of things.

11. THE HANDICAPS OF YOUTH
Parents of two teenagers are worried about their failing eyesight. The daughter can't find anything to wear in a closet full of clothes and the son can't find anything good to eat in a refrigerator full of food.

12. SLIPPING WITH AGE
It seldom occurs to teenagers that someday they will know as little as their parents.

13. PARENTING TEENS
I'm tempted to believe Mark Twain's philosophy: When a kid turns thirteen, stick him in a barrel, nail the lid shut, and feed him through the knot hole. When he turns sixteen, plug the hole.

14. GETTING IT DONE
There are three ways to get something done:
1. Do it yourself.
2. Hire someone to do it.
3. Forbid your kids to do it.

15. TEENAGE AWARENESS
First mother of a teenager: "My daughter doesn't tell me anything. I'm a nervous wreck!"

Second mother of a teenager: "My daughter tells me everything, and I'm a nervous wreck!"

16. VALUE OF AN EDUCATION
Friend: "Has your son's education proved to be of any real value?"
Father: "Yes, indeed. It has entirely cured his mother of bragging about his brains and accomplishments."

17. NOT LOGICAL

There's nothing wrong with teenagers that reasoning with them won't aggravate.

18. MOTIVATING TEENAGERS

A community club was discussing the proposed establishment of a youth center. A youthful member of the club spoke out in favor of having a young person oversee the center; someone young enough, she said, to know what teenagers really like to do.

"Yes," agreed an older member, "but also old enough to see that they don't."

19. WRITE BACK!

As the mother said good-bye to her son who was returning to school after spring vacation, she reminded him to write often. Another woman standing nearby heard the plea and gave this advice: "The surest way to get your son to write home is to send him a letter saying, 'Here's fifty dollars, spend it any way you like.'" "And that will make my son write home?" "Yes indeed. You forget to enclose the money."

ONE HUNDRED
FORTY-TWO

Zeal

(See also Enthusiasm)

1. AND YOU THINK YOU'RE BUSY?

I just finished reading F. Deauville Walker's biography of William Carey, pioneer missionary to India. Here is the record of one day in India reconstructed from his diary in 1806.

He rose at a quarter to six, read a chapter from the Hebrew Bible and spent some time in private devotion. At seven the servants came in for family prayers in Bengali, after which, while waiting for his *chota* (i.e., little breakfast), he spent some time reading Persian with a *munshi* and then a portion of Scripture in Hindustani. The moment breakfast was over, he settled down to the translation of the Ramayana from Sanskrit into English. At ten o'clock he went to the college, where his classes and other duties kept him until two o'clock. On returning to his lodgings he examined a proofsheet of his Bengali translation of Jeremiah until dinnertime. After this meal, assisted by the chief pundit of the college, he translated most of the eighth chapter of Matthew's Gospel into Sanskrit, until six o'clock when he sat down with a Telugu pundit more fully to study that language. At half past seven he preached in English to a congregation of forty persons, including one of the judges (from whom at the close of the service he got a subscription of five hundred rupees toward the new chapel). At nine o'clock, "the service being over and the congregation gone," he sat down and translated Ezekiel 11 into Bengali—which took him nearly two hours. He wrote a letter to a friend in England; then, after reading a chapter from his Greek Testament by way of private devotion, he went to bed.

2. SPIRITUAL ELOQUENCE IN COMMUNICATION
Eloquence isn't necessarily flowery language so much as heartfelt expression. Consider this prayer of a country preacher in Red Rock, Mississippi:

"O Lord, give Thy servant this mornin' the eyes of the eagle and the wisdom of the owl; connect his soul with the gospel telephone in the central skies; 'luminate his brow with the Sun of Heaven; possess his mind with love for the people; turpentine his imagination; grease his lips with 'possum oil; loosen his tongue with the sledge hammer of Thy power; 'lectrify his brain with the lightnin' of the word; put 'petual motion on his arms, fill him plum full of the dynamite of Thy glory; 'noint him all over with the kerosene oil of Thy salvation and set him on the fire. Amen!"

3. REASON TO CHEER
The streets were lined with crowds, cheering the marching regiments about to leave for overseas. A recruit, who had watched the crowd for some time, asked, "Who are all those people cheering?" The veteran replied, "They are people who are not going."

4. RISKS OF APPEARING FOOLISH
Author Rudyard Kipling tells how on a world tour at a certain port General Booth boarded the ship. He was seen off by a horde of tambourine-beating Salvationists. The whole thing revolted Kipling's fastidious soul. Later he got to know the general and told him how much he disapproved of this kind of thing. "Young man," said Booth, "if I thought that I could win one more soul for Christ by standing on my hands and beating a tambourine with my feet I would learn to do it." The real enthusiast does not care if others think he is a fool. WILLIAM BARCLAY, *Letters to the Corinthians*

5. LAW AND GRACE

A tyrannical husband demanded that his wife conform to rigid standards of his choosing. She was to do certain things for him as a wife, mother, and homemaker. In time she came to hate her husband as much as she hated his list of rules and regulations. Then, one day he died—mercifully as far as she was concerned.

Some time later, she fell in love with another man and married him. She and her new husband lived on a perpetual honeymoon. Joyfully, she devoted herself to his happiness and welfare. One day she ran across one of the sheets of do's and don'ts her first husband had written for her. To her amazement she found that she was doing for her second husband all the things her first husband had demanded of her, even though her new husband had never once suggested them. She did them as an expression of her love for him and her desire to please him.

6. EFFORT WITH A CAPITAL "E"

I was impressed several years ago that Eugene Ormandy dislocated a shoulder while leading the Philadelphia Orchestra. I do not know what they were playing. Certainly not Mozart. Perhaps Stravinsky. But at any rate, he was giving all of himself to it! And I have asked myself sadly, "Did I ever dislocate anything, even a necktie?" HALFORD LUCOCK

7. TOO MUCH CAUTION

Cautious, careful people, always casting about to preserve their reputation and social standing, never can bring about a reform. Those who are really in earnest must be willing to be anything or nothing in the world's estimation. SUSAN B. ANTHONY